ROGET'S THESAURUS
of
WORDS
for
Writers

ROGET'S THESAURUS of WORDS for *Writers*

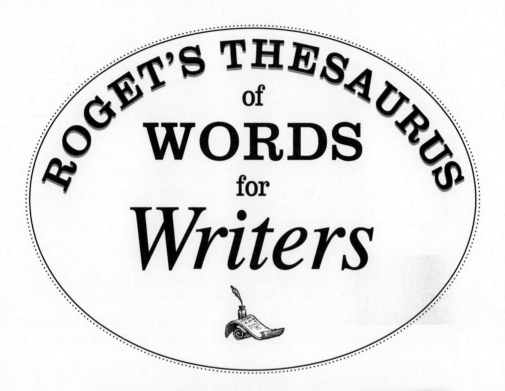

*Over 2,300 Emotive, Evocative,
Descriptive Synonyms,
Antonyms, & Related Terms*
EVERY WRITER
SHOULD KNOW

DAVID OLSEN, MICHELLE BEVILACQUA,
JUSTIN CORD HAYES, AND ROBERT BLY

Adams Media
New York London Toronto Sydney New Delhi

Adams Media
An Imprint of Simon & Schuster, LLC
100 Technology Center Drive
Stoughton, MA 02072

For information about special discounts for bulk purchases, please contact Simon & Schuster Special Sales at 1-866-506-1949 or business@simonandschuster.com.

The Simon & Schuster Speakers Bureau can bring authors to your live event. For more information or to book an event contact the Simon & Schuster Speakers Bureau at 1-866-248-3049 or visit our website at www.simonspeakers.com.

Manufactured in the United States of America

15 2024

Library of Congress Cataloging-in-Publication Data has been applied for.

ISBN 978-1-4405-7311-8
ISBN 978-1-4405-7312-5 (ebook)

Introduction

All writers, from time to time, need a reference source—a place we can go to find the term that will fit just right into our writing. Whether it's romance, mystery, science fiction, or adventure, the right word in the right place can make a huge difference.

That's where this thesaurus comes in. The object of *Roget's Thesaurus of Words for Writers* is not only to give you an array of terms related to common words; unlike a standard thesaurus, it's also intended to show you how these words are used in sentences, whether made-up examples or quotations from well-known sources. The words selected here are ones we use as writers: expressive, nuanced, and creative—as well as a bit unusual.

For each key word you'll find a list of related words sorted by their part of speech: adjectives, adverbs, nouns, verbs, and antonyms. Go through them until you find the one best suited to the sentence you're crafting. As you do so, you'll be building your word skills and making yourself a better writer.

As a creative person working with words, you respect their importance. You know the pleasure of finding just the right phrase, of contemplating it for a moment on the screen of your computer before moving on. There's an almost physical thrill from listening to a piece of great writing in which every word is like a note in a symphony, all sounding in harmony.

You also know that writing is like fine china: A single misplaced word, a turn of phrase that stumbles, and suddenly your work is in pieces at your feet, and you've got to begin the painful process of picking it up and putting it back together.

For the most part, the words we use are formed by who we are. Our vocabulary grows and is shaped by our interactions with family and friends, by our education, and by the books we read. The broader your erudition, the more versatile will be your word usage. As well, your writing will grow stronger, and your words will have more power to move your readers.

Just as a carpenter has his or her box of tools, so as a writer you have tools you use in pursuit of your trade. This thesaurus is such a tool. Use it to keep your vocabulary finely honed and you can expect to excel at your craft.

1. Abuse

(uh-BYOOZ), verb

To use insulting, harsh, or unjust language to or about; to use improperly, misuse; to harm by treating badly; to treat in an offensive way.

ADJECTIVES

contumelious (kon-too-MEE-lee-us). Insolently humiliating and abusive; contemptuous; insulting.
The defendant passively endured the prosecutor's CONTUMELIOUS speech.

opprobrious *(uh-PRO-bree-us).* Abusive; disrespectful.
Martha was caught off guard by her friend's sudden OPPROBRIOUS attack on her behavior of the previous night.

scurrilous (SKUR-ih-luss). Offensive to civilized discourse; verbally abusive; vulgar; coarse; slanderous.
Because they were made on the floor of the Senate, the senator's SCURRILOUS accusations against me were protected, but if he should dare to repeat them in another setting, I will sue him for every penny he's worth.

truculent (TRUK-yu-lent). Rude; mean; scathingly harsh.
He knew the play was not his best, but James was not prepared for the TRUCULENT reviews by all the critics.

virulent (VEER-yuh-lent). Poisonously or intensely hostile.
Marla's VIRULENT words were meant to hurt her sister deeply.

vitriolic (vit-ree-AWL-ik). Acidic; harsh; caustic.
McCarthy's VITRIOLIC attacks on organizations with no actual Communist ties went completely unchallenged in the Senate.

vituperative *(vie-TOO-per-uh-tive).* Scathing and harshly abusive, as criticism.
You can't hide your VITUPERATIVE attack behind a few surface pleasantries!

NOUNS

invective *(in-VEK-tiv).* Criticism or negative observations expressed in the strongest, harshest possible terms.
"The art of INVECTIVE resembles the art of boxing. Very few fights are won with the straight left. It is too obvious, and it can be too easily countered."—Gilbert Highet, Scottish-born American biographer and essayist

obloquy (OB-luh-kwee). Censure or verbal abuse of a person, especially by many people or the public; public discredit.
There appears to be no end to the number of celebrities whose activities result in dramatic and lengthy OBLOQUY.

VERBS

revile (rih-VILE). To curse or abuse in harsh language.
Realizing that he was REVILED by those opposing his stand on the military buildup, the senator decided to cancel his appearance at the campus.

ANTONYMS

extol (eks-TOLE). To praise with great enthusiasm.
William has not ceased to EXTOL the virtues of his new girlfriend.

laud (LAWD). Commend; praise.
Rebecca loves her history teacher and LAUDS him constantly.
See also: Criticize

2. Achievement

(uh-CHEEV-muhnt), noun

Something accomplished, especially by skill, work, courage, etc.; feat; exploit; a great deed.

ADJECTIVES

venerable (VEN-er-uh-bull). Respected and revered, especially due to achievement, intelligence, or character.
After many years of performing to the highest standards, our orchestra has achieved a VENERABLE reputation.

NOUNS

accomplishment (uh-KOM-plish-muhnt). Something successfully completed.
To the casual observer it was just a sidewalk, but Simon was proud of his ACCOMPLISHMENT.

attainment (uh-TAYN-muhnt). An achievement.
"I declare, on my soul and conscience, that the ATTAINMENT of power, or of a great name in literature, seemed to me an easier victory than a success with some young, witty, and gracious lady of high degree."—Honoré de Balzac, French novelist

capstone (CAP-stone). A crowning achievement; a finishing touch; originally, a protective stone at the top of an arch.
When she won the Pulitzer Prize for her last novel, it was the CAPSTONE to a long and distinguished literary career.

eminence (EM-ih-nence). Superiority or outstanding notability; having great achievements or high rank.
Doctor Powers's EMINENCE as a surgeon is well known.

fruition (froo-ISH-un). That which has arisen from development, possession, use, or effort; the achievement of something desired or labored for.
The novel was, in a sense, the FRUITION of a lifetime of work for Melville.

masterpiece (MAS-ter-peece). A person's greatest work; achievement of a lifetime.
"When love and skill work together, expect a MASTERPIECE."—John Ruskin, English art critic

ANTONYMS

debacle (dih-BAH-kull). Utter collapse or rout; a complete (often ludicrous) failure.
The initiative seemed promising enough, but turned out to be another of George's DEBACLES.

3. Aggrandize

(uh-GRAN-dyz), verb

To exaggerate, put on a false front, and make something look greater and grander than it really is.

ADJECTIVES

bumptious (BUMP-shuss). Loud and assertive in a crude way.
The club's golf pro was fired due to his BUMPTIOUS behavior on the links.

faux (FOH). Fake; phony; artificial.
She wore a cheap second-hand dress and a FAUX pearl necklace made out of white beads.

ostentatious (ah-sten-TAY-shuss). Pretentious; presented in a showy manner so as to impress others; meant to flaunt one's wealth or success.
"The man who is OSTENTATIOUS of his modesty is twin to the statue that wears a fig-leaf."—Mark Twain

unbridled (un-BRY-duld). Without limitations or boundaries; uncontrolled and unrestrained.
The customer's UNBRIDLED fury at being denied a refund was a sight to behold.

vainglorious (vayn-GLOR-ee-us). Conceited; boastful; prone to showing off and bragging.
Although the scion of a well-established family, Gordon is so VAINGLORIOUS that you'd think him a parvenu!

NOUNS

façade (fuh-SOD). The front of a building; a deceptive appearance masking a thing's true nature.
"A good man often appears gauche simply because he does not take advantage of the myriad mean little chances of making himself look stylish. Preferring truth to form, he is not constantly at work upon the FAÇADE of his appearance."
—Iris Murdoch, Irish writer and philosopher

hyperbole (high-PER-buh-lee). An over-exaggeration made for effect.
"The final key to the way I promote is bravado. I play to people's fantasies. People may not always think big themselves, but they can still get very excited by those who do. That's why a little HYPERBOLE never hurts."
—Donald Trump, American entrepreneur

jactitation (jak-ti-TAY-shun). A false boast, especially one that is harmful to others.
Beatrice tried impress her classmates by telling them her last name was Kennedy. However, her JACTITATION was discovered and her peers returned to ignoring her.

VERBS

bloviate (BLOH-vee-ayt). To speak pompously and at length.
Maxwell BLOVIATES about his "excellent" golf game, but everyone knows he cheats outrageously.

ANTONYMS

diffident (DIFF-ih-dent). Uncertain or unsure about making a decision or taking an action; lacking confidence and boldness.
If you feel DIFFIDENT about driving a Rolls-Royce, you can always buy a Bentley.

laconic (luh-KAWN-ik). Of few words; expressing oneself with an economy of words.
Harold may be LACONIC, but when he does speak, he is worth listening to.

4. Agree

(uh-GREE), verb

To consent or concede; to be in harmony; to have the same opinion; to come to an understanding.

ADJECTIVES

amenable (ah-MEE-nah-bull). Agreeable to the wishes and desires of others.
Mark considers himself AMENABLE, but the rest of us just think he's a pushover.

complaisant (kuhm-PLAY-zuhnt). Agreeable and eager to please.
Eleanor is far too COMPLAISANT with common strangers.

conciliatory (kon-SILL-ee-ah-tore-ee). Reconciling; able to settle a dispute or resolve a conflict in a manner that leaves no hard feelings on either side.
"If you are not very clever, you should be CONCILIATORY."
—Benjamin Disraeli, British statesmen and literary figure

palatable (PAL-uh-tuh-bull). Agreeable; acceptable.
You have two options, Mr. Mayor, neither very PALATABLE.

NOUNS

accord (uh-KORD). Official agreement or treaty; harmony.
After a prolonged strike, with the issue of healthcare benefits resolved, the representatives finally reached an ACCORD acceptable to both labor and management.

appeasement (uh-PEEZ-ment). The act of making others happy by agreeing to their demands.
Charlene realized too late that her policy of APPEASEMENT might please Warren, but it would not cause him to treat her with more respect.

assent (uh-SENT). Agreement that an opinion, view, or proposal is correct; corroboration.
You forget, Mr. Jameson, that it is only with the ASSENT of the stockholders that the CEO can be ousted.

collusion (kuh-LOO-zhun). A conspiratorial or secret understanding or agreement entered into for an illicit or fraudulent end.
The leaders were arraigned on price COLLUSION in violation of antitrust laws.

conspiracy (kun-SPEER-uh-see). A treacherous plan involving two or more persons; an agreement among conspirators.
Your contention that Bill and Hillary Clinton were part of a CONSPIRACY to assassinate Vincent Foster amounts to what, in an earlier day, would have been called seditious libel, Mr. Oliver.

VERBS

accede (ak-SEED). To give consent or approval.
The college president eventually ACCEDED to the demands of the student demonstrators.

acquiesce (ak-wee-ESS). To accept or consent silently without protest or enthusiasm.
When he saw the policeman approach with his gun drawn, the bandit ACQUIESCED to his arrest.

mollify (MOL-uh-fye). To soothe, soften in temper; pacify; appease.
The umpire's attempts to MOLLIFY the two screaming managers with some risqué humor were to no avail.

pacify (PASS-uh-fye). To appease; bring to a state of peace or calm; tranquilize.
Her suggestion that she offer a written apology to the offended client seemed to PACIFY Mr. Peters.

placate (PLAY-kayt). To reduce the anger of; appease.
Although the company was unable to raise wages, it did make an effort to PLACATE the union by extending the afternoon coffee break.

ANTONYMS

dissension (dih-SEN-shun). Disagreement, especially among people in a group.
New rules favoring older members of the club caused great DISSENSION and a fracturing of long-standing alliances.

5. Alone

(uh-LOHN), adjective, adverb

Apart from anything and anyone else; separate; within nothing more; only; solitary.

ADJECTIVES

monastic (muh-NAS-tik). Relating to the practice of withdrawing from society to live a quiet, contemplative life, often dedicated to religious faith.
Saint Pachomius founded the first organized Christian MONASTIC community.

NOUNS

monophobia (mon-uh-FOE-bee-uh). An abnormal dread of being alone.
Al's MONOPHOBIA has gotten much worse since the death of his wife.

recluse (REK-loos). A person who lives apart from society, or in seclusion, often for religious contemplation.
When Jim reaches a certain age, his solitary lifestyle might brand him as a hermit, but for now he considers himself a RECLUSE.

VERBS

disenfranchise (dis-en-FRAN-chyz). To deny someone a right or privilege; to make someone feel rejected and apart. Often specifically applied to voting rights.
"Some states specify felonies that condemn the citizen to DISENFRANCHISEMENT for life."—Andrew Hacker, American political scientist

immure (ih-MYOOR). To confine, imprison, or enclose behind walls.
Whitney remained IMMURED in her room as she pondered the itinerary for her luxury vacation to Italy.

prescind (pree-SIND). To detach, separate, or isolate; to cut off, terminate.
Working on the latest project has made me want to PRESCIND my thoughts from all contact with the team.

sequester (see-KWESS-ter). To remove and isolate a portion from a larger whole.
"A great deal of genetic engineering must be done before we have carbon-eaters SEQUESTERING carbon in sufficient quantity to counteract the burning of fossil fuels."—Freeman Dyson, English-born American physicist and mathematician

ANTONYMS

gregarious (grih-GAIR-ee-us). Enjoying the company of other people, sociable.
"We are easy to manage, a GREGARIOUS people, / Full of sentiment, clever at mechanics, and we love our luxuries."—Robinson Jeffers, American poet
See also: Eliminate, Isolated

6. Ambiguity

(am-bih-GYOO-ih-tee), noun

Uncertainty; lack of clear definition.

ADJECTIVES

amorphous (ah-MORE-fis). Without definite shape, substance, or form; lacking definition and boundaries.
"Of course the illusion of art is to make one believe that great literature is very close to life, but exactly the opposite is true. Life is AMORPHOUS, literature is formal."—Françoise Sagan, French novelist and playwright

enigmatic (en-ig-MATT-ik). Mysterious, puzzling, and difficult to figure out.
"The interest in life does not lie in what people do, nor even in their relations to each other, but largely in the power to communicate with a third party,

antagonistic, ENIGMATIC, yet perhaps persuadable, which one may call life in general."—Virginia Woolf, British essayist and novelist

nebulous (NEB-yoo-luss). Vague and not well thought out; ill-defined; lacking concretes.
Jay's plans for what he would do when he graduated from college were NEBULOUS at best.

opaque (oh-PAYK). Hard to understand; obscure.
"The bottom of being is left logically OPAQUE to us, as something which we simply come upon and find, and about which (if we wish to act) we should pause and wonder as little as possible."
—William James, American psychologist and philosopher

NOUNS

zelig (ZEH-lig). A chameleonlike person who seems omnipresent.
The parvenus try so hard to be ZELIGS, blending in seamlessly at our functions, but we can always spot them for the intruders they are.

VERBS

misconstrue (miss-kuhn-STROO). To misinterpret or to take in a wrong sense.
The disagreement over the price of the yacht was due merely to the fact that David MISCONSTRUED the terms of the offer.

vacillate (VASS-uh-layt). To swing back and forth between two points.
"But modern character is inconstant, divided, VACILLATING, lacking the stone-like certitude of archaic man. . . ."—Saul Bellow, American author

ANTONYMS

mot juste (MOW-zhoost). The perfect word or phrase to communicate precisely what you mean to say.
Years of elocution lessons have left Paulina capable of leavening every occasion with a suitable MOT JUSTE.

7. Angry

(ANG-gree), adjective

Feeling, showing, or resulting from anger, strong resentment, or wrath.

ADJECTIVES

acrimonious (ak-rih-MOAN-ee-us). Bitter or caustic, especially in language or manner; disputed.
"There is something about the literary life that repels me, all this desperate building of castles on cobwebs, the long-drawn ACRIMONIOUS struggle to make something important which we all know will be gone forever in a few years . . ."
—*Raymond Chandler, American author*

apoplectic (ap-uh-PLECK-tik). In an extremely agitated state of rage.
Emily's careless event planning makes me APOPLECTIC, and I just want to step in and plan the luncheon myself.

fractious (FRAK-shuss). Easily angered or irritable; quarrelsome; unruly.
In movies of a certain vintage, the local police were always portrayed as FRACTIOUS.

livid (LIHV-id). Enraged or extremely angry.
Jennifer was LIVID when we suggested that her new outfit was out of date.

NOUNS

cholers (KOH-lers). The mood of anger, irritability, grumpiness, or being short-tempered and impatient.
When Franklin is in the grip of CHOLERS, even his closest friends avoid his table at the club.

ANTONYMS

placid (PLASS-id). Calm; peaceful; serene.
In contrast to my excitable and angry father, my mother was always PLACID and able to keep the peace in our household.

8. Animals

(AN-uh-muhls), noun

Any living organisms capable of locomotion but not of making their own food by photosynthesis; distinguished from plants; members of the kingdom Animalia.

ADJECTIVES

anthropomorphic (an-thruh-puh-MOOR-fik). Attributing human characteristics to animals.
Children's literature, and much adult fantasy, is filled with ANTHROPOMORPHIC animals.

aquiline (ACK-wuh-line). Resembling an eagle or curving like an eagle's beak.
Neil wasn't sure that it was a compliment when Julie described his features as AQUILINE.

bovine (BO-vine). Of or resembling a cow or ox; dull.
The hardest part of teaching high school for me has been getting used to the look of BOVINE submissiveness on most of my students' faces.

leonine (LEE-uh-nine). Having characteristics of a lion.
Ben's LEONINE mane of hair makes most of his girlfriends jealous.

lupine (LOO-pine). Like a wolf; savage and predatory.
Sid's LUPINE behavior makes you feel like you should go home and take a shower after you've been around him for a little while.

ophidian (oh-FIDD-ee-un). Of snakes or snakelike; dishonest or mean-spirited.
The lawyer's OPHIDIAN eyes made me second-guess myself with every question he asked.

ovine (OH-vine). Characteristic of sheep.
The earliest classes at school were marked by the OVINE migration of students to lecture halls.

oviparous (oh-VIP-er-uss). Producing eggs that mature and hatch after being deposited outside the body, as birds, most reptiles, and fishes.
Because they are unprotected much of the time, eggs of OVIPAROUS animals often have a tough and leathery shell.

ovoviviparous (oh-voh-vye-VIP-er-uss). Producing eggs that are hatched within the mother's body so that the young are born alive, as certain reptiles and fishes.
It seems as if OVOVIVIPAROUS animals couldn't decide whether to lay eggs or produce live young.

porcine (PORE-sine). Reminiscent of, resembling, or pertaining to a pig.
Mike's constant description of his heavyset blind date as "my PORCINE companion" may have had something to do with her early departure from the party.

simian (SIM-ee-uhn). Characteristic of or pertaining to apes or monkeys.
Taking care of the children for the day was fun, even if their SIMIAN antics resulted in a lot of misunderstandings and tears.

ursine (UR-sine). Characteristic of bears.
Mr. Hess was so glad to see me that he ran across the hall and gave me a fierce (I might say URSINE!) embrace.

viviparous (vye-VIP-er-uss). Producing live young instead of eggs, as mammals and some reptiles and fishes.
The young of VIVIPAROUS animals require a long period of care before they can survive on their own.

vulpine (VUHL-pine). Like a fox; cunning or crafty.
My son's VULPINE grin let me know he was up to something of which I would not approve.

zoomorphic (zoh-uh-MOOR-fik). Pertaining to a deity or other being conceived of in animal form or with animal features.
Some cultures worshipped ZOOMORPHIC beings that had special qualities.

NOUNS

fauna (FAW-nuh). The animal population of a particular region or time period.
According to this article, the FAUNA of Australia include more marsupials than are found on any other continent.

marsupial (mar-SOOP-ee-uhl). A mammal that carries its young in a pouch on the outside of her body, where the baby continues to develop.
The kangaroo is the best-known MARSUPIAL, but wombats also carry their babies in a pouch.

ANTONYMS

herbaceous (hur-BAY-shuss). Characteristic of an herb; plantlike.
Some wines can have an HERBACEOUS odor and a taste that is quite disagreeable.

9. Annoy

(uh-NOY), verb

To irritate or bother, as by a repeated action; to make angry.

ADJECTIVES

irascible (ih-RASS-uh-bull). Easily irritated or annoyed; prone to losing one's temper; quick to anger.
"I have never known anyone worth a damn who wasn't IRASCIBLE."
—Ezra Pound, American expatriate poet

niggling (NIG-ling). Petty; annoying.
I could usually deal with my roommate's NIGGLING complaints about hairs in the sink and my forgetting to take out the trash, but I was in no mood for it today.

officious (oh-FISH-us). Asserting authority or power in an obnoxious, overbearing, or pompous manner.
"There is immunity in reading, immunity in formal society, in office routine, in the company of old friends and in the giving of OFFICIOUS help to strangers, but there is no sanctuary in one bed from the memory of another."
—Cyril Connolly, British literary critic and writer

NOUNS

gadfly (GAD-fly). A fly that bites livestock; also, a person who annoys, irritates, or provokes.
With his constant grumbling and irritating habits, Morton has turned into the GADFLY of our department.

vexation (vek-SAY-shun). Frustration, annoyance, or irritation resulting from some action, occurrence, or statement.
"There is not much less VEXATION in the government of a private family than in the managing of an entire state."
—Michel de Montaigne, Renaissance scholar

VERBS

glower (GLOU-ur). To give a brooding, annoyed, or angry look.
Mark hoped GLOWERING at our mother would convey that he didn't appreciate her telling his new girlfriend how difficult he had been to toilet train, but Mom didn't seem to notice.

nettle (NET-uhl). To provoke, irritate, or annoy.
"The comic spirit is given to us in order that we may analyze, weigh, and clarify things in us which NETTLE us, or which we are outgrowing, or trying to reshape."—Thornton Wilder, American playwright and novelist

ANTONYMS

affable (AF-uh-bull). Pleasant and polite; agreeable; warm.
No one we knew had a more AFFABLE personality than Grace, and we always enjoyed being in her company no matter the occasion.

complaisant (kuhm-PLAY-zuhnt). Agreeable and eager to please.
Eleanor is far too COMPLAISANT with common strangers.

10. Answer

(AN-ser), verb

To reply to a question, argument, letter, etc.; to respond in kind; to retaliate.

NOUNS

acknowledgment (ak-NOL-ij-muhnt). A recognition and expression of receipt.
June always sent a formal ACKNOWLEDGMENT in answer to any invitation.

rejoinder (rih-JOIN-der). A clever or witty reply to a question or comment.
Lydia's often catty REJOINDERS quickly made her the bane of our group.

riposte (rih-POST). A quick, often witty or cutting, response to a comment or question.
Eileen was unable to offer one of her usual RIPOSTES when we decried her decision to eschew the season's fashion.

VERBS

countervail (KOWN-tur-VAIL). To use equal force against; to compensate.
The challenger hit the champion with two quick left jabs and a right uppercut, but the champion COUNTERVAILED with a left hook.

rebut (ree-BUT). To provide a reply that opposes a position.
Bill never simply answered questions; he saw them as opportunities to REBUT other peoples' opinions.

reciprocate (rih-SIP-ruh-kayt). To give or act in turn following the lead of another; to reply with a courtesy, gift, or example from another.
Mr. Powers has shown evidence that he wants to end the feud; the least you can do is RECIPROCATE.

refute (ree-FYOOT). To produce evidence or proof that an argument is incorrect; to deny the truth or accuracy of something.
My lawyer could REFUTE his own existence if necessary.

retort (rih-TORT). To reply in a sharp, retaliatory manner.
Carl had to bite back a sharp RETORT when Sallee criticized the couture gown his mother wore to the soiree.

ANTONYMS

inquisitorial (in-kwiz-ih-TOR-ee-uhl). Having the nature of an investigator; extremely curious; inquisitive.
As Nick was growing up, he would face an INQUISITORIAL confrontation with his mother every time he came home late.

11. Anxiety

(ang-ZY-uh-tee), noun

A state of unease, apprehension, or misgiving.

ADJECTIVES

frenetic (fruh-NET-ik). Frantic and frenzied.
"I love my work with a FRENETIC and perverse love, as an ascetic loves the hair shirt which scratches his belly."—Gustave Flaubert, French writer

NOUNS

angst (ANGKST). A feeling of anxiety, dread, or anguish.
Carolyn's self-doubts caused her much ANGST prior to the meeting with her potential in-laws.

apprehension (ap-ruh-HEN-shun). Uneasiness about the future; suspicion of impending bad fortune.
A vague feeling of APPREHENSION came over Gordon as he stepped into the old house.

compunction (kuhm-PUNGK-shun). Anxiety caused by regret for doing another harm.
Thomas never feels COMPUNCTION for the bruises he leaves on the lacrosse field.

inquietude (in-KWY-ih-tood). A state of disturbance; restlessness; uneasiness.
Amy's INQUIETUDE at the prospect of going to school made her feel physically sick.

solicitude (suh-LIS-ih-tood). The state of being concerned and anxious.
The number of comments on the local blog indicated the town's growing SOLICITUDE over a possible increase in property taxes.

trepidation (trep-ih-DAY-shun). A state of fear or agitation.
At first, I approached the task of writing this book with some TREPIDATION.

VERBS

disquiet (dis-KWY-it). To make anxious, restless, or uneasy; disturb.
The absolute silence of the forest would DISQUIET anyone.

ANTONYMS

aplomb (uh-PLOM). Self-possession; assurance; poise.
Even under conditions that would make the most resolute among us anxious, Ralph's APLOMB was intact.

certitude (SUR-ti-tood). Absence of doubt; assurance.
For the first time in his college career, Arthur had studied sufficiently for the exam and walked to class with a pleasant feeling of CERTITUDE.

12. Appropriate

(ah-PRO-pree-it), adjective

Fitting or suitable for a particular purpose; proper; especially compatible.

ADJECTIVES

apposite (APP-uh-zit). Relevant, pertinent, or appropriate to a given situation.
Your objections are extremely APPOSITE, but I wish you would let me finish describing my plan before you shoot it full of holes!

apt (APT). Suitable for the purpose or occasion; fitting.
Roger could always be counted on to provide an APT comment, whatever the occasion.

concinnous (kon-SIN-us). Characterized by a harmonious arrangement of parts; a congruous style especially in literary works.
Peter found the CONCINNOUS expressions of baroque symphonies particularly pleasing and satisfying.

condign (kon-DINE). Fitting, suitable; deserved: used especially in connection with punishment for wrongdoing.
Twenty years at hard labor was a perfectly CONDIGN punishment for Bill's vicious crime.

de rigueur (duh-rih-GUR). Conforming to current standards of behavior, fashion, style, and etiquette.
A two-carat diamond engagement ring that cost a young man a year's salary was DE RIGUEUR for proposing to a girl in the 1950s.

felicitous (fih-LISS-ih-tuss). Well suited for a particular occasion.
"O to be a dragon / a symbol of the power of Heaven—of silkworm / size or immense; at times invisible. FELICITOUS phenomenon!"—Marianne Moore, Modernist American poet and writer

germane (jer-MANE). Relevant, pertinent, and fitting.
"Quotes from Mao, Castro, and Che Guevara . . . are as GERMANE to our highly technological, computerized society as a stagecoach on a jet runway at Kennedy airport."—Saul Alinksy, American activist

ADVERBS

apropos (ap-rih-POE). Appropriate, or at an opportune time.
Charlie began screaming the words "Too late! Too late!" APROPOS of nothing.

NOUNS

decorum (dih-COR-um). Social propriety; dignified conduct.
Though the delegates were extremely frustrated at the chairman's move, they betrayed no emotion, and strict DECORUM was observed in the meeting hall.

ANTONYMS

aberrant (AB-uh-runt). Abandoning the correct, expected, or proper way of doing things; straying from the "right" or norm.
Alice's decision to quit college and tour the country on a motorcycle seemed so ABERRANT to her parents that they asked her to get a psychiatric evaluation.

gratuitous (grah-TOO-ih-tuss). Unnecessary; inappropriately excessive; uncalled for.
"Being accused of making money by selling sex in Hollywood, home of the casting couch and the GRATUITOUS nude scene, is so rich with irony that it's a better subject for a comic novel than a column."—Anna Quindlen, American author and opinion columnist

impropriety (im-pro-PRY-ih-tee). Something that has the quality of being improper.
Beverly's minor IMPROPRIETY at the dinner table was overlooked; the conversation turned quickly to other topics.

incongruous (in-KONG-groo-us). Describes something that does not belong in its current place, setting, or role; out of place; not fitting in.
"The taste for quotations (and for the juxtaposition of INCONGRUOUS quotations) is a Surrealist taste."—Susan Sontag, American literary theorist, philosopher, and political activist

solecism (SOLL-ih-siz-um). Something that deviates from the normal, accepted, or proper order; inconsistency.
She told her husband not to worry, that forgetting a host's name was only a minor SOLECISM and certainly nothing to be concerned about.

unseemly (un-SEEM-ly). Inappropriate; unbecoming.
The family felt that Bill's presence at the memorial service would have been UNSEEMLY, as he had been my sister-in-law's bitterest business rival.

unsuitable (un-SOO-tuh-bull). Not suitable, inappropriate; unfitting.
"This mode of electioneering suited neither my taste nor my principles. I thought it equally UNSUITABLE to my personal character and to the station in which I am placed."—John Quincy Adams, American president

13. Approval

(uh-PROOV-uhl), noun

The act of approving; a favorable attitude or opinion; consent; sanction.

NOUNS

approbation (ap-ruh-BAY-shun). Official approval or commendation.
"In a virtuous and free state, no rewards can be so pleasing to sensible minds, as those which include the APPROBATION of our fellow citizens. My great pain is, lest my poor endeavours should fall short of the kind expectations of my country."—Thomas Jefferson

commendation (komm-uhn-DAY-shun). Something that commends; a recommendation; approval; praise.
For bravery beyond the call, Jones received an official COMMENDATION at the ceremony.

imprimatur (im-pruh-MAW-ter). Sanction; approval, usually by the Roman Catholic Church, to publish a book.
After directing several revisions of the controversial book's text, the Church finally gave its IMPRIMATUR.

VERBS

acclaim (uh-KLAYM). To greet with loud and boisterous approval; applaud.
Not content with applause and shouts of joy, the citizens would ACCLAIM the dictator by firing rifles into the air.

countenance (KOUN-tih-nunce). To indicate approval of, to sanction.
I'm afraid I can't COUNTENANCE your dangerous exploits, so please take me home.

ANTONYMS

askance (uh-SKANTS). With suspicion, mistrust, or disapproval; with an oblique look at an object, person, or situation.
I looked ASKANCE at Philip when he left the store without paying for his bubble gum.

stigmatize (STIG-muh-tyz). To mark or describe something in a way that shows disgrace or strong disapproval.
Many people with AIDS find that coping with the physical trauma of their disease is only part of their difficulty; another part is being STIGMATIZED by others as somehow deserving of punishment.
See also: Help, Support

14. Argue

(AR-gyoo), verb

To present reasons for or against a proposal, proposition, etc.; to dispute or contend something with or against another person.

ADJECTIVES

bellicose (BELL-ih-kohss). Belligerent, surly, ready to argue or fight at the slightest provocation.
Doug is so touchy about his new car that he'll instantly turn BELLICOSE if you so much as brush against it.

contentious (kuhn-TEN-shuss). Having the tendency to argue; quarrelsome; characterized by dispute or controversy.
I walked away when the discussion heated up and became too CONTENTIOUS.

dialectical (die-uh-LEK-tih-kul). Having to do with logical arguments.
Paul employed a DIALECTICAL thoroughness to destroy an opponent's argument.

eristic (ur-ISS-tik). Characterized by argument or controversy with often subtle and superficial reasoning.
Henry tried to understand, but Martha's ERISTIC explanation left him as clueless as he had been before she started speaking.

pugnacious (pug-NAY-shuss). Always wanting to argue and debate every last thing; quarrelsome.
Teenagers are PUGNACIOUS by nature: if I say "no," he invariably asks "why?"

NOUNS

imbroglio (im-BRO-lee-oh). An involved and confusing or bitter disagreement, as between persons or nations.
Our inability to decide which New Year's Eve party to attend created an IMBROGLIO that disrupted our social calendar for months.

logomachy (low-GOM-uh-kee). An argument or dispute distinguished by the incorrect or reckless use of words; meaningless battle of words.
One of the primary sources of entertainment during election season is the candidates' LOGOMACHY.

polemic (puh-LEM-ik). An aggressive argument against or refutation of the opinions of another; a person who argues in opposition to another; controversialist.
"He had a strong will and a talent for POLEMIC."—Saul Bellow, American author

sophistry (SOFF-iss-tree). A seemingly convincing argument that is logically flawed.
I believe this jury is too sophisticated to be taken in by the SOPHISTRIES the defense has offered.

VERBS

controvert (KON-truh-vert). To oppose with logical reasoning; to dispute or contradict.
No matter how many attempts the defense makes to CONTROVERT the details of this sequence of events, the fact remains that the defendant was seen leaving the building immediately after the murder.

expostulate (ek-SPOSS-chuh-layt). To reason earnestly with a person in opposition to something he has done or intends to do.
I EXPOSTULATED with Nora about the mistake I believed she was about to make, but she was immutable.

oppugn (uh-PYOON). To reason against; oppose with argument; call in question; fight against.
Alice bridled easily and would OPPUGN every judgment her boss made about her work.

quibble (KWIB-ul). To argue over a minor matter; to voice a niggling objection.
If you are not 100 percent satisfied, your money will promptly be refunded without question or QUIBBLE.

remonstrate (rih-MON-strayt). To protest, object, or show disapproval.
When Carlotta REMONSTRATED our snubbing of Julia, we simply began to snub Carlotta as well.

ANTONYMS

incontestable (in-kuhn-TES-tuh-bull). Inarguable because unquestionable.
The fact that Lloyd thinks his talent for birdcalls will be found attractive by women is INCONTESTABLE proof that he will remain a lifelong bachelor.

indubitable (in-DOO-bih-tuh-bull). Absolutely unquestionable and completely beyond doubt.
Warren's confidence in his judgment is INDUBITABLE, which is not to say that it is warranted.

unimpeachable (un-ihm-PEE-chuh-bull). Above reproach; impossible to discredit or slander.
Jason is not a great manager, but his technical credentials are UNIMPEACHABLE.

15. Arrogance

(AIR-uh-gunce), noun

Condition of unjustified pride or self-importance.

ADJECTIVES

fastuous (FASS-chew-us). Patronizing and supercilious.
Despite her beauty, Jenny rarely got asked out, due to her FASTUOUS behavior.

haughty (HAW-tee). Snobbish and disdainful.
"The HAUGHTY sommelier, with his talismanic tasting cup and sometimes irritating self-assurance, is perceived more as the high priest of some arcane rite than as a dining room functionary paid to help you enjoy the evening."
—Frank J. Prial, former New York Times *wine columnist*

imperious (im-PEER-ee-us). Self-important; dictatorial.
Mrs. Banks rushed around the kitchen, issuing a series of IMPERIOUS commands to the cook.

presumptuous (pri-ZUMP-choo-us). Too bold or forward; showing overconfidence; taking too much for granted; taking liberties.
Michael was PRESUMPTUOUS in assuming on his first day that he would be invited to board meetings.

supercilious (soo-per-SILL-ee-us). Having a low opinion of or contempt for others based on a belief in one's superiority.
Too many get-rich-quick promoters imbue their advertisements with a SUPERCILIOUS attitude toward the wealth-seekers they profess to want to help.

NOUNS

braggadocio (brag-uh-DOH-see-oh). Empty boasting or bragging.
Eric claims he is a consummate wine connoisseur, but it is just BRAGGADOCIO.

jackanapes (JACK-uh-napes). An arrogant or impertinent person; especially, an impudent young man.
If that JACKANAPES tells you to put his photo on the book jacket one more time, it will be the last day he works here as an editor.

ANTONYMS

unassuming (un-uh-SOOM-ing). Modest and unpretentious.
The Binghamtons just bought a lovely, UNASSUMING starter home in the town where their families live.

16. Art

(ARHT), noun

The ability to make things; creativeness; the creative process applied to aesthetic principles; the objects subject to aesthetic standards; works of art including painting, sculpture, architecture, music, literature, drama, the dance, etc.

NOUNS

art nouveau (ART noo-VOH). A popular form of design that originated in the 1880s, characterized by wavy objects such as flower stems, flowing hair, flames, etc.
That museum's collection of ART NOUVEAU jewelry is one of the town's best-kept secrets.

auteur (oh-TUR). A filmmaker who establishes complete control and imposes his distinctive style on a film.
"Miles is so caught up with being an AUTEUR that he's ruining the production!" Marla complained.

avant-garde (uh-vahnt GARD). Relating to the latest trends, especially in the world of art; of a new or experimental nature.
As a sculptor, Milton found keeping pace with the AVANT-GARDE both challenging and rewarding for his own work.

baroque (buh-ROKE). A style of art and architecture originating in Italy in the early seventeenth century and characterized by much ornamentation and curved lines.
Paula decided not to buy the house because she feared its BAROQUE decor would make it a difficult resell.

chiaroscuro (kee-are-uh-SKURE-oh). A pattern of light and dark (or light and shadow) in a painting or literary work.
The power of the painting comes from its CHIAROSCURO, which seems to indicate looming disaster.

expressionism (ex-PRESH-uh-niz-um). An art movement with roots in the late nineteenth and early twentieth centuries in which external forms of reality are distorted as a means of communicating an interior vision of the artist.
For Edvard Munch, whose painting The Scream *is perhaps the single most recognizable image of EXPRESSIONISM, the themes of isolation and anxiety were of paramount importance.*

futurism (FYOO-chur-iz-um). An early twentieth-century arts movement stressing the dynamics and movements of the industrial age.
Jones was fascinated by early industrial art; last semester he took a course on FUTURISM.

genre (ZHAWN-ruh). A particular style that characterizes a type of music, art, literature, film, etc.
Though their GENRE doesn't make for pleasant or easy reading, one has to admire muckrakers like Upton Sinclair, who aimed to bring about important social reforms with their novels.

impressionism (im-PRESH-uh-niz-um). An art movement of the late nineteenth century dedicated to reproducing the effect of light on objects, typically by means of short brush strokes.
The painter and sculptor Edgar Degas was one of the foremost practitioners of IMPRESSIONISM.

Labanotation (la-beh-no-TAY-shun). A nomenclature used to choreograph ballets, modern dance, and other performances so the dancers can follow the steps.
Even with the best-available LABANOTATION, Walker was unable to adequately perform a Viennese waltz at Natasha's coming-out party.

leitmotif (LIGHT-moe-teef). A recurring theme in a musical or opera associated with a particular character, situation, setting, etc.; a dominant theme.
Ian's LEITMOTIF is the smell of never-washed and often-worn clothing.

libretto (li-BRET-oh). The text of a musical work, such as a cantata or opera, often accompanied by a translation.
As she is fluent in Italian, Maria rarely needs to refer to the LIBRETTO when attending the opera.

mimesis (mi-MEE-sis). Imitation or representation, especially of human speech, behavior, etc.
The play's MIMESIS made me temporarily forget I was watching actors.

minimalism (MIN-ih-mull-iz-um). A school of art in which "less is more"—clean and uncluttered paintings; sculpture with simple lines; fiction written in a lean and spare style; music with uncomplicated scores and minimal instruments.
John Cage's MINIMALIST composition 4'33" consists of four and a half minutes of silence.

modernism (MOD-er-niz-um). Describes a modern avant-garde style of painting, sculpture, or architecture.
"Postmodernism is MODERNISM with the optimism taken out."
—Robert Hewison, British historian

montage (mon-TAHZH). A work of art made up of a variety of visuals—photographs, film clips, etc.—brought together to present an idea.
The documentary's excellent use of MONTAGE really brought to life the triumphs and heartbreaks of World War II.

muse (MEWS). The source of one's creative or artistic inspiration, named after the mythical Greek Muses said to be patrons of the fine arts.
"O for a MUSE of fire, that would ascend / The brightest heaven of invention."
—William Shakespeare

pastiche (pah-STEESH). A piece of music, writing, or art made up mostly of material taken from existing sources.
Some folks consider hip-hop music nothing but mindless PASTICHE, but I heartily disagree.

repertoire (REH-per-twahr). A library of works that a group knows and regularly performs.
The philharmonic's REPERTOIRE includes most of the classical standards from Bach, Beethoven, Brahms, and Mozart.

rococo (ruh-KOH-koh). A style of architecture and design developed in France from the baroque and characterized by elaborate and profuse delicate ornamentation.
Henry enjoys the elaborate shell designs of ROCOCO art, although I consider it excessively ornate.

surrealism (suh-REE-uh-liz-um). A twentieth-century movement in art and literature that emphasized the subconscious or irrational nature of perceived forms through the illogical placing and presentation of subject matter.
Dali's The Persistence of Memory, *which features the now-famous melting watches, was immediately hailed as a masterpiece of SURREALISM.*

thespian (THESS-pee-un). An actor; especially a person who performs onstage in a play.
Sir Laurence Olivier was rightly regarded as the most versatile THESPIAN of his era.

tragedian (truh-JEE-dee-un). An actor noted for performing tragic parts.
Richard Burbage was the premier TRAGEDIAN of the Elizabethan era.

triptych (TRIP-tik). A picture or carving on three panels, or a set of three associated paintings or other works of art.
Scott wanted to buy just the center painting, but the gallery owner refused to break up the TRIPTYCH.

trompe l'oeil (tromp LOY). An instance of visual trickery, as, for instance, an optical illusion giving the impression of three dimensions in a two-dimensional artistic medium.
The painter specialized in TROMPE L'OEIL murals that often fooled passersby into thinking they were walking toward a storefront.

verism (VAIR-iz-uhm). The theory that art and literature should closely represent reality, including the ugly and distasteful.
The artists from the VERISM school are usually responsible for the works that create the most public outrage.

virtu (ver-TOO). A knowledge of or appreciation for artistic objects or curios; the quality of being artistic, beautiful, rare, or otherwise of interest to collectors.
Uncle David was known for his VIRTU and his gifts were eagerly anticipated.

ANTONYMS

elemental (el-uh-MEN-tul). Primitive; starkly simple; basic.
It was clear even to the untrained eye how the artist's work progressed from ELEMENTAL depictions to more sophisticated forms later in his career.

vestigial (ve-STIJ-ee-uhl). Imperfectly developed.
This pottery shows VESTIGIAL attempts at artistry that would mature later.

17. Ask

(ASK), verb

To seek the answer to a question; inquire of; request; solicit; beg.

ADJECTIVES

precatory (PREK-uh-tor-ee). Expressing or characterized by an entreaty or wish.
The government ministers listened intently to the PRECATORY address and after thirty seconds of consideration, dismissed it as impractical.

suppliant (SUH-plee-unt). Characterized by humble imploring.
After he had an affair, Steve's SUPPLIANT behavior toward his wife became almost nauseating to his friends.

NOUNS

invocation (in-vuh-KAY-shun). The process or act of invoking; a call to a higher power (usually God) for help.
The priest offered a special INVOCATION at the beginning of the service.

mendicant (MEN-dih-kunt). Beggar.
There, among the castoffs of society, the lepers, MENDICANTS, and prostitutes of the city, he decided to begin his ministry.

VERBS

adjure (uh-JOOR). To entreat earnestly or request solemnly.
The witnesses were ADJURED to avoid any contact with the accused.

beseech (bih-SEECH). To beg, implore, or ask, with great politeness, fawning, or urgency.
We BESEECH you, Mr. Prime Minister: think twice before committing the lives of so many of our countrymen to this cause.

canvass (KAN-vus). To solicit support, opinions, votes, subscriptions, etc.
Virgil and I spent all Sunday walking around the city CANVASSING for our candidate.

catechize (KAT-ih-kyz). To question fully or closely; to question with reference to someone's beliefs.
The hiring manager CATECHIZED every applicant to weed out any with negative attitudes.

entreat (en-TREET). To ask earnestly for (something); appeal; supplicate.
Smitten by remorse, Ted ENTREATED Lorna to take him back once again.

exhort (ig-ZORT). To urge; to plead with (usually in an attempt to warn or advise).
"The function of the moralist is not to EXHORT men to be good but to elucidate what the good is."—Walter Lippmann, American journalist

implore (im-PLORE). To beseech or beg for fervently; crave; to demand urgently.
She IMPLORED him to attend the party.

importune (im-poor-TOON). To bother with requests or demands; urge or demand persistently or repeatedly.
After months of IMPORTUNING his employer for promotion to a position that did not yet exist, Hank was asked to leave the company.

interpellate (in-tur-PELL-ayt). To formally ask about an official action or policy or personal conduct.
Protocol dictated that the ambassador INTERPELLATE through proper channels.

obtest (ob-TEST). To beg for; supplicate; beseech.
Higgins decided that he would wait as long as necessary in order to OBTEST the king for clemency.

supplicate (SUP-lih-kayt). To make a humble, sincere, and earnest request of someone.
The department heads decided their best bet was to assemble as a group in the president's office and SUPPLICATE her to approve the budget increases.

ANTONYMS

affirm (uh-FURM). To state positively; declare; assert to be true.
"The more I read, the more I meditate; and the more I acquire, the more I am enabled to AFFIRM that I know nothing"—Voltaire, French philosopher and writer

profess (pro-FESS). To make an open declaration of; affirm.
Marcia was quick to PROFESS her involvement in the scheme when asked.

18. Attractive

(uh-TRAK-tihv), adjective

Pleasing in appearance or manner; alluring.

ADJECTIVES

aesthetic (ess-THET-ik). Of or related to a sense of what is attractive or beautiful.
Covering your walls with pictures torn from the newspaper does not testify to a genuine AESTHETIC sense, Harold.

beguiling (bee-GUY-ling). Charming; bewitching; enchanting.
The BEGUILING charm Monica learned at finishing school more than makes up for her vapid personality.

bucolic (byoo-KALL-ik). Expressive of rural serenity and charm.
We bought a weekend place in a BUCOLIC little village.

comely (KUM-lee). Pleasing or attractive.
Jane is COMELY, but her mother fears that the men she attracts will not make her happy.

idyllic (eye-DILL-ik). Pleasing; peaceful; ideal.
Our IDYLLIC honeymoon in the tropics was interrupted by a hurricane.

meretricious (mer-i-TRISH-us). Attracting attention in an unseemly or inappropriate fashion.
His favorite brand of beer used MERETRICIOUS ads—TV commercials showing scantily clad young women—to attract more attention.

pulchritudinous (pul-krih-TOOD-in-us). Having or characterized by physical beauty; comely.
Many in the crowd were not particularly interested in the football game itself, but attended the event to observe firsthand the PULCHRITUDINOUS cheerleaders.

statuesque (statch-oo-ESK). Having a tall and well-proportioned form; like or resembling a statue; graceful; shapely.
Although he had won many gold medals, news reporters only focused on the swimmer's STATUESQUE physique.

winsome (WIN-suhm). Winning and engaging; charming.
Lydia looked quite WINSOME throughout her coming-out party.

NOUNS

siren (SY-ren). A destructive but seductively beautiful, beguiling woman; anything considered dangerously seductive.
"It is natural to indulge in the illusions of hope. We are apt to shut our eyes to that SIREN until she 'allures' us to our death."—Gertrude Stein, American author

VERBS

captivate (KAP-tih-vayt). To capture the affection or attention of, as by beauty; charm.
Of all the girls at the dance, only Betty could CAPTIVATE the boys without seeming to try.

enthrall (en-THRAWL). To charm or captivate; to put under strong influence; enchant.
Garbo's performance was simply ENTHRALLING.

entice (en-TYSS). To tempt in a pleasing fashion; to attract or lure.
The delicious aroma emanating from the bakeshop often ENTICES me to stop in and pick up a doughnut or muffin on my way to work.

inveigle (in-VAY-gull). To lure, entice; to win over by ingenuity or flattery.
Craig INVEIGLED the dean into allowing him to graduate even though he failed to meet the foreign-language requirement of the university.

ANTONYMS

repugnant (rih-PUG-nunt). Distasteful; objectionable.
"The very word 'secrecy' is REPUGNANT in a free and open society; and we are as a people inherently and historically opposed to secret societies, to secret oaths, and to secret proceedings."—John F. Kennedy, American president

repulsive (rih-PUHL-siv). Causing strong dislike or aversion; offensive; disgusting.
Kathy was surprised by the new art exhibit; instead of beautiful, well-formed, and harmonious images, they were distinctly and utterly REPULSIVE.

19. Augur

(AW-ger), verb

To predict or foretell the future.

ADJECTIVES

arcane (ar-KAYN). Strange and mysterious; understood by only a few.
Bill's ARCANE knowledge of all Lexus models and their accessories is just a waste of gray matter.

auspicious (aw-SPISH-us). Promising; seemingly favorable or likely to be accompanied by good fortune; having encouraging signals or reasons for optimism at the beginning of an undertaking.
The blind date did not have an AUSPICIOUS start because Max kept calling his friend's cousin "Mallory" instead of "Mary."

inscrutable (in-SKROO-tuh-bull). Mysterious and not easy to understand.
"I suppose I now have the reputation of being an INSCRUTABLE dipsomaniac. One woman here originated the rumour that I am extremely lazy and will never do or finish anything."—James Joyce, Irish author and playwright

premonitory (preh-MAWN-ih-tor-ee). Strongly indicative that something is going to happen.
The Harrisons sold their stock in that company because they had a PREMONITORY vision that the company would soon go bankrupt.

NOUNS

bellwether (BELL-weh-thur). A leading indicator or important factor in determining a course of action or outcome.
The fact that Robert got thrown out of Groton and Exeter was a BELLWETHER for his lackadaisical years at Dartmouth.

harbinger (HAR-bin-jer). A forerunner or warning sign of a future event or trend.
The asteroid's shadow blotted out the sun as it speeded on a collision course with Earth, a HARBINGER of impending doom.

portent (POOR-tent). A sign that something is going to happen
In Ray Bradbury's novel Something Wicked This Way Comes, *the carnival coming to town is a PORTENT of evil things to come.*

VERBS

betoken (bee-TOE-kin). To foreshadow; to indicate something is about to occur.
For Mary and Paul, the breakdown of their new Porsche while they were still two hours away from their summer home BETOKENED a disastrous vacation.

ANTONYMS

belie (bee-LYE). To contradict or misrepresent.
Luther's mild-mannered, almost sickly appearance BELIED his physical conditioning and surprising strength.

educe (ee-DYOOCE). To come to a conclusion or solve a problem through reasoning based on thoughtful consideration of the facts.
After Roger's family purchased a Mercedes C class, rather than its usual Mercedes E class, we EDUCED the Wallertons were enduring financial difficulties.

misconstrue (miss-kuhn-STROO). To misinterpret or to take in a wrong sense.
The disagreement over the price of the yacht was due merely to the fact that David MISCONSTRUED the terms of the offer.

20. Authority

(uh-THAWR-ih-tee), noun

The power or right to give commands, enforce obedience, take action, or make final decisions; jurisdiction.

ADJECTIVES

contumacious (kon-too-MAY-shuss). Obstinately resisting authority; disobedient; insubordinate.
The CONTUMACIOUS defendant eventually had to be gagged.

insubordinate (in-suh-BOR-dn-it). Failing to accept or obey proper authority.
Frank, not eager to be branded INSUBORDINATE, did his best to carry out the colonel's strange orders.

magisterial (madj-ih-STEER-ee-uhl). Having the authority, weight, and gravity of someone considered a master of a particular art, task, ability, etc.
With MAGISTERIAL grace, the conductor lifted her baton.

martial (MAR-shull). Appropriate to wartime; pertaining to military control over a civilian population.
After capturing Richmond, the commander issued an order placing it under MARTIAL law.

officious (oh-FISH-us). Asserting authority or power in an obnoxious, overbearing, or pompous manner.
Bill was an old-school manager who believed it was proper to be OFFICIOUS and condescending in the treatment of his employees.

NOUNS

bureaucracy (byoo-RAWK-ruh-see). The concentration of power and authority in administrative bodies; an administrative body; a group of nonelective government officials.
As the company grew, the entrenched BUREAUCRACIES in the accounting and finance departments gained more and more influence.

fiat (FEE-aht). An authoritative decree or order.
Everyone interested in receiving a sizeable portion of his inheritance simply allows grandfather to rule the household by FIAT.

hegemony (hih-JEM-uh-nee). Domination of a region or the entire world by a single nation, or the authority of one individual over an entire group.
Alison should not achieve HEGEMONY over the rest of us merely because her list of social contacts is slightly longer than ours.

hierarchy (HIGH-uh-rahr-key). A pecking order or ranking according to status or level of authority.
In the HIERARCHY of the military, a medical doctor, who is assigned the rank of captain but is not a military man, automatically outranks a lieutenant, who may have years of battle experience.

judicature (JOO-dih-kuh-choor). The authority of jurisdiction of a court of law.
This case is in fact within my JUDICATURE, despite counsel's arguments to the contrary.

purview (PURR-vyoo). A person's range of authority and control.
Yes, Junior, I'm afraid that taking out the garbage DOES in fact fall into your PURVIEW.

recusancy (REK-yuh-zun-see). The refusal to recognize or obey established authority.
At one time, an individual's religious RECUSANCY could result in punishment.

sedition (sih-DISH-uhn). An action that promotes discontent or rebellion against authority.
In an act of childish SEDITION, Alex quit the club after we refused to play a round of golf with him.

suzerainty (SOO-zer-en-tee). Paramount, unquestioned authority.
"The account executives are sufficiently mature to manage every phase of their accounts without challenging the ultimate SUZERAINTY of the copywriter."
—David Ogilvy, British advertising executive

VERBS

arrogate (AIR-uh-gayt). To demand something for oneself or to take control without authority.
The way Nelson ARROGATES office meetings drives his coworkers crazy!

depose (dih-POZE). To oust or remove from office or a position of power and authority.
After the dictator was DEPOSED, the country set about healing the wounds of a long civil war.

usurp (yoo-SURP). To assume control forcibly and/or without right or authority; to take over.
The authority of Congress was indeed USURPED by Lincoln during the war, but legislators briskly reasserted themselves once the crisis was past.

ANTONYMS

derelict (dair-uh-LIKT). Willfully neglectful; shirking responsibility; knowingly failing to perform one's duty.
The sheriff was typically drunk, usually nasty, and always DERELICT in the performance of his duties.

lax (LAX). Not strict; careless; not stringent.
The new teacher was LAX in asserting his authority and could not control the classroom.

21. Avoid

(uh-VOID), verb

To keep away from; to prevent contact; to prevent from happening.

NOUNS

pariah (puh-RYE-uh). An outcast; one who is shunned, avoided, or despised.
After his firing, Milton had the nerve to show up unannounced at the company picnic and then seemed surprised when he was treated as a PARIAH.

VERBS

abscond (ab-SKOND). To depart quickly and in secret, especially to avoid criminal charges.
The bank robbers immediately ABSCONDED with the money to Mexico.

circumvent (sir-kum-VENT). To avoid by means of artful contrivance; to maneuver around; bypass.
In CIRCUMVENTING the will of the board of directors, the CEO knew he was taking a risk.

eschew (ess-CHOO). To shun; to stay away from, especially as a result of moral or ethical concerns.
Chuck ESCHEWED his coworkers' nights out on the town, knowing they almost always concluded with a visit to a strip club.

evade (ee-VADE). To sidestep or dodge; to flee from (a pursuer).
The fugitives EVADED the authorities for three months but were finally apprehended near Scottsdale, Arizona.

malinger (muh-LING-gur). To avoid work by making up excuses.
"There will be no MALINGERING in this office," the new supervisor said sternly.

preclude (pri-KLOOD). To hinder; prevent; make impossible, especially in advance.
"Don't rule out working with your hands. It does not PRECLUDE using your head."—Andy Rooney, American journalist and writer

shun (shun). To keep away from or avoid.
Wade's parents thought he would be glad they had agreed to chaperone the school dance and seemed surprised when he SHUNNED them for the entire evening.

ANTONYMS

accost (uh-KAWST). To approach and speak to; to confront.
As time went on, the old man became less and less stable and would ACCOST everyone he met on the street, asking questions no one could answer.

confront (kuhn-FRUHNT). To face; stand or meet face-to-face; to face in defiance; oppose.
"All of the great leaders have had one characteristic in common: It was the willingness to CONFRONT unequivocally the major anxiety of their people in their time."—John Kenneth Galbraith, Canadian-American economist

22. Aware

(uh-WEAR), adjective

Having knowledge of something through alert observation or interpretation of what one sees, hears, or feels; conscious.

ADJECTIVES

astute (uh-STUTE). Skilled; quick to learn or grasp; shrewd; sharp-witted.
Carl was an ASTUTE investor who knew when to follow the crowd and when to ignore it.

au courant (oh kuh-RONT). Up-to-date; current.
Mary Ann prided herself on her ability to stay AU COURANT with the latest trends in fashion.

cognizant (KOG-nih-zint). Aware of the realities of a situation; well informed.
The attorney angrily denied the charges that his client had been COGNIZANT of the scheme to defraud consumers.

discerning (dih-SUR-ning). Showing good insight, judgment, and understanding; discriminating.
Although Jamie is excellent at acquiring reference works, she is not the most DISCERNING editor when it comes to evaluating children's book proposals.

percipient (pur-SIP-ee-int). Keenly or readily perceiving; discriminating.
Arthur was a PERCIPIENT gourmet, so we always let him choose the restaurant for a celebratory meal.

perspicacious (pur-spi-KAY-shuss). Characterized by acute mental perception and understanding.
Amanda's PERSPICACIOUS powers of observation made her particularly effective as a psychologist.

pervious (PUR-vee-us). Open or accessible to reason, influence, or argument.
The new teacher was thrilled at the prospect of a classroom full of smiling faces and PERVIOUS minds.

sentient (SEN-tee-ent). Having or capable of perception or feeling; conscious.
"Many years ago, a particular creature was selected to develop into the dominant life form on this planet. It was given certain breaks and certain challenges, all of which, when utilized or overcome, marked it indelibly with particular traits as it moved along the road to a higher SENTIENCE."—Roger Zelazny, American science fiction writer

subliminal (sub-LIM-inn-uhl). Operating below the threshold of consciousness, but still having an effect on the mind.
SUBLIMINAL advertising was a big fad in advertising in the 1970s.

trenchant (TREN-chunt). Keen; sharply perceptive; incisive; discerning.
Michael's TRENCHANT commentary on American politics and society have made him a popular radio talk show host.

VERBS

annunciate (uh-NUN-see-ayt). To proclaim or announce.
Jackie chose to ANNUNCIATE her engagement at her sister's birthday party and turned the attention on herself.

apprise (uh-PRYZ). To notify; to cause to be aware of.
Have you been APPRISED of the most recent news from home?

disabuse (diss-uh-BYOOZ). To free oneself or someone else from an incorrect assumption or belief.
We had to DISABUSE Lorraine of her belief that her family connections would immediately make her a member of our group.

promulgate (PROM-ul-gayt). To put forward publicly; to announce in an official capacity.
The news of the British attack was PROMULGATED by town criers.

ANTONYMS

heedless (HEED-liss). Unmindful; careless; thoughtless.
Jack was HEEDLESS of the effects of his comments and, without meaning to, often hurt the feelings of his friends and family.

nescience (NESH-uhns). Ignorance; lack of knowledge.
The townspeople were not evil by nature, but from their NESCIENCE were afraid of and hostile to strangers.

23. Bad

(bad), adjective

Not good; defective in quality; not sound; not an acceptable standard; lacking worth; unfit.

ADJECTIVES

calamitous (kuh-LAM-uh-tuss). Catastrophic; disastrous.
The stock market's CALAMITOUS crash gave rise to a nationwide panic.

cataclysmic (kat-uh-KLIZ-mihk). Of or caused by a cataclysm (deluge); disastrous.
The assassination of the prime minister was a CATACLYSMIC event that led to a lengthy civil war.

egregious (eh-GREE-juss). Remarkable in a bad way; having extremely undesirable qualities.
Pauline made the EGREGIOUS mistake of asking the price of a piece of jewelry that caught her eye, rather than simply asking to purchase the necklace.

grievous (GREE-vuhss). Flagrant and outrageous; atrocious; causing grief and great sorrow.
"Jealousy is a GRIEVOUS passion that jealously seeks what causes grief."
—Franz Grillparzer, Austrian poet

hellacious (hel-AYE-shuss). Extremely brutal, violent, and severe; remarkably difficult.
Madison's HELLACIOUS foray into the corporate world resulted in her quickly going back to being supported solely by her trust fund.

macabre (muh-KAH-bruh). Horrifying; ghastly; reminiscent of death.
The old man's MACABRE tales frightened the children.

odious (OH-dee-us). Offensive or disgusting; causing revulsion.
"To depend upon a profession is a less ODIOUS form of slavery than to depend upon a father."—Virginia Woolf, British essayist and novelist

odoriferous (oh-duh-RIFF-er-us). Bad-smelling; foul.
Eleanor believed she would enjoy her weekend trek through the South American rainforest, but she found the animals too noisy, the constant rain unpleasant, and the forest's ODORIFEROUS vegetation distasteful.

putrescent (pyoo-TRESS-unht). Rotten; decayed; decomposed.
Roger was concerned only with the welfare of big cats and after many years in the field wasn't bothered by the PUTRESCENT remains of their prey animals.

NOUNS

abomination (uh-bom-ih-NAY-shen). Anything disgusting or hateful; a shameful, vile, or disgusting act or condition.
"Not just a vile act, your honor, the defendant committed an ABOMINATION!" thundered the prosecutor, pointing at my client.

nadir (NAY-der). Rock-bottom, the worst a situation can get or become; point of greatest despair or adversity.
We always have to attend the Wallingtons' Christmas party, because of their standing, but in truth, that dreadfully boring event is always the NADIR of our social calendar.

ANTONYMS

pukka (PUCK-uh). Authentic; genuine; proper; first-class.
He had never driven one before, but Frank could recognize immediately that this classic automobile was a PUKKA.

recherché (ruh-shair-SHAY). Sought with care; rare; choice; uncommon.
Brian was not content having the same possessions as other people and continually searched for RECHERCHÉ items to show off.
See also: Abuse, Crimes, Evil

24. Banter

(BAN-ter), noun

Good-natured teasing or light, playful remarks.

NOUNS

badinage (bah-dih-NAHZH). Light-hearted banter, not meant to be taken seriously.
"If you don't care for me, you can move out now. I'm frankly not up to BADINAGE."—Harlan Ellison, American author

chaff (CHAF). Good-natured teasing or ridicule.
It seemed easy at first, but keeping up the CHAFF throughout the party turned out to be quite a chore.

facetiousness (fuh-SEE-shuss-ness). Conversation that lacks serious intent and is concerned with something nonessential and amusing.
I could see by the amount of liquor flowing that the party would be characterized by awkward dancing and FACETIOUSNESS.

persiflage (PUR-suh-flahzh). A light, flippant, or frivolous style of writing or speaking; banter.
The room was filled with the sounds of the string quartet and the guests' PERSIFLAGE.

pleasantry (PLEZ-uhn-tree). The quality of being pleasant or playful in conversation; courteous social remark.
He now faced an enemy on the battlefield who was once his good neighbor with whom he had exchanged many PLEASANTRIES.

raillery (RAY-luh-ree). Good-natured teasing.
"RAILLERY," said Montesquieu, is "a way of speaking in favor of one's wit at the expense of one's better nature."

repartee (rep-er-TAY). Conversation characterized by witty banter.
Our galas and balls are always marked by delightful REPARTEE around the grand dinner table.

ANTONYMS

churlishness (CHUR-lish-ness). A mean, boorish, or rude outlook; lack of civility or graciousness.
Neil was surprised by Susan's CHURLISHNESS when discussing a mutual friend.

disputatious (dis-pyoo-TAY-shuss). Inclined to dispute; fond of arguing; contentious.
Laura brought her DISPUTATIOUS brother with her to the movie, so we were prepared for an unpleasant evening.

25. Bathos

(BAY-thoss), noun

A sudden change in mood from the solemn and serious to a more light-hearted, relaxed, and humorous outlook. Also, insincere pathos.

ADJECTIVES

capricious (kuh-PREE-shuss). Prone to quickly changing one's mind, decision, or course of action at the drop of a hat or on impulse.
"I do not understand the CAPRICIOUS lewdness of the sleeping mind."
—John Cheever, American novelist

effervescent (ef-ur-VESS-ent). Bubbly; upbeat; cheerful; possessing a positive attitude and joyful personality.
After getting the acceptance letter from Cornell, Sabrina was EFFERVESCENT and celebrated with a trip to Neiman Marcus.

NOUNS

bonhomie (bon-uh-MEE). A good-natured, genial manner.
Even though he has no family pedigree, Walker is accepted into our group because of his contagious BONHOMIE.

VERBS

prattle (PRAT-l). To babble; to talk nonstop without regard to whether what you are saying makes sense or is of any interest to the listener.
"Infancy conforms to nobody: all conform to it, so that one babe commonly makes four or five out of the adults who PRATTLE and play to it."
—Ralph Waldo Emerson, American poet, essayist, and transcendentalist

ANTONYMS

dyslogistic (diss-luh-JISS-tik). Showing disapproval or censure.
We gave Elizabeth DYSLOGISTIC glances when she told us she had decided to stop shopping at Cartier.

equable (ECK-wuh-bull). Unvarying, steady, and free from extremes.
"He spake of love, such love as spirits feel / In worlds whose course is EQUABLE and pure."—William Wordsworth, British Romantic poet

26. Behave

(bee-HAYV), verb

To manage or conduct oneself, especially in a proper or correct way; to act or react.

ADJECTIVES

inveterate (in-VET-er-it). Never changing; persisting by habit.
"Take all the garden spills, / INVETERATE, / prodigal spender / just as summer goes."—Hilda Doolittle, American poet and memoirist

NOUNS

demeanor (dih-MEE-ner). Outward conduct; deportment.
In an effort to teach behavior, primary schools graded students on their DEMEANOR.

habitude (HAB-uh-tyood). Customary behavior or customary procedure.
Alistair's HABITUDE is for the servants to awake him just prior to noon.

portance (PORT-ens). Conduct; carriage, bearing; demeanor.
My grandmother grew up in a more civilized period, or so she claimed, and appreciated the value of proper PORTANCE.

praxis (PRAK-sis). Established practice; custom.
At one time, killing and stuffing specimens was the PRAXIS for many branches of biology.

propriety (pro-PRY-uh-tee). Behaving in a way that conforms to the manners and morals of polite society.
"PROPRIETY is the least of all laws, and the most observed."—François de La Rochefoucauld, French author

VERBS

acquit (uh-KWIT). To behave in accordance with a person's position or obligations.
It had been years since the actors had worked together on stage, but they both ACQUITED themselves like professionals.

bestir (bee-STUR). To rouse to action; stir up; busy or exert (oneself).
Having made elaborate preparations to watch the game without interruption, Arthur did not plan to BESTIR himself for the rest of the afternoon.

comport (kum-PORT). To conduct oneself; to behave in a particular way.
Roger always embarrasses us because he seems to think his family name frees him to COMPORT himself foolishly.

discharge (dis-CHARJ). To perform, execute, or fulfill a duty or function.
The soldier took his position seriously and always DISCHARGED his duties to the best of his ability.

ANTONYMS

dysfunctional (diss-FUNK-shun-uhl). Characterized by abnormal functioning, or poor interpersonal behavior within a group.
Charlie always blames his rotten behavior on being the product of a DYSFUNCTIONAL family.

27. Belief

(bee-LEEF), noun

A state of mind in which confidence is placed in a person or thing; a conviction that certain things are true; faith.

ADJECTIVES

existential (eggs-ih-STEN-shul). Pertaining to ideas, beliefs, and philosophies that support the concept of free will and the freedom of the individual.
"No phallic hero, no matter what he does to himself or to another to prove his courage, ever matches the solitary, EXISTENTIAL courage of the woman who gives birth."—Andrea Dworkin, American radical feminist and author

implausible (im-PLAWZ-ih-bull). Difficult to believe; highly unlikely to be true.
"At first glance, most famous fairy tales seem so IMPLAUSIBLE and irrelevant to contemporary life that their survival is hard to understand."—Alison Lurie, American novelist and academic

monistic (moh-NIS-tik). Characterized by the idea that everything—including philosophy, religion, and mysticism—can be reduced to a single substance or explained by a single principle.
Of course we believe the world is MONISTIC. Wealth is the source of everything in the universe.

orthodox (OR-thuh-docks). Mainstream; conventional; adhering to the strictest interpretation of a law or religion.
ORTHODOX medicine has long ignored the obvious effect diet and nutrition have on health and illness.

staunch (stonch). Firm in resolution or belief; fixed.
Mr. West, a STAUNCH conservative, believed that government waste was the main problem requiring attention in Washington.

syncretistic (sin-krih-TIH-stik). Pertaining to a set of beliefs obtained by combining elements of multiple cultures, religions, societies, or schools of thought.
Pauline's SYNCRETISTIC worldview comes from the fact that her family has traveled extensively across the globe.

teleological (tee-lee-uh-LOJ-ih-kuhl). Concerning the belief that things exist for a purpose.

The fact that we have unsurpassable wealth and taste, while others who are less important endure hardship, is surely proof that we live in a TELEOLOGICAL universe.

NOUNS

agnostic (ag-NOS-tik). A person who believes it is impossible to know the essential nature of things and whether or not an ultimate cause (as God) exists.

Frank, who had been raised in a deeply religious home, knew that it would hurt his parents if they discovered he was an AGNOSTIC.

determinism (dih-TUR-muh-niz-um). The belief that a person's course of action is not free but predetermined by external circumstances.

A true disciple of DETERMINISM, Jerry felt he should not be held accountable for having married three women—since, as he argued, each of the relationships had been "meant to be."

ethos (EE-thos). The core principles or beliefs of a religion, culture, or community.

Even the eating of cheese violates the ETHOS of the vegan culture.

humanism (HEW-muh-niz-um). The philosophy or belief that the highest ideals of human existence can be fulfilled without regard to religion or supernatural intervention.

"The four characteristics of HUMANISM are curiosity, a free mind, belief in good taste, and belief in the human race."—E. M. Forster, English novelist

hypothesis (hy-POTH-uh-sis). A principle derived from limited evidence, seen as sensible based on an analysis of available data, but not proven to the point where it is an accepted theory, rule, or law.

"In order to shake a HYPOTHESIS, it is sometimes not necessary to do anything more than push it as far as it will go."—Denis Diderot, French philosopher

iconoclast (eye-KAHN-uh-clast). An individual who is contrarian in thought, rebellious in spirit, and oppositional, and who applies himself to battling established institutions, existing governments, religious doctrine, and popular notions and beliefs.

The late George Carlin saw the role of the comic in society as one of ICONOCLAST.

ideologue (EYE-dee-uh-log). A person who rigidly adheres to an ideology with a closed mind regarding other points of view.
"An IDEOLOGUE may be defined as a mad intellectual."—Clifton Fadiman, American critic

martyrdom (MAR-ter-dum). The condition of having suffered death as a martyr, a person who has died or been killed rather than give up his faith or principles.
Many say that John Brown's MARTYRDOM served his cause more effectively than anything he did at Harper's Ferry.

mores (MORE-ayz). The accepted norms of social behavior for the time and society in which one lives.
Grant learned the hard way that MORES vary from country to country when he made the faux pas of trying to shake the hand of the Thai businessman.

nihilism (NIE-uh-liz-im). The belief that life is meaningless.
A profound NIHILISM seems to have fallen over the poet during the last six months she spent in London; her letters to her mother indicate a severe depression.

pragmatism (PRAG-muh-tiz-um). The belief that one's actions should be guided primarily based on knowledge or opinion of what is likely to work best in a given situation; the imperative to always do what is practical and effective.
Our families have succeeded in amassing great wealth over many generations because we are all, at heart, practitioners of PRAGMATISM.

predestination (pree-dess-tih-NAY-shun). The belief that we do not have free will and that our lives and destinies are preordained and beyond our control.
The problem with PREDESTINATION is that whatever happens, you can say that it was meant to be, and no one can prove you wrong.

solipsism (SAHL-ip-sihz-uhm). The notion that one's own experiences and thoughts are the only source of true knowledge.
The SOLIPSISM of some members of the leisure class is distasteful to those of us who, for example, know what our servants need even more than they do.

tabula rasa (TAB-yuh-luh RAH-suh). A clean slate; lacking preconceived notions, prejudices, beliefs, and attitudes; receptive to instruction and information.
"Classic writer's fear of the blank page: call it TABULA-RASA-phobia."
—John Jerome, American nonfiction writer

Taoism (DOW-is-um). A system of philosophy identified with the sage Lao-tzu and embodied most notably in his work *Tao Te Ching*, which holds that life lived simply and in accordance with natural laws and events is most in keeping with the Tao, or way, that underlies all existence.

Scholars may debate the fine points of a rational understanding of TAOISM, but a true practitioner probably expresses it best when she gracefully and thankfully accepts a proffered cup of tea.

tenet (TEN-it). A central doctrine; a core belief; a rule or principle one lives by.

"Christian writers from the third century on pointed out the deleterious effect of Platonism on Christian belief—even while adopting many of its fundamental TENETS."—Harold Attridge, Dean of Yale University Divinity School

weltschmerz (VELT-shmertz). A lingering sorrow that some believe is a given in life.

When we snubbed Margaret for buying so many fashion knockoffs, her WELTSCHMERZ lasted until we forgave her.

zealot (ZEL-it). A rabid follower; a true believer; a fanatical advocate.

"What a noble aim is that of the ZEALOT who tortures himself like a madman in order to desire nothing, love nothing, feel nothing, and who, if he succeeded, would end up a complete monster!"—Denis Diderot, French philosopher

zeitgeist (ZITE-gyst). The prevailing viewpoints, attitudes, and beliefs of a given generation or period in history.

In the twenty-first century, "going green" is very much at the forefront of the nation's ZEITGEIST, as people have been made aware of the importance of being good stewards of our planet's natural resources.

ANTONYMS

apostasy (uh-POSS-tah-see). The act of abandoning, ignoring, or openly flouting an accepted principle or belief.

Paul was a believer in his parents' religion for most of his life, until his faith was overrun and crushed by unstoppable APOSTASY.

dubiety (doo-BY-ih-tee). The state of doubt; doubtfulness; uncertainty.

The financial reports were inconsistent and confusing, and they caused rampant DUBIETY within both chambers of Congress.

28. Best

(BEST), adjective

Having the highest quality, standing, or excellence; most suitable, desirable, or advantageous; superior to all others.

ADJECTIVES

efflorescent (ef-luh-RESS-uhnt). Describes something that has reached the final stage of its development or is at the peak of perfection.
Thomas is convinced that the Bugatti Veyron Fbg represents the EFFLORESCENT automobile.

empyreal (em-PEER-ee-uhl). Elevated and sublime; or, of the sky.
The beautiful three-carat sapphire her fiancé gave her shone with an EMPYREAL, almost celestial, light.

maximal (MAK-suh-mull). The highest or greatest possible; at the upper limit.
Once it reached its MAXIMAL height, the test plane could be returned to base for examination.

nonpareil (non-pah-RELL). Without equal or peer.
We could tell Jeanette was a typical parvenu when she attempted to convince us that Bennington Posh Couture golf bags are NONPAREIL.

optimum (OP-tih-mum). The most favorable degree, point, or condition; the best result for given conditions.
George knew his fish and arrived at the best spot on the lake at the OPTIMUM moment.

paramount (PAIR-uh-mount). Supreme; superior; excellent.
It is of PARAMOUNT importance that we complete this project on time.

peerless (PEER-luss). Without peer; above others with regard to ability or quality; beyond compare.
Mrs. Reilly's PEERLESS skills as a mediator soon earned her a special position of respect on the school board.

quintessential (kwin-tuh-SEN-shul). The most nearly perfect or typical example of its category or kind.

"Craving that old sweet oneness yet dreading engulfment, wishing to be our mother's and yet be our own, we stormily swing from mood to mood, advancing and retreating—the QUINTESSENTIAL model of two-mindedness."
—Judith Viorst, American author and psychoanalyst

rarefied (RAIR-uh-fyed). Lofty; exalted; of high class or caliber.
Most copywriters don't operate in the RAREFIED environment in which Clayton makes his millions.

superlative (soo-PURR-luh-tiv). The quality of something's being the best in its class.
Our family's show horses are SUPERLATIVE in every way.

NOUNS

apotheosis (ah-paw-thee-OH-sis). The culmination or highest point.
Winning the Silver Gutter Award at his local bowling alley was the APOTHEOSIS of Wendell's less-than-stellar sports legacy.

epitome (ee-PIT-uh-mee). The highest or supreme example.
Many people consider The Mary Tyler Moore Show *to be the EPITOME of a 1970s situation comedy.*

exemplar (ig-ZEM-plar). A role model, a shining example of a desired state, status, or behavior.
"The system—the American one, at least—is a vast and noble experiment. It has been polestar and EXAMPLAR for other nations."—Phyllis McGinley, American poet

ne plus ultra (nay plooce OOL-truh). The highest possible embodiment (of something).
Many consider Oedipus Rex *tragic drama's NE PLUS ULTRA.*

paragon (PAIR-uh-gone). A peerless model or pattern of perfection.
Even if we could live our lives in accordance with the PARAGONS of right living, would we not still experience conflict and misunderstanding with others?

primacy (PRY-muh-see). Quality of being first in order, rank, or importance.
Physics is thought, by physicists, to hold PRIMACY over other sciences.

zenith (ZEE-nith). The highest point attained; the peak.
"This dead of midnight is the noon of thought, / And Wisdom mounts her ZENITH with the stars."—Anna Laetitia Barbauld, English poet and children's author

ANTONYMS

nadir (NAY-der). Rock-bottom, the worst a thing can get or become; point of greatest despair or adversity.
Everyone quietly prayed that the market had reached its NADIR and would bounce back quickly and completely.
See also: Grand

29. Bona fide

(BO-nah fyed), adjective

Legitimate, the real thing, the genuine article.

ADJECTIVES

unimpeachable (un-ihm-PEE-chuh-bull). Above reproach; impossible to discredit or slander.
We promoted Carla to upstairs maid because her job performance has been UNIMPEACHABLE.

veritable (VER-ih-tuh-bull). Genuine; the real thing; representing a perfect specimen or example.
"For me, the child is a VERITABLE image of becoming, of possibility, poised to reach towards what is not yet, towards a growing that cannot be predetermined or prescribed."—Maxine Greene, American philosopher and educator

NOUNS

exemplar (ig-ZEM-plar). A role model, a shining example of a desired state, status, or behavior.
"The system—the American one, at least—is a vast and noble experiment. It has been polestar and EXAMPLAR for other nations."—Phyllis McGinley, American poet

rectitude (REHK-tih-tood). Moral virtue; rightness.
"The mind that's conscious of its RECTITUDE, / Laughs at the lies of rumor."
—Ovid, Roman poet

veracity (ver-ASS-ih-tee). The characteristic or habit of being truthful
and conforming to accepted standards of behavior.
"The world is upheld by the VERACITY of good men: they make the earth whole-
some."—Ralph Waldo Emerson, American poet, essayist, and transcendentalist

VERBS

vindicate (VIN-dih-kayt). To prove your opinion is correct, or your action
justified, or that you are innocent of a misdeed you stand accused of, despite
opinions and evidence to the contrary.
We laughed at Paulette's predictions about the imminent fall fashions, but
once the couture was unveiled, Paulette was VINDICATED.

ANTONYMS

aggrandize (uh-GRAN-dyz). To exaggerate, put on a false front, and make
something look greater and grander than it really is.
Phil tries to AGGRANDIZE his reputation by stating that he is a charter
member of the Bill O'Reilly fan club, but everybody just thinks this "feat"
makes him pathetic.

clandestine (klan-DES-tin). Pertaining to activities that are secret, covert,
and perhaps not fully authorized or sanctioned.
"CLANDESTINE steps upon imagined stairs / Climb through the night, because
his cuckoos call."—Wallace Stevens, American poet

fallacious (fuh-LAY-shuss). Based on one or more false assumptions.
Since my online subscriber list is double opt-in, accusing me of being a
spammer is a wholly FALLACIOUS assumption.

faux (FOH). Fake; phony; artificial.
She wore a cheap second-hand dress and a FAUX pearl necklace made out of
white beads.

inveigle (in-VAY-gull). To convince or persuade someone through trickery, dishonesty, or flattery.
Craig INVEIGLED the dean into allowing him to graduate even though he failed to meet the foreign language requirement of the university.

traduce (truh-DOOCE). To speak maliciously of; slander.
We have snubbed Katrina permanently because she has, at one time or another, TRADUCED each one of us in the society pages.

usurper (you-SIR-per). A person who seizes a position of power through illegal means, force, or deception.
"A USURPER in the guise of a benefactor is the enemy that we are now to encounter and overcome."—William Leggett, American poet and fiction writer

30. Brave

(BRAYV), adjective

The characteristic of fearlessness in meeting danger or difficulty; having courage.

ADJECTIVES

audacious (aw-DAY-shuss). Extremely bold; reckless; daring; adventurous; defiant in the face of convention.
His AUDACIOUS behavior at the family reunion shocked even his brothers and sisters.

dauntless (DAWNT-liss). Fearless, intrepid, and bold.
"For Thought has a pair of DAUNTLESS wings."—Robert Frost, American poet

intrepid (in-TREP-id). Resolutely brave.
The INTREPID climber made her way down the icy mountain alone.

valorous (VAL-er-uss). Characterized by fearlessness and bravery, especially in battle.
My uncle's office was filled with citations commemorating his many VALOROUS acts in World War II.

NOUNS

bravado (bruh-VAW-doe). An open show of bravery; characterized by a display of boldness.
The mayor's swaggering attitude of BRAVADO was of little help when the town was finally attacked.

sangfroid (san-FWAH). The attitude or state of possessing a cool head and steadfast composure in the face of danger, adversity, or stressful situations.
The car crash shook him, but within seconds he recovered his SANGFROID and went to check on his driver.

ANTONYMS

pavid (PAV-id). Timid and fearful.
Charlie's cat must have been abused as a kitten, because it sleeps with one PAVID eye open.

pusillanimous (pyoo-suh-LAN-ih-muss). Being mild or timid by nature; a shrinking violet; a person who seeks to avoid conflict, challenge, and danger.
L. Frank Baum's most PUSILLANIMOUS fictional creation is the Cowardly Lion of Oz.

recreant (REHK-ree-ant). Craven; cowardly; crying for mercy.
Victory seemed likely because we were facing a reputedly RECREANT foe.

tremulous (TREHM-yuh-luss). Timid and fearful.
With TREMULOUS mien, Anthony asked Gwendolyn if she would consent to a joining of their families.

trepidation (trep-ih-DAY-shun). A state of fear or agitation.
Continual tremors created TREPIDATION in the entire population.

31. Burgeon

(BURR-jin), verb

To sprout, to grow; to blossom and flourish.

ADJECTIVES

ebullient (eh-BULL-yuhnt). Feeling joy and positive emotions at an extreme level; the state of being wildly enthusiastic about something.
Lorne was EBULLIENT when he found that his mother had given the college enough money to overturn his rejection.

efflorescent (ef-luh-RESS-uhnt). Having reached the final stage of its development, or being at the peak of perfection.
Thomas is convinced that the Bugati Veyron Fbg represents the EFFLORESCENT automobile.

fervent (FUR-vuhnt). Showing great enthusiasm and intensity of spirit.
Packing up the family's castoffs for myriad charities each December places Contessa in a FERVENT state.

germinal (JUHR-mih-nuhl). Related to the earliest stage of development.
Roland's foray into art-buying is in its GERMINAL phase.

NOUNS

apotheosis (ah-paw-thee-OH-siss). The culmination or highest point.
Winning the Silver Gutter Award at his local bowling alley was the APOTHEOSIS of Wendell's less-than-stellar sports legacy.

concupiscence (kon-KYOO-pih-suhns). Unbridled lust in the extreme—horniness.
"You're talking to a young vampire, a fountain of CONCUPISCENCE."
—Mario Acevedo, American fantasy author

VERBS

foment (foe-MENT). To rouse or incite.
"If perticuliar care and attention is not paid to the Laidies we are determined to FOMENT a Rebelion, and will not hold ourselves bound by any Laws in which we have no voice, or Representation."—Abigail Adams, second First Lady of the United States

metastasize (meh-TASS-tih-size). To spread harmfully from an original source, as with cancer cells.
Byron's ugly nature quickly METASTASIZED in our group, as he spread lies and gossip among more and more of our social contacts.

ANTONYMS

entropy (EN-troh-pee). The tendency of any system to run down and revert to total chaos.
"Just as the constant increase of ENTROPY is the basic law of the universe, so it is the basic law of life to be ever more highly structured and to struggle against ENTROPY."—Václav Havel, Czech playwright, writer, and politician

32. Cabal

(kuh-BAHL), noun

An underground society, secret religious sect, or other private group assembled for purposes hidden from those around them.

ADJECTIVES

furtive (FUR-tihv). Acting guilty of some misstep or possessing knowledge one would just as soon keep secret.
"For a while the two stared at each other—Denison embarrassed, Selene almost FURTIVE."—Isaac Asimov, Russian-born American author and biochemist

inscrutable (in-SKROO-tuh-bull). Mysterious and not easy to understand.
"I suppose I now have the reputation of being an INSCRUTABLE dipsomaniac. One woman here originated the rumour that I am extremely lazy and will never do or finish anything."—James Joyce, Irish author and playwright

Machiavellian (mack-ee-uh-VEL-ee-uhn). Unscrupulous and self-centered; manipulative; cunning.
We can hardly be called MACHIAVELLIAN simply because we do what we need to do to hold onto the luxurious lifestyle to which we have become accustomed.

NOUNS

coup (koo). Forcible seizure of power or control.
Sophia took control of her father's company while he was in the hospital, an act the investors considered a bit of a COUP.

minion (MIN-yuhn). A follower of someone in an important position.
"I caught this morning morning's MINION, king- / dom of daylight's dauphin, dapple-dawn-drawn Falcon, in his riding."—Gerard Manley Hopkins, English poet and Jesuit priest

oligarchy (OH-lih-gar-kee). A nation, state, or other place where the population is governed by a relatively small group of people, especially when all are members of the same family.
Most family owned businesses are OLIGARCHIES, not democracies.

sedition (sih-DISH-uhn). An action that promotes discontent or rebellion.
In an act of childish SEDITION, Alex quit the club after we refused to play a round of golf with him.

VERBS

encipher (en-SY-fur). To scramble or convert data into a secret code, prior to transmission.
Mathematicians were employed by the Army to crack ENCIPHERED messages during the war.

ANTONYMS

gregarious (greh-GAIR-ee-us). Extroverted; outgoing; friendly and cheerful in nature.
"We are easy to manage, a GREGARIOUS people, / Full of sentiment, clever at mechanics, and we love our luxuries."—Robinson Jeffers, American poet

ostentatious (awe-sten-TAY-shuss). Pretentious; presented in a showy manner so as to impress others; meant to flaunt one's wealth or success.
"The man who is OSTENTATIOUS of his modesty is twin to the statue that wears a fig-leaf."—Mark Twain

33. Careful

(KAYR-full), adjective

Exercising caution; dealing thoughtfully with a situation; wary; showing close attention or great concern.

ADJECTIVES

chary (CHAIR-ee). Very cautious or wary.
I was CHARY of Lillian's new business scheme because her "great" ideas always result in spectacular disasters.

circumspect (SIR-kum-spekt). Prudent, cautious; considering from all sides.
"I smiled, / I waited, / I was CIRCUMSPECT; / O never, never, never write that I / missed life or loving."—Hilda Doolittle, American poet and memoirist

fastidious (fah-STID-ee-us). Particular about things, expecially good housekeeping and personal hygiene; placing great importance on even the smallest of details.
"A FASTIDIOUS person in the throes of love is a rich source of mirth."
—Martha Duffy, Arts editor, Time *magazine*

meticulous (meh-TIK-yuh-luhss). Extremely precise; fussy about details.
As a radiologist, Arthur was required to give METICULOUS attention to reading test results.

parsimonious (par-sih-MOAN-ee-us). Conservative in spending and tight with a dollar; parting with money or other resources only grudgingly and after much cajoling.
Esmerelda can be surprisingly PARSIMONIOUS, considering that her family's fortune is among the greatest possessed by our social contacts.

punctilious (punk-TILL-ee-uss). Overly attentive to trifling details; taking great care to dispose of seemingly small matters in a formally correct way.
The PUNCTILIOUS Mrs. Smith took issue with the seating arrangements we had suggested.

scrupulous (SKROO-pyoo-luss). Characterized by a conscientious adherence to what is considered true, right, or accurate.
The CFO was replaced by a financial expert who also exercised SCRUPULOUS control of the company's expense accounts, much to the chagrin of the sales force.

NOUNS

preciosity (presh-ee-OSS-uh-tee). Carefully affected or fastidious refinement.
It was unclear why Ralph adopted his PRECIOSITY, but we know he didn't inherit it from his guileless parents.

ANTONYMS

prodigal (PRAHD-ih-gull). Characterized by reckless wastefulness; spendthrift; excessively generous.
Known for his PRODIGAL spending habits, William always caused a stir among waitstaff in the restaurants he frequented.

profligate (PROF-lih-git). Extravagant; wasteful; excessive.
"The official account of the Church's development viewed alternative voices as expressing the views of a misguided minority, craven followers of contemporary culture, PROFLIGATE sinners, or worse."—Harold Attridge, Dean of Yale University Divinity School

slatternly (SLAT-urn-lee). Untidy and careless; slovenly; disorderly.
Dorothy's SLATTERNLY habits make her an interesting choice for "mother of the year."

slovenly (SLUHV-in-lee). Dirty or untidy in one's personal habits.
Burt's SLOVENLY room is at odds with his tidy personal appearance.

34. Chance

(CHANSS), noun

Happenings that occur unpredictably in the absence of cause or design; fortuity; luck; uncertainty.

ADJECTIVES

aleatory (A-lee-uh-tore-ee). Unplanned, spontaneous, or spur of the moment; depending on luck, randomness, or chance.
"Of course you lost the election!" Miranda yelled. "An ALEATORY, fly-by-the-seat-of-your-pants campaign is never going to be a recipe for success!"

auspicious (aw-SPISH-us). Promising; seemingly favorable or likely to be accompanied by good fortune; encouraging optimism at the beginning of an undertaking.
The trip did not begin AUSPICIOUSLY; our car broke down within an hour.

fortuitous (for-TOO-ih-tuss). A happy event taking place by accident or chance.
"The most FORTUITOUS event of my entire life was meeting my wife Eleanor."—Franklin Delano Roosevelt

hapless (HAP-liss). Luckless; unfortunate.
Oliver presented a rather HAPLESS figure during his first few days on the job, but he soon mastered his new responsibilities.

inauspicious (in-aw-SPISH-uss). Accompanied by or predictive of ill luck; not favorable in portent.
Who could have predicted that from such INAUSPICIOUS beginnings Grant would rise to command great armies and, eventually, lead his nation?

precarious (prih-KAIR-ee-us). Tenuous; dependent upon circumstances; uncertain; unsecured.
During that time of civil unrest, Jack thought frequently about his PRECARIOUS future.

propitious (pruh-PISH-us). Presenting a good omen; auspicious.
We all hoped that the beautiful sunset was a PROPITIOUS omen for our camping vacation.

providential (prahv-uh-DEN-shul). Fortunate; as if occurring by or resulting from divine intervention.
Fastening my seat belt was a PROVIDENTIAL act, as the accident made apparent.

NOUNS

deus ex machina (DAY-uhs eks MA-keh-nuh). An unexpected and fortunate event solving a problem or saving someone from disaster; a stroke of good luck.
Harry had reached a financial threshold, and it would take a DEUX EX MACHINA to rescue him from bankruptcy.

entropy (EN-troh-pee). The tendency of any system to run down and revert to total chaos.
"Just as the constant increase of ENTROPY is the basic law of the universe, so it is the basic law of life to be ever more highly structured and to struggle against ENTROPY."—Václav Havel, Czech playwright, writer, and politician

kismet (KIHZ-met). Fate or destiny.
A hopeless romantic, Brian believed KISMET was responsible for his arranged marriage.

serendipity (ser-en-DIP-ih-tee). The attaining of success, good fortune, or an object of desire through luck and random circumstance.
What made him an Internet billionaire was SERENDIPITY more than brains or talent.

ANTONYMS

ascribe (uh-SKRYBE). To attribute or assign causal responsibility to a person or thing.
This work has been ASCRIBED to Rousseau, but his authorship now seems uncertain.

etiology (ee-tee-OL-uh-gee). The assignment of a cause; the science of origins or causes.
The ETIOLOGY of the disease was clear; David developed mesothelioma from his years of working, unprotected, with asbestos.

35. Change

(CHEYNJ), noun, verb

A transformation; substitution; alteration or modification; to cause to become different; convert

ADJECTIVES

capricious (kuh-PREE-shuss). Prone to quickly changing one's mind, decision, or course of action at the drop of a hat or on impulse.
"I do not understand the CAPRICIOUS lewdness of the sleeping mind."
—John Cheever, American novelist

malleable (MAL-yuh-bull). Easily molded into different shapes; easily influenced to change one's opinion or actions.
"I did not know that mankind was suffering for want of gold. I have seen a little of it. I know that it is very MALLEABLE, but not so MALLEABLE as wit."—Henry David Thoreau, American author and transcendentalist

mercurial (mer-KYOOR-ee-uhl). Volatile, fickle, and erratic.
Joe thought his MERCURIAL boss was exhausting but highly entertaining.

pliable (PLY-uh-bull). Able to be changed in shape, form, or inclination; capable of being directed or influenced.
Gold, one of the world's most valuable metals, is also one of the most PLIABLE.

protean (PRO-tee-en). Highly changeable; readily taking on different characters or forms.
A willing, brave, and PROTEAN actress will tend to be employed more frequently.

NOUNS

acculturation (ah-kul-chuh-RAY-shin). The process of adapting to a different culture; cultural modification.
New citizens are formed through ACCULTURATION at the cost of their heritage and culture.

flux (FLUKS). Unceasing change.
The organization's plans were in a state of constant FLUX.

mutability (myoo-tuh-BIL-ih-tee). The condition of being able to change at a moment's notice.
"It is the same! For, be it joy or sorrow, / The path of its departure still is free: / Man's yesterday may ne'er be like his morrow; / Nought may endure but MUTABILITY"—Percy Bysshe Shelley, English Romantic poet

permutation (per-myoo-TAY-shun). A transformation leading to a complete change.
After exploring numerous PERMUTATIONS of its style, the band returned to the sound with which it had first attracted fans.

transubstantiation (tran-sub-stan-she-A-shun). The changing of one substance into another; transmutation; transformation.
TRANSUBSTANTIATION is used as a technique in marketing, transforming shabby and gauche items into supposed examples of tasteful luxury.

vicissitudes (vhi-SISS-ih-toods). The constant changes in one's situation or condition, common throughout life.
"VICISSITUDES of fortune, which spares neither man nor the proudest of his works, which buries empires and cities in a common grave."—Edward Gibbon, British historian

VERBS

abrade (uh-BRADE). To wear away or rub off; to wear down in spirit.
The campaign had hoped for a hard-hitting, informative television commercial, but the ad—widely perceived as negative and mean-spirited—served only to ABRADE voter support.

acclimate (AK-lih-mayt). To adapt or become accustomed to a new altitude, climate, environment, or situation.
At first Joan found college life lonely and stressful, but after a few weeks she was able to ACCLIMATE, and she never longed for home again.

assimilate (uh-SIM-uh-layt). To acquire and incorporate as one's own; to absorb; to alter by adoption.
Dorothy could ASSIMILATE information more quickly and thoroughly than any other student in the school.

emend (ee-MEND). To change by means of editing; to correct (a text or reading).
Many of Shakespeare's most famous lines, such as "A rose by any other name would smell as sweet," are the result of a critic's choice to EMEND a troublesome source text.

macerate (MASS-uh-rayt). To waste away; to become thin or emaciated; to soften or decompose.
It was painful for his family to watch Harold, who had been so vigorous and robust, slowly MACERATE.

metamorphose (met-uh-MORE-fohz). To change completely in character or nature; to change into a different physical form.
The boarding school experience gave Martha new friends and the impetus to METAMORPHOSE into a young woman.

permute (per-MYOOT). To alter; to make different; to change the order or sequence of.
John had spent more than fifty hours creating what he thought was the perfect presentation until his boss asked him to PERMUTE much of the statistical data.

shunt (SHUNT). To change the direction of; to divert.
When his proposal was dismissed after less than a minute of discussion, Mark felt more than ever that his ideas were being SHUNTED aside without due consideration.

ANTONYMS

immutable (ih-MYOO-tuh-bull). Unchangeable.
"I don't know what IMMUTABLE differences exist between men and women apart from differences in their genitals."—Naomi Weisstein, American feminist

incorrigible (in-KORE-ih-juh-bull). Incapable of being reformed; not easily changed or influenced.
Young Pete was an INCORRIGIBLE boy, forever getting into scrapes and causing mischief.

ossify (OS-uh-fye). To harden and become unable to change.
Due to his lack of contact with others, Jack's opinions have OSSIFIED.

Rubicon (ROO-bih-kawn). A point beyond which permanent change is unavoidable.
In signing the bill, the governor may have crossed the RUBICON and forever closed the door on his prison reform program.
See also: Reduce

36. Cogent

(KOH-jent), adjective

Reasoned; well-thought-out; logical; compelling; persuasive.

ADJECTIVES

apropos (ap-rih-POE). Appropriate, or at an opportune time.
Charlie began screaming the words "Too late! Too late!" APROPOS of nothing.

cognizant (KOG-nih-sint). Aware of the realities of a situation.
Amanda is always COGNIZANT of her acquaintances' pedigrees.

germane (jehr-MANE). Relevant, pertinent, and fitting.
"Quotes from Mao, Castro, and Che Guevara . . . are as GERMANE to our highly technological, computerized society as a stagecoach on a jet runway at Kennedy airport."—Saul Alinksy, American activist

salient (SALE-yent). Relevant; germane; important; something that stands out and gets noticed.
The pond in the front yard is the most SALIENT feature of our new home.

tendentious (ten-DEN-shuss). Promoting one's beliefs or point of view.
Laura is TENDENTIOUS in extolling her belief in the efficacy of prayer in healing all illnesses.

NOUNS

raison d'être (RAY-zohn deh-truh). The core reason why something exists; its central purpose and, literally, "reason for being."
When Jane's children went off to college, her RAISON D'ÊTRE disappeared, and she fell into a deep depression.

sagacity (suh-GASS-ih-tee). Wisdom; soundness of judgment.
"Our minds are endowed by nature with such activity and SAGACITY that the soul is believed to be produced from heaven."—Quintilian, Roman rhetorician

VERBS

adjudicate (uh-JOO-dih-kayt). To preside over or listen to opposing arguments and help two parties settle their differences and come to an agreement.
As my daughters pummeled each other while screaming at top volume, I tried desperately to ADJUDICATE their quarrel.

educe (ee-DYOOCE). To come to a conclusion or solve a problem through reasoning based on thoughtful consideration of the facts.
After Roger's family purchased a Mercedes C class, rather than its usual Mercedes E class, we EDUCED the Wallertons were enduring financial difficulties.

ANTONYMS

feckless (FEK-less). Possessing an air of casual indifference; lacking definitiveness of purpose.
Some accuse us of being FECKLESS, but they have no idea how difficult it is to live a wealth-infused lifestyle.

obtuse (ob-TOOCE). Lacking understanding, intelligence, and perception; unable to comprehend; having a dense mind.
Thomas was so OBTUSE that he didn't realize his inappropriate behavior was making his friends uncomfortable.

opaque (oh-PAYK). Hard to understand; obscure.
"The bottom of being is left logically OPAQUE to us, as something which we simply come upon and find, and about which (if we wish to act) we should pause and wonder as little as possible."—William James, American psychologist and philosopher

tangential (tan-JEHN-shull). Divergent or digressive; having little to do with the subject or matter at hand.

"New York is full of people . . . with a feeling for the TANGENTIAL adventure, the risky adventure, the interlude that's not likely to end in any double-ring ceremony."—Joan Didion, American journalist

37. Color

(KULL-er), noun

The portion of the visible light spectrum reflected by an object; the resulting sensation of light waves on the eye.

ADJECTIVES

cerulean (suh-RUE-lee-uhn). Being the blue of the sky.
Boys lined up everywhere that Janis went just to look into her CERULEAN eyes.

monochromatic (mawn-owe-kruh-MAT-ik). Of a single color.
The sweep and power of Ansel Adams's MONOCHROMATIC photography proves how much can be accomplished with a roll of black-and-white film.

olivaceous (all-uh-VAY-shuss). Dark green, olive.
The Springfield Golf Club was known for its OLIVACEOUS fairways.

pallid (PAL-id). Pale; faint; lacking in color.
Nancy's PALLID complexion was the result of poor health rather than a desire to avoid UV rays.

pavonine (PAHV-uh-nine). Resembling the colors of a peacock; rainbowlike.
Nature at its finest is demonstrated by the peacock's PAVONINE tail feathers.

pied (PYED). Having blotches of two or more colors.
The poet Gerard Manley Hopkins believed the strangeness of PIED creatures and plants was a sign of God's grace.

polychrome (PAWL-ee-krome). Having many colors.
The office was a more cheerful place with Mary's POLYCHROME outfits.

roseate (ROH-zee-it). Rosy; rose-colored.
The ROSEATE glass in the windows gave the room a faintly bordello flavor.

sallow (SAL-low). Sickly; grayish greenish yellow.
The SALLOW tone of Melanie's skin led us to wonder whether she was ill.

spadiceous (spay-DISH-uhs). Of a bright brown color.
It took years for the paint maker to develop a bright brown, but they finally released a SPADICEOUS enamel.

variegated (VAIR-ee-uh-gay-tid). Changing color or containing different hues of the same color.
A lawn covered in VARIEGATED fallen leaves is the sign that Autumn is finally here.

verdant (VUR-duhnt). Green, especially with foliage.
With its careful mix of plants, the Whittingtons' formal garden remains VERDANT year-round.

xanthic (ZAN-thik). Of yellow; yellowish.
Carrie's pantsuit was electrified by the addition of a XANTHIC scarf.

NOUNS

bice (BYSS). Azurite blue; medium blue.
Peter and Martha simultaneously decided that BICE would be the best color for the dining room.

cyan (SY-an). Greenish blue; one of the primary colors used in printing.
The entire printing run had to be discarded because CYAN was missing.

jacinth (JAY-sinth). Reddish orange.
JACINTH seemed like a good choice for the kitchen until John finished painting one wall.

metachromatism (met-uh-KRO-muh-tiz-um). A change of color, especially as the result of a change in temperature.
Spring causes a welcome METACHROMATISM of the forest.

murrey (MURR-ee). A dark purplish-red.
Peter's "black" eye actually had a MURREY cast.

ocher (OH-kur). Dark yellow.
The traffic lights in the artists' colony displayed red, OCHER, and green.

opalescence (OH-puh-LESS-enss). Characterized by a play of colors; iridescence.
A random mixture of tints gave the vase an OPALESCENCE that Nancy couldn't reproduce despite her best efforts.

oxblood (OKS-blud). Dark, dull red.
Greg bought OXBLOOD shoes because he believed he could wear them with blue, gray, and brown suits.

perse (PURSS). Very dark blue or purple.
Luckily, Betty thought better of buying a PERSE purse.

puce (PYOOCE). Dark or brownish purple.
Eventually, Peter's bruise turned PUCE.

raddle (RAD-uhl). Red ocher.
RADDLE was not a better choice for the dining room walls as it turned out.

sepia (SEE-pee-uh). Brown, grayish brown, or olive brown.
The SEPIA of the photographs gave them a vintage feel.

solferino (sowl-fuh-REE-noh). Vivid, purplish pink.
Jane's scarf demonstrated that a little SOLFERINO goes a long way.

vermilion (vur-MILL-yun). Scarlet red; bright red.
In her trademark VERMILION pantsuit, Carrie really stood out in a crowd.

ANTONYMS

achromatic (ak-ruh-MAT-ik). Having no color.
Marcia was quite insistent in asking us to help her interpret her ACHROMATIC dreams.

neutral (NOO-truhl). Having little or no color; not vivid.
Having become weary of her home's vibrant color scheme, Anne decided to try the opposite tack and painted all her walls with NEUTRAL shades.

38. Combine

(kuhm-BYN), verb

To bring together into a whole; gather; assemble or accumulate.

ADJECTIVES

concerted (kun-SUR-tid). Mutually devised or planned; done or performed in cooperation or together.
The two made a CONCERTED effort to get Vivian to change her mind, but she was resolute.

NOUNS

cache (KASH). Something hidden or stored.
Everyone was jealous when they learned of Moira's CACHE of acceptances to the finest schools.

miscellany (MISS-uh-lay-nee). A grouping or collection of various elements.
The volume, which featured a hodgepodge of essays, poems, and interviews relating to the Beats, was an intriguing MISCELLANY of writings from the bohemian world of the fifties.

pastiche (pah-STEESH). A haphazard collection of items from various sources.
Ronald's carefully crafted sculpture looked like a PASTICHE to our untrained eyes.

synergy (SIN-er-jee). The combined effort of two or more groups, agents, businesses, etc. to accomplish a common goal.
The SYNERGY demonstrated by the two departments quickly sparked amazing results.

synthesis (SIN-thuh-suss). A combination of elements to form a new whole.
The writer's latest book is an intriguing SYNTHESIS of classical Greek tragedy and cyberpunk elements.

VERBS

accrete (uh-KREET). To accumulate or cause to become attached.
Every time I park my car under a tree, a layer of bird droppings ACCRETES on its candy apple red finish.

agglomerate (uh-GLAHM-uh-rayt). To gather items into a ball or cluster.
Phil is so lazy he seems to think his job is just to AGGLOMERATE all the pieces of paper in the recycle bin.

aggregate (AG-rih-gayt). To combine or collect parts into a whole or mass.
Many social websites are attempting to AGGREGATE other social sites to capture as much traffic as possible.

amalgamate (uh-MAL-guh-mayt). To blend into a coherent single unit; to combine a number of elements into a whole.
The two boards voted to AMALGAMATE the firms as soon as possible.

conjoin (kuhn-JOIN). To join together or unite; to wed.
After the battling factions CONJOINED, they were able to accomplish peacefully most of their separate goals.

convene (kon-VEEN). To bring together or assemble in a body, usually for some public purpose.
The board of trustees will CONVENE on the first Tuesday of each month until further notice.

cull (KULL). To gather or collect a portion of a larger group.
Consumer behavior data was CULLED from online surveys and focus groups.

marshal (MAR-shul). To bring together all the resources at one's disposal to achieve a goal.
Patricia MARSHALED all of her social contacts to try to get a front-row ticket for fashion week.

muster (MUSS-ter). To gather or assemble (soldiers, etc.) for roll call, inspection, etc.; to summon.
The bystanders paused for a moment to MUSTER their courage before rushing into the burning building.

syncretize (SING-krih-tize). To combine or unite varying parties, ideas, principles, etc.
As the denomination's local attendance began to fall sharply, several churches SYNCRETIZED their efforts to improve overall attendance.

ANTONYMS

apportion (uh-POOR-shun). To distribute, divide, or assign appropriate shares of.
It was the lawyer's duty to APPORTION the sad remains of a once-proud manufacturing empire.

disseminate (diss-SEM-in-ayt). To distribute something so as to make it available to a large population or area.
The Internet is rapidly replacing newspapers as the primary medium for the DISSEMINATION of news.

mete (MEET). To distribute or allot.
After Elyssia's shopping spree, her father METED out substantial punishment by taking away her credit cards.

39. Command

(kuh-MAND), verb

To issue an order or orders; direct with authority; to have authority over; control.

ADJECTIVES

peremptory (puh-REMP-tuh-ree). Allowing for no rebuttal or overturning.
Kings may issue PEREMPTORY declarations of war, Mr. Secretary; presidents are obliged to discuss such matters with Congress.

83

NOUNS

imperative (im-PAIR-uh-tiv). A command or an essential objective.
Peggy's mother considered the 11:00 P.M. curfew as a nonnegotiable IMPERATIVE even if the teenager had a more casual interpretation.

mandate (MAN-dayt). Authoritative command, endorsement, or instruction; an order issued by one court of law to another, lower court.
When the MANDATE was issued, we discovered our business plan had become illegal.

VERBS

adjure (uh-JOOR). To command solemnly as if under oath, often under the threat of some sort of penalty.
The witnesses were ADJURED to avoid any contact with the accused.

enjoin (ehn-JOYN). To direct or order someone to do something.
After purchasing one too many Bentleys, Alex was ENJOINED by his father to be more frugal.

interdict (in-ter-DIKT). To prohibit; to forbid the use of something.
The court's emergency decision was designed to INTERDICT the strike and prevent the violence that had occurred during the last workers' demonstration.

proscribe (pro-SCRIBE). To forbid or prohibit.
State law PROSCRIBES the keeping of wild animals as house pets.

stipulate (STIP-yoo-layt). To make a specific demand or arrangement as a condition of agreement.
The contract was quite clear; it STIPULATED the delivery date.

ANTONYMS

countermand (KOUNT-er-mand). To cancel officially, especially to cancel a previous order.
Once Harold began smoking again, he COUNTERMANDED the no-smoking policy he'd recently adopted for his business.
See also: Authority

40. Commotion

(kuh-MOH-shun), noun

Violent motion; turmoil; agitation; confusion; disturbance.

ADJECTIVES

clamorous (KLAM-uhr-uss). Loud; expressively vehement; noisy and demanding.
The throngs in the street roared with CLAMOROUS applause.

clarion (KLAR-ee-uhn). Clear and shrill.
On the first day back to school, Robby groaned at the CLARION call of his morning alarm.

tempestuous (tem-PESS-chew-uss). Tumultuous and turbulent, as a personality.
Claire's TEMPESTUOUS personality is most likely linked to the fact that her father has married and remarried an excessive number of times.

vociferous (vo-SIF-er-uss). Loud and insistent so as to gain the listener's attention.
"Let the singing singers / With vocal voices, most VOCIFEROUS, / In sweet vociferation out-vociferize / Even sound itself."—Henry Carey, English poet

NOUNS

fracas (FRAK-us). Commotion; a noisy disagreement.
The nightly FRACAS between the couple next door is always loud enough to wake me out of a sound sleep.

hubbub (HUB-ub). Noise and confusion; an outburst.
The HUBBUB outside our window came as a surprise; the parade was not due for an hour, yet the streets were already thronged with people.

perturbation (purr-ter-BAY-shun). Any disturbance that alters the normal functioning of a system, moving object, person, or process.
"O polished PERTURBATION! golden care! / That keep'st the ports of slumber open wide / To many a watchful night."—William Shakespeare

yawp (YAWP). A raucous, clamorous noise.
"I sound my barbaric YAWP over the roofs of the world."—Walt Whitman, American poet and humanist

ANTONYMS

halcyon (HAL-see-un). Calm, peaceful, tranquil.
After a hard, stormy winter, townspeople were entranced by the HALCYON weather of our spring.

tranquility (trang-KWIL-ih-tee). The state of being tranquil; calmness; serenity; peacefulness.
After a long day in the city, Andrew longed for the TRANQUILITY of his house buried in the country.

41. Complain

(kuhm-PLAYN), verb

To express pain or dissatisfaction; to find fault; to declare annoyance, resentment, or grief.

ADJECTIVES

querulous (KWAIR-eh-luss). Habitually whining and griping.
Their QUERULOUS manner with the waiter made them unpleasant and embarrassing dinner companions.

NOUNS

malcontent (mal-kuhn-TENT). A discontented, resentful, or rebellious person. *Harvey is such a MALCONTENT that he'll argue with you if you tell him it's a nice day!*

VERBS

carp (KARP). To raise picky, trivial objections; complain peevishly. *All the CARPING at the staff meeting kept anything substantive from being done.*

cavil (KAV-il). To find fault with something; to raise objections needlessly. *Town meetings take twice as long as they should because some citizens use the event as a forum to CAVIL.*

grouse (GRAUSS). To complain or grumble about one's situation. *We decided not to return to the restaurant after the maître d' continuously GROUSED about the slovenliness of his waitstaff.*

inveigh (in-VAY). To protest strongly; to rail. *The crowd INVEIGHED against the governor's decision to commute Davidson's sentence.*

remonstrate (rih-MON-strayt). To protest, object, or show disapproval. *When Carlotta REMONSTRATED against our snubbing of Julia, we simply began to snub Carlotta as well.*

ANTONYMS

rejoice (rih-JOYCE). To be glad and take delight in. *"Time is too slow for those who wait, too swift for those who fear, too long for those who grieve, too short for those who REJOICE, but for those who love, time is eternity."—Henry Van Dyke, American short story writer and poet*

revel (REV-uhl). To take much pleasure, delight. *"From every blush that kindles in thy cheeks, / Ten thousand little loves and graces spring / To REVEL in the roses."—Nicholas Rowe, English dramatist and poet*

42. Complex

(kuhm-PLEKS), adjective

Not simple; complicated; elaborate; characterized by many related parts.

ADJECTIVES

anfractuous (an-FRACK-chuh-wuss). Full of windings and intricacies, like a good mystery novel.
The novel's ANFRACTUOUS plot worked on paper, but it became stupefyingly confusing—actually, just plain stupid—onscreen.

convoluted (KON-vuh-loo-tid). Complicated; twisted and coiled.
After listening to his CONVOLUTED directions, I thanked the farmer and drove away vowing to buy a GPS device as soon as possible.

daedal (DEE-duhl). Extremely intricate and complex; skillfully made.
I thought I could repair my computer until I got a look at the machine's DAEDAL circuitry.

inextricable (in-eck-STRICK-uh-bull). Incapable of being disentangled or untied; hopelessly complex.
The INEXTRICABLE problem remained unsolved, even after the company's best minds spent three days attacking it.

involute (IN-vuh-loot). Intricate; involved.
The INVOLUTE diagrams in the owner's manual did not help George sort out his old sports car's electrical system.

tortuous (TORE-choo-uss). Winding; full of twists and turns.
Drive safely; the road leading from the center of town up the side of the mountain is a TORTUOUS one.

VERBS

obfuscate (OB-fuss-kayt). To muddy or confuse an issue; to muddle facts important to someone else's judgment or decision.
The defense has put up with enough of these attempts to OBFUSCATE, Your Honor.

ANTONYMS

unalloyed (un-uh-LOID). Not mixed with any other materials; pure.
John found it refreshing to watch his toddler's UNALLOYED pleasure when playing with soap bubbles.

unpretentious (un-prih-TEN-shuss). Modest; without showy display; simple; plain.
"Those who are firm, enduring, simple and UNPRETENTIOUS are the nearest to virtue."—Confucius
See also: Difficult

43. Compliment

(KOM-pluh-ment), verb

To express or convey a compliment; confer admiration, respect, or praise; politely flatter.

ADJECTIVES

adulatory (AJ-uh-luh-tore-ee). Complimentary; giving effusive praise.
"He includes in his final chapter a passage of ADULATORY prose from Henry James."—Joyce Carol Oates, American author

laudable (LAW-duh-bull). Commendable; deserving of praise.
Rebecca's decision to tell her mother that she lost the emerald brooch she borrowed without permission was LAUDABLE.

NOUNS

blandishments (BLAN-dish-ments). Compliments rendered primarily to influence and gain favor with the person you are praising.
The BLANDISHMENTS heaped upon the consultant by his clients were not sufficient to persuade him to take a staff position with them.

claque (KLAK). A group of people hired to applaud at an entertainment event.
The first comedian was absolutely terrible; if it hadn't been for the CLAQUE the
management had assembled at the last minute, there wouldn't have been
any applause at all.

encomium (en-KO-me-um). Effusive praise given in a public forum.
The CEO's ENCOMIUM at Phil's retirement dinner caused his eyes to mist over.

hagiography (hag-ee-OG-ruh-fee). A biography that idealizes its subject.
The Van Gelders were disappointed with the volume written about their illustri-
ous descendants because the book fell far short of being a HAGIOGRAPHY.

hosanna (ho-ZAN-uh). An expression of praise, exaltation, and adoration
typically heard in religious ceremonies; an instance of excessive praise.
Mel's agent warned him not to take too seriously the HOSANNAS that came
his way after he won the acting award.

plaudit (PLAW-dit). An expression of gratitude or praise; applause.
I am unworthy, my friends, of the PLAUDITS you have bestowed on me this evening.

sycophant (SIK-uh-fuhnt). A self-seeking person attempting to gain an
advantage using flattery.
Outwardly polite, the rock star secretly viewed his fans as slobbering SYCOPHANTS.

VERBS

extol (eks-TOLE). To praise with great enthusiasm.
Iris has not ceased to EXTOL the virtues of her new Romain Jerome Day &
Night watch.

ANTONYMS

deprecate (DEP-rih-kayt). To express severe disapproval of another's actions.
"Those who profess to favor freedom and yet DEPRECATE agitation, are
men who want crops without plowing up the ground."—Frederick Douglass,
American abolitionist and orator

disparage (dih-SPAIR-ihj). To bring reproach or discredit upon; belittle.
"But the DISPARAGING of those we love always alienates us from them to some
extent. We must not touch our idols; the gilt comes off in our hands."—Gustave
Flaubert, French novelist

44. Concise

(kun-SICE), adjective

Brief and to the point; expressing a great deal in a few words.

ADJECTIVES

compendious (kuhm-PEN-dee-us). Concise, succinct; to the point.
Sheila is unable to tell COMPENDIOUS stories about her trips to the Riviera.

elliptical (uh-LIP-tuh-kuhl). Expressed with extreme economy, free of extraneous matter.
Ernest Hemingway was known for his ELLIPTICAL style of writing.

epigrammatic (eh-pih-gruh-MAT-ik). Similar to an epigram; terse and clever in expression.
All of us in the office looked forward to receiving one of Tony's EPIGRAMMATIC e-mail messages.

gnomic (NOH-mik). Pithy; pertaining to a writer of aphorisms.
It was difficult to grasp whether the speaker's GNOMIC remembrances were meant to be complimentary.

laconic (luh-KAWN-ik). Of few words; expressing oneself with an economy of words.
Harold may be LACONIC, but when he does speak, he is worth listening to.

pauciloquent (paw-SIL-oh-kwent). Using few words; concise in speech.
My father, PAUCILOQUENT to the end, simply said "Goodbye" and expired.

sententious (sen-TEN-shuss). Tending to use many pithy aphorisms or maxims in order to enlighten others.
Polonius's SENTENTIOUS manner of speaking clearly irritates Hamlet in this scene.

succinct (suck-SINKT). Brief; pithy; concise.
Norman preferred to say a SUCCINCT goodbye to his brother before getting into the cab, rather than engaging in a long, drawn-out scene at the train station.

synoptic (sin-OP-tik). Forming or involving a synopsis or summary.
The close of a presentation should be SYNOPTIC in nature.

taciturn (TASS-ih-turn). Reserved; uncommunicative; speaking few words.
"Nature is garrulous to the point of confusion, let the artist be truly TACITURN."
—Paul Klee, German-born Swiss painter

NOUNS

brevity (BREV-ih-tee). Shortness; terseness.
Paine's argument was stated with such BREVITY and passion that within one short month of its publication every colonist seemed to be in favor of independence from Britain.

VERBS

recapitulate (ree-kuh-PITCH-uh-layt). To summarize in concise form; restate briefly.
Sgt. Dennis, an eyewitness, RECAPITULATED the incident to his superiors at headquarters.

ANTONYMS

diffuse (dih-FYOOS). Widely spread; characterized by great length in writing or speech; wordy.
"To get the right word in the right place is a rare achievement. To condense the DIFFUSED light of a page of thought into the luminous flash of a single sentence, is worthy to rank as a prize composition just by itself."—Mark Twain, American humorist and writer

expansive (ik-SPAN-siv). Widely extended; broad; extensive.
Having been severely criticized for his reticence during previous press conferences, the spokesman gave an EXPANSIVE account of the situation for the audience.
See also: Change, Reduce

45. Conflict

(KON-flikt), noun

A fight, battle, or struggle; controversy; incompatibility.

NOUNS

contention (kuhn-TEN-shun). Strife, especially verbal conflict; argument.
Suddenly, the town meeting was the scene of heated political CONTENTION.

contravention (kon-truh-VEN-shun). An instance of contradiction or
opposition; violation; the condition of being overruled or disobeyed.
*Your appearance here without the full report is in blatant CONTRAVENTION of
the instructions laid out in my memo.*

discord (DIS-kord). Lack of harmony; disagreement; quarreling between parties.
Lack of communication skills is responsible for much marital DISCORD.

dissension (dih-SEN-shun). Disagreement, especially among people in a group.
*New rules favoring older members of the club caused great DISSENSION and
a fracturing of long-standing alliances.*

melee (MAY-lay). A confused struggle involving many people.
*"The man who is in the MELEE knows what blows are being struck and what
blood is being drawn."—Woodrow Wilson*

nemesis (NEM-uh-sis). An opponent one is unable to defeat.
*"How wonderful to live with one's NEMESIS! You may be miserable, but you
feel forever in the right."—Erica Jong, American author and teacher*

rancor (RANG-ker). Conflict between individuals or groups, usually resulting
from disagreement over an action or issue, and accompanied by ill will, bad
feelings, and an escalation of the dispute over time.
*"They no longer assume responsibility (as beat cops used to do) for averting
RANCOR between antagonistic neighbors."—Harlan Ellison, American author*

ANTONYMS

conciliation (kuhn-sill-ee-A-shun). The act of making peace; reconciliation; appeasement.
"I appeal to all Irishmen to pause, to stretch out the hand of forbearance and CONCILIATION, to forgive and forget, and to join with me in making for the land they love a new era of peace, contentment and goodwill."—George V, English king

concord (KON-kord). Friendly and peaceful relations, as between nations; agreement; harmony.
"If there is a country in the world where CONCORD, according to common calculation, would be least expected, it is America."—Thomas Paine, English-American writer and political pamphleteer

46. Confused

(kon-FYOOZD), adjective

Perplexed or disconcerted; disordered; mixed up.

ADJECTIVES

addled (ADD-ulld). Thrown into confusion; confounded.
After studying all night, Aaron's ADDLED brain couldn't focus on the exam.

bemused (bee-MYOOZD). Bewildered, perplexed, or lost in reflection.
Victor stared BEMUSED at the photograph of his father in full military dress—a man he had never thought of in quite that way.

discombobulated (diss-kum-BOB-yoo-layt-ed). Confused or thrown into an awkward predicament; utterly disconcerted.
The frenzied pace of eight hours on the trading floor had left me utterly DISCOMBOBULATED.

flummoxed (FLUHM-uckst). Completely bewildered.
The appearance of his ex-wife was so unexpected that Jason was momentarily FLUMMOXED.

nebulous (NEB-yoo-luss). Vague and not well thought out; ill-defined; lacking concretes.
Jay's plans for what he would do when he graduated college were NEBULOUS at best.

obscurant (uhb-SKYOOR-unt). Tending to make obscure; preventing understanding.
Jason often used OBSCURANT terms when talking with people he didn't like.

quizzical (KWIHZ-ih-kuhl). Showing puzzled amusement or disbelief.
The QUIZZICAL look on Amanda's face, when a perfect stranger proposed marriage, was absolutely priceless.

NOUNS

farrago (fuh-RAWG-oh). A careless, confused mixture; mish-mash.
My four-year-old, who picked out his own outfit for the first time this morning, walked into the kitchen sporting a FARRAGO of mismatched clothing.

nonplussed (non-PLUSST). A state of utter perplexity in which one is unable to act further.
Arthur admitted later that he was NONPLUSSED by Jean's unexpected admission of complicity in the plot to steal the physics final exam.

quandary (KWON-dree). A state of uncertainty about one's next move.
Estelle realized that her unrestrained comments to the society pages had left the rest of us quite upset, and she was in a QUANDARY as to how to repair the situation.

snafu (snah-FOO). An egregious but common error.
Supposedly, the word "SNAFU" is an acronym of the phrase "Situation normal, all fouled up" or something similar.

VERBS

conflate (kuhn-FLAYT). To fuse together; especially to mistakenly think of separate concepts, actions, or things as identical.
The lawyer told the jury they should not CONFLATE a warning with a threat.

obfuscate (AHB-fuh-skayt). To talk or write about a subject in a way that deliberately makes it unclear, selectively omits certain facts, or communicates wrong ideas or impressions, so that the listener or reader does not grasp the whole truth of the situation.
Despite his Ivy League education, Alexander seems able only to OBFUSCATE any subject upon which he touches.

ANTONYMS

decipher (dih-SY-fer). To translate from meaningless code; to discover the meaning of; to interpret.
"All in all, the creative act is not performed by the artist alone; the spectator brings the work in contact with the external world by DECIPHERING and inter-preting its inner qualifications and thus adds his contribution to the creative act."—Marcel Duchamp, French artist

illuminate (ih-LOO-muh-nayt). To make clear; to enlighten intellectually.
"Derive happiness in oneself from a good day's work, from ILLUMINATING the fog that surrounds us."—Henri Matisse, French painter

47. Consistent

(kuhn-SIS-tuhnt), adjective

Holding to the same practice or principles; constant adherence; compat-ible; harmonious.

ADJECTIVES

assiduous (uh-SID-joo-us). Constant; unceasing in effort; persistent; diligent; unremitting and attentive.
Karen was ASSIDUOUS in completing her final project, but was still one day late.

coherent (koh-HEER-uhnt). Logically arranged; consistent; harmonious.
The marketing team was able to develop a COHERENT promotional plan for maximum effect.

homogeneous (ho-mo-JEE-nee-uss). The same throughout; made up of like parts; not heterogeneous.
The island supported a small HOMOGENEOUS population of aboriginal tribes.

isochronous (eye-SOCK-ruh-ness). Occurring consistently at regular intervals.
The ticking of a clock is ISOCHRONOUS, but the arrival of the elevator at different floors is not.

symmetrical (sih-MET-rih-kuhl). Having a shape or form that is regular and uniform.
Because the disease was SYMMETRICAL in its progression, treatment could be directed more accurately.

ANTONYMS

erratic (ih-RAT-ik). Inconsistent; lacking a set course; wandering or fluctuating unpredictably.
Elaine's ERRATIC writing style irritated her superiors, who had no time to puzzle over an indecipherable and meandering memo.

oscillate (OSS-ih-layt). To sway back and forth; vacillate.
My two-year-old nephew was mesmerized by the fish tank, with its colorful fish, OSCILLATING plants, and soft lighting.

48. Correct

(kuh-REKT), verb

To make right, accurate, or true; remove errors from; to cause to conform to a standard; to point out the errors; to scold (someone) in order to make improvements.

ADJECTIVES

curative (KYOOR-uh-tiv). Providing a remedy; able to provide alleviation of an ailment.
The CURATIVE measures were slow but effective; Joseph eventually recovered completely.

VERBS

ameliorate (uh-MEEL-yuh-rayt). To improve or upgrade; to make an unacceptable state of affairs better or put right.
The ambassador's midnight visit was the first step taken to AMELIORATE the poor relations between the two countries, and may actually have averted war.

amend (uh-MEND). To modify or update; to remove or correct faults; improve.
In light of the testimony we've heard tonight, Madame President, I'd like to AMEND my earlier remarks.

castigate (KAS-tuh-gayt). To scold or criticize harshly, with the objective of assigning blame and motivating others to correct their errors.
The bartender was CASTIGATED by his boss for serving alcohol to two teenage girls without checking their IDs first.

emend (ee-MEND). To correct or remove faults, as from a text.
Blanche EMENDED her holiday wish list, removing the Ferrari watch and replacing it with a Versace dinner plate.

rectify (REK-tih-fy). To put right; to correct.
Ellen RECTIFIED her previous mistakes and filed the report.

redress (ree-DRESS). To remedy; rectify.
"When griping grief the heart doth wound, / and doleful dumps the mind opress, then music, with her silver sound, / with speedy help doth lend REDRESS."—William Shakespeare

revamp (ree-VAMP). To redo; to renovate thoroughly.
The playwright decided to REVAMP several of the weaker scenes in the first act.

ANTONYMS

irremediable (ihr-ree-MEE-dee-uh-bull). Unable to be repaired, cured, or remedied.
One too many arguments between Rose and Jim finally caused an IRREMEDIABLE rift in their fragile relationship.

49. Crimes

(KRYMZ), noun

Acts committed in violation of a law prohibiting them or omitted in violation of a law ordering them; wrongful acts that are punishable by law.

ADJECTIVES

felonious (fuh-LONE-ee-uss). Criminal; villainous; reminiscent of or relating to a felony crime.
Although no court in the land would consider it FELONIOUS, my brother's attempt to blackmail me over that little dent I put in my parent's car was, in my mind, worthy of a long jail sentence.

illicit (ih-LISS-it). Illegal or morally unjustifiable; something not sanctioned by custom or law.
We all know now that the money was acquired through ILLICIT means, don't we?

NOUNS

arson (AR-suhn). The act of destroying property with fire.
After Councilor Perry's campaign headquarters burned down, his supporters were quick to accuse their opponents of ARSON; in fact, one of their own neglected cigarette butts was to blame.

bigamy (BIG-uh-mee). The crime of taking marriage vows while still legally married to someone else.
By marrying June before her divorce was finalized, Stanley was technically guilty of BIGAMY.

complicity (kum-PLISS-uh-tee). To be involved in or associated with, or to participate in or have previous knowledge of, an instance of wrongdoing.
Although he did not receive money for throwing the 1919 World Series, Buck Weaver was nevertheless suspended from baseball for life, because his failure to expose the scheme was seen as COMPLICITY in his teammates' plans.

contraband (KON-truh-band). Illegal or prohibited goods.
Jean tried to smuggle a tape recorder into the concert, but her CONTRABAND was quickly discovered and taken from her.

pyromania (pye-roe-MAY-nee-uh). The compulsion to set fires.
Police believe that the blaze is not the work of an arsonist out for commercial gain, as was initially suspected, but an act of PYROMANIA.

transgression (trans-GRESH-un). A violation of a rule; the breaking of a law or guideline.
David was perhaps a little too eager to cross over into Mr. Peterson's yard to play ball, but this was a minor TRANSGRESSION.

uxoricide (uk-SOR-ih-syd). The crime of murdering one's wife.
Eventually, the defendant was acquitted of UXORICIDE when his wife's death was ruled a suicide.

vaticide (VAT-uh-syd). The act of murdering a prophet.
Tom took the reviewer's negative article on his religious poetry as an act tantamount to VATICIDE.

VERBS

embezzle (im-BEZ-ul). To appropriate for oneself funds that were placed in one's care for another party.
Bill had always seemed to be a model employee, so the news that he had been EMBEZZLING money from the company for some years came as a complete shock to us all.

indict (in-DITE). To charge formally with a crime or offense.
Rumors that Mr. Brown would soon be INDICTED for his part in the scandal swept the city.

pilfer (PIL-fer). To take without authorization or permission; to steal.
I had a feeling the tickets Wayne was trying to sell me had been PILFERED from someone, but he assured me that was not the case.

ANTONYMS

sanctioned (SANGK-shund). Officially authorized; approved; allowed; permitted.
"The principles on which we engaged, of which the charter of our independence is the record, were SANCTIONED by the laws of our being, and we but obeyed them in pursuing undeviatingly the course they called for."—Thomas Jefferson, American president

scrupulous (SKROO-pyoo-lus). Characterized by a conscientious adherence to what is considered true, right, or accurate; honest.
The success of John's nefarious plan depended on his assumption that law enforcement was less SCRUPULOUS in that part of the world.
See also: Dishonest

50. Criticize

(KRIT-uh-syz), verb

To analyze and judge as a critic; to find fault with or censure; to make judgments.

ADJECTIVES

censorious (sen-SOR-ee-us). Critical; easily finding fault.
When it came to grading term papers, Mrs. Edwards was seen by many as overly CENSORIOUS, even taking off points for using a paper clip instead of a staple.

hypercritical (hy-purr-KRIT-ih-kuhl). Excessively or meticulously critical.
"Good writers have two things in common: they would rather be understood than admired, and they do not write for hairsplitting and HYPERCRITICAL readers."—Friedrich Nietzsche, German philosopher

NOUNS

diatribe (DIE-uh-tryb). A speech railing against injustice; a vehement denunciation.
The editorial was a mean-spirited DIATRIBE against school vouchers, written to prevent children from other towns from being sent by bus to Centerville High School.

screed (SKREED). A long written argument; an argumentative essay; a long, monotonous speech or piece of writing; a diatribe.
The newspaper's editor was the recipient of a mountain of SCREEDS from outraged citizens criticizing the board of selectmen's policies.

VERBS

castigate (KAS-tuh-gayt). To scold or criticize harshly, with the objective of assigning blame and motivating the other person to correct his or her error.
The bartender was CASTIGATED by his boss for serving alcohol to two teenage girls without checking their ID first.

cavil (KAV-uhl). To find fault in trivial matters or raise petty objections.
Susan CAVILLED for some time about the lateness of the milk delivery, but since it was only a matter of minutes, she eventually gave in and paid the bill.

chide (chyd). To scold or lecture; to reprove.
My brother CHIDED me for neglecting to visit our grandparents during my trip to California.

disparage (dih-SPAIR-ihj). To bring reproach or discredit upon; belittle.
"Man's constant need to DISPARAGE woman, to humble her, to deny her equal rights, and to belittle her achievements—all are expressions of his innate envy and fear."—Elizabeth Gould Davis, American feminist and author

excoriate (ik-SKORE-ee-ayt). To criticize; to attempt to censure or punish.
We EXCORIATED Melanie for inviting people with no family connections to her birthday party.

fulminate (FULL-mih-nayt). To explode. Also: to denounce loudly or forcefully.
Edmond FULMINATED against the bill on the floor of the Senate, but he knew he did not have the votes to defeat it.

lambaste (lam-BAYST). To berate or criticize harshly, especially in an unkind way.
We LAMBASTED Marla for not visiting Comme des Garçons during her recent weekender to Beijing.

objurgate (OB-jur-gayt). To chide sharply; rebuke; upbraid vehemently; berate.
Mr. Williams worked himself into a frenzy waiting to OBJURGATE his new salesman for losing the Duckhorn account.

oppugn (uh-PYOON). To reason against; oppose with argument; call in question.
Matt made a critical mistake when he OPPUGNED his rival's credentials.

reprehend (rep-ruh-HEND). To find fault with; voice disapproval of.
That Arnold REPREHENDS his daughter's wayward behavior seems somewhat hypocritical to those of us who knew him in his youth.

reprove (ree-PROOV). To criticize and correct others.
We had to REPROVE Elyssia for some of her questionable fashion choices.

scarify (SKAIR-ih-fy). To wound with harsh criticism.
We deemed it necessary to SCARIFY Eileen for having the nerve to criticize our motives.

upbraid (up-BRAYD). To censure or to find fault with.
Roger UPBRAIDED the butler severely when we learned he was gossiping to other members of our staff.

ANTONYMS

unimpeachable (un-ihm-PEE-chuh-bull). Above reproach; impossible to discredit or slander.
We promoted Carla to upstairs maid because her job performance has been UNIMPEACHABLE.
See also: Abuse

51. Cross

(KRAWSS), adjective

Contrary; ill-tempered; cranky; easily annoyed.

ADJECTIVES

bellicose (BELL-ih-kohss). Belligerent, surly, ready to argue or fight at the slightest provocation.
Doug is so touchy about his new car that he'll instantly turn BELLICOSE if you so much as brush against it.

cantankerous (kan-TANG-ker-us). Ill-tempered; grumpy.
"You kids stay off my lawn!" our CANTANKEROUS old neighbor barked.

captious (KAP-shuss). Fond of finding faults in others; ill-natured and overly critical; carping.
Ed's CAPTIOUS remarks were entirely inappropriate and showed his lack of self-esteem.

churlish (CHUR-lish). Surly; mean; boorish; rude; characterized by a lack of civility or graciousness.
We found it almost impossible to believe that Diane's new boyfriend was more CHURLISH than his predecessor.

dyspeptic (diss-PEP-tik). Irritable and ill-humored.
No wonder Fred can't get a girlfriend. His DYSPEPTIC temperament drives all potential mates away.

farouche (fuh-ROOSH). Unsociable; cranky; withdrawn; fierce.
Your FAROUCHE behavior will not win you any friends. In fact, it will simply alienate you from everyone.

peevish (PEE-vish). Irritable; fretful; hard to please; easily and often showing impatience or ill humor.
Brock is normally pleasant and good-humored, but his illness with its persistent fever has made him PEEVISH.

petulant (PETCH-uh-lunt). Impatiently peevish; showing great annoyance or irritation with minor problems.
He dismissed their questions with a PETULANT wave of the hand and quickly changed the subject.

pugnacious (pug-NAY-shuss). Inclined to argue and debate every last thing.
Joey was PUGNACIOUS by nature and could never let go of an argument until he believed he had won.

splenetic (splih-NET-ik). Bad-tempered; irritable; spiteful; malevolent.
As soon as we met her mother, we could see that Jane's SPLENETIC comments were a self-defense mechanism.

waspish (WAWS-pish). Irascible and petulant; given to resentment.
Rebecca can be WASPISH, but we forgive her because she throws the best galas.

NOUNS

Xanthippe (zan-TIP-ee). Wife of Socrates; an ill-tempered, shrewish woman.
Felicia is far from a XANTHIPPE simply because she interacts only with certain members of the household staff.

ANTONYMS

affable (AFF-uh-bull). Pleasant and polite; agreeable; warm.
We believed that Grace had such an AFFABLE personality because she grew up with seven siblings.

sympathetic (sim-puh-THET-ik). In agreement with another's mood, feelings, disposition, etc.; congenial.
"Resolve to be tender with the young, compassionate with the aged, SYMPA-THETIC with the striving, and tolerant with the weak and the wrong. Sometime in your life you will have been all of these."—Robert Goddard, American rocket engineer

D

52. Deceitful

(dih-SEET-fuhl), adjective

Tending or apt to deceive, lie, or cheat; misleading; false; fraudulent.

ADJECTIVES

duplicitous (doo-PLIS-ih-tus). Characterized by hypocritical deception or cunning; double-dealing.
His DUPLICITOUS behavior disappointed and hurt his friends, and eventually Mike found himself alone.

gullible (GULL-ih-bull). Easily cheated, tricked, or deceived.
I'm afraid Terry is a little too GULLIBLE to survive for long as an aspiring actor in a city like New York.

illusory (ih-LOO-suh-ree). Giving a false appearance of being real; seeming genuine but probably fake or deceptive.
After she moved to the beach, Lorna expected to feel joy but instead found that joy ILLUSORY.

insidious (in-SIHD-ee-uss). Designed to entrap; happening or spreading harmfully but subtly; stealthily and seductively treacherous.
Mark's chess games were full of INSIDIOUS traps meant to lull his opponent into a sense of complacency.

Machiavellian (mack-ee-uh-VEL-ee-uhn). Unscrupulous and self-centered; manipulative; cunning.
We can hardly be called MACHIAVELLIAN simply because we do what we need to do to hold on to the luxurious lifestyle to which we have become accustomed.

perfidious (per-FID-ee-us). Faithless; treacherous; not able to be trusted.
Once again, Heather's heart was broken by a PERFIDIOUS lover.

sanctimonious (sank-tih-MOWN-ee-us). Overbearingly self-righteous; smug; hypocritically righteous.
"Not but I've every reason not to care / What happens to him if it only takes / Some of the SANCTIMONIOUS conceit / Out of one of those pious scalawags."—Robert Frost, American poet

unctuous (UNK-chew-us). Possessing an untrustworthy or dubious nature; characterized by an insincere manner.
Local car dealers doing their own TV commercials often communicate in an UNCTUOUS, almost laughable manner.

NOUNS

artifice (AR-tih-fiss). The use of clever strategies and cunning methods to fool or best others and tip an outcome in one's favor.
"Every art and ARTIFICE has been practiced and perpetrated to destroy the rights of man."—Robert Ingersoll, American orator

charlatan (SHAR-luh-tun). A fake; fraud; a person falsely claiming to possess a given level of status, skills, or knowledge in order to deceive others.
The defendant, it has been claimed, is a CHARLATAN and a liar—but where is the evidence for this?

chicanery (shih-KAIN-uh-ree). Cheating or deception, especially through the use of language.
The way the candidate consistently quibbled about the precise meaning of his statements made me feel he was guilty of CHICANERY.

mountebank (MOUNT-uh-bank). A charlatan; one who sells worthless medicines, potions, and the like; a fake; an unscrupulous pretender.
The line between visionary romantic and common MOUNTEBANK, for my father, was often a thin one.

poseur (poh-ZUR). A person who attempts to impress or obtain the approval of others by assuming characteristics not truly his own; an affected person.
Whenever Bobby saw a POSEUR, he would comment, "Big hat, no cattle."

red herring (red HAIR-ing). Something intended to mislead others from the real issue or problem; a deception.
The board of selectmen's discussion of sewers was a RED HERRING and had nothing to do with the increase in taxes.

sophistry (SOF-iss-tree). Subtly misleading argument or reasoning.
I believe this jury is too sophisticated to be taken in by the SOPHISTRIES the defense has offered.

subterfuge (SUB-tur-fyooj). A misleading ruse or cunning evasion; a strategic avoidance employing deceit.
Nick knew he would have to come up with a clever SUBTERFUGE to get out of going to another boring Sunday dinner at his grandparents' home.

wile (WYL). A clever trick meant to attain a goal; an instance of or talent for beguiling deceit.
Headquarters trusts, as always, that the information you have been given is secure even from the WILES of a spy of the opposite sex.

VERBS

bamboozle (bam-BOO-zul). To deceive; trick.
Fred was BAMBOOZLED out of $15,000 by a con artist who convinced him to invest money in nonexistent real estate.

dissemble (dih-SEM-bul). To act with an insincere or disguised motive.
Although many on the committee were convinced that the undersecretary was DISSEMBLING about how much he knew of rebel activities, there was no hard proof to support this view.

finagle (fih-NAY-gul). To wangle; to use clever, often underhanded methods to achieve one's desires.
Justin FINAGLED his way into the press conference by borrowing a pass from another reporter.

purport (per-PORT). To claim to be something you are not; to pretend to do something you aren't in fact doing.
"Doris Lessing PURPORTS to remember in the most minute detail the moth-eaten party dresses she pulled, at age thirteen, from her mother's trunk."
—Tim Parks, British novelist

wangle (WANG-guhl). To accomplish by underhanded methods.
Jennifer managed to WANGLE an invitation to the Clarksons' party, even though she is the gauchest of the area's newcomers.

ANTONYMS

guileless (GYL-liss). Without guile; candid; frank.
"There is a strange glow on the face of a GUILELESS person. Inner cleanliness has its own soap and water—the soap of strong faith and the water of constant practice."—Sri Sathya Sai Baba, Indian spiritual leader

veracious (vuh-RAY-shuss). Honest; truthful.
Your Honor, I ask that the defense's assertion that none of the prosecution's witnesses are VERACIOUS be stricken from the record.

53. Declare

(dih-KLAIR), verb

To make clearly known; state or announce in definite or formal terms; to announce officially or emphatically.

NOUNS

avowal (uh-VOW-uhl). An open admission or statement.
He had run as a Democrat for over thirty years, so his AVOWAL of support for the Republican ticket shocked many voters.

VERBS

allege (uh-LEJ). To state without proof; to declare as a reason or excuse.
The media are usually quick to ALLEGE a celebrity's mistake or wrongdoing in order to create interest.

aver (uh-VER). To assert the truthfulness of a statement.
"'Has she no faults, then (Envy says), sir?' / Yes, she has one, I must AVER: / When all the world conspires to praise her, / The woman's deaf, and does not hear."—Alexander Pope, British poet

contend (kuhn-TEND). To maintain; to hold to be a fact; assert.
After years in prison, Arthur still CONTENDS that he is innocent.

postulate (POSS-chuh-layt). A theory, belief, hypothesis, or principle based on an analysis of known facts.
"The primacy of human personality has been a POSTULATE both of Christianity and of liberal democracy."—Julian Huxley, English evolutionary biologist

tout (TOWT). To publicize in a boastful, extravagant manner.
The studio TOUTED its latest picture as "the greatest story ever told."

ANTONYMS

gainsay (GANE-say). To deny, dispute, or contradict.
Michael has made no attempt to GAINSAY the persistent rumors that his family's fortune rests solely on insider trading.

recant (rih-KANT). To withdraw or disavow formally.
"I cannot and will not RECANT anything, for to go against conscience is neither right nor safe."—Martin Luther, the father of Protestantism

54. Defense

(dee-FENSE), noun

Protection from harm or danger; guarding from attack; support against a foe.

NOUNS

aegis (EE-jis). The protection, support, and help rendered by a guardian, supporter, backer, or mentor.
Jill thinks she's above reproach because she's under the AEGIS of that marketing vice president with a penchant for younger women.

bastion (BASS-chuhn). An institution, individual, or something else protecting or preserving a particular way of life, society, set of beliefs, or moral code.
Cliff graduated from Yale, a BASTION of respectability and privilege.

bulwark (BULL-werk). A defensive, protective barrier, wall, or force.
"Since he aims at great souls, he cannot miss. But if someone should slander me in this way, no one would believe him. For envy goes against the powerful. Yet slight men, apart from the great, are but a weak BULWARK."
—*Sophocles, Greek tragedian*

cannonade (kan-uh-NAYD). A continuous, relentless bombardment or effort.
A CANNONADE of questioning greeted Eva's statement that she was quitting the club's tennis team.

muniment (MYOO-nuh-munt). A means of defense; in law, a document, such as a title or deed, used to defend or maintain rights or privileges.
Sam was prepared to support his claims to ownership and brought all the necessary MUNIMENTS to the hearing.

paladin (PAL-uh-din). A knight or heroic champion, a defender or advocate of a noble cause; any of the twelve peers who attended Charlemagne.
The fictional character of Superman represented society's need for a PALADIN during the 1950s.

palisade (pal-ih-SADE). A defensive barrier or fence comprising a row of tall stakes driven into the ground; also, a line of steep cliffs along a river.
As we drove along the PALISADES of the river gorge, my wife and I lamented that we had forgotten to bring our camera.

VERBS

adduce (uh-DUCE). To cite as an example or justification; to bring something forward for consideration.
I would ADDUCE the following reasons in support of rewriting the club charter.

forfend (for-FEND). To protect, defend, secure, etc.
After he bought a television with a fifty-five-inch screen, Keith bought an alarm system to FORFEND it.

indemnify (in-DEM-nih-fy). To protect from or provide compensation for damages; to shield against the loss, destruction, or damage of something.
This policy INDEMNIFIES my house against fire, flood, and burglary.

vindicate (VIN-dih-kayt). To prove an opinion correct or an action justified; to prove innocence; to defend one's rights; to avenge.
We laughed at Paulette's predictions about the imminent fall fashions, but, once the couture was unveiled, Paulette was VINDICATED.

ANTONYMS

untenable (uhn-TEN-uh-bull). Not possible to defend, as an argument or position.
"Are the legitimate compensation and honors that should come as the result of ability and merit to be denied on the UNTENABLE ground of sex aristocracy?"—Bertha Honore Potter Palmer, American socialite

55. Defiant

(dih-FYE-unht), adjective

Characterized by defiance; resistant or challenging; rebellious

ADJECTIVES

contumacious (kon-teh-MAY-shuss). Obstinately resisting authority; disobedient; insubordinate.
The CONTUMACIOUS defendant eventually had to be gagged.

obstreperous (ob-STREP-er-us). Uncontrollably aggressive; defiant, boisterous.
Before announcing the plan for massive layoffs to his workers, the boss hired an extra security force to prevent certain OBSTREPEROUS persons from inciting a riot.

recalcitrant (rih-KAL-sih-trunt). Unwilling to cooperate voluntarily; resisting control or authority; hesitant to step forward and do what one is asked or told to do.
On the witness stand, the mobster was RECALCITRANT and uncommunicative.

renitent (REN-eh-tent). Steadfastly resisting pressure, constraint, or compulsion.
Dorothy's RENITENT efforts proved superior to her mother's attempts to modify her behavior.

subversive (sub-VER-sihv). Describes an act performed to challenge or overthrow the authority of those in power.
"If sex and creativity are often seen by dictators as SUBVERSIVE activities, it's because they lead to the knowledge that you own your own body."
—Erica Jong, American author and teacher

NOUNS

dissentient (dih-SEN-shunt). A person who dissents, especially in opposition to the majority opinion.
The group of close-knit political activists, for all their discussion of free thought, could never tolerate a true DISSENTIENT.

recusancy (REK-yuh-zun-see). The refusal to recognize or obey established authority.
At one time, an individual's religious RECUSANCY could result in punishment.

sedition (sih-DISH-uhn). An action that promotes discontent or rebellion against authority.
In an act of childish SEDITION, Alex quit the club after we refused to play a round of golf with him.

VERBS

beard (BEERD). To defy boldly; oppose.
To ensure the measure would pass, supporters needed to be ready to BEARD the opposition.

contravene (kawn-truh-VEEN). To go against or deny; to oppose something by action or argument.
The orders I left were to be CONTRAVENED by no one but the colonel.

remonstrate (rih-MON-strayt). To protest, object, or show disapproval.
When Carlotta REMONSTRATED our snubbing of Julia, we simply began to snub Carlotta as well.

restive (RESS-tiv). Impatient and stubborn; contrary.
Audrey was RESTIVE about her upcoming vacation abroad and thus found it difficult to concentrate on her schoolwork.

ANTONYMS

milquetoast (MILK-toast). An unassertive, timid, spineless person who is easily intimidated.
Unless you just want to be a pencil-pusher all your life, you've got to stop being such a MILQUETOAST, Arthur!

verecund (VER-ih-kuhnd). Bashful; modest.
Paul's VERECUND manner makes it difficult to carry on a conversation with him.

56. Descant

(des-KANT), verb

To talk freely and without inhibition.

ADJECTIVES

convivial (kuhn-VIV-ee-ull). Fond of feasting, drinking, and companionship.
"One does not leave a CONVIVIAL party before closing time."
—Winston Churchill, British statesman and orator

discursive (dis-KER-siv). A manner or style of lecturing in which the speaker rambles among many topics.
Paul's DISCURSIVE lectures on American history jumped from century to century, yet it all came together in an understandable and fresh fashion.

facile (FASS-ul). Accomplished easily and with little effort.
"The hunger for FACILE wisdom is the root of all false philosophy."
—George Santayana, author and philosopher

loquacious (loh-KWAY-shuss). Verbose; chatty; given to talking nonstop.
Amy and Donna are both so LOQUACIOUS, their average phone call lasts ninety minutes.

mellifluous (meh-LIH-flu-us). Of music, speech, or other sound that is sweet and pleasant to listen to.
The MELLIFLUOUS tones of his voice brought Martin many high-paying gigs for voice-overs.

verbose (ver-BOHSS). Describes a person or composition using more words than are needed to get the point across.
Long-winded and VERBOSE, Mitch made his team members groan whenever he stood up to speak at a charity event.

NOUNS

badinage (bah-dih-NAHZH). Light, good-natured, even playful banter.
"If you don't care for me, you can move out now. I'm frankly not up to BADINAGE."—Harlan Ellison, American author

diatribe (DYE-uh-tryb). A speech railing against injustice; a vehement denunciation.
The editorial was a mean-spirited DIATRIBE against school vouchers written to prevent children from other towns from being sent by bus to Centerville High School.

filibuster (FILL-ih-bus-ter). A prolonged speech or other tactics to delay legislative actions or other important decisions.
The room breathed a collective sigh when the senator finally ended his eight-hour FILIBUSTER.

garrulity (gah-ROO-lih-tee). The habit of talking way too much.
"The interview is an intimate conversation between journalist and politician wherein the journalist seeks to take advantage of the GARRULITY of the politician and the politician of the credulity of the journalist"—Emory Klein, American journalist

kaffeeklatsch (KAW-fee-klatch). An informal social gathering, typically including coffee and gossip.
Jeanette is not welcome at our KAFFEEKLATSCH because she refuses to gossip about her social contacts.

VERBS

bloviate (BLOH-vee-ayt). To speak pompously and at length.
Maxwell BLOVIATES about his "excellent" golf game, but everyone knows he cheats outrageously.

confabulate (kuhn-FAB-yuh-layt). To chat or converse informally.
Jarod proceeded to CONFABULATE about the wines most recently added to the family cellar.

natter (NATT-er). To talk ceaselessly; babble.
The way Emily NATTERS endlessly about her family's new yacht is revolting to those of us who have owned several yachts over the years.

prattle (PRAT-l). To babble; to talk nonstop without regard as to whether what you are saying makes sense or is of any interest to the listener.
"Infancy conforms to nobody: all conform to it, so that one babe commonly makes four or five out of the adults who PRATTLE and play to it."—Ralph Waldo Emerson, American poet, essayist, and transcendentalist

ANTONYMS

farouche (fah-ROOSH). To become sullen, shy, or withdrawn in the presence of company.
His FAROUCHE demeanor gave people the impression that he didn't like them, when in fact he was merely an introvert.

laconic (luh-KAWN-ik). Of few words; expressing oneself with an economy of words.
Harold may be LACONIC, but when he does speak, he is worth listening to.

taciturn (TASS-ih-turn). Reserved; uncommunicative; a person of few words.
"Nature is garrulous to the point of confusion, let the artist be truly TACITURN."—Paul Klee, German-born Swiss painter

57. Desire

(dih-ZYR), verb

To want or crave.

ADJECTIVES

esurient (ih-SOOR-ee-uhnt). Hungry; greedy; voracious.
Because he was raised by wolves, Jack often displayed ESURIENT habits.

orectic (aw-REK-tik). Characterized by appetite or desire.
Unfortunately, Michael was obsessed with ORECTIC thoughts about girls to the exclusion of any interest in schoolwork.

wistful (WIHST-full). Yearning, pensive; having an unfulfilled desire.
"I never saw a man who looked / With such a WISTFUL eye / Upon that little tent of blue / Which prisoners call the sky."—Oscar Wilde, Irish playwright and poet

NOUNS

ardor (AR-der). Emotional warmth; passion; eagerness; intense devotion.
The author's ARDOR for the environment is obvious in all of his writings.

aspiration (ass-puh-RAY-shun). Goal; desire; something one wishes to achieve.
Marco, whose ASPIRATION was to be a concert violinist, practiced his instrument at least eight hours a day.

desideratum (deh-sih-deh-RAY-tum). Something that one covets or desires.
Ever since she was an adolescent, Evangeline's DESIDERATUM has been a first edition of Virginia Woolf's first novel, The Voyage Out.

ebullition (ebb-uh-LISH-un). A sudden outpouring of strong emotion; passion.
The concert closed with an inspired EBULLITION from the entire orchestra.

yen (YEN). A strong desire or urge.
"Perhaps one subtext of the health care debate is a YEN to be treated like a whole person, not just an eye, an ear, a nose or a throat."—Anna Quindlen, American author and opinion columnist

VERBS

covet (KUHV-it). To strongly desire; to desire something that another person has.
As a young boy, I was taught not to COVET my neighbor's tricycle.

ANTONYMS

animosity (an-ih-MOSS-ih-tee). Strong dislike for; open and active hostility toward.
"Life appears to me too short to be spent nursing ANIMOSITY, or registering wrongs."—Charlotte Brontë, English novelist

spurn (SPURN). To reject with scorn; disdain.
"If the riches of the Indies, or the crowns of all the kingdoms of Europe, were laid at my feet in exchange for my love of reading, I would SPURN them all."
—Ralph Waldo Emerson, American poet

58. Determined

(dih-TUR-minnd), adjective

Having one's mind made up; settled; decided; resolved.

ADJECTIVES

indefatigable (in-deh-FAT-uh-guh-bull). Capable of continuing along one's current course of action without wavering, tiring, or faltering.
"We are truly INDEFATIGABLE in providing for the needs of the body, but we starve the soul."—Ellen Wood, British playwright

indomitable (in-DOM-ih-tuh-bull). Not easily discouraged or subdued; unyielding; unconquerable.
When it came to a cause she believed in, Paula's INDOMITABLE spirit was not to be denied.

intractable (in-TRAK-tuh-bull). Difficult to control or manage; stubborn.
"It is precisely here, where the writer fights with the raw, the INTRACTABLE, that poetry is born."—Doris Lessing, British author

intransigent (in-TRAN-zih-jent). Stubborn; refusing to consider opinions other than one's own.
"Lamont stared for a moment in frustration but Burt's expression was a clearly INTRANSIGENT one now."—Isaac Asimov, Russian-born American author and biochemist

obdurate (OB-doo-rit). Stubborn and unyielding; hardhearted; unsympathetic.
"The fates are not quite OBDURATE; / They have a grim, sardonic way / Of granting them who supplicate / The thing they wanted yesterday."—Roselle Mercier Montgomery, American poet

obstinate (OB-stih-nit). Inflexible in one's opinions and attitudes; refusing to change or accede to the wishes of others.
"The male sex still constitutes in many ways the most OBSTINATE vested interest one can find."—Francis Pakenham, British social reformer

pertinacious (per-tih-NAY-shuss). Persistent or obstinate to the point of annoyance.
The car salesman's PERTINACIOUS patter caused me to leave the lot immediately.

resolute (REZ-uh-loot). Unyielding in determination; firm of purpose.
We remain RESOLUTE on the question of the hostages: they must be released without precondition.

sedulous (SEJ-yuh-luss). Done or crafted with perseverance, diligence, and care.
The teen's SEDULOUS labors at the desert site were rewarded by the discovery of triceratops bones in the third week of the dig.

staunch (STONCH). Firm in resolution or belief; fixed.
Mr. West, a STAUNCH conservative, believed that government waste was the main problem requiring attention in Washington.

tenacious (tuh-NAY-shuss). Persistent, stubborn, obstinate.
"Women are TENACIOUS, and all of them should be TENACIOUS of respect; without esteem they cannot exist; esteem is the first demand that they make of love."—Honoré de Balzac, French novelist and playwright

VERBS

indurate (IN-duh-rayt). To become hard; harden; stubborn.
His friends were concerned that Paul's rejection by his latest girlfriend would INDURATE him to future relationships.

ANTONYMS

falter (FAWL-ter). To act hesitantly; show uncertainty; waver.
"We shall neither fail nor FALTER; we shall not weaken or tire. . . . Give us the tools and we will finish the job."—Winston Churchill, British statesman and orator

vacillate (VASS-uh-layt). To waver; show indecision; be irresolute.
"It seems to me that the problem with diaries, and the reason that most of them are so boring, is that every day we VACILLATE between examining our hangnails and speculating on cosmic order."—Ann Beattie, American novelist

59. Didactic

(dy-DAK-tik), adjective

Designed, made, or tailored for purposes of education, self-improvement, or ethical betterment.

ADJECTIVES

erudite (AIR-yoo-dyte). Sophisticated; well educated; deeply learned; knowledgeable; scholarly.
Beneath his ERUDITE image, Dr. John Brinkley was a money-grubbing con man.

hypercritical (hy-per-KRIT-ih-kuhl). Excessively or meticulously critical.
"Good writers have two things in common: they would rather be understood than admired, and they do not write for hairsplitting and HYPERCRITICAL readers."—Friedrich Nietzche, German philosopher

meticulous (meh-TIK-yuh-luss). Extremely precise; fussy.
The overly METICULOUS maître d' made us self-conscious and detracted from our enjoyment of the meal.

niggling (NIG-ling). Demanding a great deal of care, attention, or time; or, trifling and insignificant.
People just don't understand how difficult it is for us to attend to all the NIGGLING needs of our servants.

NOUNS

autodidact (aw-toe-DY-dakt). A self-educated person.
In the twentieth century, the library was the university of the AUTODIDACT; in the twenty-first century, it is the Internet.

lyceum (LIE-see-um). A school or other place of learning.
"[Television] should be our LYCEUM, our Chautauqua, our Minsky's, and our Camelot."—E.B. White, American author

pedagogue (PED-ah-gog). A strict, humorless, no-nonsense teacher.
"The negative cautions of science are never popular. If the experimental-ist would not commit himself, the social philosopher, the preacher, and the PEDAGOGUE tried the harder to give a short-cut answer."—Margaret Mead, American cultural anthropologist

VERBS

elucubrate (ih-LOO-kyoo-brayt). To produce a written work through lengthy, intensive effort.
Thanks to a few hundred bucks passed along to a classmate, Miles did not have to ELUCUBRATE his term paper and could, instead, attend parties with us.

quibble (KWIB-ul). To argue over a minor matter; to voice a niggling objection.
If you are not 100 percent satisfied, your money will promptly be refunded with-out question or QUIBBLE.

ANTONYMS

dilettante (DILL-ih-tont). A person who studies a subject in a casual fashion, learning the topic for the fun of it rather than to apply it to solve real problems.
Joseph Priestly could be considered a DILETTANTE, and yet his work led to the discovery of oxygen.

vacuous (VAK-yoo-uss). Devoid of emotion, intelligence, or any normal human thought processes; stupid; moronic.
The VACUOUS stare from her two eyes, looking like raisins pushed into a lump of dough, made him shiver with loathing and contempt.

60. Difficult

(DIF-ih-kult), adjective

Not easy to do, make, or understand; requiring significant labor, skill, or knowledge to be performed successfully.

ADJECTIVES

abstruse (ab-STROOS). Arcane, complex, difficult to understand and learn.
Bob began to wish there was, in fact, a Santa Claus because he found the "simple instructions" to his son's bicycle far too ABSTRUSE.

anfractuous (an-FRACK-chuh-wuss). Full of windings and intricacies, like a good mystery novel.
The novel's ANFRACTUOUS plot worked on paper, but it became stupefyingly confusing—actually, just plain stupid—onscreen.

arduous (AR-joo-us). Requiring exceptional effort or care; mentally or physically challenging; laborious.
Stacy has been preparing all week for the ARDUOUS marathon competition.

byzantine (BIZ-un-teen). Convoluted; overly complicated; difficult to figure out because of its complexity.
We found it impossible to follow the BYZANTINE plot of how Eileen made Mariah a laughingstock by replacing her Prada shoes with nearly identical knockoffs.

circuitous (sir-KYOO-uh-tuss). Extremely twisty and winding; indirect.
*Blanche called it a shortcut, but her CIRCUITOUS route caused us to arrive
very late to the party.*

herculean (her-kyuh-LEE-uhn). Of extraordinary power or difficulty. Often
capitalized because the word alludes to Hercules.
*"We found it a HERCULEAN effort not to chortle at the outlandish clothing of
the nouveau riche attendees of our party," said Lillian.*

impalpable (im-PAL-puh-bull). Difficult to understand; intangible.
*"The soul is so IMPALPABLE, so often useless, and sometimes such a nuisance,
that I felt no more emotion on losing it than if, on a stroll, I had mislaid my visiting card."—Charles Baudelaire, French poet, critic, and translator*

insuperable (in-SOO-per-uh-bull). Impossible to overcome or surmount.
*"Conceit is an INSUPERABLE obstacle to all progress."—Ellen Terry,
British actress*

onerous (OH-nerr-us). Difficult; imposing heavy responsibility.
*Caring for his son's large aquarium quickly went from an interesting hobby to
an ONEROUS burden.*

NOUNS

asperity (ah-SPAIR-ih-tee). Roughness; harshness.
Sorry, I can't handle the ASPERITY of his politics. Could we skip the speech?

conundrum (kuh-NUN-drum). A difficult problem or situation that is not
easily resolved.
*Choosing whether to attend MIT, Yale, or Harvard was quite a CONUNDRUM: MIT
had the courses he wanted, but Harvard and Yale offered him full sports scholarships.*

labyrinth (LAB-uh-rinth). A mazelike series of connected tunnels and passages.
He ran, terrified, as the Minotaur chased him through the LABYRINTH.

morass (muh-RASS). A confusing or troublesome situation from which it is
difficult to disentangle oneself.
*"One idea is enough to organize a life and project it / Into unusual but viable
forms, but many ideas merely / Lead one thither into a MORASS of their own
good intentions."—John Ashbery, American poet*

nodus (NOH-dus). A difficult point; a knotty situation.
Jason reached a NODUS in his relationship with Gail and was determined to find a solution while there was still a chance.

straits (STRAYTS). A position of difficulty and challenge.
After a series of bad investments, I found myself in dire financial STRAITS.

ANTONYMS

elementary (el-uh-MEN-tuh-ree). Of first principles; of the rudiments or fundamentals of something; introductory; simple.
"By respect for life we become religious in a way that is ELEMENTARY, profound, and alive."—Albert Schweitzer, German missionary and theologian

facile (FASS-ul). Accomplished easily and with little effort.
"Sometimes there is a greater lack of communication in FACILE talking than in silence."—Faith Baldwin, American author

61. Dirty

(DUR-tee), adjective

Unclean; soiled with dirt; foul; vile; mean.

ADJECTIVES

bedraggled (bee-DRAG-uld). Harried or in a condition of disarray; unkempt; dirty and limp.
A group of BEDRAGGLED orphans stood outside begging by the flickering gaslight.

sordid (SOR-did). Characterized by grossness or baseness; vile; wretched; squalid.
The movie opened with a scene showing the hero boldly walking into a SORDID tenement house to find the villain.

NOUNS

squalor (SKWALL-ur). The state or quality of being filthy.
My mother knew full well that my roommates were not the tidiest men in the world, but she still seemed shocked when confronted with the unrepentant SQUALOR of our apartment.

VERBS

contaminate (kuhn-TAM-uh-nayt). To make unclean, impure, or corrupt by contact; to make unusable or harmful by adding impure materials.
If the reactor is breached, the cooling water will CONTAMINATE the bay and render its marine life radioactive.

defile (dih-FYL). To pollute; to corrupt or make unclean.
The river that only a few years ago ran clean and clear is now DEFILED with a witches' brew of chemicals, thanks to the new tanning plant.

sully (SUL-ee). To besmear or make foul; to cast aspersions.
I will not allow you to SULLY the good name of my family with such baseless accusations.

taint (TAYNT). To make morally corrupt; to infect, contaminate, or spoil; to affect with something harmful or unpleasant.
The senator's actions, no matter how noble in intent, are forever TAINTED by his previous transgressions.

ANTONYMS

hygienic (hy-jee-EN-ik). Promoting health; healthful; sanitary.
Aunt Charlotte's HYGIENIC practices made it quite safe to eat off her floors.

immaculate (ih-MAK-yuh-lit). Perfectly clean; without a spot or stain; unsoiled.
"His words are bonds, his oaths are oracles; his love sincere, his thoughts IMMACULATE; his tears pure messengers sent from his heart; his heart as far from fraud, as heaven from earth."—William Shakespeare, English dramatist

62. Disagree

(dis-uh-GREE), verb

To differ; dissent; to quarrel about or disapprove of something.

ADJECTIVES

bilious (BILL-yuss). Having a nasty temperament or disagreeable disposition; to be "full of bile" and hatred.
The polo team's BILIOUS captain made his team miserable as he proceeded to criticize their every move.

discordant (dis-KOR-dunt). Conflicting; lacking in harmony.
I find that composer's DISCORDANT style difficult to listen to.

dyslogistic (diss-luh-JISS-tik). Showing disapproval or censure.
We gave Elizabeth DYSLOGISTIC glances when she told us she had decided to stop shopping at Cartier.

NOUNS

apostasy (uh-POSS-tah-see). The act of abandoning, ignoring, or openly flouting an accepted principle or belief.
"It was his idea of grand APOSTASY to drive to the reform synagogue on the high holidays and park his pink-eye nag among the luxurious, whirl-wired touring cars of the rich."—Saul Bellow, American author

dissidence (DISS-uh-dehnts). Strong disagreement, especially with a government.
The newly formed government decided to crack down on DISSIDENCE by jailing anyone who disagreed with governmental policies.

VERBS

demur (di-MURR). To make an objection on the grounds of scruples.
"Assent, and you are sane; / DEMUR,—you're straightway dangerous, / And handled with a chain."—Emily Dickinson, American poet

deprecate (DEP-rih-kayt). To express severe disapproval of another's actions.
"Those who profess to favor freedom and yet DEPRECATE agitation, are
men who want crops without plowing up the ground."—Frederick Douglass,
American abolitionist and orator

gainsay (GANE-say). To deny, dispute, or contradict.
Michael has made no attempt to GAINSAY the persistent rumors that his fam-
ily's fortune rests solely on insider trading.

harangue (huh-RANG). Verbally accost; yell at; berate.
"But on that hot July day she breaks—HARANGUING strangers in the street."
—Oliver Sacks, British neurologist

inveigh (in-VAY). To protest or complain strongly.
The crowd INVEIGHED against the governor's decision to commute Davidson's
sentence.

negate (nih-GAYT). To cause to be ineffectual; to deny; to reverse.
I imagine that double hot fudge sundae I ate completely NEGATED the effects of
my morning exercises.

ANTONYMS

amenable (ah-MEE-nuh-bull). Readily agreeable to the wishes and desires of
others.
Mark considers himself AMENABLE, but the rest of us just think he's a pushover.

complaisant (kuhm-PLAY-zuhnt). Agreeable and eager to please.
Eleanor is far too COMPLAISANT with common strangers.

63. Dishonest

(dis-AWN-ist), adjective

Not honest; the tendency to lie, cheat, or steal; untrustworthy;
fraudulent.

ADJECTIVES

collusive (kuh-LOO-siv). Involving or characterized by collusion; conspiring for fraudulent purposes.
The brothers' COLLUSIVE tendencies were well known to high school administrators.

disingenuous (diss-in-JEN-yoo-uss). Not inclined toward open dealing; less than truthful; other than appearances would suggest; insincere.
The mayor's carefully worded denials never explicitly touched on her involvement in her campaign's alleged effort to buy votes, leading many to conclude that she was being DISINGENUOUS.

duplicitous (doo-PLIS-ih-tus). Characterized by hypocritical deception or cunning; double-dealing; intentionally deceptive.
His DUPLICITOUS acts were second nature to Jim after years of living on the mean streets of Newark.

knavish (NAYV-ish). Untrustworthy, dishonest, and mischievous.
Despite, or perhaps because of, his KNAVISH behavior, Jonathan is always a success at our society balls.

smarmy (SMAR-mee). Insincerely earnest.
In between syrupy love songs, the SMARMY lounge singer repeatedly assured the crowd they were by far the best audience he'd ever performed for.

unconscionable (un-KON-shu-nuh-bull). Lacking in principles or conscience; beyond any reasonable boundary.
Your decision to destroy those letters without attempting to get permission from the poet's widow was UNCONSCIONABLE.

NOUNS

covin (KUV-in). In law, a conspiracy of two or more people to defraud or swindle others.
After the coven members were found guilty, their COVIN made newspaper headline fodder for days.

grifter (GRIFF-ter). A person who engages in unseemly activities; a swindler, a dishonest gambler, etc.
The small-town bar was filled with reprobates, toothless legions, and GRIFTERS. I felt right at home.

pettifoggery (PET-ee-fog-er-ee). Petty dishonesty or trickery.
"Let's put all this PETTIFOGGERY behind us," said Mr. Powers, "and start dealing with each other in a more straightforward manner."

rogue (rohg). A scoundrel; a dishonest person; a person known to have low morals and habits.
Everyone in Savannah knew that Rhett was a ROGUE, but somehow he managed to use that fact to his advantage.

VERBS

bilk (bilk). To swindle or cheat.
The accountant, investigators learned, had been BILKING the company of nearly a quarter of a million dollars a year.

filch (FILCH). To steal, especially to steal petty amounts or inexpensive goods.
Brian is proud of how many motel towels he's FILCHED over the years.

mulct (MUHLKT). To get something from someone else by fraud or extortion; swindle.
The con man MULCTED ten bucks from the unsuspecting couple.

perjure (PUR-jer). To lie or give false and misleading testimony; to commit the crime of testifying to something one knows is untrue.
Although Mr. Frattori was not convicted on the main charges he faced, he may serve time in prison for having PERJURED himself during the trial.

purloin (PUR-loyn). To steal or to take by dishonest means.
Bobby PURLOINED almost all the contents of his dad's change jar before being discovered.

ANTONYMS

conscionable (KON-shuh-nuh-bull). That which agrees with one's ideas of right and wrong; just.
Arthur and Carolyn considered their relationship with friends and neighbors and tried to treat everyone as CONSCIONABLE people would.

reputable (REP-yuh-tuh-bull). Respectable; honorable.
When a natural disaster occurs, one unfortunate result is the appearance of charitable organizations that are not completely REPUTABLE.

64. Dull

(DUHL), adjective

Lacking sensitivity or spirit; causing boredom; tedious.

ADJECTIVES

aseptic (uh-SEP-tik). Lacking emotion or vibrancy.
Jordan's ASEPTIC performance at the job interview is probably the reason he didn't get the job, despite his qualifications.

banal (buh-NAL). Trite; lacking originality.
Aaron always dismissed the insights of the other philosophers as BANAL, but I for one never heard him utter a single profound idea.

bourgeois (boor-ZHWA). Characteristic of the middle class; having material concerns, an interest in respectability, and a tendency toward mediocrity.
Dave is so BOURGEOIS he goes to a liquor store across town so his neighbors won't know he drinks.

bromidic (bro-MIHD-ik). Trite and commonplace.
The marketing executive groaned as one BROMIDIC ad campaign after another crossed her desk.

insipid (in-SIP-id). Lacking in vigor; unexciting.
In Frank's opinion, the novel's plot was INSIPID and left much to be desired.

jaded (JAY-did). Worn out; dulled or satiated due to overindulgence.
Her parents thought that providing Tracy with everything her heart desired as a child would make her a happy person, but she grew up to be a JADED and selfish woman.

lackluster (LACK-lus-ter). Flat; not shiny or brilliant.
Wanda's LACKLUSTER performance as Hedda Gabler led one critic to remark that she probably had a long career ahead of her in the theater—as a stage weight.

mundane (mun-DAYN). Ordinary, practical, or everyday.
Everett's concerns were MUNDANE enough: keep a roof over his head, track down the occasional meal.

pedestrian (puh-DESS-tree-uhn). Lacking in originality or vitality.
If you really want to advance in this company, you're going to have to come up with something better than the PEDESTRIAN ideas we've already tried and rejected.

trite (TRYT). Lacking in effectiveness or freshness due to continual use and excessive repetition; hackneyed; stale.
"The TRITE subjects of human efforts, possessions, outward success, luxury have always seemed to me contemptible."—Albert Einstein

vapid (VAP-id). Void of intellectual curiosity or intelligence; lacking spirit and enthusiasm; routine, unchallenging.
What irked him most about his sister-in-law was her VAPID stares in response to simple questions, conversation, and jokes.

NOUNS

pabulum (PAB-yuh-lum). Writing or speech that is simplistic, insipid, or bland.
Christie could be counted on to deliver the sort of PABULUM that would distract the media from the real and sordid activities of the actor.

ANTONYMS

exuberant (ig-ZOO-ber-uhnt). Overflowing with spirit; uninhibitedly enthusiastic; abounding in vitality.
"Nothing ever succeeds which EXUBERANT spirits have not helped to produce."—Friedrich Nietzsche, German philosopher

provocative (pruh-VAWK-uh-tiv). Tending to provoke; inciting; stimulating.
Andrew's visits to the art museum filled him with PROVOCATIVE images and gave him new energy.

65. Eat

(EET), verb

To consume for nourishment; take in food.

ADJECTIVES

bibulous (BIB-yuh-luss). Related to drinking or to drunkenness; fond of alcoholic beverages.
You may think you're "fine," but your BIBULOUS activities will put you in the poorhouse or in jail one of these days!

crapulous (KRAP-yuh-luss). Pertaining to eating and drinking too much, or the consequences of eating and drinking too much.
Jim spent the day after the party in a CRAPULOUS state.

dipsomaniacal (dip-suh-muh-NIE-ih-kul). Having an uncontrolled craving for alcohol.
The private detective summed up his latest client, a booze-loving gold digger, as the "DIPSOMANIACAL dame."

gustatory (GUSS-tuh-tore-ee). Of the sense of taste.
"Food has it over sex for variety. Hedonistically, GUSTATORY possibilities are much broader than copulatory ones."—Joseph Epstein, American author and critic

herbivorous (hur-BIV-er-us). Eating plants rather than meat.
The HERBIVOROUS animals are not considered predators unless plants can be thought of as prey.

macrobiotic (mack-row-by-OT-ik). Of a diet rich in whole grains and beans, which some believe lengthens one's lifespan.
After she had a few health scares, Jean turned to a MACROBIOTIC diet.

omnivorous (om-NIV-er-uss). Accustomed to eating both animal and vegetable food items.
The Cantonese, I am told, are OMNIVOROUS, and it is said that the traveler is best advised not to inquire too closely into exactly what he is eating.

omophagous (oh-MOH-fuh-guss). Eating raw food, especially raw meat.
Peggy considered becoming OMOPHAGOUS, but was concerned about her ability to digest raw food.

seminivorous (sem-uh-NIV-er-us). Eating seeds.
Now that Diane has adopted SEMINIVOROUS habits, we often see her hovering near bird feeders.

voracious (vuh-RAY-shuss). Possessing a huge and insatiable appetite, whether for food, knowledge, amusement, or something else.
Her son always had a VORACIOUS desire for knowledge. He read anything he could get his hands on and was always willing to experience something new.

NOUNS

polydipsia (pol-ee-DIP-see-uh). An abnormal or excessive thirst.
The bartender, clearly uninterested in Ralph's claim to suffer from POLYDIPSIA, told him flatly that he'd had enough.

polyphagia (pol-ee-FAY-jee-uh). An excessive desire to eat.
Ray's POLYPHAGIA was successfully diverted into an excessive desire to talk.

refection (ri-FEK-shun). Food and drink; nourishment; refreshment.
As I recall, REFECTIONS were not the high point of my college experience.

repast (ri-PAST). Food provided or consumed for a meal.
Obviously a frustrated comedian, Jack entitled his most recent painting The Last REPAST.

vegan (VEE-guhn). A person who eats only vegetables, fruits, and grains and no animal products whatsoever.
A VEGAN since college, Wanda had a hard time finding restaurants that offered entrees she could eat.

viand (VY-und). An article of food.
Chef Jacques thought that any VIAND, whether prime rib or meatloaf, should be served to the customer in a visually appealing way.

VERBS

gormandize (GORE-mun-dyz). To eat like a glutton, as if one were starving.
We find GORMANDIZING on even the finest French cuisine to be quite tasteless and, therefore, to be avoided.

imbibe (im-BYB). To drink, especially alcoholic beverages.
Donald once had a drinking problem, but now he no longer IMBIBES.

masticate (MASS-tih-kayt). To chew, especially to chew thoroughly.
The best way to appreciate the gustatory arts is to MASTICATE your personal chef's creations at as relaxed a pace as possible.

quaff (KWOFF). To drink with gusto and in large volume.
"We QUAFF the cup of life with eager haste without draining it, instead of which it only overflows the brim."—William Hazlitt, English literary critic and philosopher

raven (RAV-un). To eat or feed greedily or voraciously.
To watch Harold RAVEN his meals is to observe the most primitive of human instincts.

ANTONYMS

emaciated (ih-MAY-see-a-tihd). Abnormally lean; wasted away as from starvation.
Janet had lost the will to live and the desire to eat, becoming more EMACIATED with each passing week.

malnourished (mal-NUR-isht). Poorly nourished; badly fed; suffering from malnutrition.
Experts in the field believe that we already have the means to help all the MALNOURISHED of the world.
See also: Foods

66. Élan

(a-LON), noun

Enthusiasm, energy, flair, zest.

ADJECTIVES

ebullient (eh-BULL-yuhnt). Feeling joy and positive emotions at an extreme level; the state of being wildly enthusiastic about something.
Lorne was EBULLIENT when he found that his mother had given the college enough money to overturn his rejection.

effervescent (ef-ur-VESS-ent). Bubbly; upbeat; cheerful; possessing a positive attitude and joyful personality.
After getting the acceptance letter from Cornell, Sabrina was EFFERVESCENT and celebrated with a trip to Neiman Marcus.

effulgent (ih-FULL-jent). Shining brightly; glowing; radiant.
The lightning storm made the evening sky positively EFFULGENT.

fervent (FUR-vuhnt). Showing great enthusiasm and intensity of spirit.
Packing up the family's castoffs for myriad charities each December places Contessa in a FERVENT state.

jocund (JOE-kund). Having a lust for life; possessing a positive attitude and desire to enjoy life to the fullest.
Ron's JOCUND façade shattered when he found himself the victim of identity theft.

NOUNS

alacrity (uh-LAK-rih-tee). Cheerful cooperation rendered with enthusiasm, promptness, and politeness.
The ALACRITY with which Steve responded to Helen's invitation is nothing short of astonishing.

fillip (FILL-uhp). Something that revives or arouses excitement.
"Faithful horoscope-watching, practiced daily, provides just the sort of small, but warm and infinitely reassuring FILLIP that gets matters off to a spirited start."
—Shana Alexander, American author

zeal (ZEEL). Great enthusiasm and energy for a cause or activity.
"The living, vital truth of social and economic well-being will become a reality only through the ZEAL, courage, the non-compromising determination of intelligent minorities, and not through the mass."—Emma Goldman, Bolshevik anarchist

zest (ZEHST). Extreme enjoyment; a lust for life.
"Such epithets, like pepper, / Give ZEST to what you write; / And, if you strew them sparely, / They whet the appetite: / But if you lay them on too thick, / You spoil the matter quite!"—Lewis Carroll, English author and logician

ANTONYMS

enervate (EN-er-vayt). To rob a person, organization, place, or thing of its energy, strength, and vitality.
Greenhouse gases ENERVATE the protective ozone layer surrounding the Earth.

lassitude (LASS-ih-tood). Having little energy or motivation; weariness.
"We know what boredom is: it is a dull / Impatience or a fierce velleity, / A champing wish, stalled by our LASSITUDE, / To make or do."—Richard Wilbur, American poet

logy (LOW-gee). Characterized by lethargy and sluggishness.
"To be scared is such a release from all the LOGY weight of procrastination, of dallying and pokiness! You burn into work. It is as though gravity were removed and you walked lightly to the moon like an angel."—Brenda Ueland, American author

pallid (PAL-id). Having a wan, sickly, washed-out appearance indicating illness or weakness, or lack of energy, strength, and vitality.
Many of us maintain a PALLID pallor because we want to make it clear that we do not need to go outdoors unless we so choose.

tepid (TEHP-id). Characterized by a lack of enthusiasm.
We greeted the new opera, with its mawkish plot and poor acting, with TEPID applause.

67. Eliminate

(uh-LIM-uh-nayt), verb

To take out; remove; get rid of; to remove from consideration; reject; eradicate.

NOUNS

catharsis (kuh-THAR-siss). The purging of the senses through tragic drama or through music; or, in general, a discharge of negative emotions.
After losing matches at the club's courts, Celeste finds that Puccini's Madama Butterfly *always leads to CATHARSIS.*

VERBS

depose (dih-POZE). To oust or remove from office or a position of power and authority.
After the dictator was DEPOSED, the country set about healing the wounds of a long civil war.

deracinate (dee-RASS-ih-nayt). To uproot or to remove by force.
The hurricane DERACINATED populations all over the island.

efface (ih-FAYSS). To erase, obliterate, make inconspicuous.
"It is also true that one can write nothing readable unless one constantly struggles to EFFACE one's own personality. Good prose is like a windowpane."
—George Orwell, British author

estrange (ih-STRANJ). To alienate or remove from a position or relationship.
Michelle's refusal to give up her self-destructive habits ESTRANGED her brother.

eviscerate (ee-VISS-uh-rayt). To disembowel; to remove essential components.
Having EVISCERATED the novel's key chapter, the censor was content to let the earlier exposition stand.

excise (EK-syz). To cut a passage from a text or, in general, to cut something out or off.
I went to the dermatologist and had that mole EXCISED.

expunge (eks-PUHNJ). To rid oneself of an annoyance; to cast out; to get rid of; to forcibly eject.
"There is no man, however wise, who has not at some period of his youth said things, or lived in a way the consciousness of which is so unpleasant to him in later life that he would gladly, if he could, EXPUNGE it from his memory."
—Marcel Proust, French novelist, essayist, and critic

expurgate (EK-spur-gayt). To purge sexually inappropriate, objectionable, or otherwise undesirable material prior to presentation.
For her parents' benefit, Marina EXPURGATED stories related to the weekend she spent slumming in Greenwich Village.

extirpate (EK-ster-payt). To do away with; remove or destroy completely; exterminate.
John hoped that his new insecticide would successfully EXTIRPATE the ants in his kitchen.

extricate (EK-strih-kayt). To remove from an entanglement.
Having gotten us into an impossible dilemma, Warren appeared to have no idea how we should go about EXTRICATING ourselves from it.

ostracize (OS-truh-syz). To exclude from society, friendship, community, etc.
Once we learned that Sasha had been planting stories about us in the society pages, we, of course, had to OSTRACIZE her permanently from our group.

redact (ree-DAKT). To remove a comment, thought, or passage from a written document before going public with it.
"You may want to REDACT your opinion on your opponent's health care policies," his campaign manager warned him.

rescind (ree-SIND). Take away, revoke, cancel, withdraw, remove.
Richard RESCINDED his order for a yacht, opting instead to purchase a private aircraft.

winnow (WIN-oh). To analyze carefully in order to separate valuable parts from worthless parts.
I WINNOWED through the stack of personal papers, looking for the ones I needed to present to the IRS.

ANTONYMS

adjoin (uh-joyn). To be close to or in contact with; to attach or append.
The architect's plans clearly show a number of secondary buildings ADJOINING the main structure.

annex (uh-NEKS). To add on or attach, as a smaller thing to a larger; to add; to incorporate, as a country or territory.
"Every other sin hath some pleasure ANNEXED to it, or will admit of an excuse: envy alone wants both."—Robert Burton, English writer and clergyman

68. Embarrassment

(em-BAYR-uhs-ment), noun

The state of being ill at ease and losing composure; self-consciousness; confusion; disconcertment.

ADJECTIVES

invidious (in-VID-ee-us). Designed to give offense or to create ill will.
"In the name of all lechers and boozers I most solemnly protest against the INVIDIOUS distinction made to our prejudice."—Aldous Huxley, British author and humanist

NOUNS

effrontery (eh-FRON-ter-ee). Offensive and aggressive behavior; audacity.
After doing a terrible job on the project, he had the EFFRONTERY to ask me, "Can I do extra credit?"

humiliation (hyoo-mill-ee-A-shun). The state in which one's pride or dignity is reduced or feelings hurt.
When she was discovered with her arms around Harry, Janet's HUMILIATION was so profound that she could never again look him in the eye.

ignominy (ig-NOM-uh-nee). Personal shame and disgrace.
After he accidentally burned down the writer's home, Wally's IGNOMINY was such that he was forced to move out of town.

opprobrium (uh-PRO-bree-uhm). Disgrace incurred by outrageously shameful conduct.
Natasha incurred OPPROBRIUM when, in a fit of anger, she deliberately smashed her Waterford crystal wine glass at the Smythingtons' annual Thanksgiving gala.

VERBS

discomfit (diss-KUM-fit). To embarrass someone to the point where they become uncomfortable.
Maggie's public mispronunciation of the organizer's name at the charity benefit DISCOMFITED her mother.

mortify (MOR-tuh-fy). To shame or humiliate; to injure someone's pride or dignity.
Oscar had no shame, and when discovered in compromising situations that would MORTIFY anyone else, he was unrepentant.

ANTONYMS

amenity (uh-MEN-ih-tee). Any feature that provides comfort or convenience; a courteous act; civility.
Edith, unsure of herself and terribly shy, was buoyed by her mentor's AMENITY.

reassure (ree-uh-SHOOR). To restore to confidence.
"It is far better to grasp the Universe as it really is than to persist in delusion, however satisfying and reassuring."—Carl Sagan, American astronomer and writer

69. Empty

(EMP-tee), adjective

Containing or having nothing; vacant; unoccupied.

ADJECTIVES

arid (AIR-id). Unproductive due to lack of rain; unfertile; barren; sterile.
The instructor's presentation, rote and ARID, put the entire class to sleep.

bereft (beh-REFT). Lacking a certain characteristic, possession, or trait.
"A woman moved is like a fountain troubled. / Muddy, ill-seeming, thick, BEREFT of beauty, / And while it is so, none so dry or thirsty / Will deign to sip or touch one drop of it."—William Shakespeare

desolate (DESS-uh-let). Lacking signs of life; barren; deserted.
We drove over a hill and suddenly the landscape was as DESOLATE as if we had landed on the moon.

devoid (dih-VOYD). Lacking utterly; without.
"No matter how skilled a surgeon you become," Dr. Smith told the intern, "you'll fail as a doctor if you continue to be DEVOID of compassion and sympathy for patients."

vacuous (VAK-yoo-uss). Lacking content or substance; empty.
Televised debates are so potentially dangerous that most candidates settle for offering VACUOUS recitations of campaign speeches rather than saying something new and unexpected.

VERBS

deplete (dih-PLEET). To use up completely; to exhaust.
Once the coal deposits in the valley had been DEPLETED, the town of Harlenville, which had thrived for thirty years, virtually ceased to exist.

disembogue (dis-em-BOHG). To empty by discharging; to pour forth.
Many streams DISEMBOGUE into and create a large river that empties into the ocean.

purge (purj). To free (someone or something) of all that is perceived as bad; to take steps to cleanse or purify.
I tried to PURGE my system of the flu virus by drinking endless glasses of fruit juice, but I still ended up missing a week of work.

ANTONYMS

permeated (PER-mee-ayt-ed). Diffused through; saturated; pervaded.
As the concert started, a feeling of goodwill and brotherhood PERMEATED the crowd.

turgescent (tur-JESS-ent). Becoming or appearing swollen or distended.
The rains overnight were so intense that by morning all the region's rivers were TURGESCENT with water.

70. End

(END), verb

To conclude.

ADJECTIVES

climactic (kly-MAK-tik). Of or pertaining to a climax; concerning the last point in a series of events.
The CLIMACTIC moment of the play comes when Hamlet finally kills Claudius.

defunct (dih-FUNKT). No longer existing or functioning.
"Practical men, who believe themselves to be quite exempt from any intellectual influence, are usually the slaves of some DEFUNCT economist."
—John Maynard Keynes, British economist

moribund (MOR-ih-bund). Lacking vigor; soon to be dead or defunct.
Ever since its head chef left for the Food Network, that gourmet restaurant has become MORIBUND and is likely to close soon.

NOUNS

cessation (sess-SAY-shun). The condition of drawing to a close; ceasing or reaching a point of abatement.
Continued diplomatic effort may well bring about a CESSATION of hostilities.

coup de grace (koo-deh-GRAHS). Deathblow; a decisive act or event that brings a situation to a close; the finishing blow.
The COUP DE GRACE came when Paul threw his bowl of oatmeal at Mona's feet, leading her to reevaluate their relationship.

dénouement (day-noo-MAH). The resolution of any complex series of events, especially in a drama or novel.
I was disappointed with the play because I felt its DENOUEMENT left too many loose ends.

desuetude (DESS-wih-tood). Disuse; discontinuance.
Telephones plugged into walls are one of many once-ubiquitous items that have fallen into DESUETUDE.

dissolution (diss-so-LOO-shun). The condition of dissolving into fragments or parts; disintegration.
The union's DISSOLUTION seemed imminent, but a change of leadership forestalled that crisis.

perdition (per-DISH-in). Complete and irreversible loss; the condition of final spiritual ruin.
Her mother's confiscation of Laura's phone and iPod cast her into teenaged PERDITION.

quietus (kwy-EE-tuhs). Something that ends or settles a situation.
"For who would bear the whips and scorns of time, / Th'oppressor's wrong, the proud man's contumely, / The pangs of disprized love, the law's delay, / The insolence of office, and the spurns / That patient merit of th'unworthy takes, / When he himself might his QUIETUS make / With a bare bodkin?"—William Shakespeare

VERBS

abrogate (AB-ro-gayt). To nullify or cancel; to formally and unilaterally conclude an agreement or deed.
The United States ABROGATED the treaty after evidence appeared suggesting that the other nations had failed to honor the agreement.

consummate (KON-sum-mayt). To complete or finalize; to bring to a point of finality or a desired end.
The real estate agent CONSUMMATING the deal realized a substantial commission.

wane (WAYN). To gradually decrease; to fade away; to become diminished.
Once she finally received the Cartier watch from her father, Karen's interest in the timepiece quickly WANED.

ANTONYMS

ad infinitum (ad in-fi-NY-tum). Without end or limit.
Wilbur remarked wryly that he could probably discuss the treatment facility's weaknesses AD INFINITUM.

interminably (in-TUR-min-uh-blee). Seemingly without end or going on for an indeterminate period of time.
"The body dies; the body's beauty lives. / So evenings die, in their green going, / A wave, INTERMINABLY flowing."—Wallace Stevens, American modernist poet

perpetuity (pur-pih-TOO-ih-tee). The state or quality of being perpetual; of indefinite duration; endless.
In his will, Horace bequeathed his home and property to the town in PERPETUITY.

Sisyphean (siss-uh-FEE-uhn). Unavailing and endless, as a task.
Some days, keeping paperwork under control seems a SISYPHEAN task.

71. Enthusiasm

(en-THOO-zee-az-im), noun

Intense or eager interest; zeal; fervor.

ADJECTIVES

ardent (AR-dent). Intense, passionate, devoted; characterized by high emotion.
Barbara, an ARDENT stamp collector, has the most impressive collection of French stamps in the school.

fervent (FUR-vuhnt). Showing great enthusiasm and intensity of spirit.
Packing up the family's castoffs for myriad charities each December places Contessa in a FERVENT state.

perfervid (per-FUR-vid). Overly intense and passionate; overblown and dramatic.
We laughed at the distastefully PERFERVID love letters that Roland sent to Germaine.

rambunctious (ram-BUNGK-shuss). Difficult to handle; wild and boisterous.
"The golden age, when RAMBUNCTIOUS spirits were regarded as the source of evil."—Friedrich Nietzsche, nineteenth-century German philosopher

unbridled (un-BRY-duld). Without limitations or boundaries; uncontrolled and unrestrained.
The customer's UNBRIDLED fury at being denied a refund was a sight to behold.

NOUNS

aficionado (uh-fish-ee-uh-NAW-doe). A devotee; someone who is enthralled with and supports a particular activity; enthusiast.
My dad can't get enough of it, but I've never really been a baseball AFICIONADO.

alacrity (uh-LAK-rih-tee). Cheerful cooperation rendered with enthusiasm, promptness, and politeness.
The ALACRITY with which Steve responded to Helen's invitation is nothing short of astonishing.

élan (a-LON). Enthusiasm, energy, flair, zest.
Bryanna reacted with ÉLAN when she was tapped to be part of a feature for Elite Travel magazine.

monomania (mon-uh-MAY-nee-uh). An excessive or obsessive interest in a single thing; a psychosis characterized by focus on a single subject.
Bird watching has become a MONOMANIA for my parents, but it's harmless and appears to make them happy.

verve (vurv). A spirited and enthusiastic manner, particularly when embodied in an artistic performance; an air of vitality.
The critics were unanimous in their opinion that, although the plot of the play was implausible and its production values poor, the actress playing the librarian brought a unique VERVE to the role.

ANTONYMS

tepid (TEHP-id). Characterized by a lack of enthusiasm.
We greeted the new opera, with its mawkish plot and poor acting, with TEPID applause.

72. Essence

(ESS-uhns), noun

Something that exists; the intrinsic, fundamental nature and features of something.

ADJECTIVES

basal (BAY-suhl). Fundamental and basic.
"The BASAL issue here," Donny said, "is what is right versus what is wrong!"

fundamental (fuhn-duh-MEN-tul). Of or forming a foundation or basis; basic; underlying; essential.
The discussion was wide-ranging, but Roger insisted on bringing the focus back to the FUNDAMENTAL issues facing the company.

intrinsic (in-TRIN-zik). In the essential nature of a thing.
The INTRINSIC value of gold was one of the few common economic factors the nations could take advantage of.

NOUNS

milieu (mill-YEW). Cultural, social, and physical surroundings; environment.
When I walked into the skateboard store, I knew immediately that I was out of my MILIEU.

ontology (on-TALL-uh-jee). A branch of metaphysics concerned with the nature of being and existence.
For several minutes, we had a lively conversation about the ONTOLOGY of human perceptions.

quintessence (kwin-TESS-uhns). The pure, concentrated embodiment of something.
"The earth is the very QUINTESSENCE of the human condition."—Hannah Arendt, German-American political theorist

status quo (STA-tus KWO). The existing state of affairs or condition.
Although Bill desperately wanted to get married, Melanie was more interested in preserving the STATUS QUO.

ANTONYMS

nihility (ny-HILL-uh-tee). The condition of nothingness.
Benjamin wondered if anything existed after this life or if death brought about NIHILITY.

nonexistence (non-ig-ZIS-tehns). The condition of not existing; something that does not exist.
"Excepting for knowledge nothing has any meaning, and to have no meaning is to be NONEXISTENCE."—Richard Burdon Haldane, British politician and philosopher

73. Ethos

(EE-thoss), noun

The core principles or beliefs of a religion, culture, or community.

ADJECTIVES

dogmatic (DAWG-matt-ik). A person who adheres rigidly to principles, rules, and beliefs, even when there is ample evidence that doing so may not be the best course of action.
Leroy is DOGMATIC in his assertion that the Maserati Gran Turismo is superior to the Mercedes-Benz SLR McLaren.

egalitarian (ih-gal-uh-TAIR-ee-uhn). To be fair and balanced in the extreme; to act in the belief that all people are created equal and should be treated so.
"Chinks in America's EGALITARIAN armor are not hard to find. Democracy is the fig leaf of elitism."—Florence King, American author

holistic (ho-LISS-tik). Concerning the whole person and not just a specific organ, condition, or disease.
Marsha's HOLISTIC approach to healing involves channeling energy through crystals.

NOUNS

demiurge (DEM-ee-urj). A powerful creative force or a creative personality.
After trying a few different professions, Jackson realized that his ability with artifice, combined with his family connections, would make him a marketing DEMIURGE.

gestalt (geh-SHTALT). A unified whole.
"Feminism is an entire world view or GESTALT, not just a laundry list of women's issues."—Charlotte Bunch, American feminist

humanism (HEW-mun-iz-um). The philosophy or belief that the highest ideals of human existence can be fulfilled without regard to religion or supernatural intervention.
"The four characteristics of HUMANISM are curiosity, a free mind, belief in good taste, and belief in the human race."—E. M. Forster, English novelist

ideologue (EYE-dee-uh-log). A person who rigidly adheres to an ideology with a closed mind regarding other points of view.
"An IDEOLOGUE may be defined as a mad intellectual."—Clifton Fadiman, American critic

monotheism (mawn-uh-THEE-iz-um). A belief in one omnipotent, omniscient God who is actively involved in the workings of both the physical universe that He created and the society of people who dwell in it.
Christianity, Judaism, and Islam are all examples of MONOTHEISM.

nationalism (NASH-eh-nul-iz-um). The idea that citizens should take great pride in their country and support it to the hilt; extreme patriotism.
Albert Einstein called NATIONALISM "the measles of mankind."

nominalism (NOM-ih-nuh-liz-um). A philosophy that denies the existence of universal truths.
Some scientists suspect that, rather than being universal, the laws of physics may vary in different regions of the universe—a strong supporting argument for NOMINALISM.

pragmatism (PRAG-muh-tiz-um). The belief that one's actions should be guided primarily based on knowledge or opinion of what is likely to work best in a given situation; the imperative to always do what is practical and effective.
Our families have succeeded in amassing great wealth over many generations because we are all, at heart, practitioners of PRAGMATISM.

ANTONYMS

abjure (ab-JOOR). To renounce or turn your back on a belief or position you once held near and dear.
Once Jodi tasted my mouth-watering, medium-rare filet mignon, she ABJURED the vegetarian lifestyle forever.

apostasy (uh-POSS-tah-see). The act of abandoning, ignoring, or openly flouting an accepted principle or belief.
"It was his idea of grand APOSTASY to drive to the reform synagogue on the high holidays and park his pink-eye nag among the luxurious, whirl-wired touring cars of the rich."—Saul Bellow, American author

sacrilegious (sak-reh-LIJ-uss). Openly insulting or disrespectful to the beliefs, religion, ideas, and practices of others—especially the ones they hold most sacred.
Bryson's insistence that Miró is more collectible than Warhol is positively SACRILEGIOUS.

74. Evil

(EE-vuhl), adjective

Wrong or bad morally; wicked.

ADJECTIVES

abhorrent (ab-HOR-ent). Loathsome or contemptible; reprehensible; repulsive; repugnant; detestable.
Julie found the book's recounting of the details of serial murders particularly ABHORRENT.

barbarous (BAR-ber-uss). Uncivilized or primitive; characterized by brutality or savagery; cruel and brutal.
Their captivity was marked by BARBAROUS living conditions, psychological abuse, and little or no news of outside events.

diabolical (dy-uh-BAWL-ih-kul). Devilish, evil; wicked or cruel.
The terrorists, the papers claimed, had a DIABOLICAL agenda.

draconian (dray-KO-nee-ihn). Strict; mean-spirited; excessively harsh; cruel, as punishment or restriction.
Ophelia was distraught over the DRACONIAN way that her father forced her to stay with her chaperone throughout their vacation on the Greek Isles.

execrable (EK-si-kruh-bull). Disgusting; detestable; vulgar.
Collectors of unauthorized Beatles records must be prepared to pay high prices for the illegal discs, which often feature tracks of EXECRABLE recording quality.

Faustian (FOW-stee-in). Relating to actions taken for selfish present gain without care for future consequences, as in a pact with the Devil.
The candidate made a FAUSTIAN bargain and aligned himself with a popular rabble rouser.

flagitious (fluh-JISH-uss). Shamefully wicked or particularly heinous.
Now that that the paparazzi hang on her every move, Natasha goes out of her way to engage in FLAGITIOUS behavior.

heinous (HAY-nuss). Evil; reprehensible; exceeding the bounds of morality.
Because of the HEINOUS nature of this crime, I am forced to pass a stern sentence.

infernal (in-FER-nul). Fiendish; devilish; of or pertaining to hell.
This INFERNAL copier keeps breaking down!

malicious (muh-LISH-uss). Spitefully mean; evil; bad in intent.
Fred said his comments were all intended as constructive criticism, but I detected a MALICIOUS note in some of his suggestions.

miscreant (MISS-kree-unt). Villainous; depraved; vicious.
Examples of Arthur's MISCREANT behavior filled police files in three cities.

nefarious (nih-FAIR-ee-us). Inherently evil, malicious, and unjust.
"You were preceded by your NEFARIOUS reputation," the sheriff said to the gunslinger who had just sidled up to the bar.

reprehensible (rep-ri-HEN-sih-bull). Abhorrent; morally inexcusable.
I agree that the crimes were REPREHENSIBLE; they were not, however, committed by my client.

sadistic (suh-DISS-tik). Marked by delight in being cruel to others.
Only a SADISTIC creep would give out as much homework as Mr. Thomas.

sinister (SIN-uh-ster). Unfavorable and potentially harmful or dangerous; having an evil appearance.
The SINISTER music gave me gooseflesh.

venal (VEE-null). Able to be bought, bribed, or otherwise persuaded to deviate from their beliefs and purpose; mercenary; corrupt.
"Give me but the liberty of the press, and I will give to the minister a VENAL House of Commons."—Richard Brinsley Sheridan, Irish playwright and statesman

NOUNS

anathema (uh-NATH-eh-muh). A person or thing regarded as wrong in the highest degree; a loathsome, detestable entity.
The ambassador warned us not to attempt to discuss the issue of dropping sanctions against the dictator; that subject is ANATHEMA to his government.

iniquity (ih-NIK-wih-tee). Injustice or immoral action.
The many INIQUITIES suffered by Native Americans at the hands of government authorities are now being widely acknowledged.

maleficence (muh-LEF-ih-sence). The undertaking of evil or harmful acts.
The long-ignored MALEFICENCE of the county's corrupt prison system was finally exposed by a rookie Globe *reporter.*

reprobate (REH-pro-bait). A person who routinely commits illegal, immoral, or unethical acts without hesitation or remorse.
One reason that Anthony continues to be a REPROBATE is because his father, as well as his social contacts, keeps bailing him out of jail.

turpitude (TUR-phi-tood). Vileness; baseness; depravity.
It's astonishing how many untalented musicians have turned a case of TURPITUDE into a successful career.

ANTONYMS

benign (bih-NYN). Kindly, gentle, generous of spirit, not harmful.
"The universe seems neither BENIGN nor hostile, merely indifferent."
—Carl Sagan, American astronomer and writer

clement (KLEM-uhnt). Forbearing; lenient; merciful in disposition or character.
The defendant was fortunate that his trial was held before a CLEMENT judge.

75. Exaggerate

(ig-ZAJ-uh-rayt), verb

To think, write, or speak of something as greater than it is; magnify beyond the truth; overstate.

ADJECTIVES

magniloquent (mag-NILL-uh-kwuhnt). Pompous, bombastic, and boastful.
The nouveau riche try to atone for their lack of polish with MAGNILOQUENT speech, but the result is ludicrous.

NOUNS

hyperbole (hy-PUR-buh-lee). Extravagant overstatement.
I think you can safely regard his promise to eat his hat if proven wrong as HYPERBOLE.

jactitation (jak-ti-TAY-shun). A false boast, especially one that is harmful to others.
Beatrice tried to impress her classmates by telling them her last name was Kennedy. However, her JACTITATION was discovered and her peers returned to ignoring her.

VERBS

aggrandize (uh-GRAN-dyz). To exaggerate, put on a false front, and make something look greater and grander than it really is.
Phil tries to AGGRANDIZE his reputation by stating that he belongs to the yacht club, but everybody just thinks this elaboration makes him pathetic.

apotheosize (uh-POTH-ee-uh-syz). To make into a god; deify; glorify.
Mark APOTHEOSIZED his new girlfriend for the rest of the evening.

embellish (em-BELL-ish). To ornament and beautify; to improve in appearance by adornment; a convenient exaggeration of the facts.
Marie's gown was EMBELLISHED with tiny pearls.

embroider (em-BROY-dur). To add fanciful details to; embellish.
Matt has been known to EMBROIDER the history of his love life.

ANTONYMS

deemphasize (dee-EM-fuh-syz). To reduce in importance; place lower emphasis upon.
After sideswiping a telephone pole with my father's car on the way home from a date, I did my best to DEEMPHASIZE the damage.

understate (uhn-der-STAYT). To make a weaker statement than is warranted by truth, accuracy, or importance; to state something weakly.
Understatement can be seen as a virtue in the friend or acquaintance, but when companies UNDERSTATE their debt and misrepresent themselves to investors and the public, the practice is distinctly malicious.

76. Excite

(ek-SYT), verb

To arouse or provoke sensations, feelings, or emotions; to awaken; to stir to action.

ADJECTIVES

incendiary (in-SEN-dee-ayr-ee). Inflammatory or exciting; deliberately provocative.
Adam's INCENDIARY remarks about my mother's parentage resulted in a bloody nose for him and a night in jail for me.

lascivious (luh-SIV-ee-us). Arousing sexual desire.
Grandmother Jones, upon being informed that the dancers at the club had done a can-can for us, denounced such LASCIVIOUS goings-on.

NOUNS

brouhaha (BROO-ha-ha). An event that involves or invokes excitement, turmoil, or conflict.
The BROUHAHA in the hotel lobby was the result of a rock star making his way from his limousine to the elevator.

fillip (FILL-uhp). Something that revives or arouses excitement.
"Faithful horoscope-watching, practiced daily, provides just the sort of small, but warm and infinitely reassuring FILLIP that gets matters off to a spirited start."—Shana Alexander, American author

frenzy (FREN-zee). A state of wild excitement; extreme emotional or mental agitation.
What with studying for the bar exam and planning her wedding, Sara had been in an almost constant FRENZY for nearly two months.

frisson (FREE-son). A sudden strong feeling of excitement, conflict, or danger.
"Pregnant women! They had that weird FRISSON, an aura of magic that combined awkwardly with an earthy sense of duty."—Ruth Morgan, American novelist

furor (FYOOR-ur). Widespread excitement or anger; fury or uproar among persons or institutions.
Governor White's indictment for embezzlement caused a FUROR in the state.

VERBS

exhilarate (ig-ZILL-uh-rayt). To make lively; to excite or energize.
Those evening runs in the cool air of the spring always EXHILARATED Tom, especially after a day spent cooped up in a stuffy office.

ferment (fur-MENT). To cause agitation or excitement, typically in order to incite drastic change.
High oil prices began to FERMENT efforts to find alternative fuel sources.

foment (foe-MENT). To rouse or incite.
"If perticuliar care and attention is not paid to the Laidies we are determined to FOMENT a Rebelion, and will not hold ourselves bound by any Laws in which we have no voice, or Representation."—Abigail Adams, second First Lady of the United States

titillate (TIT-l-ayt). To excite in an agreeable way.
With its stirring performance of Beethoven's Eroica Symphony, the full orchestra TITILLATED us at the Van Gelders' gala.

ANTONYMS

blasé (blah-ZAY). Unimpressed; bored; apathetic to pleasure because of excessive indulgence.
I told Jim that he stood a very good chance of being fired this week, but to tell you the truth, he seemed rather BLASÉ about the whole thing.

imperturbable (im-per-TUR-buh-bull). Describes someone or something incapable of being agitated or disturbed.
During the air turbulence, I felt calmer due to my father's IMPERTURBABLE demeanor.

phlegmatic (fleg-MAT-ik). Having a calm, unexcitable temperament.
Allan's PHLEGMATIC personality was certainly helpful during the deadline crunch in keeping us all from panicking.

77. Facile

(FASS-ul), adjective

Accomplished easily and with little effort.

ADJECTIVES

adroit (uh-DROYT). Skilled or clever in a particular pursuit.
"It's kind of sad," Betty said to Barbara, "that Will thinks being ADROIT at playing cat's cradle will impress women."

efficacious (eff-ih-KAY-shuss). Capable of having a desired effect.
"Example is always more EFFICACIOUS than precept."—Samuel Johnson, British moralist and poet

lissome (LISS-um). Lithe; supple; flexible.
Moira acquired her LISSOME frame from years of swimming in her family's Olympic-sized pool.

lithe (lythe). Having a body and/or mind that is limber, flexible, and supple.
"The coconut trees, LITHE and graceful, crowd the beach . . . like a minuet of slender elderly virgins adopting flippant poses."—William Manchester, American historian

tractable (TRAK-tuh-bull). Easygoing; easily managed.
The occasional kind comment seems rather enough to keep our servants TRACTABLE.

NOUNS

alacrity (uh-LAK-rih-tee). Cheerful cooperation rendered with enthusiasm, promptness, and politeness.
The ALACRITY with which Steve responded to Helen's invitation is nothing short of astonishing.

fecundity (fe-KUN-di-tee). The quality of being exceptionally productive, creative, fertile, or fruitful.
"Blistering heat suddenly took the place of Carboniferous moisture and FECUNDITY."—Simon Winchester, British author and journalist

ANTONYMS

abstruse (ab-STROOS). Arcane, complex, difficult to understand and learn.
Bob began to wish there was, in fact, a Santa Claus because he found the "simple instructions" to his son's bicycle far too ABSTRUSE.

obtuse (ob-TOOS). Lacking understanding, intelligence, and perception; unable to comprehend; having a dense mind.
Thomas was so OBTUSE, he didn't realize his inappropriate behavior was making his friends uncomfortable.

quagmire (KWAG-myer). A thorny problem for which there is no ready solution; a messy situation from which there is no expeditious means of escape.
"Your home is regarded as a model home, your life as a model life. But all this splendor, and you along with it . . . it's just as though it were built upon a shifting QUAGMIRE."—Henrik Ibsen, Norwegian playwright

78. False

(FALCE), adjective

Not correct or true; fake; deceptive; not genuine; erroneous.

ADJECTIVES

ersatz (AIR-zotz). Phony, fake, counterfeit; inferior as an imitation of an original.
Before his sentencing and jail term, the artist made an impressive living selling ERSATZ Rembrandt paintings.

factitious (fak-TISH-uss). Contrived; fabricated.
At first, we thought the rumor FACTITIOUS, but then we learned that Hermes does, in fact, plan to design and market a helicopter.

fallacious (fuh-LAY-shuss). Based on one or more false assumptions.
Since my online subscriber list is double opt-in, accusing me of being a spammer is wholly FALLACIOUS.

faux (FOH). Fake; phony; artificial.
She wore a cheap second-hand dress and a FAUX pearl necklace made out of white beads.

sophistic (suh-FIS-tik). Sounding reasonable, yet patently false.
One can argue that what is learned in law school is largely the skill of making SOPHISTIC arguments that a jury can believe.

specious (SPEE-shuss). Something that appears correct on the surface but is in fact wrong.
The judge summarily rejected the SPECIOUS arguments put forth by the defendant, which seemed to have no evidence to back them up.

spurious (SPYOOR-ee-us). False; inauthentic; not well thought out.
Every week I get SPURIOUS accusations of being a spammer even though my list is entirely double opt-in.

supposititious (suh-poz-ih-TISH-us). Substituted with the intent of deceiving or defrauding; counterfeit.
The SUPPOSITITIOUS documents looked genuine, even bearing the secret markings designed to prevent deception.

NOUNS

canard (kuh-NARD). A fabrication or unfounded story.
The claim that the president of the company is likely to resign soon has been thoroughly discredited, but you will still hear some members of the opposition spreading the CANARD.

fallacy (FOWL-uh-see). A misconception; an erroneous perception; a deceit.
For some, childhood is a time of innocence; but it's a FALLACY to say it is like this for all children.

feint (faynt). A false advance or attack intended to catch an opponent off guard.
Jim made a FEINT with his left before decking his opponent with a fierce right cross.

subreption (sub-REP-shun). The dishonest misrepresentation or concealment of facts.
The board's report was replete with statistics, but as a summary of the situation, it was a complete SUBREPTION.

VERBS

gainsay (GAYN-say). To declare false; to oppose or contradict.
The principles of the Bill of Rights, Mr. Secretary, will admit no GAINSAYING.

misconstrue (miss-kuhn-STROO). To misinterpret or to take in a wrong sense.
The disagreement over the price of the yacht was due merely to the fact that David MISCONSTRUED the terms of the offer.

ANTONYMS

unerring (uhn-UR-ing). Consistently accurate; invariably precise or correct.
"The British public has always had an UNERRING taste for ungifted amateurs."—John Osborne, British playwright

veracious (vuh-RAY-shuss). Honest; truthful.
Many readers of a novel will feel cheated and complain if it fails to provide a VERACIOUS account of fictional circumstances.
See also: Mistake

79. Fealty

(FEE-ul-tee), noun

A sense of obligation or loyalty, usually existing because one person feels beholden to another.

ADJECTIVES

obsequious *(uhb-SEE-kwee-us)*. Subservient; eager to listen and to please others to an excessive degree; behaving in the manner of a servant or slave.
"[The political mind] is a strange mixture of vanity and timidity, of an OBSEQUIOUS attitude at one time and a delusion of grandeur at another time.—Calvin Coolidge

NOUNS

encomium (en-KO-me-um). Effusive praise given in a public forum.
The CEO's ENCOMIUM at Phil's retirement dinner caused his eyes to mist over.

hierarchy (HY-uh-rar-kee). A pecking order or ranking according to status or level of authority.
In the HIERARCHY of the military, a medical doctor, who is assigned the rank of captain but is not a military man, automatically outranks a lieutenant who may have years of battle experience.

homage (HOM-ij). Respect paid and deference shown to a superior or other person one admires, fears, or wishes to emulate or praise.
Gary took black and white photos with a nondigital camera in HOMAGE to Ansel Adams, whose works he greatly admired.

honorific (on-uh-RIFF-ik). A tribute or reward given in an effort to honor someone as a sign of deep respect.
Lifetime achievement awards aren't for any single work, but an HONORIFIC for long service and a track record of excellence.

obeisance (o-BAY-since). Deferential respect or homage, or an act or gesture expressing the same.
Rachael expressed OBEISANCE by allowing the elderly woman to sit in her plush opera box, rather than in the mezzanine.

VERBS

truckle (TRUK-uhl). To submit obsequiously to a command.
We have trained our servants to TRUCKLE to our every whim.

ANTONYMS

antidisestablishmentarianism (ant-eye-diss-es-STAB-lish-men-tare-ee-uh-nizm). A movement or protest against an established institution or authority.
No, Walter, bringing your own coffee to Starbucks is not an example of ANTIDISESTABLISHMENTARIANISM. It's just foolish.

quisling (KWIZ-ling). A traitor; a person who conspires with the enemy.
The leader of Norway's National Unity movement was executed for being a QUISLING in 1945.

sedition (sih-DISH-uhn). An action that promotes discontent or rebellion.
In an act of childish SEDITION, Alex quit the club after we refused to play a round of golf with him.

80. Fight

(FYT), verb

To be involved in a physical struggle or battle; to try to overcome someone or something; contend.

ADJECTIVES

bellicose (BELL-ih-kohss). Belligerent, surly, ready to argue or fight at the slightest provocation.
Doug is so touchy about his new Jaguar that he'll instantly turn BELLICOSE if you so much as brush against it.

belligerent (buh-LIJ-er-ent). Aggressive or pugnacious; eager to instigate a fight.
Don became overbearing and BELLIGERENT with his employees after his divorce, causing many of them to resign.

internecine (in-ter-NEH-seen). Involving or relating to conflict within a group.
The INTERNECINE conflict became so intense that it prevented the board from functioning.

pugnacious (pug-NAY-shuss). Inclined to fight or quarrel; belligerent; quarrelsome.
Teenagers are PUGNACIOUS by nature: if I say "no," he invariably asks "why?"

truculent (TRUK-yu-lent). Belligerent; argumentative; always ready for a fight.
Short-tempered and TRUCULENT, Lucy could be set off by the slightest incident or comment.

NOUNS

donnybrook (DAWN-ee-brook). A free-for-all, knock-down, drag-out fight.
Police expected a DONNYBROOK at the protest march, but both those for and those against the issue were peaceful and courteous.

guerrilla (guh-RILL-uh). A member of an informal group of fighters that attacks enemies with surprise raids, sabotage, booby traps, etc.
The nation's army could not defeat the GUERRILLAS, who seemed to swoop down invisibly from the mountains, wreak havoc, and then disappear.

pugilist (PYOO-juh-list). A person who fistfights; a boxer.
Finally, the two PUGILISTS stepped into the ring; the match was about to begin.

sciamachy (sy-AM-uh-kee). Fighting with imaginary enemies; a sham fight.
Arthur refused to believe that we supported him; believing the worst, he engaged in a SCIAMACHY of his own making.

ANTONYMS

conciliatory (kon-SILL-ee-ah-tor-ee). Actions or words meant to settle a dispute or resolve a conflict in a manner that leaves no hard feelings on either side.
"If you are not very clever, you should be CONCILIATORY."—Benjamin Disraeli, British statesman and literary figure

harmony (HAR-muh-nee). Agreement in feeling, action, ideas, interests, etc.; peaceable or friendly relations.
"With an eye made quiet by the power of HARMONY, and the deep power of joy, we see into the life of things."—William Wordsworth, English poet

81. Flawed

(FLAWD), adjective

Imperfect or defective in a way that impairs the quality of, and detracts from, one's character.

ADJECTIVES

bibulous (BIB-yuh-luss). Related to drinking or to drunkenness.
Arthur thinks he's "fine," but his BIBULOUS activities are causing the club to consider permanent expulsion.

bilious (BILL-yuss). Having a nasty temperament or disagreeable disposition; to be "full of bile" and hatred.
The polo team's BILIOUS captain made his team miserable as he proceeded to criticize their every move.

bumptious (BUMP-shuss). Overbearing or crudely assertive; overly pushy or impertinent.
We had difficulty crossing the border because Nan got into a squabble with a BUMPTIOUS border guard.

capricious (kuh-PREE-shuss). Prone to quickly changing one's mind, decision, or course of action at the drop of a hat or on impulse.
"I do not understand the CAPRICIOUS lewdness of the sleeping mind."
—John Cheever, American novelist

captious (KAP-shuss). Fond of finding faults in others; ill-natured and overly critical; carping.
Ed's CAPTIOUS remarks were entirely inappropriate and showed his lack of self-esteem.

churlish (CHUR-lish). Surly; mean; boorish; rude; characterized by a lack of civility or graciousness.
We found it almost impossible to believe that Diane's new boyfriend was more CHURLISH than his predecessor.

déclassé (day-kluh-SAY). Of a fallen social position or inferior status.
Jean thought her imitation designer bag looked exactly like the real thing, but the other girls in her exclusive private school quickly ridiculed Jean—and her bag—for being DÉCLASSÉ.

desultory (DEH-sul-tor-ee). Lacking guidance or progressing randomly; aimless; fitful.
Unable to believe it was his last day on the job, Bill's DESULTORY thoughts wandered through his mind.

effete (eh-FEET). Depleted and lacking in vigor due to decadence or self-indulgence.
The Eddingtons belong to an American club of EFFETE snobs who claim to trace their lineage back to the British royal family

farouche (fuh-ROOSH). Unsociable; cranky; withdrawn; fierce.
Your FAROUCHE behavior will not win you any friends. In fact, it will simply alienate you from everyone.

gauche (GOHSH). Sorely lacking in the social graces and good manners; crude behavior.
Rhett was under the impression that one needed only money to join the country club. However, his GAUCHE demeanor caused him to be denied membership.

hapless (HAP-liss). Luckless; unfortunate.
Oliver presented a rather HAPLESS figure during his first few days on the job, but he soon mastered his new responsibilities.

hidebound (HYD-bownd). Inflexible and holding narrow opinions.
Arthur can be rather HIDEBOUND when pontificating on the virtues of the classic era versus the condition of the automobile industry at present.

jaundiced (JAWN-dist). Demonstrating prejudice, due to envy or resentment.
The Blythingtons' JAUNDICED view of our dinner parties is due to their financial inability to entertain so lavishly.

maladroit (mal-uh-DROIT). Lacking adroitness; inept; awkward.
Ernie came in for a lot of teasing for his MALADROIT negotiations with the used-car dealer.

parasitic (pair-uh-SIT-ik). Describes something or—more often—someone who acts like a parasite and lives off of another while doing little if anything useful.
My PARASITIC brother-in-law said he was just going to stay with us until he got back on his feet, but he's been sitting around on our couch for nearly a month now!

pedantic (puh-DAN-tik). Intellectually showy or overblown; making a great display of knowledge; overly concerned with formal rules.
I found James's PEDANTIC manner quite condescending.

ungainly (un-GAYN-lee). Graceless.
Wilma, who had always thought of herself as UNGAINLY, was surprised at the ease with which she and Clive moved across the dance floor.

NOUNS

Achilles' heel (uh-KILL-eez HEEL). A vulnerable point.
Bob was a hard worker, but he often lost jobs because of his ACHILLES' HEEL, his temper.

bibliomania (bib-lee-oh-MAY-nee-uh). A preoccupation with the acquisition and ownership of books.
Lauren's BIBLIOMANIA extends only to her stockpile of catalogs for exclusive shops.

foible (FOY-bull). A small flaw, weakness, or defect.
For all his flaws and FOIBLES, Richard Nixon was perhaps the most effective president on foreign policy in the twentieth century.

histrionics (hiss-tree-ON-iks). Over-the-top, unnecessarily dramatic behavior.
"Enough with the HISTRIONICS!" his mother scolded, immediately shutting off the flow of tears and silencing his bawling.

hypocrisy (hih-POK-ruh-see). Pretending to be something one is not, or pretending, for the sake of appearance, to have high moral beliefs; pretense.
In Marilyn's view, a marriage counselor who advises others to live up to the ideal of fidelity but who cheats on his own wife exemplifies the worst kind of HYPOCRISY.

schadenfreude (SHAH-dn-froy-duh). Satisfaction or pleasure felt at the misfortune of another.
Wilson's conviction on perjury charges set off a festival of SCHADENFREUDE among his many conservative detractors.

ANTONYMS

impeccable (im-PEK-uh-bull). Without defect or error; faultless; flawless.
"No office anywhere on earth is so puritanical, IMPECCABLE, elegant, sterile or incorruptible as not to contain the yeast for at least one affair, probably more."—Helen Gurley Brown, American editor

paragon (PAIR-uh-gone). A peerless model or pattern of perfection.
"What a piece of work is a man! How noble in reason, how infinite in faculty, in form and moving how express and admirable, in action how like an angel, in apprehension how like a god—the beauty of the world, the paragon of animals!"—William Shakespeare, English dramatist

82. Foods

(FOODS), noun

Substances consumed by eating or drinking for nourishment, to provide energy, to sustain life, or promote growth.

ADJECTIVES

culinary (KYOO-lih-nare-ee). Relating to cooking or the preparation of food.
My CULINARY efforts these days are much humbler than my library of cookbooks would lead you to believe.

julienne (joo-lee-EN). In thin strips (of vegetables).
Lisa knew JULIENNE vegetables would look more elegant on the plates of her dinner guests than those cut in the normal way.

NOUNS

aperitif (uh-pair-uh-TEEF). An alcoholic beverage consumed before a meal.
The clock struck six o'clock and the guests at the dinner party were served APERITIFS.

bisque (BISK). A thick and creamy soup made with meat, fish, or shellfish.
Mom didn't care what else was on the menu, as long as the restaurant offered lobster BISQUE.

bouillabaisse (boo-yuh-BASE). A stew made from various kinds of fish, usually shellfish.
After Uncle Charlie helped us clean the fish and clams we'd caught, Aunt Pattie showed us how to make her famous BOUILLABAISSE.

compote (KOM-pote). A stewed fruit and sugar dessert.
In addition to an unidentifiable brownish meat in a dark, concealing sauce, many of the TV dinners I ate as a child included a rather leaden strawberry COMPOTE.

grenadine (GREN-uh-deen). A pomegranate-flavored syrup used in preparing mixed drinks.
Ted had planned to make Tequila Sunrises for the party, but as he had no GRENADINE to add a hint of red, he called the drinks "Tequila Sunbursts."

gruel (GROOL). A thin, soup-like dish made from cooked cereal or grain.
In one of the most memorable scenes Dickens ever wrote, young Oliver Twist loses a lottery among the workhouse boys and must ask for an unprecedented second helping of GRUEL.

haggis (HAG-iss). A dish originating in Scotland made by combing the diced heart, liver, and lungs of a sheep or cow with onions, suet, oatmeal, and seasonings, and placing the mixture into the animal's stomach, and boiling it.
Ivan had been enjoying the HAGGIS Mrs. MacIntyre had prepared for him until he asked her how it was made.

hardtack (HARD-tak). A hard biscuit once common in the rations of sailors and soldiers. Hardtack did not spoil—a major logistical benefit.
By the end of the war, the Union soldiers were thoroughly sick of the HARDTACK and vegetable soup that had been the mainstay of their diet.

jambalaya (jam-buh-LY-uh). A spicy Cajun dish featuring rice cooked with ham, sausage, chicken, shrimp, or oysters, and seasoned with herbs.
Anna had so much ham left over from Easter dinner that she decided to try to whip up a JAMBALAYA.

marzipan (MAR-zuh-pan). A popular candy made from almonds, egg whites, and sugar, often molded into the shapes of animals.
In Europe it is quite common to decorate a Christmas tree with edible decorations, including gingerbread men, MARZIPAN animals, and miniature fruitcakes.

petit four (PET-ee FOR). A small decorated cake. Plural: petits fours (PET-ee FORS).
Aunt Marcia always served tea and PETITS FOURS at three o'clock.

quahog (KO-hawg). An edible clam found off of the Atlantic coastline of North America.
Every summer Grandpa would take us to his beach house in Maine, where we'd fish and dig for QUAHOGS in the quiet hours before dawn.

sake (SAH-kee). A wine-like Japanese beverage made with fermented rice.
When he returned from California, my father and I dined on sushi and drank warm SAKE at his favorite Japanese restaurant.

tangelo (TAN-juh-lo). A kind of citrus fruit; hybrid of a tangerine and a grapefruit.
The corner fruit market specialized in stocking the more exotic fruits and vegetables, and for most of the year was the only place in town where one could regularly purchase TANGELOS.

VERBS

flambé (flom-BAY). To serve in flaming liquor (usually brandy).
Although the dinner was only so-so, the raspberry custard that the waiter FLAMBÉD at our table was both dramatic and delicious.

ANTONYMS

abstain (ub-STAYN). To refrain from; to refuse to partake in; to go without voluntarily.
Maria, who had ABSTAINED from eating meat while in high school, was persuaded to try a cheeseburger on her graduation night.

83. Fool

(FOOL), verb

To trick; deceive; dupe.

ADJECTIVES

oblique (oh-BLEEK). Indirectly or deviously achieved; evasive; underhanded.
If direct appeals do not work, Amanda is always quick to use OBLIQUE methods in order to get her father to buy her whatever luxury item she wants.

NOUNS

artifice (AR-ti-fiss). The use of clever strategies and cunning methods to fool or best others and tip an outcome in your favor.
"Every art and ARTIFICE has been practiced and perpetrated to destroy the rights of man."—Robert Ingersoll, American orator

gambit (GAM-bit). A remark used to redirect a conversation; or, a maneuver used to seek advantage.
"The catchphrase positively rejoices in being a formula, an accepted GAMBIT, a ready-made reaction."—John Gross, British literary critic

guile (GYL). Deceit; treachery.
I was amazed at the GUILE Richard displayed in going after my biggest account.

legerdemain (lej-uhr-duh-MAYN). Magic tricks; generally speaking, trickery and deception.
The Wilkinsons are one of the few of our families whose initial wealth did not come as a result of financial LEGERDEMAIN.

VERBS

equivocate (ee-KWIV-uh-kayt). To deceive through the use of ambiguous language.
The candidate seemed to EQUIVOCATE on the energy crisis with each speech he made.

palter (PAWL-ter). To talk or act insincerely; deal crookedly.
It seemed that in every conversation I had with her, Janice would PALTER and I would pretend to believe it.

prevaricate (pruh-VAIR-uh-kayt). To avoid revealing the true nature of one's position, actions, feelings, etcetera; to be untruthful.
My opponent has chosen to PREVARICATE rather than address his role in the scandal.

temporize (TEM-puh-ryz). To gain time by being evasive or indecisive.
I unleashed a longwinded backstory in an effort to TEMPORIZE and come up with a logical explanation for my earlier behavior.

ANTONYMS

ingenuous (in-JEN-yoo-us). Candid; frank; open; sincere; free from reserve or restraint.
Dorothy's INGENUOUS remarks revealed the depth of her friendship toward the deceased.

naïveté (nah-eev-TAY). The state of being naïve; simplicity; artlessness.
Mother's NAÏVETÉ was no act; she could not deceive and firmly believed everyone else was just as honest.

84. Forgive

(fer-GIV), verb

To give up the desire to punish or resentment against; to stop being angry with; grant remission of an offense; pardon.

ADJECTIVES

venial (VEE-nee-uhl). Forgivable; not serious; excusable.
Stealing a kiss may be a VENIAL offense depending on the circumstances.

NOUNS

amnesty (AM-nuh-stee). Freedom from imprisonment for large numbers of people, initiated by a government.
The prisoners of war waited years for AMNESTY.

clemency (KLEM-uhn-see). Forbearance or mercy toward a wrongdoer or opponent; lenience in cases where circumstances warrant.
The governor's show of CLEMENCY for Callahan may come back to haunt him at election time.

VERBS

absolve (ab-ZOLV). To formally pronounce guiltless or blameless; to relieve of any responsibility for an actual or alleged misdeed.
The judge ABSOLVED the accused of any wrongdoing.

acquit (uh-KWIT). To release from a duty or obligation; to declare not guilty (of something); exonerate.
With little evidence of guilt, the jury had to ACQUIT the defendant.

exculpate (EK-skull-payt). To free someone from an obligation or burden, or prove the innocence of someone suspected of being guilty.
Gerald Ford's pardon EXCULPATED Richard Nixon legally, but history consigned him to the role of a disgraced president forever.

exonerate (ig-ZON-uh-rayt). To clear or free from blame or guilt; to restore (one's reputation).
After the charges were thrown out and Brian was completely EXONERATED, he was free to continue his work in the securities industry.

ANTONYMS

chastise (chass-TYZ). To punish in order to correct; to criticize severely.
The boarding school lived up to its reputation as a severe environment where a boy would be CHASTIZED for every infraction no matter how small.

oppressed (uh-PREST). Kept down by the unjust or cruel use of authority or power; burdened with harsh, rigorous impositions.
"Freedom is never voluntarily given by the oppressor; it must be demanded by the OPPRESSED."—Martin Luther King, Jr., American minister and civil-rights leader

85. Fun

(FUHN), noun

A source or cause of amusement or merriment; enjoyment.

ADJECTIVES

facetious (fuh-SEE-shuss). Meant to get a laugh rather than to be taken seriously; sarcastic.
"Boarding school manners and attitudes—stoic denial, FACETIOUS irony—are still deeply entrenched in the character of the country."—Jonathan Raban, British travel writer and novelist

gamesome (GAYM-suhm). Playful and frolicsome.
"[Nature] is GAMESOME and good, / But of mutable mood,— / No dreary repeater now and again, / She will be all things to all men."—Ralph Waldo Emerson, American poet, essayist, and transcendentalist

risible (RIZZ-uh-bull). Capable of causing laughter due to its ludicrous nature.
Janine's decision to summer in the Hamptons instead of on the French Riviera was deemed RISIBLE by the rest of us.

waggish (WAG-ish). Joking, witty, and mischievous; occasionally, dog-like.
"This species of 'fame' a WAGGISH acquaintance says can be manufactured to order, and sometimes is so manufactured."—Herman Melville, American author

NOUNS

disport (dih-SPORT). A diversion or amusement.
Felicia has turned the act of arguing with the proprietors of her favorite boutiques into a DISPORT.

revelry (REV-uhl-ree). Boisterous festivity and merrymaking.
"Midnight shout and REVELRY, / Tipsy dance and jollity."—John Milton, English poet

VERBS

carouse (kuh-ROWZ). To engage in boisterous social activity.
We CAROUSED until dawn at the New Year's Eve party that the Weathertons hold every year.

gambol (GAM-bull). To run, skip, or jump about in a playful or joyous fashion.
"We all have these places where shy humiliations GAMBOL on sunny afternoons."—W. H. Auden, Anglo-American poet

ANTONYMS

dishearten (dis-HAR-tun). To deprive of enthusiasm; to depress the spirits or courage of; discourage.
"A cynic can chill and DISHEARTEN with a single word."—Ralph Waldo Emerson, American poet

somber (SAWM-ber). Depressed or depressing; gloomy; dismal, melancholy; sad.
Due to the seriousness of the situation, the television announcer spoke in SOMBER tones.

G

86. Gauche

(GOHSH), adjective

Sorely lacking in the social graces and good manners; crude behavior.

ADJECTIVES

benighted (bee-NYE-ted). To be lost, ignorant, or unenlightened.
The medieval period was a BENIGHTED era of superstition.

bumptious (BUMP-shuss). Loud and assertive in a crude way.
The club's golf pro was fired due to his BUMPTIOUS behavior on the links.

fatuous (FATCH-oo-us). Trivial, silly, absurd, unimportant, pointless.
"I'm sick of pretending that some FATUOUS male's self-important pronounce-ments are the objects of my undivided attention."—Germaine Greer, Australian writer and scholar

odious (OH-dee-us). Offensive or disgusting; causing revulsion.
"To depend upon a profession is a less ODIOUS form of slavery than to depend upon a father."—Virginia Woolf, British essayist and novelist

ribald (RIB-uld). Lewd; off-color; somewhat dirty and inappropriate.
"It is . . . useful to distinguish between the pornographic, condemned in every society, and the bawdy, the RIBALD, the shared vulgarities and jokes, which are the safety valves of most social systems."—Margaret Mead, American cultural anthropologist

NOUNS

philistine (FILL-ih-steen). A crude and ignorant person who is disinterested in and does not appreciate culture and the arts.
"A PHILISTINE is a full-grown person whose interests are of a material and commonplace nature, and whose mentality is formed of the stock ideas and conventional ideals of his or her group and time."—Vladimir Nabokov, Russian-American novelist

troglodyte (TRAWG-luh-dyt). A person considered to be primitive, out of date, coarse, uncouth, ill-mannered, or brutish.
Sick and tired of going out with TROGLODYTES, Janet told her friends she was through with blind dates.

yahoo (YAH-hoo). A boorish, uncultivated, common person.
"Factory windows are always broken. / Somebody's always throwing bricks, / Somebody's always heaving cinders, / Playing ugly YAHOO tricks."—Vachel Lindsay, American poet

yob (YAWB). A cruel and loutish young man; a bully.
"Mick Jagger, alternately slurring YOB and lisping lordling, is classlessness apotheosised."—Philip Norman, British author

VERBS

yawp (YAWP). To make a raucous, clamorous noise.
"I sound my barbaric YAWP over the roofs of the world."—Walt Whitman, American poet and humanist

ANTONYMS

beguiling (bee-GY-ling). Charming; bewitching; enchanting.
The BEGUILING charm Monica learned at finishing school more than makes up for her vapid personality.

savoir faire (SAV-wahr-FAYR). An evident sense of confidence, optimism, and proficiency in the task at hand.
Eileen hosted a charity luncheon for forty people with her usual SAVOIR FAIRE.

87. Gift

(GIFT), noun

Something given or bestowed; a present.

ADJECTIVES

eleemosynary (ell-uh-MOSS-uh-nair-ee). Having to do with charity or charitable activity.
Our boss is always reminding us that we're a for-profit business, not an ELEEMOSYNARY organization.

NOUNS

bequest (bih-KWEST). Something (property, etc.) given to another in a will; a legacy.
My uncle's BEQUEST was the stuff of fantasy: a house in the south of France.

douceur (doo-SIR). A bribe or a conciliatory gift.
After Francine's father refused to buy her another polo pony, he offered her the DOUCEUR of a weekend at an exclusive spa.

endowment (en-DOW-munt). Income derived from donations; a grant.
The research project did not need to campaign for money, as its expenses were funded by an ENDOWMENT.

lagniappe (lan-YAP). An unexpected bonus gift or extra benefit; the icing on the cake.
Frederick would have bought the expensive car, even without the LAGNIAPPE of a voice-activated navigation system.

largesse (lar-JESS). The generous bestowal of gifts; generosity in general.
"A LARGESS universal, like the sun, / His liberal eye doth give to everyone, / Thawing cold fear."—William Shakespeare

oblation (uh-BLAY-shun). A religious offering; a holy gift typically offered at an altar or shrine.
Sophia could be counted on to say a prayer and offer an OBLATION every day she was healthy enough to walk to church.

offertory (AW-fer-tor-ee). An element used during a Christian communion service.
The OFFERTORY is preceded and followed by a prayer.

recompense (REK-um-pence). Something of value given to make up for injury or inconvenience, either accidental or deliberate.
"To be remembered after we are dead, is but poor RECOMPENSE for being treated with contempt while we are living."—William Hazlitt, English literary critic and philosopher

subvention (sub-VEN-shun). Money granted, usually from a government or other authority, to be used in the support of an institution, study, or program; subsidy; grant.
Many nonprofit art and humanitarian organizations owe their existence to government's SUBVENTION.

ANTONYMS

forfeit (FOR-fit). Something a person loses or has to give up; a fine; penalty.
"If once you FORFEIT the confidence of your fellow citizens, you can never regain their respect and esteem."—Abraham Lincoln, American president

relinquish (ri-LING-kwish). To give up; to surrender or forswear something.
"Time does not RELIQUISH its rights, either over human beings or over mountains."—Johann Wolfgang von Goethe, German playwright and novelist

88. Grand

(GRAND), adjective

Imposing because of size, beauty, or extent; magnificent; splendid; majestic.

ADJECTIVES

august (aw-GUHST). Inspiring awe, reverence, or admiration; imposing; eminent.
After waiting for hours, we were finally escorted to the dean's office and found ourselves in his AUGUST presence.

epic (EP-ik). Of major proportions; extraordinary.
Rosa Park's refusal to sit at the back of the bus would take on legendary status in the EPIC struggle for civil rights.

regal (REE-gull). Fit for or characteristic of a king; royal.
The king exercised his REGAL powers for the benefit of his subjects and kingdom.

reginal (ri-JY-nul). Like or characteristic of a queen; queenly; royal.
In the event she rise to the throne, the princess was given instruction and training in REGINAL duties and conduct.

resplendent (reh-SPLEN-dent). Full of splendor; shining brightly; dazzling.
The bride was RESPLENDENT in a beaded silk gown.

sublime (suh-BLYM). Reaching new levels of quality and perfection unduplicated elsewhere; of such immense beauty that the viewer's breath is taken away, metaphorically speaking.
"The SUBLIME and the ridiculous are often so nearly related, that it is difficult to class them separately. One step above the SUBLIME makes the ridiculous, and one step above the ridiculous makes the SUBLIME again."—Thomas Paine, English revolutionary and intellectual

sui generis (SOO-aye JEN-er-is). Of its own kind; individual; unique.
The royal wedding was a SUI GENERIS event.

sumptuous (SUMP-choo-us). Extravagant; lavish.
A SUMPTUOUS feast awaited the couple at the hotel.

transcendent (tran-SEN-dent). Going beyond normal everyday experience; existing beyond the known physical universe and its limitations.
*"Genius . . . means the TRANSCENDENT capacity of taking trouble."
—Thomas Carlyle, Scottish satirist and historian*

ANTONYMS

menial (MEE-nee-uhl). Of or fit for servants; low; mean.
"Such MENIAL duties; but her way / Of looking at them lent a grace / To things the world deemed commonplace."—Ella Wheeler Wilcox, American poet and writer

unassuming (un-uh-SOOM-ing). Modest and unpretentious.
The Binghamtons just bought a lovely, UNASSUMING starter home in the town where their families live.

89. Greed

(GREED), noun

Excessive desire to acquire possessions, wealth, etc.; craving more than is necessary or appropriate.

ADJECTIVES

edacious (ih-DAY-shuss). Greedy, eager, and consumed with consumption.
It's not fair to label Rosella EDACIOUS because she only wants the same luxury items the rest of us desire.

rapacious (ruh-PAY-shuss). Taking by force; plundering; predatory.
It appeared that Jon set out to prove that power corrupts with his RAPACIOUS habits.

voracious (vuh-RAY-shuss). Possessing a huge and insatiable appetite, whether for food, knowledge, amusement, or something else.
Her son always had a VORACIOUS desire for knowledge. He read anything he could get his hands on and was always willing to experience something new.

ANTONYMS

munificent (myoo-NIFF-uh-suhnt). Characterized by great generosity.
The Pattersons are so MUNIFICENT that they give to charity year-round rather than merely at times when giving offers tax benefits.

noblesse oblige (no-BLESS oh-BLEEZH). An act of generosity, charity, or kindness performed by a rich person for the benefit of someone less fortunate than himself, viewed by the giver as paying the universe back for his good fortune.
Donald gave the young man a job not out of a sense of pity or guilt, but out of a sense of NOBLESSE OBLIGE.

philanthropist (fill-ANN-throw-pist). A person who generously gives of his or her time, energy, and money to charity.
Bill Gates is the most proactive PHILANTHROPIST out of all the billionaires who care to invest their time in contributing to charitable causes.

90. Group

(GROOP), noun

A collection or assembly of persons or things; a meeting.

ADJECTIVES

sectarian (sek-TARE-ee-in). Relating to the practices, nature, or activities of a sect.
"In the early 1990s, as the insurgency took on a more unambiguously religious and SECTARIAN flavor, several Pandits were killed, and most of the rest fled for their lives."—William Dalrymple, Scottish historian and author

NOUNS

cabal (kuh-BAL). An underground society, secret religious sect, or other private group assembled for purposes hidden from those around them.
I was shocked when our neighbors asked us to join a CABAL of devil worshippers; after all, he is a deacon at the local church!

cadre (KAH-dray). A group of trained personnel capable of forming and training a larger organization, typically a government or military agency.
Even after the war ended, a number of officers were left to form a CADRE in order to quell future unrest in the region.

cartel (kar-TELL). A group assembled with the objective of establishing mutual control over prices, production, and marketing of goods by the members; a coalition of political figures united for a particular cause.
The oil CARTEL had succeeded in driving world energy prices up significantly.

confraternity (kahn-fruh-TUR-nih-tee). An association of people united for a common cause.
Eager to improve the condition of our neighborhood playgrounds, Carol and I joined a town CONFRATERNITY that had formed for that purpose.

consortium (kun-SOR-tee-um). A union, partnership, or alliance, especially one among financial or business entities.
Mr. Sparks represented a CONSORTIUM of firms.

convocation (kon-vo-KAY-shun). An assembly of people gathered in response to a summons.
The address Mr. Freling gave at the CONVOCATION challenged all graduates to excel.

coterie (KOH-tuh-ree). an exclusive group of people, often meeting with a specific goal in mind.
Those in favor of the proposal formed a COTERIE that quickly became a very vocal minority.

faction (FAK-shin). A small dissenting group within a larger one.
"I will keep where there is wit stirring, and leave the FACTION of fools."
—William Shakespeare

guild (gild). A group of people dedicated to common interests or goals; an association of like-minded individuals.
Although she knew it was only a first step, Andrea couldn't help feeling that joining the Screen Actors GUILD meant she was on her way to becoming a star.

kaffeeklatsch (KAW-fee-klatch). An informal social gathering, typically including coffee and gossip.
Jeanette is not welcome at our KAFFEEKLATSCH because she refuses to gossip about her social contacts.

phalanx (FAY-lanks). A group of closely assembled people or animals, usually working together for a specific purpose, such as launching an attack. *The geek tried not to show his fear in the hallway, as the PHALANX of jocks walked in his direction.*

retinue (RET-n-oo). A group of companions or followers (of a person of great importance); an entourage. *The president and his RETINUE are expected here just before noon.*

ANTONYMS

anchorite (ANG-kuh-ryt). A person who lives alone and apart from society for religious meditation; recluse; hermit. *"And even in the most refined circles and with the best surroundings and circumstances, one must keep something of the original character of an ANCHORITE, for otherwise one has no root in oneself."—Vincent van Gogh, Dutch painter*

eremite (AIR-uh-myt). A hermit; religious recluse. *John chose the life of an EREMITE as the way to spiritual salvation and moral redemption.*

ochlophobia (ock-luh-FO-be-uh). An illogical fear or dread of crowds. *Betty never realized she suffered from OCHLOPHOBIA until she moved to the city, where she had great difficulty walking to and from work during rush hour.*

91. Grouse

(GROUSS), verb

To complain or grumble about one's situation.

ADJECTIVES

acrimonious (ak-rih-MOAN-ee-us). Angry; bitter; disputed. *"There is something about the literary life that repels me, all this desperate building of castles on cobwebs, the long-drawn ACRIMONIOUS struggle to make something important which we all know will be gone forever in a few years . . ."—Raymond Chandler, American author*

fractious (FRAK-shuss). Easily angered or irritable; quarrelsome; unruly.
"Sex is metaphysical for men, as it is not for women. Women have no problem to solve through sex. Physically and psychologically, they are serenely self-contained. They may choose to achieve, but they do not need it. They are not thrust into the beyond by their own FRACTIOUS bodies."—Camille Paglia, American author, feminist, and social critic

jaundiced (JAWN-dist). Demonstrating prejudice, due to envy or resentment.
The Blythingtons' view of our dinner parties is JAUNDICED by the fact that our personal chef is superior to theirs.

querulous (KWAIR-eh-luss). Habitually whining and griping.
Their QUERULOUS manner with the waiter made them unpleasant and embarrassing dinner companions.

NOUNS

animadversion (an-uh-mad-VER-zhun). Very harsh criticism that suggests disapproval of what is being criticized.
My boss's frequent ANIMADVERSIONS have led to high staff turnover.

bête noire (bett-NWAR). A thing for which one has an intense dislike or great fear; a dreaded enemy or foe.
Sunlight was Dracula's greatest BÊTE NOIRE.

cholers (KOH-lers). The mood of anger, irritability, grumpiness, or being short-tempered and impatient.
When Franklin is in the grip of CHOLERS, even his closest friends avoid his table at the club.

jeremiad (jare-uh-MY-uhd). A document or speech in which the author bitterly rails against the injustices of society or warns of impending death, destruction, or doom.
The Unabomber's Manifesto was an intelligently written JEREMIAD.

misanthrope (MISS-un-throwp). A person of antisocial nature who dislikes other people and thinks poorly of them until they give him reason not to.
Harold has become a veritable MISANTHROPE since Anabelle refused to attend the regatta with him.

VERBS

abominate (uh-BOM-in-ayt). To loathe; hate; detest.
"For my part, I ABOMINATE all honorable respectable toils, trials, and tribulations of every kind whatsoever."—Herman Melville, American author

castigate (KAS-tuh-gayt). To scold or criticize harshly.
The bartender was CASTIGATED by his boss for serving alcohol to two teenage girls without checking their ID first.

denigrate (DEN-ih-grayt). Insult; put down; demean; belittle.
"Everything we shut our eyes to, everything we run away from, everything we deny, DENIGRATE or despise, serves to defeat us in the end."—Henry Miller, American author and painter

harry (HAIR-ee). To torment with constant attacks.
"At middle night great cats with silver claws, / Bodies of shadow and blind eyes like pearls, / Came up out of the hole, and red-eared hounds / With long white bodies came out of the air / Suddenly, and ran at them and HARRIED them."
—William Butler Yeats, Irish poet and dramatist

ANTONYMS

encomium (en-KO-me-um). Effusive praise given in a public forum.
The CEO's ENCOMIUM at Phil's retirement dinner caused his eyes to mist over.

levity (LEV-ih-tee). Lack of appropriate seriousness; or, inconstant in nature.
"Love, which is the essence of God, is not for LEVITY, but for the total worth of man."—Ralph Waldo Emerson, American poet, essayist, and transcendentalist

waggish (WAG-ish). Joking, witty, and mischievous.
"This species of 'fame' a WAGGISH acquaintance says can be manufactured to order, and sometimes is so manufactured."—Herman Melville, American author

92. Grow

(GROH), verb

To develop naturally, as any living organism; increase in size or amount.

VERBS

burgeon (BURR-jin). To sprout, to grow; to blossom and flourish.
Natalia does her part for the BURGEONING "green" movement by having her gardener turn manure from her stables into fertilizer.

coalesce (ko-uh-LESS). To unite or grow into a single whole.
No amount of pleading from Jones could convince the two unions to COALESCE.

dilate (DIE-layt). To expand.
The rock star's pupils had DILATED, leading some to believe that he had been experimenting again with narcotics, and quite recently.

maturate (MATCH-uh-rayt). To mature; ripen; develop.
The pediatrician told Alice that her son would one day MATURATE, but his teen years have come and gone and she is still waiting for the evidence.

propagate (PROP-uh-gayt). To grow, breed, or cause to multiply and flourish.
"The fiction of happiness is PROPAGATED by every tongue."—Samuel Johnson, British moralist and poet

ripen (RY-puhn). To become ripe; to reach maturity or a state of full physical and/or emotional development.
Arthur was pleased to watch his granddaughter grow and RIPEN intellectually.

ANTONYMS

subside (sub-SYD). To become less active; to become quiet; abate.
"Friendship may, and often does, grow into love, but love never SUBSIDES into friendship."—Lord Byron, English poet

wither (WITHE-er). To dry up; shrivel; to lose vigor or freshness; become wasted or decayed.
"The person who tries to live alone will not succeed as a human being. His heart WITHERS if it does not answer another heart. His mind shrinks away if he hears only the echoes of his own thoughts and finds no other inspiration."—Pearl Buck, American author

93. Happy

(HAP-ee), adjective

Having, showing, or causing a feeling of great pleasure, contentment, or joy; lucky.

ADJECTIVES

convivial (kuhn-VIV-ee-ull). Fond of feasting, drinking, and companionship.
"One does not leave a CONVIVIAL party before closing time."—Winston Churchill, British statesman and orator

ebullient (eh-BULL-yuhnt). Feeling joy and positive emotions at an extreme level; the state of being wildly enthusiastic about something.
Lorne was EBULLIENT when he found that his mother had given the college enough money to overturn his rejection.

effervescent (ef-ur-VESS-ent). Bubbly; upbeat; cheerful; possessing a positive attitude and joyful personality.
After getting the acceptance letter from Cornell, Sabrina was EFFERVESCENT and celebrated with a trip to Neiman Marcus.

gregarious (greh-GAIR-ee-us). An extrovert; an outgoing person; one who is friendly and cheerful in nature.
"We are easy to manage, a GREGARIOUS people, / Full of sentiment, clever at mechanics, and we love our luxuries."—Robinson Jeffers, American poet

halcyon (HAL-see-un). Calm, peaceful, carefree, prosperous.
"It was the most HALCYON summer I ever spent."—Rick Bass, American author and environmental activist

jocose (joe-KOSE). Humorous, playful, and characterized by good humor.
Her son's JOCOSE nature marked him for a career in sales, rather than administration.

jocund (JOE-kund). Having a lust for life; possessing a positive attitude and desire to enjoy life to the fullest.
Ron's JOCUND façade shattered when he found himself the victim of identity theft.

orgiastic (or-jee-AS-tik). Arousing unrestrained emotional release.
William becomes loathsomely ORGIASTIC when he attends and bids at art auctions.

sanguine (SANG-gwin). Accepting of circumstances with good cheer and a positive attitude.
"Many marketers were SANGUINE about the Do Not Call introduction, saying that it helped better focus their telephone communications."—Eleanor Trickett, DM News editor

NOUNS

beatitude (bee-AT-it-tood). Being in the highest possible state of happiness, good humor, and contentment.
"Kindness is a virtue neither modern nor urban. One almost unlearns it in a city. Towns have their own BEATITUDE; they are not unfriendly; they offer a vast and solacing anonymity or an equally vast and solacing gregariousness."
—Phyllis McGinley, American author and poet

bon vivant (bon vee-VAWN). A person who enjoys living well.
In Paris with her rich aunt, Janice lived the life of a BON VIVANT, shopping and dining out to her heart's content.

felicity (fih-LISS-ih-tee). A state of blissful happiness.
"Never lose sight of the fact that all human FELICITY lies in man's imagination, and that he cannot think to attain it unless he heeds all his caprices."
—Marquis de Sade, French aristocrat and revolutionary

levity (LEV-ih-tee). Lightness; insubstantiality.
Gentlemen, with all due respect, we face a crisis; this is no time for LEVITY.

roisterer (ROY-stir-er). Party-goer, celebrator, one who has a good time in a loud and boisterous manner.
The ROISTERERS' enjoyment of the party was so infectious, their neighbors joined them instead of complaining about the noise.

ANTONYMS

defeatist (dih-FEET-ist). Accepting defeat as an unavoidable consequence of life; pessimistic.
Sheldon's DEFEATIST attitude led Monica, his supervisor, to wonder whether he would ever complete the project he was working on.

malcontent (mal-kuhn-TENT). A discontented, resentful, or rebellious person.
Harvey is such a MALCONTENT that he'll argue with you if you tell him it's a nice day!

saturnine (SAT-ur-nyn). Moody; morose; gloomy; unhappy; having a pessimistic outlook on life.
Ever since his father told him he could not have another Lotus Esprit, Williams has acted positively SATURNINE.

94. Harass

(huh-RASS), verb

To bother persistently; disturb continually; pester; persecute.

VERBS

badger (BAJ-er). To torment as if baiting a badger; to urge persistently; nag.
Martha was convinced that she had to BADGER her daughter to do her homework.

beleaguer (beh-LEE-ger). To persistently surround, harry, or bother until you get what you want.
To the embarrassment of her friends, Kristen BELEAGUERED the sommelier until he brought her a satisfactory Bordeaux.

besiege (bih-SEEJ). To submit a person or body to insistent demands from all sides; to crowd around.
Everywhere he went, the movie idol was BESIEGED by crazed fans looking for autographs and even pieces of his hair or clothing.

harry (HAIR-ee). To torture with constant attacks.
"At middle night great cats with silver claws, / Bodies of shadow and blind eyes like pearls, / Came up out of the hole, and red-eared hounds / With long white bodies came out of the air / Suddenly, and ran at them and HARRIED them."
—William Butler Yeats, Irish poet and dramatist

hector (HEK-ter). To bully; dominate.
The coach HECTORED the boys so often that they quit the team in disgust.

inculcate (IN-kul-kayt). To impress an idea or belief upon someone by repeating it to that person over and over until the idea is firmly lodged in his brain.
New cult members are quickly INCULCATED with the cult leader's beliefs and world view.

ANTONYMS

facilitate (fuh-SIL-ih-tayt). To make easier; to lighten the work of; help; assist.
"Every human being must find his own way to cope with severe loss, and the only job of a true friend is to FACILITATE whatever method he chooses."
—Caleb Carr, American novelist

respite (RESS-pit). A temporary delay or postponement, especially of something distressing.
"Sweet Flower of Hope! free Nature's genial child! / That didst so fair disclose thy early bloom, / Filling the wide air with a rich perfume! / For thee in vain all heavenly aspects smiled; / From the hard world brief RESPITE could they win."—Samuel Taylor Coleridge, English poet

95. Harm

(HARM), verb

To hurt, damage, or impair; injure.

ADJECTIVES

baleful (BAIL-ful). Ominous; signaling evil to come.
It always seemed to me that Mrs. Howard had a BALEFUL gleam in her eye as she passed out her absurdly difficult tests.

baneful (BAYN-ful). Venomous; deadly; ruinous.
Austin relaxed when he learned that the outback did not contain all the BANEFUL plants and animals that he had imagined.

deleterious (dell-ih-TEER-ee-us). Harmful; damaging.
Smoking has been proven to have a DELETERIOUS effect on one's health.

internecine (in-ter-NESS-een). Characterized by slaughter; deadly.
The INTERNECINE conflict was particularly unfortunate in its thoroughness.

noisome (NOY-sum). Harmful or injurious to the health; offensive.
The NOISOME chemicals were placed in a locked room.

noxious (NOK-shuss). Morally harmful and pernicious.
Even with his wealth, good looks, and charm, Steven has such a NOXIOUS personality that we always feel awful after spending time with him.

pernicious (purr-NISH-us). Resulting in damage or harm; having a debilitating effect.
We believe that, once the producers of luxury items become publicly traded companies, the results will be PERNICIOUS.

NOUNS

juggernaut (JUG-er-nawt). A large, overpowering, destructive force.
Once he begins arguing about the superiority of Maseratis, Jefferson becomes a JUGGERNAUT, capable of deflating anyone else's arguments.

maleficence (muh-LEF-ih-sense). Action that deliberately causes harm; behavior driven by evil intentions.
Our upstairs maid's various acts of MALEFICENCE finally caused her to be released from our family's employment.

scourge (SKURJ). A cause of widespread or great affliction.
Famine is one of humanity's most horrific SCOURGES.

VERBS

debilitate (dih-BILL-uh-tayt). To make weak or feeble.
Several hours on the polo fields are enough to DEBILITATE even the most robust player.

decimate (DESS-ih-mayt). To reduce something greatly, to the point of wiping it out.
"Every doctor will allow a colleague to DECIMATE a whole countryside sooner than violate the bond of professional etiquette by giving him away."
—George Bernard Shaw, Irish playwright

deface (dih-FACE). To disfigure or damage.
It breaks my heart to see the old stone bridge, my one unchanging companion from boyhood, DEFACED with the spray-painted grumblings of drunken teenagers.

defile (dih-FYL). To pollute; to corrupt or make unclean.
The river that only a few years ago ran clean and clear is now DEFILED with a witches' brew of chemicals, thanks to the new tanning plant.

desecrate (DESS-ih-krayt). To abuse the sacred character of a thing; to treat disrespectfully or irreverently.
Such profane language from our organization's current leader serves only to DESECRATE the memory of the founder.

enervate (EN-er-vayt). To rob a person, organization, place, or thing of its energy, strength, and vitality.
Greenhouse gases ENERVATE the protective ozone layer surrounding the Earth.

exacerbate (ig-ZASS-er-bayt). To take action that makes a situation worse or aggravates it further.
The problem with the mission was further EXACERBATED when the outer tiles ripped away from the space shuttle.

raze (RAYZ). To tear down or demolish.
We had to RAZE our Cape Cod home and rebuild it entirely, due to some structural damage caused by high winds.

vitiate (VISH-ee-ayt). To spoil or impair the quality of; corrupt.
"A VITIATED state of morals, a corrupted public conscience, is incompatible with freedom."—Patrick Henry, American patriot

ANTONYMS

innocuous (ih-NAWK-yew-us). Not harmful or offensive; innocent, incidental, and hardly noticeable.
"I know those little phrases that seem so INNOCUOUS and, once you let them in, pollute the whole of speech."—Samuel Beckett, Irish writer, dramatist, and poet
See also: Abuse

96. Hate

(HAYT), verb

To have intense dislike or ill will for; despise; detest; loathe.

ADJECTIVES

contemptuous (kun-TEMP-choo-us). Feeling or expressing disdain, disapproval, deep hatred, or scorn.
The defendant's CONTEMPTUOUS behavior on the stand was, amazingly, overlooked by the judge.

xenophobic (zee-nuh-FOE-bik). Having an irrational fear or hatred of foreigners and immigrants.
We are not XENOPHOBIC; we dislike all strangers, regardless of their backgrounds, unless they are brought to us by other social contacts.

NOUNS

animadversion (an-uh-mad-VER-zhun). Very harsh criticism that suggests disapproval of what is being criticized.
My boss's frequent ANIMADVERSIONS have led to high staff turnover.

animus (AN-uh-muss). Prejudiced ill will.
Don's ANIMUS toward a former colleague drove him to thoughts of violence until therapy helped him to diminish his hatred.

aversion (uh-VUR-zhun). Extreme dislike; loathing.
My AVERSION to soap operas leaves me with little to discuss at coffee breaks.

enmity (EN-mih-tee). Mutual dislike, animosity, hatred, antagonism, or disagreement between two groups or parties.
Was the ENMITY between Muhammad Ali and Joe Frasier an act, genuine, or a combination of both?

misandry (mih-SAN-dree). Hatred of men.
After twenty years of feeling the effects of the glass ceiling, she was entitled to MISANDRY in all its manifestations.

misanthrope (MISS-en-throwp). A person of antisocial nature who dislikes other people and thinks poorly of them until they give him reason not to.
Harold has become a veritable MISANTHROPE since Anabelle refused to go on any more dates with him.

misogamy (mih-SOG-uh-mee). Hatred of marriage.
After his divorce, Brent's mistrust of marriage bordered on MISOGAMY.

misogyny (mih-SOJ-uh-nee). Hatred of women.
A lifetime of rejection had filled him with a rabid MISOGYNY.

rancor (RANG-ker). Conflict between individuals or groups, usually resulting from disagreement over an action or issue, and accompanied by ill will, bad feelings, bitterness, and an escalation of the dispute over time.
"They no longer assume responsibility (as beat cops used to do) for averting RANCOR between antagonistic neighbors."—Harlan Ellison, American author

repugnance (rih-PUG-nunce). To show strong aversion, dislike, or disgust for something.
We can greet the news of the terrorist bombing only with REPUGNANCE.

vitriol (VIT-ree-ohl). An attitude of bitterness, hatred, or mean-spiritedness.
The school board reprimanded the coach with VITRIOL.

VERBS

abhor (ab-HOR). To experience a feeling of great repugnance or disgust.
It was clear almost as soon as the dinner party had begun that Jennifer ABHORRED her half-sister.

execrate (EK-sih-krayt). To loathe; to subject to scorn and derision.
We EXECRATED William for weeks due to his casual rejection of an invitation to join Yale's Skull and Bones.

ANTONYMS

adulate (AJ-uh-layt). To show excessive praise or admiration; flatter or admire servilely.
"I have been very happy, very rich, very beautiful, much ADULATED, very famous and very unhappy."—Brigitte Bardot, French actress

esteem (ih-STEEM). To value highly; have great respect and regard for; prize.
"The harder the conflict, the more glorious the triumph. What we obtain too cheap, we ESTEEM too lightly; it is dearness only that gives everything its value."—Thomas Paine, English-American writer and political pamphleteer

97. Haughty

(HAW-tee), adjective

Snobbish and arrogant.

ADJECTIVES

austere (aw-STEER). Stern; grim and lacking humor or warmth; clean and unornamented; severe or strict in manner.
In the movie Dead Poets Society, *Robin Williams clashes with an AUSTERE headmaster at a private boys' school.*

de rigueur (duh-rih-GUR). Conforming to current standards of behavior, fashion, style, and etiquette.
A two-carat diamond engagement ring that cost a young man a year's salary was DE RIGUEUR for proposing to a girl in the 1950s.

vainglorious (vayn-GLOR-ee-us). Conceited; boastful; prone to showing off and bragging.
Although the scion of a well-established family, Gordon is so VAINGLORIOUS that you'd think him a parvenu!

NOUNS

affectation (ah-fek-TAY-shun). Behaviors or mannerisms that are exaggerated, extreme, eccentric, and deliberately showy, often an effort to attract attention.
"AFFECTATION is awkward and forces imitation of what should be genuine and easy."—John Locke, British philosopher

doyen/doyenne (doy-EN). A man or woman who is the senior member of a group, based on rank, age, experience, etc.
Though she is the youngest member of our group, Brittany is our DOYENNE, based on her extensive family connections.

haute couture (OAT ko-TOOR). Highly fashionable clothing on the cutting edge of the latest design fads and trends.
"HAUTE COUTURE should be fun, foolish, and almost unwearable."
—Christian Lacroix, French fashion designer

haut monde (oh MOND). High society.
"The literary wiseacres prognosticate in many languages, as they have through-out so many centuries, setting the stage for new HAUT MONDE in letters and making up the public's mind."—Fannie Hurst, American novelist

ANTONYMS

déclassé (day-kluh-SAY). Of a fallen social position or inferior status.
Jean thought her imitation designer bag looked exactly like the real thing, but the other girls in her exclusive private school quickly ridiculed Jean—and her bag—for being DÉCLASSÉ.

egalitarian (ih-gal-uh-TAIR-ee-uhn). Fair and balanced in the extreme; of the belief that all people are created equal and should be treated so.
"Chinks in America's EGALITARIAN armor are not hard to find. Democracy is the fig leaf of elitism."—Florence King, American author

gauche (GOHSH). Sorely lacking in the social graces and good manners; crude behavior.
Rhett was under the impression that one needed only money to join the country club. However, his GAUCHE demeanor caused him to be denied membership.

hoi polloi (HOY puh-LOY). A pejorative term used to describe the masses or the common people.
"My practice is to ignore the pathetic wishes and desires of the HOI POLLOI,"
the governor said haughtily.

98. Help

(HELP), verb

To give assistance and make it possible or easier to accomplish a task; to aid.

NOUNS

aegis (EE-jis). The protection, support, and help rendered by a guardian, supporter, backer, or mentor.
Jill thinks she's above reproach because she's under the AEGIS of that
marketing vice-president with a penchant for younger women.

VERBS

abet (uh-BET). To encourage or assist a plan or activity, usually a misdeed.
Though Michael did not participate in the actual kidnapping, he ABETTED the
perpetrators by hiding them from the police.

adjudicate (uh-JOO-dih-kayt). To preside over or listen to opposing arguments and help two parties settle their differences and come to an agreement.
As my daughters pummeled each other while screaming at top volume, I tried
desperately to ADJUDICATE their quarrel.

assuage (uh-SWAYJ). To put someone at ease; to comfort or soothe; to erase doubts and fears.
"But history must not yet tell the tragedies enacted here; let time intervene in
some measure to ASSUAGE and lend an azure tint to them."—Henry David
Thoreau, American author and transcendentalist

exhort (ig-ZORT). To urge or advise earnestly.
"The function of the moralist is not to EXHORT men to be good but to elucidate what the good is."—Walter Lippmann, American journalist

minister (MIN-us-stur). To give help; fill wants; to serve as a nurse.
It was touching to watch Calvin MINISTER to his wife during her recovery.

mitigate (MITT-ih-gayt). To make or become milder, less severe, or less painful.
The medication should MITIGATE John's symptoms within twenty-four hours.

ANTONYMS

sabotage (SAB-uh-tawzh). Intentional obstruction of or damage to some process or activity; the undermining of a cause.
"Self-SABOTAGE is when we way we want something and then go about making sure it doesn't happen."—Alyce P. Cornyn-Selby, American manager and author

thwart (THWART). To hinder, obstruct, frustrate, or defeat a person, plans, etc.
"Instinct must be THWARTED just as one prunes the branches of a tree so that it will grow better."—Henri Matisse, French painter

99. Hide

(HYD), verb

To place or keep out of sight; conceal; secrete; to keep from the knowledge of others; keep secret.

ADJECTIVES

covert (KUV-ert). Concealed; disguised; secret.
Try as we might, we never managed to get our uncle to discuss his experiences conducting COVERT ops at the CIA.

ulterior (ul-TEER-ee-er). Beyond what is being shown, as motives.
"When one has extensively pondered about men, as a career or as a vocation, one sometimes feels nostalgic for primates. At least they do not have ULTERIOR motives."—Albert Camus, Algerian-born French author and philosopher

NOUNS

occultation (awk-uhl-TAY-shin). The act of hiding or blocking from view.
With disguises offering a bit of needed OCCULTATION, we were able to hit Manhattan's hot spots away from the glare of the dreaded paparazzi.

VERBS

camouflage (KAM-uh-flazh). To hide or make something less visible by changing its appearance.
Dave became one of the company's best salesmen because he was able to CAMOUFLAGE his real feelings.

dissimulate (dih-SIM-yuh-layt). To hide one's feelings from another, often by using untruths.
Feeling extremely guilty about his affair, Jake would DISSIMULATE behind a wall of anger whenever Tricia asked him pointed questions.

seclude (sih-KLOOD). To hide or keep apart; to keep in isolation.
Jared SECLUDED himself in his room in order to meet the project's deadline.

ANTONYMS

manifest (MAN-uh-fest). To make clear or obvious; clear; plain; patent.
"MANIFEST plainness, embrace simplicity, reduce selfishness, have few desires."—Lao-tzu, Chinese Taoist philosopher

overt (oh-VURT). Open, public, and observable.
Americans must insist that local, state, and federal government operations remain OVERT.

100. Hoary

(HOAR-ee), adjective

Impressively old; ancient.

ADJECTIVES

hidebound (HYD-bownd). Inflexible and holding narrow opinions.
Wallace can be rather HIDEBOUND when pontificating on the virtues of classic Mercedes-Benz models versus the condition of the automobile company at present.

moribund (MOR-ih-bund). Lacking vigor; soon to be dead or defunct.
Ever since its head chef left for the Food Network, that gourmet restaurant has become MORIBUND and is likely to close soon.

venerable (VEN-err-uh-bull). An individual or institution that is respected and revered, sometimes because of achievement, intelligence, or character; but just as often as a result of being around a long time.
"Is the babe young? When I behold it, it seems more VENERABLE than the oldest man."—Henry David Thoreau, American author and transcendentalist

NOUNS

anachronism (uh-NAK-ruh-niz-em). A person, place, thing, or idea whose time has past and that seems to belong to an earlier age.
His three record players—and the fact that he doesn't even know what an MP3 is—make Jim something of an ANACHRONISM.

xerosis (zih-ROH-sis). The typical hardening of aging skin and tissue.
Ophelia constantly visits European spas to slow the onset of XEROSIS.

VERBS

wane (WAYN). To gradually decrease; to fade away; to become diminished.
Once she finally received the Cartier watch from her father, Karen's interest in the timepiece quickly WANED.

ANTONYMS

élan (a-LON). Enthusiasm, energy, flair, zest.
Bryanna reacted with ÉLAN when she was tapped to be part of a feature for Elite Travel Magazine.

jocund (JOE-kund). Having a lust for life; possessing a positive attitude and desire to enjoy life to the fullest.
Ron's JOCUND façade shattered when he found himself the victim of identity theft.

nascent (NAY-sent). Having just been born or invented and still in the early stages of growth and development.
It's always amusing to watch the nouveau riche during the NASCENT period of their adjustment to luxury.

101. Honor

(ON-ur), noun

Great regard or respect given or received; glory; fame; renown; strong sense of right and wrong; the application of integrity and principles.

ADJECTIVES

dauntless (DAWNT-liss). Fearless, intrepid, and bold.
"For Thought has a pair of DAUNTLESS wings."—Robert Frost, American poet

emeritus (ih-MAIR-ih-tuss). Retired but still holding an honorary title corresponding to the position held prior to retirement.
Watkins has been awarded the position of Professor EMERITUS.

honorific (on-uh-RIFF-ik). A tribute or reward given in an effort to honor someone as a sign of deep respect.
Lifetime achievement awards aren't for any single work, but an HONORIFIC for long service and a track record of excellence.

meritorious (mair-uh-TORE-ee-uss). Worthy of praise, laudable.
Earl's work at the homeless shelter was MERITORIOUS, but it left him little time for his family and friends.

NOUNS

accolade (AK-uh-layd). A mark of acknowledgment or expression of praise; that which confers praise or honor.
The firm's president had hung on his office wall many plaques, citations, and ACCOLADES.

éclat (a-KLAW). Great public acclaim; or, great public notoriety.
Although they are the height of Paris fashion, Martina's five-inch heels earned her much ÉCLAT in the society pages.

fealty (FEE-ul-tee). A sense of obligation or loyalty, usually existing because one person feels beholden to another.
The only reason that Bryson pledged FEALTY to David is because David's social connections helped Bryson get a job on Wall Street.

homage (HOM-ij). Respect paid and deference shown to a superior or other person one admires, fears, or wishes to emulate or praise.
Gary took black and white photos with a nondigital camera in HOMAGE to Ansel Adams, whose works he greatly admired.

laureate (LORE-ee-it). A person who has been singled out for a particular high honor or award.
The group included a remarkable cross-section of accomplished scientists, some of whom were Nobel LAUREATES.

obeisance (oh-BAY-since). Deferential respect or homage, or an act or gesture expressing the same.
In an act of OBEISANCE, Rachael brought the elderly woman up to sit in her plush opera box, rather than in the mezzanine.

panegyric (pan-uh-JEER-ik). Formal, elaborate praise.
After Coach Henry retired, her former athletes filled the local paper with PANEGYRICS concerning her character and accomplishments.

perquisite (PUR-kwih-zit). An incidental privilege other than payment that accompanies a position of responsibility; an extra payment beyond what is owed.
Among the president's PERQUISITES were two front-row seats to all the Celtics' regular-season home games.

ANTONYMS

ignoble (ig-NO-bull). Dishonorable in nature; not deserving respect; characterized by baseness or lowness.
Peter's IGNOBLE aims were well known to all in the room.

infidelity (in-fih-DEL-ih-tee). The quality or act of having been untrue or
inconsistent with an (often implied) standard; disloyalty; marital unfaithfulness.
*Although Gwen suspected her husband of INFIDELITY, she had not come across
any tangible proof.*

renege (ri-neg). To go back (on one's word); to break a promise or commitment.
*Dalton was supposed to have been named vice president in exchange for his sup-
port, but Peterson RENEGED on the deal after assuming control.*

102. Illness

(IL-niss), noun

An unhealthy condition of the body or mind; sickness; disease.

NOUNS

autism (AW-tiz-um). A condition characterized by difficulty with or indifference to social contact and impaired ability to communicate.
Often subjected to abuse and inhumane treatment two or three decades ago, people with AUTISM are now more likely to receive a meaningful therapeutic regimen.

bulimia (buh-LEE-mee-uh). An eating disorder in which sufferers alternately binge, then purge, forcing themselves to vomit.
The faculty health center featured a nurse with special training in dealing with BULIMIA and other eating disorders.

carbuncle (KAR-bunk-uhl). A painful inflammation of the skin similar to, but more serious than, a boil.
Jimmy's inventive excuses for his absences reached a new level when he told his teacher he had been unable to attend Spanish class because of a CARBUNCLE.

eczema (EG-zuh-muh). An inflammatory skin condition, characterized by red, itching skin that erupts into lesions that later become scaly, hard, and crusty.
The skin cleanser Noxzema was named after its supposed ability to "knock ECZEMA."

gingivitis (jin-jih-VY-tuss). A gum disease; the condition of having swollen gums.
The rinse promised lifetime protection against GINGIVITIS, a claim Fred viewed with some skepticism.

hemophilia (hee-muh-FEEL-ee-uh). A blood defect usually affecting males but transmitted by females in which the blood fails to clot normally, often leading to uncontrolled hemorrhaging.
Because so many HEMOPHILIA patients have contracted the AIDS virus from contaminated blood, many will only accept transfusions using blood that has been donated by family and friends.

hypertension (hy-pur-TEN-shun). High blood pressure.
Some over-the-counter cough, cold, and allergy medicines tend to cause elevated blood pressure, and include a warning that they may be hazardous to those suffering from HYPERTENSION.

hyperthermia (hy-pur-THUR-mee-uh). Extreme increase of body heat.
The reading is 105 degrees; we are dealing not with a simple fever, but with severe HYPERTHERMIA.

hypothermia (hy-po-THER-mee-uh). Extreme loss of body heat.
After several hours in the freezing water, the victims had already succumbed to the effects of HYPOTHERMIA.

influenza (in-floo-EN-zuh). A contagious respiratory virus characterized by inflammation of the mucous membrane, fever, prostration, aches, and pains.
David was still weak from his bout with INFLUENZA.

kyphosis (ki-FOE-sis). Excessive curvature of the spine suffered by hunchbacks.
After William's father forced him to help out the family gardener, William complained for weeks afterward that the outdoor work gave him KYPHOSIS.

migraine (MY-grayn). An excruciating headache, caused by expanding capillaries, that occurs on one (usually the left) side of the head, and causes the sufferer nausea, vomiting, and extreme sensitivity to light.
As a treatment for my MIGRAINES, the doctor gave me a new prescription, suggesting I take two tablets and lie down in a very dark room whenever I felt one coming on.

mononucleosis (mawn-oh-noo-klee-OH-siss). An infectious illness caused by an increase of mononuclear leukocytes in the blood, and characterized by extremely swollen glands, a sore throat, and exhaustion.
Erika's MONONUCLEOSIS caused her to miss nearly two months of school.

narcolepsy (NAR-kuh-lep-see). The disorder of suddenly and unpredictably falling asleep.
After learning he suffered from NARCOLEPSY, Brian realized how dangerous it would be for him to drive, and voluntarily returned his license to the registry.

osteoporosis (oss-tee-oh-puh-ROE-sis). A condition of fragile, brittle bones, particularly common in women of advanced age.
The doctor advised all of his female patients over fifty to make sure they took in plenty of calcium as a precaution against OSTEOPOROSIS.

psoriasis (suh-RY-uh-suss). A chronic skin disease causing the skin to become covered with red patches and white scales.
Emmett treated his first bout of PSORIASIS by applying copious amounts of moisturizer, but it did no good.

schizophrenia (skit-suh-FREE-nee-uh). A mental condition that can cause sufferers to hallucinate, to be disoriented, and to withdraw from society.
It is a common misconception that SCHIZOPHRENIA is the condition of having multiple personalities.

ANTONYMS

eupepsia (yoo-PEP-see-uh). Good digestion.
John enjoyed EUPEPSIA and could eat almost anything, including very spicy foods, without gastric distress or physical regret.

euphoria (yoo-FOR-ee-uh). A feeling of well-being; an abnormal feeling of buoyant vigor and health.
"The writer who loses his self-doubt, who gives way as he grows old to a sudden EUPHORIA, to prolixity, should stop writing immediately: the time has come for him to lay aside his pen."—Sidonie Gabrielle Colette, French novelist

103. Imagine

(ih-MAJ-in), verb

To create a mental image of; form an idea or notion; to think or fancy; conceive in the mind.

ADJECTIVES

apocryphal (uh-POK-rih-fuhl). Of dubious authenticity; having been fabricated long after the fact.
The story of Shakespeare's having shared a mistress with Richard Burbage is almost certainly APOCRYPHAL.

factitious (fak-TISH-uss). Contrived; fabricated.
At first, we thought the rumor FACTITIOUS, but then we learned that couture-producer Hermes does, in fact, plan to design and market a helicopter.

pensive (PEN-siv). Thoughtful; having wistful or dreamy thoughts.
My girlfriend was ready for a riotous night on the town, but I was feeling PENSIVE, so we ended up going to a cafe and talking well into the night.

ADVERBS

vicariously (vye-KAIR-ee-uss-lee). To enjoy imagined feelings and experiences largely by observing or hearing about another person's life and adventures.
Married for over twenty-five years, Roger often told his single friends that he lived VICARIOUSLY through them.

NOUNS

chimera (kih-MEER-uh). An illusion of the mind or a dream that can't possibly be realized.
Leon's idea of the perfect woman is a CHIMERA that keeps him from realizing his goal of finding true love.

epiphany (ih-PIF-uh-nee). A sudden, unexpected insight that seems to come from nowhere and throws great illumination on a subject previously not well understood.
One day Marcus had an EPIPHANY and realized that, to find true happiness, he should become a philanthropist.

phantasmagoria (fan-taz-muh-GORE-ee-uh). A dreamlike, constantly changing series of visions.
The avant-garde film had no dialogue or plot in the traditional sense; it was essentially a PHANTASMAGORIA set to music.

VERBS

envisage (en-VIZ-ij). To envision, imagine, or create a mental picture.
"I don't ENVISAGE collectivism. There is no such animal, it is always individualism."—Gertrude Stein, American author

fabricate (FAB-rih-kayt). To create something; often used negatively, to suggest that one is lying, or "creating" false information.
Mom shook her head because she could tell I was just FABRICATING my explanations.

ANTONYMS

discerning (dih-SURN-ing). Showing good insight, judgment, and understanding; discriminating.
"Children, who play life, DISCERN its true law and relations more clearly than men, who fail to live it worthily, but who think that they are wiser by experience, that is, by failure."—Henry David Thoreau, American essayist, poet, and philosopher

percipient (pur-SIP-ee-int). Keenly or readily perceiving; discriminating.
Arthur was a PERCIPIENT gourmet, so we always let him choose the restaurant for a celebratory meal.

104. Impatient

(im-PAY-shunt), adjective

Feeling or showing a lack of patience; annoyance due to delay or opposition; restless.

ADJECTIVES

brusque (BRUSK). Short; abrupt or curt in manner.
Her BRUSQUE exterior put Tom off at first, but he later discussed many important issues with Ann in depth.

bumptious (BUMP-shuss). Overbearing or crudely assertive; overly pushy or impertinent.
We had difficulty crossing the border because Nan got into a squabble with a BUMPTIOUS border guard.

impetuous (im-PETCH-oo-us). Impulsive; driven by sudden force or emotion.
Dirk's impetuous remark may well cost him his job.

importunate (im-PORE-chuh-nit). Demanding or impatient in issuing repeated requests.
Two-year-olds, though lovable, can be IMPORTUNATE; Wesley seemed unprepared for this.

irascible (ih-RASS-uh-bull). Easily provoked or annoyed; prone to losing one's temper; quick to anger.
"I have never known anyone worth a damn who wasn't IRASCIBLE."
—Ezra Pound, American expatriate poet

restive (RESS-tiv). Impatient and stubborn; contrary.
Audrey was so worked up about her first summer abroad that her excitement came across as RESTIVE.

unceremonious (un-sair-uh-MONE-ee-uss). Rude or abrupt; tactlessly hasty; inappropriate.
June made an UNCEREMONIOUS exit just as the chairman was beginning his remarks on the Fentworth project.

ANTONYMS

abide (uh-BYD). To withstand, patiently wait for, or tolerate.
I could ABIDE my dinner companion's bigotry for only so long; by evening's end, I had to challenge him.

philosophic (fil-uh-SOFF-ik). Rational; sensibly composed; calm.
Harry hated to wait, but over time he saw that his impatience harmed only himself, and when necessary, was PHILOSOPHIC about periods of forced inactivity.

105. Improve

(im-PROOV), verb

To make better; to raise to a better quality or condition; increase the worth of.

ADJECTIVES

didactic (dy-DAK-tik). Designed, made, or tailored for purposes of education, self-improvement, or ethical betterment.
"The essential function of art is moral . But a passionate, implicit morality, not DIDACTIC."—D.H. Lawrence, British author

NOUNS

meliorism (MEE-lee-uh-riz-um). A philosophy of optimism that says the world is gradually improving through divine intervention or human effort—or both.
Thomas Hardy's philosophy of MELIORISM showed in his belief in the ultimate goodness of humankind.

VERBS

aggrandize (uh-GRAN-dyz). To exaggerate, put on a false front, and make something look greater and grander than it really is.
Phil tries to AGGRANDIZE his reputation by stating that he is a charter member of the Bill O'Reilly fan club, but everybody just thinks this "feat" makes him pathetic.

augment (awg-MENT). To make greater in size, amount, strength, etc.
The contributions collected for the library addition were AUGMENTED by a large anonymous donation.

bowdlerize (BODE-ler-ize). To remove obscenity, violence, and other inappropriate content from a novel, play, or story so as to make it appropriate for a younger reader.
Hollywood BOWDLERIZED his script, so, instead of being R-rated, the film was rated PG-13.

elevate (EL-ih-vayt). To raise up, make higher; to raise to a higher intellectual or moral level; to raise the spirits; lift.

Only a visit from her favorite nephew could ELEVATE Ann's spirits and calm her feelings of depression and loss.

gentrify (JENN-truh-fy). To take something rundown, such as a neighborhood, and improve it.

Attempts to GENTRIFY the historic neighborhood failed because of community apathy.

ANTONYMS

deteriorate (dih-TEER-ee-uh-rayt). To make or become worse; lower in quality or value; depreciate.

"Writing, at its best, is a lonely life. Organizations for writers palliate the writer's loneliness, but I doubt if they improve his writing. He grows in public stature as he sheds his loneliness and often his work DETERIORATES. —Ernest Hemingway, American novelist

exacerbate (ig-ZASS-er-bayt). To take action that makes a situation worse or aggravates it further.

The problem with the mission was further EXACERBATED when the outer tiles ripped away from the space shuttle.

106. Indicate

(IN-dih-kayt), verb

To show; point out, or direct attention to; to give a sign of; signify.

NOUNS

bellwether (BELL-weh-thur). A leading indicator or important factor in predicting a trend or outcome.

The fact that Robert got thrown out of Groton and Exeter was a BELLWETHER for his lackadaisical years at Dartmouth.

indicant (IN-di-kuhnt). Something that indicates or points out.
The loss of electricity was the first INDICANT that the presentation would not be successful.

premonition (pree-muh-NISH-un). A feeling of anticipation; a forewarning.
Bob had daily PREMONITIONS of disaster, but they were all unfounded.

VERBS

augur (AW-gur). To foretell future events, as though by supernatural knowledge or power; to divine; to indicate a future trend or happening.
The chairman's sour mood this morning does not AUGUR well for that budget proposal we made.

denote (de-NOTE). To indicate or make clear; to serve as sign or symbol for something else.
Her chills and discoloration, Dr. Smith observed, DENOTED severe hypothermia.

evince (ee-VINCE). To reveal or indicate the presence of a particular feeling or condition.
The blocky lines of Van Gogh's paintings EVINCE a feeling of depression and madness.

presage (PRESS-ij). To foretell or indicate.
Such provocation may PRESAGE armed conflict in the region.

ANTONYMS

ensconce (en-SKONTS). To hide something in a secure place.
Paul hoped that once the statue was ENSCONCED on board ship, they would have no trouble with customs officers.

veil (VAYL). To cover or conceal; to hide the actual nature of something; mask; disguise.
"A poet dares be just so clear and no clearer. . . . He unzips the VEIL from beauty, but does not remove it. A poet utterly clear is a trifle glaring."—E.B. White, American writer

107. Ineffable

(in-EF-uh-bull), adjective

Something so fantastic, incredible, or difficult to grasp that it cannot be described in words.

ADJECTIVES

auspicious (aw-SPISH-us). A good beginning giving rise to the belief that the venture, journey, or activity will end in success.
The blind date did not have an AUSPICIOUS start because Max kept calling his friend's cousin "Mallory" instead of "Mary."

efflorescent (ef-luh-RES-uhnt). At the final stage of development; at the peak of perfection.
Thomas is convinced that the Bugati Veyron Fbg represents the EFFLORESCENT automobile.

empyreal (em-PEER-ee-uhl). Elevated and sublime; or, of the sky.
The beautiful three-carat sapphire her fiancé gave her shone with an EMPYREAL, almost celestial, light.

ethereal (eh-THEER-ee-uhl). Light and airy; possessing a heavenly or celestial quality.
"ETHEREAL, their mauve / almost a transparent gray, / their dark veins bruise-blue."—Denise Levertov, British-born American poet

impalpable (im-PAL-puh-bull). Difficult to understand easily; or, intangible.
"The soul is so IMPALPABLE, so often useless, and sometimes such a nuisance, that I felt no more emotion on losing it than if, on a stroll, I had mislaid my visiting card."—Charles Baudelaire, French poet, critic, and translator

outré (oo-TRAY). Radically unconventional; outside the limits of expected conduct or behavior.
"One of life's intriguing paradoxes is that hierarchical social order makes cheap rents and OUTRÉ artists' colonies possible."—Florence King, American author

surreal (suh-REEL). Possessing a quality that makes something seem unreal; strange; bizarre; almost other worldly.
"He seemed to toss them all into the mixed salads of his poetry with the same indifference to form and logic, the same domesticated SURREALISM, that characterized much of the American avant-garde of the period."
—Frank O'Hara, American poet

NOUNS

chimera (kih-MEER-uh). An object, place, event, or combination of things so strange, odd, and improbable that it logically should not exist in the real world—and yet, it does.
"What a CHIMERA then is humankind. What a novelty! What a monster, what a chaos!"—Blaise Pascal, French philosopher

eidolon (eye-DOH-luhn). A phantom or apparition; or, the image of an ideal.
"By a route obscure and lonely, / Haunted by ill angels only, / Where an EIDOLON, named Night, / On a black throne reigns upright."—Edgar Allan Poe, American author and poet

metaphysics (met-uh-FIZ-iks). The study of arguments, thoughts, and principles based primarily on thinking and abstract reasoning rather than hard facts that can be demonstrated through physical evidence.
"During my METAPHYSICS final, I cheated by looking into the soul of the person sitting next to me."—Woody Allen, American film director, writer, and comedian

VERBS

postulate (POSS-chuh-layt). To arrive at a theory, belief, hypothesis, or principle based upon an analysis of known facts.
Darwin POSTULATED his theory of evolution by natural selection many years before publishing The Origin of Species *in 1859.*

zen (ZEHN). Generally speaking, to figure out the answer to a difficult problem with a flash of sudden insight.
After days of indecision regarding which gala to attend on a particular night, Danielle managed to ZEN the answer and make her choice.

ANTONYMS

orthodox (OR-thuh-dox). Mainstream; conventional; adhering to the strictest interpretation of a law or religion.
ORTHODOX medicine has long ignored the obvious effect diet and nutrition have on health and illness.

sacrilegious (sak-reh-LIJ-uss). Openly insulting or disrespectful to the beliefs, religion, ideas, and practices of others—especially the ones they hold most sacred.
Bryson's insistence that Miró is more collectible than Warhol is positively SACRILEGIOUS.

108. Inevitable

(in-EV-uh-tuh-bull), adjective

Unavoidable; sure to occur; certain; necessary.

ADJECTIVES

assured (ah-SHOORD). Certain; guaranteed; with great confidence.
"Just as I know the sun will rise tomorrow," my lawyer told me, "you can be ASSURED that you'll be acquitted."

ineluctable (in-eh-LUCK-tuh-bull). Unavoidable, inevitable, with a sense of being unfortunate, sad, or even tragic.
Our inability to procure Pratesi linens for our Colorado ski lodge created an INELUCTABLE sadness among the members of our family.

inescapable (in-eh-SKAY-puh-bull). Incapable of being avoided, ignored, or escaped.
"We are caught in an INESCAPABLE network of mutuality, tied in a single garment of destiny."—Martin Luther King, Jr., American minister and civil-rights leader

inexorable (in-EK-sur-uh-bull). Unstoppable; relentless; persistent.
"I know enough to know that most of the visible signs of aging are the result of the INEXORABLE victory of gravity over tissue."—Isaac Asimov, Russian-born American author and biochemist

irrevocable (ih-REV-uh-kuh-bull). Not to be recalled or revoked; unalterable.
"Education is our greatest opportunity to give an IRREVOCABLE gift to the next generation."—Ernie Fletcher, governor of Kentucky and U.S. representative

obligatory (uh-BLIG-uh-tor-ee). Having the nature of an obligation; binding; required; mandatory.
By making taxes OBLIGATORY, we've made them inevitable.

VERBS

ordain (or-DAYN). To decree; order; predetermine.
John felt that fate had ORDAINED that he would encounter his minister at the worst possible time.

ANTONYMS

adventitious (add-vin-TISH-us). Arising or occurring sporadically or in unusual locations; accidental.
Every time I plant a garden, ADVENTITIOUS wildflowers pop up to ruin my design.

aleatory (A-lee-uh-tore-ee). Unplanned, spontaneous, on the spur of the moment rather than deliberately thought out and carefully considered; dependent on luck, randomness, or chance.
Most sporting events have rules that attempt to eliminate or at least diminish ALEATORY factors so the skill of the participants becomes the primary influence on the outcome.

109. Insane

(in-SANE), adjective

Not sane; mentally ill or deranged; completely senseless.

ADJECTIVES

frenetic (fruh-NET-ik). Wild; frenzied; excessively excited.
Wilbur's FRENETIC behavior has resulted in hospitalization on more than one occasion.

ludicrous (LOO-dih-kruss). Absurd to the point of being laughable; obviously implausible or impractical.
Your proposal that I accept a 75 percent pay cut is LUDICROUS, Mr. Robinson.

maniacal (muh-NYE-uh-kull). Overly emphatic; frenzied; having a fanatical devotion to a certain pursuit.
Chuck's obsession with baseball statistics bordered on the MANIACAL.

non compos mentis (non KAHM-puhs MEN-tiss). Not in one's right mind.
When Bryce suggested he was considering the ministry rather than joining the family bond business, we were certain he was NON COMPOS MENTIS.

pathological (path-uh-LOJ-ih-kuhl). Involving or caused by disease; evidencing or caused by an abnormal or extreme condition.
Diane's PATHOLOGICAL need for attention has caused her, on more than one occasion, to plant lies about herself in the society pages.

quixotic (kwik-SOT-ik). Absurdly romantic; impractical; impulsive and rash; in the manner of Cervantes's character Don Quixote.
We all loved Arthur dearly but could not support his continual QUIXOTIC quests to save the environment.

unhinged (uhn-HINJD). Confused; disordered; distraught; unbalanced.
Rose became UNHINGED at the news of the death of her college roommate.

NOUNS

dementia (dih-MEN-shuh). A mental illness characterized by loss of reason.
Owing to the deceased's DEMENTIA at the time the will was signed, there was considerable legal wrangling over the estate.

imbecility (im-buh-SILL-ih-tee). Foolishness; simplemindedness.
Although he disdained the IMBECILITY of mainstream television, Arnie was not above an occasional viewing of Keeping Up with the Kardashians.

megalomania (meg-uh-lo-MAY-nee-uh). A psychopathological condition in which a person is obsessed with fantasies of riches, grandeur, or authority; people whose ambitions and sense of self-importance are overblown.
Some have interpreted the tycoon's purchase of the old castle as an uncharacteristically bad real estate deal; I see it as pure MEGALOMANIA.

quirk (KWIRK). A peculiarity of one's personality or manner.
One of the most omnipresent QUIRKS of the nouveau riche is that they still ask the price of a luxury item, rather than simply offering to purchase it.

sociopath (SO-see-uh-path). A person who, because of mental illness, lacks restraint or moral responsibility toward fellow members of society.
Although motion pictures and popular fiction have shown an unending fascination with serial killers, the fact is that such SOCIOPATHS are quite rare.

ANTONYMS

lucid (LOO-sid). Possessed of a clear mental state; having full use of one's faculties; intelligible.
Although he lost consciousness for a few minutes, Glenn was LUCID before the ambulance arrived.

rational (RASH-uh-nul). Having the ability to reason logically without emotion.
"Man is a RATIONAL animal who always loses his temper when he is called upon to act in accordance with the dictates of reason."—Oscar Wilde, Irish poet, novelist, and dramatist

110. Insensitive

(in-SEN-sih-tiv), adjective

Lacking in human sensibility; not capable of being impressed or influenced.

ADJECTIVES

aloof (uh-LOOF). Indifferent or uninterested; unsociable.
Chuck's ALOOF attitude at our dinner party made us wonder if our usually talkative friend was trying to tell us something.

blithe (blythe). Cheerful or merry in disposition; carefree or indifferent; unconcerned with petty cares or problems.
Rod dismissed the accountant's objections with a BLITHE wave of his hand.

callous (KAL-uss). Unfeeling; insensitive; hardened.
*The chauffeur couldn't understand how Mr. Jensen could be so CALLOUS
as to ride by the crowd of homeless people every day without taking the least
notice of them.*

pachydermatous (pak-uh-DER-mah-tus). Having a thick skin; not sensitive
to criticism, ridicule, etc.
As a used car salesman, Ed had developed a PACHYDERMATOUS outlook on life.

reflexive (reh-FLEK-siv). Happening through reflex or habit rather than
considered action.
*We don't mean to act imperiously toward the nouveau riche; it's just a
REFLEXIVE and conditioned response.*

stoic (STOH-ik). Able to endure pain or suffering without complaining.
"He soldiered through his duties with what looked like cheerful STOICISM."
—Thomas Pynchon, American author

stolid (STALL-id). Unemotional and impassive.
Thomas's STOLID demeanor hides the heart of a jet-setting playboy.

ANTONYMS

impressionable (im-PRESH-uh-nuh-bull). Easily affected by impressions;
capable of being influenced; sensitive.
*Brian was a good friend and quite bright, but he was as IMPRESSIONABLE as
the average twelve-year-old child.*

susceptible (suh-SEP-tuh-bull). Easily affected emotionally; having a
sensitive nature or feelings; responsive.
*"History has informed us that bodies of men as well as individuals are
SUSCEPTIBLE of the spirit of tyranny."—Thomas Jefferson, American president*

111. Insular

(IN-suh-ler), adjective

Self-contained and therefore isolated from the world and unaffected by outside influences, usually to one's detriment.

ADJECTIVES

geopolitical (jee-oh-poh-LIH-tih-kull). Anything having to do with the politics affecting the relationships of two or more countries, especially when influenced by geographical factors.
GEOPOLITICAL instability in the Middle East is fueling rising crude oil prices.

hermetic (her-MET-ik). Isolated, or unaffected by outside influences.
"Reality, whether approached imaginatively or empirically, remains a surface, HERMETIC."—Samuel Beckett, Irish writer, dramatist, and poet

monastic (muh-NAS-tik). Relating to the practice of withdrawing from society to live a quiet, contemplative life, often dedicated to religious faith.
Saint Pachomius founded the first organized Christian MONASTIC community.

NOUNS

cabotage (KAB-uh-tazh). The right of a country to control all air traffic flying in its skies.
After 9/11, CABOTAGE became a major concern of New York City and its mayor.

isolationism (eye-suh-LAY-shin-iz-um). A foreign policy in which a country deliberately keeps its relationships and interactions with other nations to a bare minimum, effectively isolating itself from world affairs.
In the early twentieth century, American ISOLATIONISM stopped the U.S. from joining the League of Nations.

jingoism (JIN-go-iz-um). Extreme nationalism, backed up by the explicit or implied threat of military force; more broadly, extreme enthusiasm and support for an idea or position without being open to contrary arguments or notions.
We cannot countenance JINGOISM, especially since it has such a negative impact on overseas markets.

separatists (SEP-rah-tists). Those who believe a particular region or group should be separated from a larger whole.
Some Canadian SEPARATISTS want Québec to be a separate nation from the rest of Canada.

solipsism (SOLL-ip-sihz-um). The notion that one's own experiences and thoughts are the only source of true knowledge.
The SOLIPSISM of some members of the leisure class is distasteful to those of us who, for example, know what our servants need even better than they do.

ANTONYMS

acculturation (ah-kul-chuh-RAY-shin). The process of adapting to a different culture.
Just because sushi makes me queasy, that doesn't mean I'm opposed to ACCULTURATION.

disseminate (diss-SEM-in-ayt). To distribute something so as to make it available to a large population or area.
The Internet is rapidly replacing newspapers as the primary medium for the DISSEMINATION of news.

éclat (a-KLAW). Great public acclaim; or, great public notoriety.
Although they are the height of Paris fashion, Martina's five-inch heels earned her much ÉCLAT in the society pages.

globalization (glow-bull-ih-ZAY-shun). The movement toward a true world economy with open and free trading across national borders.
"Proponents of GLOBALIZATION insist that, as trade and investment move across borders, economic efficiencies raise the standards of living on both sides of the exchange."—Arthur Goldwag, American author

populism (POP-yuh-liz-um). A political movement or policy that appeals to the masses—the average working man or woman—not the upper class.
"Being naked approaches being revolutionary; going barefoot is mere POPULISM."—John Updike, American novelist and literary critic

urbane (ur-BANE). Suave, sophisticated, refined, cosmopolitan, and well versed in the ways of high society.
Even in his knock-around tennis whites, Brett always manages to appear URBANE.

112. Insult

(in-SULT), verb

To attack the feelings of another; to treat with scorn and indignity.

ADJECTIVES

derogatory (dih-ROG-uh-tor-ee). Tending to lessen or impair someone or something; disparaging and negative.
Butch's DEROGATORY remarks about my girlfriend were meant to goad me into a fight, but I was determined to keep my cool.

insolent (IN-suh-luhnt). Rude and arrogant; insulting and contemptuous.
Her INSOLENT retorts to Joan's well-intentioned queries stunned the dinner party.

pejorative (pih-JOR-uh-tiv). Insulting; meant as a put-down or to belittle.
"Wordsmith" is a corporate term used to denote someone who is a good writer, but professional writers see it as PEJORATIVE.

NOUNS

defamation (def-uh-MAY-shun). False, baseless attack on a person's or group's reputation.
After the last of the magazine's articles on her, Virginia decided she had put up with enough DEFAMATION and decided to sue.

umbrage (UM-brij). To take exception to and be offended by a comment or action seen as a slight or insult.
"I take UMBRAGE with people who post comments on my blog that are patently false," Bob said.

VERBS

denigrate (DEN-ih-grayt). Insult; put down; demean; belittle.
"Everything we shut our eyes to, everything we run away from, everything we deny, DENIGRATE or despise, serves to defeat us in the end."—Henry Miller, American author and painter

malign (muh-LINE). To defame; to besmirch (the reputation of).
The much-MALIGNED team owner's decision to trade his star quarterback turned out to be one of the best moves he ever made.

traduce (truh-DOOCE). To speak maliciously of; slander.
We have snubbed Katrina permanently because she has, at one time or another, TRADUCED each one of us in the society pages.

vilify (VILL-ih-fy). To defame; to slander.
My opponent's ceaseless attempts to VILIFY me during this campaign reached a new low when she accused me of being a neo-Nazi.

ANTONYMS

felicitate (fih-LISS-ih-tayt). To compliment; to congratulate; wish happiness to.
"Remind me," said Robin's mother, "to FELICITATE your sister on having received an 'A' in biology."

plaudit (PLAW-dit). An expression of gratitude or praise; applause.
"Not in the shouts and PLAUDITS of the throng, but in ourselves, are triumph and defeat."—Henry Wadsworth Longfellow, American poet

113. Introduce

(in-truh-DOOCE), verb

To put into place; insert.

VERBS

infuse (in-FYOOZ). To introduce; cause to penetrate; instill.
The dynamic commissioner INFUSED a new sense of pride into the beleaguered department.

insinuate (in-SIN-yu-ayt). To introduce slowly, indirectly, but skillfully.
I had great confidence that we were headed in the right direction until the guide's comments INSINUATED doubts in my mind.

intercalate (in-TUR-kuh-layt). To interpose between or among existing elements; to insert one or more days into the calendar.
The book's design was improved by INTERCALATING quotations and aphorisms between sections of straight text.

interject (in-ter-JEKT). To insert in between; interpose.
My mother always tried to INTERJECT herself when my brother and I were fighting.

interpolate (in-TER-puh-layt). To introduce something—often something unnecessary or incorrect—between other things or parts.
Dexter could not help but continuously INTERPOLATE critical remarks into the descriptions of the latest Parisian designs.

interpose (in-ter-POZE). To aggressively insert unsolicited opinion, assistance, or presence into a situation.
"I hope I am not INTERPOSING," Eileen said as she walked in on our meeting—which of course, she was.

intersperse (in-ter-SPURSE). To scatter here and there; to distribute or place at intervals.
INTERSPERSED throughout the studio audience were "clappers" whose sole purpose was to motivate the rest of the crowd into laughing and applauding for the show.

intromit (in-truh-MIT). To admit; to cause to enter; put in.
"I never tire of INTROMITTING a hardboiled egg into a milk bottle, shell and all."—Raymond Sokolov

obtrude (ub-TROOD). To impose oneself or one's ideas on others.
Paul saw no problem OBTRUDING his opinions on complete strangers.

ANTONYMS

rescind (re-SIND). Take away, revoke, cancel, withdraw, remove.
The town RESCINDED all their restrictions on water use after we received two weeks of heavy rain.

revoke (rih-VOKE). To take back or withdraw; reverse; rescind.
"Knowledge is that possession that no misfortune can destroy, no authority can revoke, and no enemy can control. This makes knowledge the greatest of all freedoms."—Bryant H. McGill, American editor and author

114. Isolated

(EYE-suh-lay-ted), adjective

Separated from other persons.

ADJECTIVES

cloistered (KLOI-sturd). Secluded; isolated; removed or hidden.
Shocked by the news of the shooting on our street, we remained CLOISTERED in our house for days afterward.

hermetic (her-MET-ik). Isolated, or unaffected by outside influences.
"Reality, whether approached imaginatively or empirically, remains a surface, HERMETIC."—Samuel Beckett, Irish writer, dramatist, and poet

insular (IN-suh-ler). Self-contained and therefore isolated from the world and unaffected by outside influences, usually to one's detriment.
The Pricewaters moved from the family's traditional home to a more INSULAR compound farther up the coast.

taciturn (TASS-ih-turn). Reserved; uncommunicative; a person of few words.
"Nature is garrulous to the point of confusion, let the artist be truly TACITURN."—Paul Klee, German-born Swiss painter

NOUNS

segregation (seg-ruh-GAY-shun). The separation of people by class, race, or ethnicity, either enforced or voluntarily, geographically or by the restriction of access to facilities or services.
As the judge seemed doomed to have to point out for the rest of his life, his order affected only those school districts whose officials deliberately practiced SEGREGATION in violation of law—not SEGREGATION that was purely the result of existing demographic patterns.

solitude (SAWL-ih-tood). The state of seclusion.
Although Peter maintained that he thought better in SOLITUDE, we considered him antisocial.

VERBS

quarantine (KWOR-un-teen). To set apart; to isolate from others in order to prevent the spread of disease.
An elementary knowledge of public health procedures would have led you to QUARANTINE this area immediately, Dr. Miller.

ANTONYMS

commingle (kuh-MING-guhl). To mix together; combine.
"All human beings are COMMINGLED out of good and evil."—Robert Louis Stevenson, Scottish essayist, poet, and author

integrate (IN-tih-grayt). To bring together or combine parts into a whole; to unite or combine.
"If we make room for everybody, there will be more room for everybody. An INTEGRATED America, where each and every American is treated with the same dignity and respect, is a better America for everyone."—General Wesley Clark, American general

115. Jaunt

(JAWNT), noun

A short journey taken for pleasure.

ADJECTIVES

gamesome (GAYM-suhm). Playful and frolicsome.
"[Nature] is GAMESOME and good, / But of mutable mood,— / No dreary repeater now and again, / She will be all things to all men."—Ralph Waldo Emerson, American poet, essayist, and transcendentalist

peripatetic (per-ih-pa-TET-ik). Wandering from career to career, job to job, company to company, or place to place, seemingly without a clear goal or definiteness of purpose.
While waiting to receive his trust fund at age thirty, Giles lived a PERIPATETIC lifestyle.

wayfaring (WAY-fair-ing). Traveling on foot.
We spent many WAYFARING weekends during our month-long jaunt in France last year.

NOUNS

disport (dih-SPORT). A diversion or amusement.
Felicia has turned the act of arguing with the proprietors of her favorite boutiques into a DISPORT.

pied-à-terre (pyay-duh-TARE). A second home or apartment, usually small, used as a place to stay for short trips to the location in lieu of renting a hotel room.
We were amazed that Alison and her family could survive in a PIED-À-TERRE containing just 2,500 square feet.

wanderlust (WAWN-der-lust). A strong and innate desire to travel far from home. *"In our WANDERLUST, we are lovers looking for consummation."—Anatole Broyard, literary critic for the* New York Times

VERBS

gallivant (GAL-ih-vant). To wander widely; to constantly travel to many different places, without an itinerary or plan; to freely go wherever and whenever the mood strikes you, and doing so frequently.
Some accuse us of GALLIVANTING around the world, but cultural knowledge is de rigueur for cocktail conversation.

gambol (GAM-bull). To run, skip, or jump about in a playful or joyous fashion. *"We all have these places where shy humiliations GAMBOL on sunny afternoons."—W. H. Auden, Anglo-American poet*

meander (me-AN-duhr). To wander aimlessly.
We fired that particular servant because he MEANDERED far too slowly from task to task.

wend (WEND). To go; to proceed.
"As they WEND away / A voice is heard singing / Of Kitty, or Katy, / As if the name meant once / All love, all beauty."—Philip Larkin, British poet, novelist, and jazz critic

ANTONYMS

laggard (LAG-urd). A person who loiters; one who is sluggish and reacts slowly.
"Reviewers . . . must normally function as huff-and-puff artists blowing LAGGARD theatergoers stageward."—Walter Kerr, American theater critic

116. Jinn

(JIN), noun

A mythical creature created from fire long before man inhabited the Earth.

ADJECTIVES

arcane (ar-KAYN). Strange and mysterious; understood by only a few.
Bill's ARCANE knowledge of all Lexus models and their accessories is just a waste of gray matter.

Brobdingnagian (brahb-ding-NAG-ian). Of enormous size; huge.
Andre the Giant was a man of BROBDINGNAGIAN proportions, standing seven-foot-five-inches and weighing over five hundred pounds.

resplendent (reh-SPLEN-dent). Garbed or decorated in lush fabrics and rich, vibrant colors.
The bride was RESPLENDENT in a beaded silk gown.

transcendent (tran-SEN-dent). Going beyond normal everyday experience; existing beyond the known physical universe and its limitations.
"Genius . . . means the TRANSCENDENT capacity of taking trouble."
—Thomas Carlyle, Scottish satirist and historian

NOUNS

allegory (AL-eh-gor-ee). A story told to communicate a hidden meaning or deeper theme.
Many of the Grimm Brothers' fairy tales are clear ALLEGORIES of the consequences of children's rotten behavior.

juggernaut (JUG-er-nawt). A large, overpowering, destructive force.
Once he begins arguing about the superiority of Maseratis, Jefferson becomes a JUGGERNAUT, capable of deflating anyone else's arguments.

legerdemain (le-juhr-duh-MAYN). Magic tricks; or, generally speaking, trickery and deception.
The Wilkinsons are one of the few of our families whose initial wealth did not come as a result of financial LEGERDEMAIN.

leviathan (le-VY-uh-thun). A gigantic creature, structure, or thing, awe-inspiring in its sheer size.
"Wilson looked out through the window at the LEVIATHAN glitter of the terminal."
—Richard Matheson, American science fiction writer

ANTONYMS

Lilliputian (lil-uh-PEW-shen). Small in stature; tiny in comparison to one's peers.
Jules Vern's LILLIPUTIAN appearance made people treat him like a child.

minimalism (MIN-ih-mull-iz-um). A school of art in which "less is more"—clean and uncluttered paintings; sculpture with simple lines; fiction written in a lean and spare style; and music with uncomplicated scores and minimal instruments.
John Cage's MINIMALIST composition 4'33" consists of four and a half minutes of silence.

117. Judgment

(JUHJ-muhnt), noun

A formed opinion; a decision made by objective deliberation; the capacity to judge.

ADJECTIVES

sagacious (suh-GAY-shuss). Perceptive; showing sound judgment.
Brian is the perfect candidate for chairman of the board; experienced, patient, and SAGACIOUS enough to help us counter the threat from our competitor.

NOUNS

acumen (uh-CUE-men). Keenness of judgment; the ability to make quick, accurate decisions and evaluations; characterized by rapid discernment and insight.
After only two years as a restaurant owner, Clyde developed a remarkable business ACUMEN; in a "bad location," he attracted many customers.

inference (IN-fer-ence). The process of reaching a logical conclusion by examining and analyzing the evidence.
Watson solved cases through INFERENCE, while Sherlock Holmes was seemingly gifted with flashes of brilliant insight.

noesis (no-EE-sis). The functioning of the intellect; the exercise of reason.
Researchers in the field of artificial intelligence dedicate much of their time to the study of human NOESIS.

osmosis (oz-MOW-siss). A subtle and effortless assimilation of ideas or influences.
Just hanging out with Bob, who was an A student, seemed to help Vincent improve his grades, as if he were learning what Bob knew through OSMOSIS.

rumination (roo-muh-NAY-shun). The act of thinking about something in great detail, weighing the pros and cons over and over in your mind.
For busy people under stress, RUMINATION after going to bed is a frequent contributor to insomnia.

VERBS

glean (GLEEN). To discover or learn slowly and deliberately.
Jacob GLEANED from the drop in Ferrari sales that a looming recession even had some of his social contacts feeling nervous.

ANTONYMS

impolitic (im-PAWL-uh-tik). Not prudent; injudicious; unwise.
After a few drinks, Uncle Roland has an unfortunate habit of making IMPOLITIC remarks about my father's failed business ventures.

indiscreet (in-dih-SKREET). Lacking good judgment and prudence; apt to talk about things that others would like left private.
Don't get alcohol near Melanie. It makes her go from prudent to INDISCREET in less than sixty seconds!

indiscriminate (in-dih-SKRIM-uh-net). Lacking clear judgment and careful distinction; haphazard; random.
The INDISCRIMINATE shelving of books made it almost impossible to do any successful browsing in the bookshop.

myopic (my-OP-ik). Narrow-mindedness or short-sightedness in one's views; lack of discernment.
Your MYOPIC views will win you few votes during the election, Senator.

promiscuous (prom-ih-SKYOO-uhs). Not restricted by type; indiscriminate; casual; irregular.
The comparatively tolerant attitude toward the PROMISCUOUS behavior of the late 1970s and early 1980s changed dramatically with the onset of the AIDS crisis.

See also: Learn, Think, Understanding

118. Kill

(KIL), verb

To cause the death of; deprive of life; put an end to.

NOUNS

fratricide (FRAT-rih-syd). The act of killing a brother; the murder of a male sibling.
It is only when Hamlet is told of the king's FRATRICIDE that a tragic chain of events is initiated.

genocide (JENN-uh-syd). The deliberate, systematic destruction of a culture, people, or nation.
The Holocaust has been the most dramatic example of a government attempting to commit GENOCIDE against an entire people—in this case, the Jews.

herbicide (URB-ih-syd). A chemical that kills plants, especially that which eradicates weeds.
Although originally described as a comparatively harmless HERBICIDE, Agent Orange was (as thousands of soldiers learned much later) anything but.

sororicide (suh-RAWR-uh-syd). The act of killing one's own sister.
Once past their teenage years, most sisters get over the urge to commit SORORICIDE.

uxoricide (uk-SOR-ih-syd). The crime of murdering one's wife.
Eventually, the defendant was acquitted of UXORICIDE; his wife's death was ruled a suicide.

vaticide (VAT-uh-syd). The act of murdering a prophet.
Tom took the reviewer's negative article on his religious poetry as an act tantamount to VATICIDE.

VERBS

decapitate (dee-KAP-ih-tayt). To remove the head of.
Although the guillotine was initially proposed as a humane method of execution, the idea of using a machine to DECAPITATE criminals now strikes most people as barbaric.

defenestrate (de-FEN-uh-strayt). To throw something or someone through or from a window.
Successful completion of the plan to DEFENESTRATE the dictator depended upon timing, luck, and courage.

fumigate (FYOO-mih-gayt). To release fumes in order to get rid of insects or other pests.
We had the place FUMIGATED, used sound waves, and set dozens of traps, but our house continued to be plagued by cockroaches.

immolate (IM-uh-layt). To kill as if as a sacrifice, especially by fire.
The monk's dramatic act of self-IMMOLATION made headlines around the world.

lapidate (LAP-ih-dayt). To stone to death.
Because of worldwide outrage and diplomatic pressure, the decision to LAPIDATE a person for infidelity was rescinded.

martyr (MAR-ter). To put to death for adhering to a belief or particular faith.
Many religions have historically seen fit to MARTYR disbelievers.

ANTONYMS

contrive (kuhn-TRYV). To invent; design; fabricate; to bring about.
"There is nothing which has yet been CONTRIVED by man, by which so much happiness is produced as by a good tavern."—Samuel Johnson, English poet, critic and writer

spawn (SPAWN). To bring forth or be the source of; to give birth to; to give rise to.
The national games served to SPAWN athletes for future Olympic competitions.

119. Kind

(KYND), adjective

Possessing sympathetic or generous qualities; of a benevolent nature.

ADJECTIVES

avuncular (A-VUNG-kyew-ler).Tolerant; genial; like an uncle.
*Myron's AVUNCULAR personality makes women think of him as a friend,
not as a lover.*

beneficent (beh-NEF-ih-sent). Magnanimous in action, purpose, or speech.
*In a BENEFICENT gesture, the neighborhood raised $10,000 to help pay for the
young boy's leukemia treatments.*

benevolent (beh-NEV-uh-lent). Characterized by feelings of charity and
good will.
*As spring approaches and the weather warms, it seems that BENEVOLENT
attitudes are in greater supply.*

benign (beh-NYN). Softhearted; gentle; mild; not harmful.
We thought Amanda BENIGN until she began to inflate her family pedigree.

magnanimous (mag-NAN-ih-muss). Forgiving; unselfish; noble.
*"In a serious struggle there is no worse cruelty than to be MAGNANIMOUS at an
inopportune time."—Leon Trotsky, Bolshevik revolutionary and Marxist theorist*

NOUNS

bonhomie (bon-uh-MEE). A good-natured, genial manner.
*Even though he has no family pedigree, Walker is accepted into our group
because of his contagious BONHOMIE.*

chivalry (SHIV-ul-ree). Brave, kind, courteous, or gentlemanly behavior.
*"We hear much of CHIVALRY of men towards women; but . . . it vanishes like
dew before the summer sun when one of us comes into competition with the
manly sex."—Martha Coston, American author*

ANTONYMS

malevolent (muh-LEV-uh-luhnt). Wishing harm or evil to others; having ill will; malicious.
"Writers take words seriously . . . and they struggle to steer their own through the crosswinds of meddling editors and careless typesetters and obtuse and MALEVO-LENT reviewers into the lap of the ideal reader."—John Updike, American writer

malignant (muh-LIG-nuhnt). Having an evil influence; wishing evil; very harmful.
"Doubtless criticism was originally benignant, pointing out the beauties of a work rather that its defects. The passions of men have made it MALIGNANT."—Henry Wadsworth Longfellow, American poet

120. Kismet

(KIZ-met), noun

Fate or destiny.

ADJECTIVES

ineffable (in-EFF-uh-bull). Something so fantastic, incredible, or difficult to grasp it cannot be described in words.
Poet Ezra Pound wrote of "the infinite and INEFFABLE quality of the British empire."

NOUNS

afflatus (uh-FLAY-tuss). Inspiration that seems to come from divine origin.
The Nobel Prize–winning novelist attributed her abilities to AFFLATUS, rather than to her own abilities.

humanism (HEW-man-iz-um). The philosophy or belief that the highest ideals of human existence can be fulfilled without regard to religion or supernatural intervention.
"The four characteristics of HUMANISM are curiosity, a free mind, belief in good taste, and belief in the human race."—E.M. Forster, English novelist

manifest destiny (MAN-ih-fest DESS-tin-ee). Expansion into foreign lands, justified as being necessary or benevolent.

"It's not greed and ambition that makes wars—it's goodness. Wars are always fought for the best of reasons, for liberation or MANIFEST DESTINY, always against tyranny and always in the best interests of humanity."—James Garner in The Americanization of Emily

ANTONYMS

iconoclast (eye-KAHN-uh-klasst). An individual who is contrarian in thought, rebellious in spirit, and oppositional, and who applies himself to battling established institutions, existing governments, religious doctrine, and popular notions and beliefs.

The late George Carlin saw the role of the comic in society as one of ICONOCLAST.

121. Kowtow

(kao-TAO), verb

To give in to someone's every wish; to grovel and behave in a subservient manner.

ADJECTIVES

complaisant (kuhm-PLAY-zuhnt). Agreeable and eager to please.
Eleanor is far too COMPLAISANT with common strangers.

conciliatory (kon-SILL-ee-ah-tore-ee). Actions or words meant to settle a dispute or resolve a conflict in a manner that leaves no hard feelings on either side.
"If you are not very clever, you should be CONCILIATORY."—Benjamin Disraeli, British statesman and literary figure

malleable (MAL-yuh-bull). Easily molded into different shapes; easily influenced to change one's opinion or actions.
"I did not know that mankind was suffering for want of gold. I have seen a little of it. I know that it is very MALLEABLE, but not so MALLEABLE as wit."
—Henry David Thoreau, American author and transcendentalist

NOUNS

appeasement (uh-PEEZ-meant). The act of making others happy by agreeing to their demands.
Charlene realized too late that her policy of APPEASEMENT might please Warren, but it would not cause him to treat her with more respect.

capitulation (kuh-pitch-uh-LAY-shun). The act of surrendering or giving up.
Ross offered James no CAPITULATION during the confrontational lacrosse game.

homage (HOM-ij). Respect paid and deference shown to a superior or other person one admires, fears, or wishes to emulate or praise.
Gary took black and white photos with a nondigital camera in HOMAGE to Ansel Adams, whose works he greatly admired.

zealot (ZEL-it). A rabid follower; a true believer; a fanatical advocate.
"What a noble aim is that of the ZEALOT who tortures himself like a madman in order to desire nothing, love nothing, feel nothing, and who, if he succeeded, would end up a complete monster!"—Denis Diderot, French philosopher

VERBS

abjure (ab-JOOR). To renounce or turn your back on a belief or position you once held near and dear.
Once Jodi tasted my mouth-watering, medium-rare filet mignon, she ABJURED the vegetarian lifestyle forever.

assuage (uh-SWAYJ). To put someone at ease; to comfort or soothe; to erase doubts and fears.
"But history must not yet tell the tragedies enacted here; let time intervene in some measure to ASSUAGE and lend an azure tint to them."—Henry David Thoreau, American author and transcendentalist

propitiate (pro-PISH-ee-ayt). To win over; to gain the approval and admiration of.
"The life that went on in [many of the street's houses] seemed to me made up of evasions and negations; shifts to save cooking, to save washing and cleaning, devices to PROPITIATE the tongue of gossip."—Willa Cather, American author

ANTONYMS

anathema (uh-NATH-eh-muh). A person or thing regarded as wrong in the highest degree; a loathsome, detestable entity.
Religious services were an ANATHEMA to Russ, what with him being a dedicated atheist and all.

intransigent (in-TRAN-zih-jent). Stubborn; refusing to consider opinions other than one's own.
"Lamont stared for a moment in frustration but Burt's expression was a clearly INTRANSIGENT one now."—Isaac Asimov, Russian-born American author and biochemist

122. Laconic

(luh-KAWN-ik), adjective

Of few words; expressing oneself with an economy of words.

ADJECTIVES

austere (aw-STEER). Stern; grim and lacking humor or warmth; clean and unornamented; severe or strict in manner.
In the movie Dead Poets Society, *Robin Williams clashes with an AUSTERE headmaster at a private boys' school.*

farouche (fah-ROOSH). To become sullen, shy, or withdrawn in the presence of company.
His FAROUCHE demeanor gave people the impression that he didn't like them, when in fact, he was merely an introvert.

opaque (oh-PAYK). Hard to understand; obscure.
"The bottom of being is left logically OPAQUE to us, as something which we simply come upon and find, and about which (if we wish to act) we should pause and wonder as little as possible."—William James, American psychologist and philosopher

quiescent (kwee-ESS-ehnt). Being at rest, inactive, or motionless.
"There is a brief time for sex, and a long time when sex is out of place. But when it is out of place as an activity there still should be the large and quiet space in the consciousness where it lives QUIESCENT."—D.H. Lawrence, British author

taciturn (TASS-ih-turn). Reserved; uncommunicative; a person of few words.
"Nature is garrulous to the point of confusion, let the artist be truly TACITURN."—Paul Klee, German-born Swiss painter

ANTONYMS

badinage (bah-dih-NAHZH). Light, good-natured, even playful banter.
"If you don't care for me, you can move out now. I'm frankly not up to
BADINAGE."—Harlan Ellison, American author

garrulity (gah-ROO-lih-tee). The habit of talking way too much.
"The interview is an intimate conversation between journalist and politician wherein
the journalist seeks to take advantage of the GARRULITY of the politician and the
politician of the credulity of the journalist"—Emory Klein, American journalist

natter (NATT-er). To talk ceaselessly; babble.
The way Emily NATTERS endlessly about her family's new yacht is revolting to
those of us who have owned several yachts over the years.

palaver (pa-LAH-ver). A rambling, meandering stream-of-consciousness
conversation spoken to prove or make a point.
Don't ask Eileen about collecting art. The result will be twenty minutes of
mind-numbing PALAVER.

prattle (PRAT-l). To babble; to talk nonstop without regard as to whether
what you are saying makes sense or is of any interest to the listener.
"Infancy conforms to nobody: all conform to it, so that one babe commonly
makes four or five out of the adults who PRATTLE and play to it."—Ralph Waldo
Emerson, American poet, essayist, and transcendentalist

123. Language

(LANG-gwij), noun

A collection of words and the rules and methods for their use common to
a people living in a community, geographical area, or nation; the means
of communicating through sounds and symbols; speech.

ADJECTIVES

colloquial (kuh-LOW-kwee-ul). Informal, conversational, everyday language.
"COLLOQUIAL poetry is to the real art as the barber's wax dummy is to
sculpture."—Ezra Pound, American expatriate poet

demotic (dih-MAH-tik). Relating to simplified, common language.
Eileen always avoids DEMOTIC speech because she does not want to be mistaken for someone from the middle class.

proverbial (pruh-VER-bee-ul). Calling to mind (a familiar) proverb; showing an immediate parallel with a well-known saying, story, or maxim.
Stan considered his younger brother about as useful as the PROVERBIAL fifth wheel.

sesquipedalian (ses-kwi-pih-DAL-yin). Preferring or having long, complex words with many syllables.
"Recently a strange whimsy has started to creep in among the SESQUIPEDALIAN prose of scientific journals."—Stephen Hall, American architect

stilted (STILL-tihd). Stiff and formal; rigid and unspontaneous in nature.
The letter was composed in such STILTED, elaborately correct language that Sergeant Ryan surmised it was written by someone whose native language was not English.

NOUNS

aphasia (uh-FAY-zhuh). The inability, brought on by brain damage, to understand words and/or ideas.
After his car accident, Marcus retained all of his physical faculties but suffered minor APHASIA that made it difficult for him to speak coherently.

argot (ar-GO). Special words and idioms used by particular groups or professions.
With the advent of text messaging, it has become even more difficult to follow the ARGOT of teenagers.

circumlocution (sir-kum-low-KEW-shun). Language that is pompous, overly formal, wordy, and redundant.
Grant's CIRCUMLOCUTION was an attempt to suggest that he attended a prep school, but all of us know he is a product of public education.

etymology (et-ih-MOLL-uh-gee). The study of the development and history of words; the derivation of a word.
I took a little Greek in school, so I think I can make an educated guess at this word's ETYMOLOGY.

euphemism (YU-feh-miz-im). A synonym that is less offensive than the word it is used to replace.
"The doctor told me I'm big boned," said Chuck defensively. "That's just a EUPHEMISM for fat," his brother said meanly.

euphuism (YU-few-iz-im). Ornate, flowery, overly elaborate language, often making the exact meaning difficult to discern.
Felicia's words are full of EUPHUISM, particularly when describing the architecture of her family's various houses.

homonym (HOM-uh-nim). A word with the same pronunciation and spelling as another but with a different meaning.
Most serious writing does not use HOMONYMS except occasionally by accident.

lexicon (LEK-sih-kahn). The language or vocabulary of a specialized discipline or profession.
"In the LEXICON of lip-smacking, an epicure is fastidious in his choice and enjoyment of food, just a soupçon more expert than a gastronome."
—William Safire, American journalist and presidential speechwriter

neologism (nee-AHL-uh-jiz-uhm). A new word, or an "old" word used in a new way.
William Shakespeare coined such NEOLOGISMS as "gossip," "swagger," and "domineering."

nomenclature (NO-men-klay-cherr). A labeling or naming system used in a specialized field or industry.
Even an activity as seemingly simple as gardening has a NOMENCLATURE all its own, indecipherable to the layperson or newbie.

onomatopoeia (on-uh-mat-uh-PEE-uh). Words that sound like, or suggest, their meaning.
The spring gala, with its popping corks, fizzing champagne glasses, and thumping music was a cornucopia of ONOMATOPOEIA.

oxymoron (awk-see-MORE-on). A phrase made by combining two words that are contradictory or incongruous.
Melissa sheepishly used the OXYMORON "accidentally on purpose" to explain to her father why her emergency credit card included a charge for $500 Manolo Blahnik heels.

palindrome (PAL-in-drohm). A word or sentence that reads the same forward as backward.
In English class, Evelyn learned about PALINDROMES, including, "Madam, I'm Adam."

philology (fi-LOL-uh-gee). The study of ancient written records and texts.
Arthur's interest in linguistics and the origins of words naturally led him to a serious involvement in PHILOLOGY.

pidgin (PIJ-in). A type of language created by the interaction of two distinct languages, used to help people communicate across language barriers.
We spoke PIDGIN to each other, and I finally was able to understand how to get to the nearest bathroom.

polyglot (PAWL-ee-glot). A person who speaks a number of languages.
The president's translator, a POLYGLOT, served him well in missions to Germany, Portugal, and Mexico.

rhetoric (RET-er-ik). The art or science of using words effectively in writing or speaking as a means of communication and persuasion.
Plato called RHETORIC "the art of ruling the minds of men."

semantics (suh-MAN-tix). The science of the way meaning is communicated through language.
Whether we say the compensation will be "appropriate" or "competitive" is really a matter of SEMANTICS; we know exactly how much we intend to pay the person we finally hire.

solecism (SOLL-ih-siz-um). A violation of rules of grammar and usage.
We all waited eagerly for the president's next SOLECISM.

synecdoche (sih-NEK-duh-kee). A type of shorthand speech in which a partial description is understood by the reader or listener to represent the whole; e.g., saying "New York" in a discussion of baseball when you mean "the New York Yankees."
Marla could not stop using SYNECDOCHE after she returned from her trip to England during which she met the royal family, saying repeatedly that she had met and socialized with "the crown."

vernacular (ver-NAK-yu-ler). The language of a particular region or specific group of people.
Communicating with stockbrokers is difficult for many investors because they do not speak the VERNACULAR of the financial world.

ANTONYMS

abridge (uh-BRIJ). To shorten by decreasing the number of words; shorten; curtail.
"Many a long dispute among divines may be thus ABRIDGED: It is so. It is not so. It is so. It is not so."—Benjamin Franklin, American statesman and scientist
See also: Speech, Talk

124. Learn

(LURN), verb

To acquire knowledge or skill by study; to become well informed.

NOUNS

clerisy (KLARE-uh-see). Learned persons as a class; intellectuals collectively.
The society struggled for recognition because it could not support a CLERISY.

cognoscente (kon-yuh-SHEN-tee). Person with superior knowledge or understanding of a particular field.
As a result of my many years living in the Bordeaux region of France, I am very much a COGNOSCENTE of wine and winemaking.

intelligentsia (in-tell-ih-JENT-see-uh). The class of people who are cultured, educated, intellectual, and interested in art and literature.
"You see these gray hairs? Well, making whoopee with the INTELLIGENTSIA was the way I earned them."—Dorothy Parker, American author and poet

literati (lit-uh-RAH-tee). The segment of society made up of learned or literary men and women.
We attract the LITERATI because of our constantly carefree and exciting exploits.

luminary (LOO-muh-nair-ee). A person recognized as an inspirational leader in his or her field.
Frederick's father is a LUMINARY in the field of circumventing most income tax.

lyceum (LIE-see-um). A school or other place of learning.
"[Television] should be our LYCEUM, our Chautauqua, our Minsky's, and our Camelot."—E.B. White, American author

mentat (MEN-tat). A human being capable of performing mental tasks with the accuracy and speed of a computer. The word was invented by author Frank Herbert for his science fiction classic *Dune*.
Our accountant is a veritable MENTAT! Did you see how fast he determined all of our charitable deductions!

oracle (OR-uh-kul). Someone who is seen as wise and authoritative, who offers completely dependable counsel or advice.
After Appomattox, Grant's words seemed (much to his surprise) to be regarded as having issued from an ORACLE.

pedagogue (PED-ah-gog). A strict, humorless, no-nonsense teacher.
"The negative cautions of science are never popular. If the experimentalist would not commit himself, the social philosopher, the preacher, and the PEDAGOGUE tried the harder to give a short-cut answer."—Margaret Mead, American cultural anthropologist

polymath (PAWL-ee-math). A person with a wide range of intellectual interests or a broad base of knowledge in many different disciplines.
"I had a terrible vision: I saw an encyclopedia walk up to a POLYMATH and open him up."—Karl Kraus, Austrian writer

savant (sah-VONT). A person with a natural talent or genius in a particular field or skill.
With her family's background in finance, it was a given that Francine would be a Wall Street SAVANT.

tutelage (toot-uhl-ij). Guided instruction or protection.
It was under Dr. Clay's TUTELAGE that he came to understand how much craft was required to write a solid play.

yeshiva (yeh-SHEE-vuh). A place of instruction in the Orthodox Jewish tradition for children of elementary school age.
When the YESHIVA released its children in the afternoon, the sounds of laughter echoed through the neighborhood.

VERBS

indoctrinate (in-DOK-truh-nayt). To teach; to impart with the knowledge or views of a particular group, philosophy, or theory.
Max's earnest attempts to INDOCTRINATE me with the ideals of the Communist Party left me unimpressed.

ANTONYMS

illiteracy (ih-LIT-er-uh-see). The inability to read and write; lack of education.
"Ignorance and ILLITERACY are obviously not synonymous; even illiterate masses can cast their ballots with intelligence, once they are informed."
—*William Douglas, associate Supreme Court justice*
See also: Judgment, Think, Understanding

125. Limited

(LIM-ih-tid), adjective

Confined within bounds; restricted.

ADJECTIVES

topical (TOP-uh-kul). Having to do with matters of local or current interest.
John wanted to learn about events in the Middle East, but the newscast only covered TOPICAL occurrences.

VERBS

circumscribe (SUR-kuhm-skryb). To encircle or encompass; confine.
After the incident in the student union, our social activities were CIRCUMSCRIBED for the remainder of the semester.

constrain (kuhn-STRAYN). To force into or hold in boundaries; confine.
Alice felt the social mores of her family and friends would eventually CONSTRAIN her to a life of mediocrity and unhappiness.

constrict (kuhn-STRIKT). To make smaller or tighter by binding or compressing.
Refusing to be CONSTRICTED, Jack joyfully colored outside the lines.

delimit (dih-LIM-it). To establish or mark the boundaries or limits of; demarcate.
After squabbling with the neighbors for years, we had professional surveyors DELIMIT the property once and for all.

demarcate (dih-MAHR-kayt). To set the limits of; to distinguish; separate.
All of our working areas were DEMARCATED with cubicles of various sizes.

prescribe (prih-SKRYB). To set down or give rules or directions to be followed; direct.
We thought we could build whatever we wanted on the land, but discovered that the town had PRESCRIBED the nature of all construction.

ANTONYMS

boundless (BOWND-liss). Unlimited; infinite; vast.
"The world of reality has its limits; the world of the imagination is BOUNDLESS."—Jean-Jacques Rousseau, French philosopher and writer

fathomless (FATH-uhm-lis). Too deep to be measured; bottomless; boundless.
Try as we might, none of the students in class have stumped the professor with a question on any topic; his knowledge seems FATHOMLESS.

126. Literature

(LIT-er-uh-chur), noun

The body of writings of a specific language, people, or period; the profession and output of an author, especially creative prose or verse.

NOUNS

belles-lettres (bell-LET-ruh). Literature considered as fine art; fictional work having a solely aesthetic function.
Those who study rhetoric speak derisively of literature that exists for an aesthetic purpose only, and therefore ignore BELLES-LETTRES.

bibliomania (bib-lee-oh-MAY-nee-uh). A preoccupation with the acquisition and ownership of books.
Lauren's BIBLIOMANIA extends only to her stockpile of catalogs for exclusive shops.

bildungsroman (BILL-dungs-roh-man). A coming-of-age novel, such as *The Catcher in the Rye* or *A Portrait of the Artist as a Young Man.*
Alex has started writing a BILDUNGSROMAN about his experiences in prep school.

breviary (BREE-vee-air-ee). A brief summary or abridgement.
She called it a BREVIARY, but Lana's recounting of her family's month on the Riviera was anything but short.

corrigendum (kor-ih-JEN-dum). An error to be corrected in a manuscript.
The proofreader handed the manuscript back to Bill, who was horrified to find that it still contained hundreds of CORRIGENDA.

gazetteer (gaz-ih-TEER). A geographical index or dictionary of places organized by name.
The Rothschilds prefer their pilot simply head for the sun, rather than consult a GAZETTEER prior to short flights.

lexicography (lex-ih-KOG-ruh-fee). The compiling, writing, and editing of dictionaries.
Though he had never intended to pursue a career in LEXICOGRAPHY, Jeremy spent twenty years with Merriam-Webster, working his way up from researcher to editor.

lexicon (LEK-sih-kawn). A dictionary composed for a specific, narrowly defined (professional) audience; the vocabulary associated with a specific discipline or group.
Arthur, though not a doctor, was well versed in the LEXICON of medicine.

magnum opus (MAG-num OH-pess). A great work, especially of art or literature; the chief work of an artist or author.
All the King's Men *could be considered Robert Penn Warren's MAGNUM OPUS.*

monograph (MON-uh-graff). A scholarly article or essay on a certain topic, usually intended for an academic audience and not for the general public.
Peterson's MONOGRAPH on theoretical physics was well received in the scientific community, although it certainly makes for tough reading for the layman.

necrology (nuh-KROL-uh-jee). A list of people who have recently died; an obituary.
Benjamin scoured the long NECROLOGY for the name of his father, but it was not there.

oeuvre (OO-vruh). An artist's, writer's, or composer's body of work, treated as a whole.
Esmerelda is familiar with and adores all of Puccini's OEUVRE, but many find his operas overly mawkish.

opus (OH-puss). A major literary or musical work.
The Breckinridges commissioned the composer's next OPUS, which will be debuted at the family's fall ball.

paleography (pay-lee-OG-ruh-fee). The study of ancient writings and inscriptions.
In order to understand their discoveries, archeologists study PALEOGRAPHY.

palimpsest (PAL-imp-sest). A parchment manuscript on which the text is written over older, earlier text, much like an oil portrait or landscape painted over another painting.
The newest addition to the Pattersons' rare manuscript collection turned out to be a PALIMPSEST, covering a text nearly one thousand years old.

précis (pray-SEE). A concise summary; abridgement; abstract.
The authors were too invested in the work to be able to write an acceptable PRÉCIS.

protagonist (pro-TAG-uh-nist). The lead character in a story, play, novel, etc.
I stopped reading the book because I found the PROTAGONIST so unbelievable.

recension (ree-SEN-shun). A critical revision of a literary work.
Changes in literary tastes make a RECENSION of standard works seem like a good idea.

roman à clef (ro-MON ah KLAY). A purportedly fictional work that only thinly veils the actual experiences of the author or of characters based on real personages.
Truman Capote was ostracized by those in his circle when he published a devastating excerpt from a ROMAN À CLEF, Unanswered Prayers, that lampooned the frailties and indiscretions of the people who had been closest to him.

strophe (STRO-fee). A stanza containing lines that do not conform to the type, style, or form of the poem in which they appear.
Those not wearing haute couture stick out at our gatherings like STROPHES stick out in short poems.

tome (TOAM). A large or scholarly book.
"She carries a book but it is not / the TOME of the ancient wisdom, / the pages, I imagine, are the blank pages / of the unwritten volume of the new."
—Hilda Doolittle, American poet and memoirist

tractate (TRAK-tayt). A treatise.
Jason spent more than six months polishing his first TRACTATE.

treatise (TREE-tiss). A formal and systematic written work on the principles, facts, evidence, and conclusions of a subject.
Mill's TREATISE on the equality of women was revolutionary for its time.

variorum (vair-ee-OR-em). An edition of a literary work containing alternative readings or notes by various editors or scholars.
The publisher believed that the quantity of reviews warranted issuing a VARIORUM.

vignette (vin-YET). A brief story, incident, or episode, usually told to illustrate some point.
Adding a VIGNETTE or two to a speech can help make abstract ideas clearer.

VERBS

emend (ee-MEND). To change by means of editing; to correct (a text or reading).
Many of Shakespeare's most famous lines, such as "A rose by any other name would smell as sweet," are the result of a critic's choice to EMEND a troublesome source text.

ANTONYMS

token (TOH-kuhn). Something used to represent a fact or event.
Archaeologists have evidence that the use of TOKENS predated writing.

127. Livid

(LIHV-id), adjective

Enraged or extremely angry.

ADJECTIVES

acrimonious (ak-rih-MOAN-ee-us). Angry; bitter; disputed.
"There is something about the literary life that repels me, all this desperate building of castles on cobwebs, the long-drawn ACRIMONIOUS struggle to make something important which we all know will be gone forever in a few years . . ."—Raymond Chandler, American author

apoplectic (ap-up-PLECK-tic). An extremely agitated state of rage.
Emily's careless event planning makes me so APOPLECTIC that I just want to step in and plan the luncheon myself.

bellicose (BELL-ih-kohss). Belligerent, surly, ready to argue or fight at the slightest provocation.
Doug is so touchy about his new Jaguar that he'll instantly grow BELLICOSE if you so much as brush against it.

intemperate (in-TEM-prit). Indulging one's own whims and fancies without regard to other people's feelings or inconvenience; immoderate, particularly in drinking alcoholic beverages.
"Certainly it was ordained as a scourge upon the pride of human wisdom, that the wisest of us all, should thus outwit ourselves, and eternally forego our purposes in the INTEMPERATE act of pursuing them."—Laurence Sterne, Irish-born English novelist and Anglican clergyman

irascible (ih-RASS-uh-bull). Easily irritated or annoyed; prone to losing one's temper; quick to anger.
"I have never known anyone worth a damn who wasn't IRASCIBLE."
—Ezra Pound, American expatriate poet

NOUNS

anathema (uh-NATH-eh-muh). A person or thing regarded as wrong in the highest degree; a loathsome, detestable entity.
Religious services were an ANATHEMA to Russ, what with him being a dedicated atheist and all.

cholers (KOH-lers). The mood of anger, irritability, grumpiness, or being short-tempered and impatient.
When Franklin is in the grip of CHOLERS, even his closest friends avoid his table at the club.

rancor (RANG-ker). Conflict between individuals or groups, usually resulting from disagreement over an action or issue, and accompanied by ill will, bad feelings, and an escalation of the dispute over time.
"They no longer assume responsibility (as beat cops used to do) for averting RANCOR between antagonistic neighbors."—Harlan Ellison, American author

Xanthippe (zan-TIP-ee). An ill-tempered, shrewish woman.
Felicia is far from a XANTHIPPE simply because she interacts only with certain members of the household staff.

VERBS

abominate (uh-BOM-in-ayt). To loathe; hate; detest.
"For my part, I ABOMINATE all honorable respectable toils, trials, and tribulations of every kind whatsoever."—Herman Melville, American author

execrate (EK-sih-krayt). To loathe; to subject to scorn and derision.
We EXECRATED William for weeks due to his casual rejection of an invitation to join Yale's Skull and Bones.

ANTONYMS

effervescent (ef-ur-VESS-ent). Bubbly; upbeat; cheerful; possessing a positive attitude and joyful personality.
After getting the acceptance letter from Cornell, Sabrina was EFFERVESCENT and celebrated with a trip to Neiman Marcus.

felicity (fih-LISS-ih-tee). A state of blissful happiness.
"Never lose sight of the fact that all human FELICITY lies in man's imagination, and that he cannot think to attain it unless he heeds all his caprices."
—Marquis de Sade, French aristocrat and revolutionary

gambol (GAM-bull). To run, skip, or jump about in a playful or joyous fashion.
"We all have these places where shy humiliations GAMBOL on sunny afternoons."—W.H. Auden, Anglo-American poet

jocose (joe-KOSS). Humorous, playful, and characterized by good humor.
The pony's JOCOSE antics marked it for a career in polo, rather than on the racetrack.

vivacious (vih-VAY-shuss). Joyful; happy, spirited; possessing a positive attitude about and enthusiasm for life; a person who lives life to the fullest.
Even after her family maintained some steep revenue losses, Sandra retained her VIVACIOUS character.

128. Love

(LUHV), noun

A strong and passionate affection or attachment to another person or persons.

ADJECTIVES

amatory (AM-uh-tore-ee). Having to do with sexual love.
Pete hasn't stopped sulking since Alice spurned his AMATORY advances at the office Christmas party.

narcissistic (nar-sis-SIS-tik). Self-loving; egotistic; indifferent to others.
Self-promotion is one thing; the NARCISSISTIC zeal with which Gerald asserts himself is quite another.

smitten (SMIT-uhn). Very much in love; struck, as though by a hard blow.
Warren is so SMITTEN with Ellen that he's no longer productive.

uxorious (uk-SORE-ee-us). Submissive or doting toward one's wife.
Although Grandpa makes a show of rebellion against Grandma's strictures
every now and then for our sake, he's as UXORIOUS as they come.

NOUNS

agape (ah-GAH-pay). In Christianity, divine love for humanity, or human love
that transcends customary boundaries; often used to describe an unselfish love
that goes beyond sexuality or worldly concerns.
The nurse's work among the poor and dispossessed seemed rooted not in a
well-meaning and temporary humanitarian instinct but in a deeper and more
profound AGAPE totally unfamiliar to most of us.

billet-doux (bill-a-DOO). A love letter. Plural: billets-doux (bill-a-dooz).
The young couple exchanged BILLETS-DOUX almost every day the summer
they were apart.

Casanova (kass-uh-NO-vuh). A man noted for his amorous activities.
Phil likes to think of himself as a CASANOVA, but most women just think he's
pathetic.

paramour (PAIR-uh-more). An illicit lover.
Although the women in her circle made high-minded speeches about her moral-
ity, Mrs. Able knew full well that most of them had had a PARAMOUR at one
time or another.

philogyny (fi-LOJ-uh-nee). The love of or fondness for women.
Zack's PHILOGYNY came naturally to him, having grown up with seven sisters.

polyandry (PAWL-ee-an-dree). The practice of having two or more husbands
at the same time.
Women who practice POLYANDRY, when questioned closely, typically advise
against it.

polygamy (puh-LIG-uh-mee). The societal practice of having more than one
spouse (especially, more than one wife) at a time.
The sect's advocacy of POLYGAMY and group parenting eventually brought it
into bitter conflict with the stern-minded townsfolk of Harris Hollow.

polygyny (puh-LIJ-uh-nee). The practice of having two or more wives at the same time.
POLYGYNY is more common than most people realize, but when revealed, such examples always create public outrage.

swain (SWAYN). A male lover.
The regency romance was teeming with would-be SWAINS.

tryst (TRIST). An appointment made by lovers to meet at a certain place and time.
Since their families are of equal station, no one worries much about the supposedly secret TRYSTS between Josephine and Brock.

VERBS

ogle (OH-guhl). To look at in an amorous or impertinent way.
No one would want to trade places with us if they only knew how tiresome it becomes to have the paparazzi constantly OGLING you.

osculate (OS-kyuh-layt). To kiss.
With practice, Jack was able to perfect his ability to OSCULATE.

ANTONYMS

abhor (ab-HOR). To experience a feeling of great repugnance or disgust.
It was clear almost as soon as the dinner party had begun that Jennifer ABHORRED her half-sister.

antagonistic (an-tag-uh-NISS-tik). Acting in a hostile, unfriendly manner; in opposition.
"There must always remain something that is ANTAGONISTIC to good."
—Plato, Greek philosopher
See also: Sex

129. Magniloquent

(mag-NILL-uh-kwuhnt), adjective

Pompous, bombastic, and boastful.

ADJECTIVES

adulatory (AJ-uh-luh-tore-ee). Complimentary; giving of effusive praise.
"He includes in his final chapter a passage of ADULATORY prose from Henry James."—Joyce Carol Oates, American author

bumptious (BUMP-shuss). Loud and assertive in a crude way.
The club's golf pro was fired due to his BUMPTIOUS behavior on the links.

grandiloquent (grand-EL-oh-kwent). Having a pompous, overly inflated, hyperbolic, or pretentious way of presenting oneself in speech and mannerism.
The architect waxed GRANDILOQUENT about the visionary design of his new skyscraper.

verbose (ver-BOHS). Describes a person or composition using more words than are needed to get the point across.
Long-winded and VERBOSE, Mitch made his team members groan whenever he stood up to speak at a charity event.

NOUNS

braggadocio (brag-uh-DOH-see-oh). Empty boasting or bragging.
Eric claims he is a consummate wine connoisseur, but it is just BRAGGADOCIO.

demagogue (DEM-ah-gog). A politician who owes his popularity largely to pandering to popular opinion and catering to the wishes of his constituency.
"A DEMAGOGUE is a person with whom we disagree as to which gang should mismanage the country."—Don Marquis, American journalist and humorist

litany (LIT-n-ee). A prolonged and boring account.
"With the supermarket as our temple and the singing commercial as our LITANY, are we likely to fire the world with an irresistible vision of America's exalted purpose and inspiring way of life?"—Adlai Stevenson, American politician

locution (low-KEW-shin). A person's manner and style of speaking.
Neil prides himself on his precise LOCUTION, but some of the guys think he sounds rather prissy.

VERBS

aggrandize (uh-GRAN-dyz). To exaggerate, put on a false front, and make something look greater and grander than it really is.
Phil tries to AGGRANDIZE his reputation by stating that he is a charter member of the Bill O'Reilly fan club, but everybody just thinks this "feat" makes him pathetic.

bloviate (BLOH-vee-ayt). To speak pompously and at length.
Maxwell BLOVIATES about his "excellent" golf game, but everyone knows he cheats outrageously.

descant (des-KANT). To talk freely and without inhibition.
Eloise is always more than willing to DESCANT concerning her past liaisons.

harangue (huh-RANG). Verbally accost; yell at; berate.
*"But on that hot July day she breaks—HARANGUING strangers in the street."
—Oliver Sacks, British neurologist*

ANTONYMS

austere (aw-STEER). Stern; grim and lacking humor or warmth; clean and unornamented; severe or strict in manner.
In the movie Dead Poets Society, *Robin Williams clashes with an AUSTERE headmaster at a private boys' school.*

colloquial (kuh-LOW-kwee-ul). Informal, conversational, everyday language.
"COLLOQUIAL poetry is to the real art as the barber's wax dummy is to sculpture."—Ezra Pound, American expatriate poet

diffident (DIFF-ih-dent). Uncertain or unsure about making a decision or taking an action; lacking confidence and boldness.
If you feel DIFFIDENT about driving a Rolls-Royce, you can always buy a Bentley.

laconic (luh-KAWN-ik). Of few words; expressing oneself with an economy of words.
Harold may be LACONIC, but when he does speak, he is worth listening to.

stolid (STAHL-id). Unemotional and impassive.
Thomas's STOLID demeanor hides the heart of a jet-setting playboy.

130. Meeting

(MEE-ting), noun

The process by which people come together; an assembly of or encounter between people.

NOUNS

assignation (ass-ig-NAY-shun). A secret meeting between lovers.
The countess's ASSIGNATIONS with the stable boy caused tongues to wag throughout the town.

conclave (KON-klave). A secret meeting; also, the room in which this meeting is held.
Fearing he might crack under pressure, the rebels did not include Eli in the CONCLAVE in which they planned their attack strategy.

confluence (KON-flu-ence). A point of meeting or flowing together.
It is on the issue of human spiritual growth that the two philosophies find their CONFLUENCE.

forum (FOR-um). A gathering, meeting, or program held for the purpose of discussing matters of public or common concern.
"Although I am sure your neighbor's constantly barking dog is irritating, Mrs. Wakefield," the chairman intoned, "the purpose of this FORUM is to discuss the proposed waste site."

liaison (lee-A-zawn). A romantic affair; the meeting of lovers.
My LIAISONS with Margaret were held in such romantic locales that I believed we should arrive on horseback to complete the image.

rendezvous (RON-day-voo). A meeting; especially, a secret meeting between lovers.
Claire knew that if her mother found out about her RENDEZVOUS with Elton, she would be grounded for at least a week.

symposium (sim-POZE-ee-um). A gathering of experts before an audience whose members may pose questions.
The SYMPOSIUM was a disaster; both professors arrived an hour late, after most of the audience had given up and left.

tête-à-tête (TET-ah-tet). A face-to-face meeting.
Some of us had begun to believe that neighborhood children were pilfering from us, so we sat down the allegedly guilty parties and had a TÊTE-À-TÊTE.

tryst (TRIST). An appointment made by lovers to meet at a certain place and time.
Since their families are of equal station, no one worries much about the supposedly secret TRYSTS between Josephine and Brock.

VERBS

convoke (kuhn-VOKE). To call together for a meeting; to summon.
An announcement went out over the intercom to CONVOKE seminar participants.

ANTONYMS

discrete (dih-SKREET). Separate and distinct; apart or detached from others.
Each work was DISCRETE and stood on its own.

divergent (dih-VUR-juhnt). Differing; diverging from others.
"Music creates order out of chaos: for rhythm imposes unanimity upon the DIVER-GENT, melody imposes continuity upon the disjointed, and harmony imposes compatibility upon the incongruous"—Yehudi Menuhin, Russian-American violinist

131. Memory

(MEM-uh-ree), noun

The act or process of remembering; the mental ability to retain and revive facts, events, or impressions; the sum of what one remembers.

ADJECTIVES

eidetic (EYE-det-ik). Describes a memory or mental image recalled with perfect clarity.
I'd studied the travel brochures so much that I had a perfectly EIDETIC vision of what to expect on the cruise ship.

nepenthean (ni-PEN-thee-uhn). Inducing a pleasurable feeling of forgetfulness, especially that of sorrow or trouble.
Attending the concert and losing himself in the beautiful melodies had a NEPENTHEAN effect on Jack.

NOUNS

anamnesis (an-am-NEE-sis). A recalling or recollection of the past.
Jack's anamneses were vivid and painful, evoking powerful recollections of the one true love of his life, now lost.

memoir (MEM-wahr). A series of written reminiscences about people, places, and events composed by and from the point of view of someone with intimate knowledge of the details.
Since Richard Nixon, virtually all American presidents have felt compelled to publish MEMOIRS focusing on their time in office.

memorabilia (mem-er-uh-BIL-ee-uh). Things worth remembering or recording; things that stir recollections; mementos; souvenirs.
John had a separate collection of MEMORABILIA for each of the family's vacations.

mnemonic (neh-MON-ik). A rhyme, sentence, or other word pattern designed to help one memorize facts.
"Roy G. Biv" is a MNEMONIC for the colors of a rainbow: red, orange, yellow, green, blue, indigo, violet.

reminiscence (rem-uh-NISS-uhns). The act of remembering; a mental impression; memory.
Confined to her bed, unable to read due to failing eyesight, Jane's dying grandmother hung on to the many happy REMINISCENCES of her life.

VERBS

evoke (ee-VOKE). To call forth or summon; to bring back to life through appeal to memory.
The sight of the old mansion EVOKED many bittersweet memories for Charles.

ANTONYMS

amnesia (am-NEE-zhuh). Partial or total loss of memory.
"A nation that forgets its past can function no better than an individual with AMNESIA."—David McCullough, American author

oblivion (uh-BLIV-ee-un). The state of being beyond memory and utterly forgotten; lost to human recollection.
To Tim, the fact that his book was being allowed to go out of print meant that he as an author had been consigned to OBLIVION.

132. Minion

(MIN-yuhn), noun

A follower of someone in an important position.

NOUNS

aficionado (uh-fish-ee-uh-NAH-doe). A devotee, someone who is enthralled with and supports a particular activity.
Dwight often refers to himself as an AFICIONADO of American-made microbrews.

faction (FAK-shin). A small dissenting group within a larger one.
"I will keep where there is wit stirring, and leave the FACTION of fools."
—William Shakespeare

fealty (FEE-ul-tee). A sense of obligation or loyalty, usually existing because one person feels beholden to another.
The only reason that Bryson pledged FEALTY to David is because David's social connections helped Bryson get a job on Wall Street.

ideologue (EYE-dee-uh-log). A person who rigidly adheres to an ideology with a closed mind regarding other points of view.
"An IDEOLOGUE may be defined as a mad intellectual."—Clifton Fadiman, American critic

phalanx (FAY-lanks). A large division or group of soldiers grouped closely together in an orderly fashion for marching or fighting.
Philip of Macedon armed each man with a long spear so the PHALANX bristled like a porcupine.

VERBS

inculcate (IN-kul-kayt). To impress an idea or belief upon someone by repeating it to that person over and over until the idea is firmly lodged in his brain.
New cult members are quickly INCULCATED with the cult leader's beliefs and world view.

ANTONYMS

iconoclast (eye-KAHN-uh-clast). An individual who is contrarian in thought, rebellious in spirit, and oppositional, and who applies himself to battling established institutions, existing governments, religious doctrine, and popular notions and beliefs.
The late George Carlin saw the role of the comic in society as one of ICONOCLAST.

maverick (MAH-ver-ik). An unorthodox or unconventional person who does what it takes to get things done.
"The rugged individualist is too often mistaken for the misfit, the MAVERICK, the spoilsport, the sore thumb."—Lewis H. Lapham, former editor of Harper's Magazine

quisling (KWIZ-ling). A traitor; a person who conspires with the enemy.
In 1945 the leader of Norway's National Unity movement was executed for being a QUISLING.

133. Mistake

(mi-STAYK), noun

An error in understanding or perception; a blunder; fault.

NOUNS

aberration (ab-uh-RAY-shun). A departure from what is true, correct, or right; a deviation from the normal or typical.
"When will we reach the point that hunting, the pleasure in killing animals for sport, will be regarded as a mental ABERRATION?"—Albert Schweitzer, German missionary and philosopher

blunder (BLUHN-der). A significant, foolish, or thoughtless mistake; stupid and careless error.
Driving drunk is a BLUNDER that most thoughtful people make only once.

contretemps (KON-treh-tahn). An inopportune occurrence with embarrassing results.
"Pan had been amongst them . . . the little god Pan, who presides over social CONTRETEMPS and unsuccessful picnics."—E. M. Forster, English novelist

faux pas (FOH pah). A serious breach of social protocol or etiquette.
Looking a Japanese business customer directly in the eye during conversation is considered an egregious FAUX PAS.

gaffe (GAF). A social blunder.
When he was shown the door, Jack realized that his latest thoughtless remark was a bigger GAFFE than he'd suspected.

mea culpa (me-uh-KULP-uh). An acknowledgement, usually public, of a blunder or mistake.
After the politician made racially tinged comments, he spent the better part of a month offering MEA CULPAS on national television.

solecism (SOLL-ih-siz-um). Something that deviates from the normal, accepted, or proper order; inconsistency.
She was sure that her SOLECISM would be forgiven and forgotten in time.

ANTONYMS

definitude (dih-FIN-ih-tyood). Definiteness; precision.
There was no question about the solution; Jason had studied the problem and could provide the correct answer with DEFINITUDE.

faultless (FAWLT-lis). Without fault or defect; perfect.
"Whoever thinks a FAULTLESS piece to see, / Thinks what ne'er was, nor is, nor e'er shall be."—Alexander Pope, English poet
See also: False

134. Moderation

(mod-uh-RAY-shun), noun

An absence of excess or extremes; calmness; the practice of restraint.

ADJECTIVES

abstemious (ab-STEE-me-us). Eating plain and simple food in moderation, avoiding overindulgence in drink and gluttony at the table.
Gandhi led an ABSTEMIOUS life.

monastic (muh-NAS-tik). Relating to the practice of withdrawing from society to live a quiet, contemplative life, often dedicated to religious faith.
Saint Pachomius founded the first organized Christian MONASTIC community.

spartan (SPAR-tin). Self-disciplined, frugal, and stoic. People who lived in the ancient Greek city of Sparta were known for their discipline and austerity.
Paul lives such a SPARTAN life that his apartment has more exercise equipment than furniture.

staid (STAYD). Fixed and settled; not distinctive; sedate; prim.
Even though the Sandersons are an important family, we could hardly last the requisite hour at the family's STAID winter ball.

NOUNS

abstinence (AB-steh-nence). The voluntarily forgoing of the indulgence of an appetite; denial of certain foods and drinks thought to be harmful to one's health; refraining from behavior considered immoral.
After years of indulgence, it was difficult for Evelyn to follow her doctor's order of complete ABSTINENCE from liquor.

ascetic (uh-SET-ik). A person who deliberately chooses to live a plain and simple life; characterized by lack of material possessions and strong self-discipline in all matters of behavior.
When Steve Jobs started Apple, a magazine profile portrayed him as an ASCETIC, noting that he had no furniture in his apartment.

temperance (TEM-per-ence). Moderation in eating and drinking; abstinence from consuming alcoholic beverages.
Cicero said that TEMPERANCE is "the firm and moderate dominion of reason over passion and other unrighteous impulses of the mind."

VERBS

sublimate (SUB-lih-mayt). To transfer the force of an unacceptable inclination or impulse to a pursuit considered proper or wholesome.
There is a popular—but unproven—notion that butchers are secretly violent, and that they choose their profession as a means of SUBLIMATING their passions.

ANTONYMS

libertine (LIB-er-teen). Licentious and free of moral restraint; or, a person so characterized.
"It is easier to make a saint out of a LIBERTINE than out of a prig."
—George Santayana, author and philosopher

licentious (ly-SEN-shuss). Promiscuous; slutty; someone who is sexually uninhibited and free.
Janine's LICENTIOUS behavior was really a cry for attention, the school psychologist was convinced.

profligate (PROF-lih-git). Extravagant; wasteful; give to activity, expenditures, or indulgences beyond those of any reasonable person.
My PROFLIGATE expenditures quickly came to a halt when my bank account reached zero.

roué (roo-AY). A licentious man; a libertine or lecher.
Although Ernest's dalliances might have been understandable when he was a young man, they were more difficult for his family to forgive in his later years, when he came to resemble nothing so much as a tired and lonely old ROUÉ.

135. Modest

(MOD-ist), adjective

Having or showing an unassuming or humble opinion of one's own achievements, merits, abilities, etc.; free from vanity or pretension.

ADJECTIVES

chary (CHAIR-ee). Shy; timid; careful; wary.
Martha was CHARY of trying anything new, whether restaurants, movies, vacation destinations, or even grocery stores.

circumspect (SIR-kum-spekt). Prudent, cautious, considering from all sides.
"I smiled, / I waited, / I was CIRCUMSPECT; / O never, never, never write that I / missed life or loving."—Hilda Doolittle, American poet and memoirist

deferential (def-uh-REN-shul). Showing respect to someone as a superior; having a humble demeanor.
A DEFERENTIAL attitude has no place in a respectful relationship.

demure (di-MYOOR). Affecting a reserved and shy appearance; outwardly retiring.
Mr. Atkins found the Hallis twins DEMURE, and wondered what they would say about him when he left.

diffident (DIFF-ih-dent). Uncertain or unsure about making a decision or taking an action; lacking confidence and boldness.
If you feel DIFFIDENT about driving a Rolls-Royce, you can always buy a Bentley.

dubious (DOO-bee-uss). Tending to be skeptical, uncertain, or doubtful.
His lack of esteem made him DUBIOUS about forming relationships.

reticent (REH-tih-sent). Reluctance to openly express one's thoughts, feelings, and personal business to other people; reserved; behaving like an introvert in social situations.
"The shorter poems tend to be RETICENT, psychologically acute love poems about the shifting inequalities of love."—Edward Mendelson, Professor of English and Comparative Literature at Columbia University

unassuming (un-uh-SOOM-ing). Modest and unpretentious.
The Binghamtons just bought a lovely, UNASSUMING starter home in the town where their families live.

verecund (VER-ih-kuhnd). Bashful; modest.
Paul's VERECUND manner makes it difficult to carry on a conversation with him.

ANTONYMS

brazen (BRAY-zuhn). Having no shame; impudent; bold.
The prosecutor expertly summarized the defendant's BRAZEN disregard for the health and safety of innocent bystanders in the commission of his heinous crime.

depraved (dih-PRAYVD). Morally bad; corrupt; perverted.
"We Americans have always considered Hollywood, at best, a sinkhole of DEPRAVED venality. And, of course, it is."—David Mamet, American playwright
See also: Moderation

136. Mourn

(MAWRN), verb

To feel or express sorrow; lament; grieve; to show the conventional signs of grief.

ADJECTIVES

bereaved (bih-REEVD). In a state of mourning; deeply sorrowful because of the loss of a loved one.
The most difficult part of Father Maurice's job was providing solace for those in his parish who were BEREAVED.

funereal (fyoo-NEER-ee-uhl). Reminiscent of a funeral; dark, brooding, and mournful.
The funereal tone of the meeting was not at all what we had in mind to raise morale.

lugubrious (loo-GOO-bree-us). Mournful in the extreme.
You may consider Steven's poems "dark"; to me, they are simply LUGUBRIOUS.

plaintive (PLAIN-tive). Expressing sorrow or sadness; mournful.
Even the singing of birds had a PLAINTIVE sound at the house for weeks after our dog Sasha died.

NOUNS

dirge (durj). A funeral song; a song of mourning.
The DIRGE from Cymbeline, *according to Professor Alpert, is the only worthwhile passage to be found in that seldom-produced Shakespeare play.*

elegy (ELL-uh-jee). A poem of mourning; a poem reflecting on and praising the deceased.
At the funeral, Mitch read a touching ELEGY for his grandmother, reminding all present of the life of kindness and sacrifice she had led.

eulogy (YOO-luh-jee). Speech or writing in praise of a person, typically used for a person who has recently died.
Diane delivered a EULOGY for her uncle that managed to be simultaneously sad and heart-warming.

lamentation (lam-en-TAY-shun). An expression of mourning.
Karl heard groans of LAMENTATION from his mother's room.

solace (SOL-uss). Consolation; to sympathize with and console.
The fact that he had thrown three touchdowns was little SOLACE to Jim: all he could think about was losing the game.

VERBS

rue (roo). To be sorrowful; to mourn or regret bitterly.
After spending prom night at home watching movies by herself, Susan began to RUE the day she had rejected Mark so cruelly.

ANTONYMS

exult (ig-ZULT). To rejoice greatly; be jubilant; to feel triumphant joy.
"Arms are instruments of ill omen. When one is compelled to use them, it is best to do so without relish. There is no glory in victory, and to glorify it despite this is to EXULT in the killing of men."—Lao Tzu, Chinese Taoist philosopher

fete (FAYT). To celebrate; to honor or entertain.
In honor of their victory, the baseball team was FETED at a celebratory dinner sponsored by the town's recreation department.
See also: Sad

137. Mysterious

(mih-STEER-ee-us), adjective

Of, containing, implying, or characterized by mystery; that which excites curiosity and wonder but is difficult or impossible to explain.

ADJECTIVES

arcane (ar-KAYN). Strange and mysterious; understood only by the initiated.
Bill's ARCANE knowledge of all Lexus models and their accessories is just a waste of gray matter.

enigmatic (en-ig-MATT-ik). Mysterious, puzzling, and difficult to figure out.
"The interest in life does not lie in what people do, nor even in their relations to each other, but largely in the power to communicate with a third party, antagonistic, ENIGMATIC, yet perhaps persuadable, which one may call life in general."
—Virginia Woolf, British essayist and novelist

inscrutable (in-SKROO-tuh-bull). Mysterious and not easy to understand.
"I suppose I now have the reputation of being an INSCRUTABLE dipsomaniac. One woman here originated the rumour that I am extremely lazy and will never do or finish anything."—James Joyce, Irish author and playwright

metaphysical (met-uh-FIZ-ih-kuhl). Beyond the physical or material; supernatural or transcendental.
"Art is the highest task and proper METAPHYSICAL activity of this life."
—Friedrich Nietzsche, German philosopher

spiritual (SPIR-ih-choo-uhl). Of or pertaining to the spirit as distinguished from the body; supernatural.
"Military power wins battles, but SPIRITUAL power wins wars."—General George Marshall, American military commander

NOUNS

prestidigitation (PRESS-tih-dih-ji-TAY-shun). The performance of sleight-of-hand magic tricks.
The New Year's Eve gala at the Worthingtons included sumptuous meals, a full orchestra, and even a practitioner of PRESTIDIGITATION who amazed the children with her performance.

ANTONYMS

palpable (PAL-puh-bull). Capable of being touched, felt, or handled; tangible.
"Popular opinions, on subjects not PALPABLE to sense, are often true, but seldom or never the whole truth."—John Stuart Mill, English ethical theorist

tangible (TAN-juh-bull). Able to be touched or felt by hand; having form and substance; real or actual; definite.
"The distinctive nature of a child is to always live in the TANGIBLE present."
—John Ruskin, English writer and critic

138. Nanosecond

(NAN-uh-sek-uhnd), noun

A time period equal to one billionth of a second.

ADJECTIVES

capricious (kuh-PREE-shuss). Prone to quickly changing one's mind, decision, or course of action at the drop of a hat or on impulse.
"I do not understand the CAPRICIOUS lewdness of the sleeping mind."
—John Cheever, American novelist

ephemeral (eh-FEM-er-uhl). Short-lived; temporary; fleeting.
"There remain some truths too EPHEMERAL to be captured in the cold pages of a court transcript."—Irving Kaufman, Chief Judge, United States Court of Appeals

temporal (tem-POR-uhl). Relating to time.
"Science is the language of the TEMPORAL world; love is that of the spiritual world."—Honoré de Balzac, French novelist and playwright

yare (YAIR). Quick and agile; lively.
Thanks to the gymnastics she performed at finishing school, Amanda has a YARE and limber body.

NOUNS

alacrity (uh-LAK-rih-tee). Cheerful cooperation rendered with enthusiasm, promptness, and politeness.
The ALACRITY with which Steve responded to Helen's invitation is nothing short of astonishing.

celerity (suh-LAIR-ih-tee). Speed; swiftness of action or motion.
I will carry out your orders with CELERITY, sir.

tempo (TEM-po). The speed or pace of something (particularly of music).
Our aerobics instructor will only play music with a fast TEMPO and a strong beat, although there are times, generally after a hard day at work, when I feel like introducing her to the wonders of Mantovani.

ANTONYMS

interminably (in-TUR-min-uh-blee). Seemingly without end or going on for an indeterminate period of time.
"The body dies; the body's beauty lives. / So evenings die, in their green going, / A wave, INTERMINABLY flowing."—Wallace Stevens, American modernist poet

languid (LANG-gwid). Characterized by weakness and fatigue; or, lacking spirit and animation.
"In doing good, we are generally cold, and LANGUID, and sluggish; and of all things afraid of being too much in the right."—Edmund Burke, Anglo-Irish statesman, orator, and author

sedentary (SED-n-tair-ee). Resting a great deal and taking little exercise.
All we have to do is hire a personal trainer if our SEDENTARY habits begin to have negative effects on our well-being.

uniformitarianism (yu-ni-for-mih-TAIR-ee-uh-niz-uhm). The belief that change on Earth takes place slowly, gradually, and at a uniform rate rather than through short, sudden, catastrophic events.
The fact that the families of our servants have been with us for many, many generations would seem to be proof of UNIFORMITARIANISM.

139. Narrow-minded

(NAIR-oh-MYN-did), adjective

Limited in outlook; bigoted; not receptive to new ideas.

ADJECTIVES

bourgeois (boor-ZHWAH). Pertaining or relating to middle-class values; conventional viewpoints.
"The representation of the garrison thus turned out to be incomparably more moderate and BOURGEOIS than the soldier masses."—Leon Trotsky, Bolshevik revolutionary and Marxist theorist

doctrinaire (DOK-truh-NAIR). To apply theories without consideration for practical problems; impractically visionary; dictatorial.
When he returned from the management workshop, Dave was somewhat less DOCTRINAIRE in his approach with the team.

hidebound (HYD-bownd). Inflexible and holding narrow opinions.
Arthur can be rather HIDEBOUND when pontificating on the virtues of the classic era versus the condition of the automobile industry at present.

myopic (my-AHP-ik). Narrow-mindedness or short-sightedness in one's views; lack of discernment.
Your MYOPIC views will win you few votes during the election, senator.

parochial (puh-ROH-kee-uhl). Very restricted in outlook; narrow views.
They may talk "big picture" but voters can generally be counted on to express PAROCHIAL views at the ballot box.

provincial (pruh-VIN-shuhl). Having the characteristics of someone unsophisticated; limited in outlook.
From his PROVINCIAL outlook on life, you would never guess that Paul attended an Ivy League college.

puritanical (pyoor-ih-TAN-ih-kuhl). Extremely or excessively strict in matters of morals and religion.
Judith could almost see the PURITANICAL fire in her mother's eyes when they started to discuss dating habits.

sectarian (seck-TAIR-ee-un). Narrow-minded and limited in outlook.
The competing cliques' SECTARIAN squabbles captured the interest of the entire school.

NOUNS

Babbitt (BAB-it). A person who clings to narrow-minded, materialistic ideals of the middle class; the main character in Sinclair Lewis's novel *Babbitt* (1922).
Jerome may not be the most open-minded businessman, but he's no BABBITT.

ANTONYMS

catholic (KATH-uh-lik). Having broad sympathies or understanding; universal in extent; liberal.
Margaret's CATHOLIC taste in art was well known, and her house was an explosion of styles and genres.

cosmopolitan (koz-muh-POL-ih-tuhn). Belonging to the whole world, not national or local; a person who is free from local or provincial bias.
"To be really COSMOPOLITAN, a man must be at home even in his own country."—Thomas W. Higginson, American clergyman and author

140. Necessary

(NESS-uh-sare-ee), adjective

That which cannot be dispensed with; essential; indispensable.

ADJECTIVES

de rigueur (duh-rih-GUR). Strictly required by etiquette, taste, fashion, or usage.
Since black tie and tails were DE RIGUEUR for the social events his new wife attended regularly, Julian found himself buying a tuxedo for the first time in his life.

inherent (in-HAIR-unt). Intrinsic; necessary; an important or essential part of something.
Dwayne's INHERENT reluctance to entrust newcomers with tasks of any significance was a major problem for the company.

NOUNS

manifest destiny (MAN-ih-fest-DESS-tin-ee). Expansion into foreign lands, justified as being necessary or benevolent.
"It's not greed and ambition that makes wars—it's goodness. Wars are always fought for the best of reasons, for liberation or MANIFEST DESTINY, always against tyranny and always in the best interests of humanity."—James Garner in The Americanization of Emily

requisite (REK-wiz-it). A mandatory action, requirement, or condition; or, necessary and mandatory.
Being physically fit is a REQUISITE for getting a job as a fireman.

sine qua non (sin-uh kwah NON). An essential feature (of something).
Many people consider a happy ending to be the SINE QUA NON of a proper comedy.

VERBS

necessitate (nuh-SESS-ih-tayt). To make necessary; to obligate.
"Each coming together of man and wife, even if they have been mated for many years, should be a fresh adventure; each winning should NECESSITATE a fresh wooing."—Marie Carmichael Stopes, British scientist and birth-control pioneer

ANTONYMS

extrinsic (eks-TRINZ-ik). Not part of the true nature of something; not essential.
The revolution was less of a spontaneous eruption of anger against capitalism as a system, and more of a reaction to EXTRINSIC forces like the constant oil shortages that came about because of international sanctions.

gratuitous (gruh-TOO-ih-tuss). Unnecessary; inappropriately excessive; uncalled for.
His GRATUITOUS attacks on the popular governor only weakened his standing among voters.

obviate (OB-vee-ayt). To anticipate, and therefore prevent, difficulties or disadvantages; make unnecessary.
The research department provided sufficient data, thus the problem was OBVIATED before it reached crisis proportions.

rigmarole (RIG-muh-roll). Absurdly complicated procedures and instructions.
The club had some value to him in business, but he quickly grew tired of all the RIGMAROLE at meetings.

superfluous (soo-PER-flew-us). Excessive and unnecessary.
Some people never seem to be aware that wearing more than a hint of fine jewelry is SUPERFLUOUS.

141. Necromancy

(NEH-kroh-man-see), noun

The ability to gain new knowledge by communicating with the dead; magic and trickery in general.

ADJECTIVES

Faustian (FOW-stee-in). Evil; malicious; dark and brooding with malevolent intent; demonic; satanic; having sold one's soul to the devil—metaphorically or literally—in exchange for wealth and power.
In the movie The End of Days, *a group of police officers make a FAUSTIAN bargain with Satan himself.*

nefarious (nih-FAIR-ee-us). Inherently evil, malicious, and unjust.
"You were preceded by your NEFARIOUS reputation," the sheriff said to the gunslinger who had just sidled up to the bar.

nether (NETH-ur). Located below or under something else.
"I know a lady in Venice would have walked barefoot to Palestine for a touch of his NETHER lip."—William Shakespeare

odious (OH-dee-us). Offensive or disgusting; causing revulsion.
"To depend upon a profession is a less ODIOUS form of slavery than to depend upon a father."—Virginia Woolf, British essayist and novelist

sacrilegious (sak-reh-LIJ-uss). Openly insulting or disrespectful to the beliefs, religion, ideas, and practices of others—especially the ones they hold most sacred.
Bryson's insistence that Miró is more collectible than Warhol is positively SACRILEGIOUS.

NOUNS

anathema (uh-NATH-eh-muh). A person or thing regarded as wrong in the highest degree; a loathsome, detestable entity.
Religious services were an ANATHEMA to Russ, what with him being a dedicated atheist and all.

frisson (FREE-son). A sudden strong feeling of excitement, conflict, or danger.
"Pregnant women! They had that weird FRISSON, an aura of magic that combined awkwardly with an earthy sense of duty."—Ruth Morgan, American novelist

Gnosticism (NAH-stih-sih-zim). The religious belief that salvation is attained through secret knowledge rather than through prayer, ritual, faith, divine grace, or good works.
Many of the key principles of Christianity were formed as a direct response to GNOSTICISM.

legerdemain (le-juhr-duh-MAYN). Magic tricks; or, generally speaking, trickery and deception.
The Wilkinsons are one of the few of our families whose initial wealth did not come as a result of financial LEGERDEMAIN.

thaumaturge (THAW-mah-turj). A person who works miracles.
If you were ever to see Hannah early in the morning, just after she has awoken, then you would know Hannah's personal make-up artist is the epitome of a THAUMATURGE.

VERBS

gorgonize (GORE-guh-nize). To paralyze or mesmerize with one's looks or personality.
Even without her family's wealth and connections, Marla would likely GORGONIZE all the men who enter her orbit.

ANTONYMS

panacea (pan-uh-SEE-uh). A universal solution for all problems, diseases, or woes.
Parents today see buying their kids everything they want as a PANACEA for misery, boredom, and unhappiness.

phoenix (FEE-nix). A mythical bird about the size of an eagle, but with brilliantly colored plumage, that dies by fire and then is reborn from the ashes.
One day the PHOENIX appeared in the forests of France, and legend has it that all the other birds become instantly jealous.

sacrosanct (SACK-roh-sankt). Beyond criticism because it is considered sacred.
"If men could get pregnant, maternity benefits would be as SACROSANCT as the G.I. Bill."—Letty Cottin Pogrebin, American editor and writer

142. Novice

(NOV-iss), noun

One who is new to a profession, trade, or sport; a beginner.

ADJECTIVES

callow (KAL-oh). Lacking experience, immature.
Ellis, a CALLOW youth accompanying Madame Hempstead, seemed not to understand that his joke about the ambassador's choice of underwear was inappropriate for a state dinner.

fledgling (FLEJ-ling). Young or inexperienced.
The FLEDGLING reporter had little respect around the newsroom.

puerile (PYOO-er-ill). Immature, babyish, infantile.
"An admiral whose PUERILE vanity has betrayed him into a testimonial . . . [is] sufficient to lure the hopeful patient to his purchase."—Samuel Hopkins Adams, American journalist

NOUNS

abecedarian (a-bee-see-DAIR-ee-un). A beginner; someone just learning the rudiments of a task, skill, job, etc.
Paul is an expert in a sea kayak, but when it comes to snow skiing, he's an ABECEDARIAN.

ingénue (AHN-zhuh-noo). From the French, meaning "naive," an actress who specializes in playing the part of an innocent or unworldly young woman.
"I always chose sophisticated parts because you can't really be interesting as a young girl or outstanding as an INGÉNUE."—Norma Shearer, American actress

juvenilia (joo-vuh-NILL-yuh). Early work by a creative artist, usually produced when the artist was young.
Lorna turned toward the stock market and away from poetry after we read her JUVENILIA and laughed uproariously.

neophyte (NEE-uh-fyt). A recent convert; someone whose newfound zeal is not balanced by experience.
"Like footmen and upstairs maids, wine stewards are portrayed as acolytes of the privileged, ever eager to intimidate the NEOPHYTE and spurn the unwary."—Frank J. Prial, former New York Times *wine columnist*

parvenu (PAR-veh-noo). Someone who has recently gained wealth, prestige, or an important position but has not yet figured out how to act appropriately in that new position.
Jed Clampett, of classic television's Beverly Hillbillies, *is a great example of a PARVENU.*

protégé (PRO-tuh-zhay). Someone aided by another influential person; a person who is protected, encouraged, or helped (for instance, in career matters) by another of superior status or rank.
Harry was always willing to mentor new hires and would often seek out a willing PROTÉGÉ to support.

tenderfoot (TEN-der-foot). A newcomer.
Walking into the project team meeting, Alice hoped that she didn't look like a complete TENDERFOOT.

tyro (TIE-roh). From the Latin, meaning "recruit," a beginner or a novice.
Though a TYRO, Madeline quickly mastered cross-country skiing during her jaunt to Switzerland.

whelp (hwelp). The offspring of a female dog or of certain other animals.
Dorothy thought it amusing to refer to her new assistant by the term "WHELP."

wunderkind (VOON-der-kinnd). One who succeeds in business, or a similar endeavor, at a comparatively young age.
Alex would be a WUNDERKIND in the firm even without his father's connections.

yearling (YEER-ling). An animal that has entered its second year; also, a horse that is one year old, dating from the beginning of the year following its foaling.
Many of our family's racehorses are YEARLINGS, which we put to pasture after their retirement.

ANTONYMS

adroit (uh-DROYT). Skilled or clever in a particular pursuit.
Years of experience have made Janet an ADROIT organizer and her events are always flawless.

doyen/doyenne (doy-EN). A man or woman who is the senior member of a group, based on rank, age, experience, etc.
Though she is the youngest member of our group, Brittany is our DOYENNE, based on her extensive family connections.

143. Obeisance

(oh-BAY-since), noun

Deferential respect or homage, or an act or gesture expressing the same.

ADJECTIVES

adulatory (ADJ-uh-luh-tor-e). Complimentary; giving of effusive praise.
"He includes in his final chapter a passage of ADULATORY prose from Henry James."—Joyce Carol Oates, American author

complaisant (kuhm-PLAY-zuhnt). Agreeable and eager to please.
Eleanor is far too COMPLAISANT with common strangers.

fulsome (FULL-sum). Excessively praising or flattering.
Katie's introduction of the keynote speaker was so FULSOME that he led his speech with a few self-effacing remarks.

NOUNS

appeasement (ah-PEEZ-meant). The act of making others happy by agreeing to their demands.
Charlene realized too late that her policy of APPEASEMENT might please Warren, but it would not cause him to treat her with more respect.

approbation (ap-ruh-BAY-shun). Official approval or commendation.
"In a virtuous and free state, no rewards can be so pleasing to sensible minds, as those which include the APPROBATION of our fellow citizens. My great pain is, lest my poor endeavours should fall short of the kind expectations of my country."—Thomas Jefferson

capitulation (kuh-pitch-uh-LAY-shun). The act of surrendering or giving up.
Ross offered James no CAPITULATION during the confrontational lacrosse game.

hagiography (hag-ee-OG-ruh-fee). A biography that idealizes its subject.
The Van Gelders were disappointed with the volume written about their illustrious descendants because the book fell far short of being a HAGIOGRAPHY.

VERBS

assuage (uh-SWAYJ). To put someone at ease; to comfort or soothe; to erase doubts and fears.
"But history must not yet tell the tragedies enacted here; let time intervene in some measure to ASSUAGE and lend an azure tint to them."—Henry David Thoreau, American author and transcendentalist

kowtow (KOW-tow). To give in to someone's every wish; to grovel and behave in a subservient manner.
Amy told Andrew that she was sick and tired of KOWTOWING to his every need.

ANTONYMS

disparage (dih-SPAIR-ihj). To bring reproach or discredit upon through one's words or actions.
"Man's constant need to DISPARAGE woman, to humble her, to deny her equal rights, and to belittle her achievements—all are expressions of his innate envy and fear."—Elizabeth Gould Davis, American feminist and author

excoriate (ik-SKORE-ee-ayt). To criticize; to attempt to censure or punish.
We EXCORIATED Melanie for inviting people with no family connections to her birthday party.

execrate (EK-sih-krayt). To loathe; to subject to scorn and derision.
We EXECRATED William for weeks due to his casual rejection of an invitation to join Yale's Skull and Bones.

144. Obstruct

(uhb-STRUKT), verb

To block or stop up with obstacles or impediments; bar; hinder.

VERBS

encumber (en-KUHM-ber). To load something—or someone—down with burdens; in legal terms, to place a lien on something.
You can't lift your backpack if you ENCUMBER it with all sorts of stuff you don't need!

fetter (FET-er). To put restraints on; confine.
Unnatural fears FETTER David's imagination and keep him locked inside his house.

impede (im-PEED). To obstruct progress; to block.
The fire regulations are quite clear on the question of storage in this hallway; nothing is allowed to IMPEDE access to the main exit.

mire (MYR). To cause to be stuck in mire; hamper; hold back.
In the early going, the administration found itself MIRED in issues far from its stated goal of improving the economy.

occlude (uh-KLOOD). To block or obstruct; to close off a passage or entranceway.
Debris from the second-floor construction OCCLUDES the entryway to the laundry room in Linda's beach house.

stymie (STY-mee). To thwart; to prevent (another) from achieving a goal.
The reporter's attempts to get to the bottom of the scandal were STYMIED by the refusal of the principals to talk to him—either on or off the record.

trammel (TRAM-uhl). To entangle; confine; restrain.
Jason is an intelligent person, so it surprised us when he explained his theory that education TRAMMELS the thought process.

ANTONYMS

expedite (EK-spi-dyt). To speed up or make easy the progress of; hasten; facilitate.
"The art of statesmanship is to foresee the inevitable and to EXPEDITE its occurrence."—Charles M. de Talleyrand, French statesman

precipitate (pri-SIP-ih-tayt). To hasten the occurrence of; to cause to happen before expected.
"It is always one's virtues and not one's vices that PRECIPITATE one's disaster."—Rebecca West, English writer

145. Ogle

(OH-guhl), verb

To look at in an amorous or impertinent way.

ADJECTIVES

amatory (AM-uh-tore-ee). Having to do with sexual love.
Pete hasn't stopped sulking since Alice spurned his AMATORY advances at the office Christmas party.

besotted (bih-SOT-ed). Made foolish, stupid, or dull due to an infatuation with love, money, the pursuit of power, etc.
Aline thinks Jake is BESOTTED with her, but he's really BESOTTED with her father's stock portfolio.

salacious (suh-LAY-shuss). Having an unhealthy, obsessive, or addictive interest in sex.
For weeks, the society pages were rife with SALACIOUS gossip, which turned out to originate from Mallory, who had lost her beau to Jeannette.

NOUNS

concupiscence (kon-KYOO-pih-suhns). Unbridled lust in the extreme—horniness.
"You're talking to a young vampire, a fountain of CONCUPISCENCE."
—Mario Acevedo, American fantasy author

coquette (ko-KET). A woman who dresses promiscuously or flirts excessively to make men think she is sexually available when in fact she has no intention of sleeping with them.
Marla doesn't intend to play the COQUETTE at society balls, but her alluring looks attract other debutantes' dates constantly.

dalliance (DAL-ee-ance). A brief, casual flirtation with or interest in someone or something; the act of tarrying rather than proceeding swiftly and deliberately.
Her DALLIANCE with the pool boy made her husband angry and jealous.

roué (roo-AY). A dissolute man in fashionable society; a rake.
"A pretty wife is something for the fastidious vanity of a ROUÉ to retire upon."—Thomas Moore, Irish poet and songwriter

satyr (SAY-ter). A lascivious, lecherous man.
Harold's graceful manners disappear once he has had a few glasses of champagne, and he becomes a veritable SATYR.

ANTONYMS

chivalry (SHIV-ul-ree). Brave, kind, courteous, or gentlemanly behavior.
"We hear much of CHIVALRY of men towards women; but . . . it vanishes like dew before the summer sun when one of us comes into competition with the manly sex."—Martha Coston, American author

uxorious (uhk-SAWR-ee-us). Doting on one's wife to an excessive degree.
"The same things change their names at such a rate; / For instance—passion in a lover's glorious, / But in a husband is pronounced UXORIOUS."—Lord Byron, British Romantic poet

146. Opinion

(uh-PIN-yuhn), noun

A belief not based on absolute certainty or real knowledge but on what seems to be true, valid, or likely to one's own mind; what one thinks; judgment.

ADJECTIVES

heterodox (HET-uh-ruh-docks). Holding unorthodox opinions, especially opinions concerned with religion.
I believe George will grow out of his HETERODOX beliefs as he gets older.

NOUNS

manifesto (man-ih-FESS-toe). A public declaration of one's intentions or motives, typically of a political nature.
Instead of galvanizing the crowd to action, the poet's MANIFESTO collapsed the audience in laughter.

obiter dictum (OB-ih-ter DIK-tuhm). An incidental opinion or remark; an incidental and nonbinding remark expressed by a judge.
Frank couldn't refrain from offering an OBITER DICTUM every time we made a turn without consulting the map.

pundit (PUN-dit). A person who gives opinions as an authority.
The conservative political PUNDITS had all decreed that Obama would be defeated in a head-to-head contest with Mitt Romney, but the voters had other ideas.

vox populi (VOKS-POP-yu-lye). Expression of the prevailing mood, concerns, and opinions in a country.
In response to an environmentally friendly VOX POPULI, more and more corporations are "going green."

VERBS

concur (kun-KUR). To agree; to share the same opinion.
The prosecutor felt that Jim's crime deserved the maximum penalty, but the judge did not CONCUR.

counsel (KOWN-sul). To discuss ideas or opinions.
Katrina's advisor was always available to COUNSEL her about work-related issues.

opine (oh-PYNE). To give an opinion.
The way that Charlotte OPINES about fashion, you'd think she created couture rather than just purchased it.

ANTONYMS

apathetic (ap-uh-THET-ik). Feeling no emotion; not interested; indifferent.
"He wasn't exactly hostile to facts, but he was APATHETIC about them."
—Wolcott Gibbs, American writer

egocentric (ee-goh-SEN-trik). Viewing everything in relation to oneself; having little regard for interests other than one's own.
We are conditioned to anticipate the EGOCENTRIC Hollywood celebrity, and they rarely disappoint.

147. Opposite

(OP-uh-zit), adjective

In opposition to; exactly contrary in relation to.

ADJECTIVES

antipodal (an-TIP-uh-del). Directly opposite; completely opposed.
As a youngster, Harry was convinced he could dig his way to Ohio's ANTIPODAL point, China.

bipolar (by-POE-luhr). Possessing two sides or poles; marked by diametrically opposed extremes; a relationship between two opposites or counterparts.
Frank's behavior on the job was generally unremarkable, but we later learned that his severe mood swings were symptoms of a BIPOLAR personality disorder.

disparate (dis-PER-iht). Describes two or more things that differ greatly from one another and cannot be logically reconciled.
"As if, as if, as if the DISPARATE halves / Of things were waiting in a betrothal known / To none."—Wallace Stevens, American modernist poet

inimical (ih-NIM-ih-kull). Working in opposition to your goal; having a harmful effect, particularly on an enterprise or endeavor.
Clarissa's work ethic is INIMICAL to earning an advanced degree in botany.

NOUNS

antithesis (an-TITH-ih-siss). The exact opposite; a thing that is completely different from another thing.
He tries so hard to be smooth, but Charles is the ANTITHESIS of cool.

antonym (AN-tuh-nim). A word having an opposite meaning to that of another word.
"Rapid" and "slow" are ANTONYMS.

brummagem (BRUHM-uh-juhm). Describes something that looks great but performs poorly.
"Our press is certainly bankrupt in . . . reverence for nickel plate and BRUMMAGEM."—Mark Twain

dichotomy (dy-KOT-uh-me). Division into two parts, especially into two seemingly contradictory parts.
A DICHOTOMY between good and evil is present in every human heart.

ANTONYMS

coequal (koh-EE-kwuhl). Equal with another in ability, extent, etc.
The United States Congress is COEQUAL to the executive branch of government.

fungible (FUN-jih-bull). Freely exchangeable for another of like nature; interchangeable.
Stella was incensed to find that diamonds are not FUNGIBLE commodities.

148. Pallid

(PAL-id), adjective

A wan, sickly, washed-out appearance indicating illness or weakness, or lack of energy, strength, and vitality.

ADJECTIVES

diffident (DIFF-ih-dent). Uncertain or unsure about a making a decision or taking an action; lacking confidence and boldness.
If you feel DIFFIDENT about driving a Rolls-Royce, you can always buy a Bentley.

ethereal (eh-THEER-ee-uhl). Light and airy; possessing a heavenly or celestial quality.
"ETHEREAL, their mauve / almost a transparent gray, / their dark veins bruise-blue."—Denise Levertov, British-born American poet

languid (LANG-gwid). Characterized by weakness and fatigue; or, lacking spirit and animation.
"In doing good, we are generally cold, and LANGUID, and sluggish; and of all things afraid of being too much in the right."—Edmund Burke, Anglo-Irish statesman, orator, and author

wan (WAWN). Showing or suggesting ill health or unhappiness.
"So shaken as we are, so WAN with care, / Find we a time for frighted peace to pant."—William Shakespeare

NOUNS

melanin (MEL-uh-nin). The pigment that determines the color of one's hair, eyes, and skin.
Tamara is unwilling to accept that, no matter how much time she spends on the sunny beaches of the Mediterranean, she will not achieve her desired tan due to her lack of MELANIN.

miasma (my-AZ-mah). An unhealthy atmosphere or environment; an unpleasant feeling pervading the air.
"These appearances, which bewilder you, are merely electrical phenomena not uncommon—or it may be there they have their ghastly origin in the rank MIASMA of the tarn"—Edgar Allan Poe, American author and poet

VERBS

enervate (EN-er-vayt). To rob a person, organization, place, or thing of its energy, strength, and vitality.
Greenhouse gases ENERVATE the protective ozone layer surrounding the Earth.

wane (WAYN). To gradually decrease; to fade away; to become diminished.
Once she finally received the Cartier watch from her father, Karen's interest in the timepiece quickly WANED.

ANTONYMS

florid (FLOOR-id). Excessively ornate and showy, as prose.
"All men are really most attracted by the beauty of plain speech, and they even write in a FLORID style in imitation of this."—Henry David Thoreau, American author and transcendentalist

refulgent (rih-FULL-jent). Radiant, gleaming; shining brightly.
When Anastasia moved her bejeweled hand while lounging in the midday sunshine, her sparkling diamonds were REFULGENT.

stygian (STY-gee-an). So dark as to be almost pitch black.
"STAND close around, ye STYGIAN set, / With Dirce in one boat convey'd! / Or Charon, seeing, may forget / That he is old and she a shade"—Walter Savage Landor, British writer and poet

tenebrous (TEN-uh-bruss). Dark and gloomy.
Eloise and Marcus spent the day exploring the TENEBROUS forest that surrounded their family's Maine compound.

149. Pandemic

(pan-DEM-ik), noun

An outbreak of a disease that threatens to spread rapidly and endanger the population of an entire nation or planet.

ADJECTIVES

bereaved (beh-REEVD). In a state of grief as the result of the death of someone loved.
"Laughter would be BEREAVED if snobbery died."—Peter Ustinov, British writer and dramatist

endemic (en-DEM-ik). Widespread, as a condition or characteristic found in a certain region, area, or group.
Affluence and influence seem to be just ENDEMIC to our group.

irremediable (eer-ree-MEE-dee-uh-bull). Impossible to cure or remedy.
Sylvia's outdated concept of couture is completely IRREMEDIABLE.

ubiquitous (yu-BIK-wih-tuss). Everywhere; all around; constantly surrounding; inescapable.
Wireless communication in the United States became UBIQUITOUS toward the close of the twentieth century.

unbridled (un-BRY-duld). Without limitations or boundaries; uncontrolled and unrestrained.
The customer's UNBRIDLED fury at being denied a refund was a sight to behold.

NOUNS

convalescence (kon-vah-LESS-sense). The time spent recovering from an illness and getting back to full health, often while being taken care of by others.
"CONVALESCENCE is the part that makes the illness worthwhile."
—George Bernard Shaw, Irish playwright

homeopathy (ho-mee-OP-uh-thee). The medical practice of giving patients minerals, metals, herbs, and other bioactive compounds in extremely diluted form.
Most modern scientists believe the effectiveness of HOMEOPATHY in some cases is due mainly to the placebo effect.

nostrum (NAH-strum). An ineffective solution that is a quick fix or Band-Aid, covering up a problem or masking its symptoms, but never addressing its root cause for a permanent fix.
"America's present need is not NOSTRUMS but normalcy."—Warren G. Harding

VERBS

metastasize (meh-TASS-tih-size). To spread harmfully from an original source, as with cancer cells.
Byron's ugly nature quickly METASTASIZED in our group, as he spread lies and gossip among more and more of our social contacts.

permeate (PUR-mee-ayt). To penetrate; to spread throughout.
The scent of Donna's exclusive perfume quickly PERMEATED the entrance hall of the Blakelys' stately home.

sequester (see-KWESS-ter). To remove and isolate a portion from a larger whole.
"A great deal of genetic engineering must be done before we have carbon-eaters SEQUESTERING carbon in sufficient quantity to counteract the burning of fossil fuels."—Freeman Dyson, English-born American physicist and mathematician

ANTONYMS

hermetic (her-MET-ik). Isolated, or unaffected by outside influences.
"Reality, whether approached imaginatively or empirically, remains a surface, HERMETIC."—Samuel Beckett, Irish writer, dramatist, and poet

rarefied (RAIR-uh-fyed). Lofty; exalted; of high class or caliber.
Most copywriters don't operate in the RAREFIED environment in which Clayton makes his millions.

salubrious (suh-LOO-bree-us). Favorable to one's health.
After father's asthma reasserted itself, the family began to spend more time at its Arizona compound because of the area's dry weather, which is SALUBRIOUS toward asthmatics.

150. Persuade

(pur-SWAYD), verb

To influence a person to an action, belief, etc.; to urge or induce; to convince through reasoning.

ADJECTIVES

tendentious (ten-DEN-shuss). Promoting one's beliefs or point of view.
Laura is TENDENTIOUS in extolling her belief in the efficacy of prayer in healing all illnesses.

NOUNS

leverage (LEHV-er-ij). Possessing an advantage or extra degree of influence in a given situation.
With his family's connections, Eldridge required no LEVERAGE to obtain a sinecure in the financial industry.

VERBS

adumbrate (ADD-um-brayt). To suggest or disclose something partially.
The factory workers were nervous when they learned the owner had ADUMBRATED a plan for layoffs.

blandish (BLAN-dish). To coax someone to do something for you through the use of flattery.
Your attempts to BLANDISH me into giving in to your point of view will not work.

inveigle (in-VAY-gull). To convince or persuade someone through trickery, dishonesty, or flattery.
Craig INVEIGLED the dean to allow him to graduate even though he failed to meet the foreign language requirement of the university.

jawbone (JAW-bone). To attempt to get someone to do something through persuasion rather than by force.
No matter how much he JAWBONED, Karl could not get Alison to sell her stock prior to the unveiling of the company's disastrous new line of parvenu fashion.

posit (PAWZ-it). To suggest or propose a theory or explanation, especially one that represents new, unusual, or nonobvious thinking and conclusions.
Astronomers POSIT that Jupiter may sustain life in its clouds.

ANTONYMS

dissuade (dih-SWADE). To convince to take alternate action; to advise against.
Marge DISSUADED her brother from joining the army.

151. Phobia

(FO-bee-uh), noun

An irrational, excessive, and persistent fear of a particular thing or situation.

NOUNS

acrophobia (ak-ruh-FO-bee-uh). An abnormal fear of heights.
Of course, his ACROPHOBIA ruled out any ride in the hot-air balloon.

monophobia (mon-uh-FOE-bee-uh). An abnormal dread of being alone.
Susan's MONOPHOBIA never manifested until she moved to a different city to start a new job.

nyctophobia (nik-toh-FO-bee-uh). A severe fear of the dark.
William never outgrew his NYCTOPHOBIA and still sleeps with the light on.

ochlophobia (ok-luh-FO-bee-uh). An illogical fear or dread of crowds.
Betty never realized she suffered from OCHLOPHOBIA until she moved to the city, where she had great difficulty walking to and from work during rush hour.

ophidiophobia (oh-fid-ee-oh-FO-bee-uh). An abnormal fear of snakes.
My father wasn't afraid of much, but his well-developed case of OPHIDIOPHO-BIA indicated a bad experience with snakes at some point in his youth.

taphephobia (taff-uh-FOE-bee-uh). The abnormal fear of being buried alive.
After seeing the final scene of that horror film, The Grave Claims Its Own, *I couldn't sleep, and I had an inkling of what it must be like to suffer from TAPHEPHOBIA.*

trypanophobia (try-pan-uh-FO-bee-uh). An abnormal fear of medical procedures involving injections or hypodermic needles.
My nephew, suffering from TRYPANOPHOBIA, considered terminating his education before high school so as to avoid the physical exam.

xenophobia (zee-nuh-FOE-bee-uh). Having an irrational fear or hatred of foreigners and immigrants.
We are not XENOPHOBIC; we dislike all strangers, regardless of their backgrounds, unless they are brought to us by other social contacts.

ANTONYMS

impavid (im-PAV-id). Not afraid; fearless.
Our IMPAVID guide was not averse to tangling with snakes, spiders, scorpions, or any other nasty and intimidating creature we encountered on the trip.

valiant (VAL-yuhnt). Brave; courageous; stout-hearted.
"Cowards die many times before their deaths; the VALIANT never taste death but once."—William Shakespeare, English dramatist

152. Place

(PLAYSS), noun

Defined portion of space that can be occupied, whether actually or virtually; area or location real or imagined.

NOUNS

domicile (DOM-ih-syl). A residence; one's legal, permanent home.
The defendant at that time had no DOMICILE, your honor; she was a homeless person.

environs (en-VY-ruhnz). The area surrounding a town or city; suburbs; vicinity.
Washington D.C. and its ENVIRONS contain as many lobbyists as government workers.

epicenter (EP-ih-cen-tuhr). The spot on the surface of the Earth directly above the site where an earthquake occurs; the focal point or origin of an activity, event, fad, etc.
I wonder when it was that Seattle became the EPICENTER of gourmet coffee.

hinterland (HIN-ter-land). An area bordering on a coast or river; inland region; an area removed from populated areas; back country.
Tired of the pressures and compromises of urban living, Martha moved her family to the more gentle HINTERLAND.

hovel (HUV-ul). A modest, humble home or hut; a rude or dirty dwelling place.
In the storm scenes of King Lear, *Edward is disguised as Poor Tom, a lunatic who has sought shelter in a HOVEL on the barren heath.*

natatorium (nay-tuh-TOR-ee-um). An indoor swimming pool.
Although he had swum in hundreds of venues, Melvin still had a dream of competing in the world's largest NATATORIUM.

periphery (puh-RIFF-uh-ree). The area at the extreme of a given boundary.
There among the homeless, at the furthest periphery of society, Maria found her calling.

pied-à-terre (pyay-duh-TARE). A second home or apartment, usually small, used as a place to stay for short trips to the location in lieu of renting a hotel room.
Alison and her family acquired a PIED-À-TERRE in the city because her work often requires her to spend days at corporate headquarters.

sanctum (SANK-tum). A holy, sacred place; a private place; retreat.
Brandon's small home office contained little more than a computer, an encyclopedia, and a few pieces of furniture, but it was in this unprepossessing SANCTUM that he wrote his Pulitzer Prize–winning play.

VERBS

egress (ee-GRESS). Exit; to go out; to leave a place.
The stewardess's earnest request that we try to EGRESS from the burning plane in an orderly fashion had little effect.

ANTONYMS

abyss (uh-BISS). A bottomless gulf; deep fissure; vast chasm; anything profound or infinite.
"Whoever fights monsters should see to it that in the process he does not become a monster. And if you gaze long enough into an abyss, the ABYSS will gaze back into you."—Friedrich Nietzsche, German philosopher

vacuity (va-KYOO-ih-tee). The state of emptiness; without contents.
"Once you fully apprehend the VACUITY of a life without struggle, you are equipped with the basic means of salvation."—Tennessee Williams, American playwright

153. Poor

(PAWR), adjective

Lacking material possessions; having little or no means to support oneself; impoverished.

ADJECTIVES

destitute (DES-ti-toot). Without the means of self-support; unable to subsist.
"When a rich man becomes poor it is a misfortune, it is not a moral evil. When a poor man becomes DESTITUTE, it is a moral evil, teeming with consequences and injurious to society and morality."—Lord Acton, English thinker and professor

impecunious (im-puh-KYOON-ee-us). To be poor or broke; to have little or no money.
Alex has been raving about his IMPECUNIOUS state ever since his trust fund was cut.

impoverished (im-POV-er-isht). Reduced to poverty.
"The Pilgrims made seven times more graves than huts. No Americans have been more IMPOVERISHED than these who, nevertheless, set aside a day of thanksgiving."—H.U. Westermayer

indigent (IN-dih-junt). Lacking the essentials of life; impoverished.
At the shelter, I came across many INDIGENT families who had fallen victim to the failing economy.

penurious (peh-NOOR-ee-uss). Lacking in means; extremely poor; destitute.
Joan, raised in comfortable surroundings, was not cut out for such a PENURIOUS lifestyle.

proletarian (pro-luh-TAIR-ee-un). The poorest class of people; the working class.
The politician's appeals to her PROLETARIAN constituents earned her many votes during the election.

ANTONYMS

opulent (OP-yoo-luhnt). Reflecting wealth and affluence.
Donald Trump showcases his OPULENT lifestyle by wearing designer suits, drinking Cristal champagne, and traveling in private airplanes.

154. Powerful

(POW-ur-full), adjective

Having or showing great power or force; mighty; influential; strong.

ADJECTIVES

authoritarian (aw-thor-uh-TAIR-ee-un). Describes a form of social control in which the government demands absolute, blind assent of its citizens.
The eerie, AUTHORITARIAN world of George Orwell's 1984 continues to resonate today.

Herculean (hur-kyuh-LEE-un). Strong and powerful; reminiscent of the Greek hero Hercules in vitality.
Robert made a HERCULEAN effort to complete the project before midnight.

omnipotent (om-NIP-uh-tuhnt). All powerful.
"An OMNIPOTENT God is the only being with no reason to lie."
—Mason Cooley, American author

redoubtable (rih-DOW-tuh-bull). The quality of being a formidable opponent.
Michael's REDOUBTABLE nature made him a successful negotiator and trial attorney.

stalwart (STAL-wart). Strong, steadfast, loyal; a staunch supporter of a group or cause.
Although Wayne is no longer a working engineer, he is a STALWART member of the American Institute of Chemical Engineers.

vehement (VEE-uh-muhnt). Acting with great force and energy; intensely emotional; passionate.
Milly, a chronic worry wart, was VEHEMENT about her children calling her if they were going to be late getting home from school.

NOUNS

carte blanche (kart blonsh). Unrestricted power, access, or privilege; permission to act entirely as one wishes.
Jean had CARTE BLANCHE during her first month or so as office manager, but the vice president eventually came to supervise her much more closely.

forte (fort). One's niche or strong point; that at which one excels.
Interior decorating was Frank's FORTE, but he resisted making a career of it for fear of what the guys would say.

juggernaut (JUG-ur-not). An object or force so powerful that it flattens or destroys anything in its path.
The earthquake did some minor structural damage to the city, but the tornado that followed a week later was a JUGGERNAUT, destroying every home and building it touched.

magnate (MAG-nayt). An industrial leader; a powerful business figure.
Your Honor, I am no communications MAGNATE; I run a small-town newspaper.

potentate (POH-ten-tayt). A powerful dictator, king, leader, or ruler.
A much-feared POTENTATE, Victor Von Doom ruled Latveria with an iron fist.

ANTONYMS

tenuous (TEN-yu-us). Unsubstantiated and weak.
Roland's arguments to prove to us that it's better to give than to receive were TENUOUS at best.

titular (TITCH-uh-luhr). A person who is a leader by title only, but lacks any real power.
The queen is the TITULAR head of the United Kingdom.

155. Predict

(pri-DIKT), verb

To state in advance; make known beforehand; foretell.

ADJECTIVES

delphic (DELL-fik). Obscurely prophetic.
For years, other economists, reporters, and just plain folks scrambled to interpret Federal Reserve Chairman Alan Greenspan's DELPHIC comments about the strength or weakness of the economy.

prophetic (pruh-FET-ik). Of or having the powers of a prophet or prophecy; predictive.
When I was growing up, my mother seemed to have a PROPHETIC gift when it came to predicting my future.

NOUNS

bellwether (BELL-weh-thur). A leader, or something that indicates future developments.
We may have to change our plans. I'm afraid those dark clouds are a BELLWETHER of today's weather shifts.

bibliomancy (BIB-lee-oh-man-see). Telling or divining the future using a book, especially the Bible, through interpretation of a passage chosen at random.
Our experience with the practitioner of BIBLIOMANCY was brief and unprofitable.

necromancy (NEH-kroh-man-see). The ability to gain new knowledge by communicating with the dead; magic and trickery in general.
"The so-called science of poll-taking is not a science at all but mere NECROMANCY."—E.B. White, American author

numerology (noo-muh-RAWL-uh-jee). The supposed practice of divining the future through analyzing the occult significance of numbers.
Judy's interest in NUMEROLOGY is the latest in a series of mystic doings; she was very big on tarot cards last week.

presentiment (prih-ZEN-tuh-ment). A feeling that something—especially something bad—is going to happen.
The flight was uneventful, despite Clyde's PRESENTIMENT that a mid-air disaster would occur.

pyromancy (PY-ruh-man-see). Divining of the future by means of fire or flames.
Brian skillfully parlayed a love of sitting around camp fires into a profitable business of PYROMANCY.

VERBS

augur (AW-ger). To predict or foretell the future.
The three witches of Shakespeare's Macbeth *AUGUR the cataclysmic fate of the play's titular character.*

portend (por-TEND). To suggest or foretell.
The tone of Joan's voice this morning PORTENDS trouble.

prognosticate (prog-NOSS-tih-kayt). To predict; to foretell the future.
As to the game's final outcome, I refuse to PROGNOSTICATE.

vaticinate (vuh-TIS-uh-nayt). To prophesy.
The ominous dark clouds and rising wind seemed to VATICINATE the end of the world or just a thunderstorm.

ANTONYMS

myopia (mye-OH-pee-uh). Inability to see close things clearly; to lack foresight.
My feeling is that by turning down that project, Fenster showed once again that he suffers from MYOPIA when it comes to marketing new consumer products.

156. Pride

(PRYD), noun

A sense of one's own dignity or worth; self-respect; an overly high opinion of oneself; self-esteem; conceit; satisfaction in one's own achievements, possessions, children, etc.

ADJECTIVES

grandiose (GRAN-dee-ose). Pompous; having pretentions or ambitions that exceed one's abilities, sensitivities, or means.
His GRANDIOSE scheme for career advancement simply will not pan out.

haughty (HOT-ee). Snobbishly proud.
I tried to apologize for bumping into the woman, but she only gave me a HAUGHTY glance and inspected her fur coat for damage.

overweening (OH-ver-WEE-ning). Extremely presumptuous, arrogant, and overconfident.
"Golf is an open exhibition of OVERWEENING ambition, courage deflated by stupidity, skill soured by a whiff of arrogance."—Alistair Cooke, British-born American journalist and broadcaster

tumid (TOO-mid). Pompous and swollen with pride.
We cannot stand it when Katherine wins arguments about couture and art collecting because the TUMID expression that crosses her face after a conversational victory is so loathsome.

vainglorious (vayn-GLOR-ee-us). Conceited; boastful; prone to showing off and bragging.
Although the scion of a well-established family, Gordon is so VAINGLORIOUS that you'd think him a parvenu!

NOUNS

hubris (HYOO-briss). Excessive pride.
Colin may have begun as a pleasant and unassuming clerk, but by the time he took over the company in 1987 he showed signs of the HUBRIS that would accompany his downfall.

VERBS

pique (peek). To injure a person's pride and thereby engender harsh feelings.
Marcia was PIQUED at not having been invited to the party.

preen (preen). To take pride (in oneself or one's accomplishments).
Barry PREENED himself on having received Broadcaster of the Year awards for three consecutive years.

ANTONYMS

chagrin (shuh-GRIN). A feeling of disappointment, humiliation, embarrass-ment, etc. caused by failure of some kind; mortification.
Much to the team's CHAGRIN, they could not score a single point in the entire last half of the game, and lost to a much inferior opponent.

contrite (kuhn-TRYT). Crushed in spirit by a feeling of remorse or guilt.
After the media reported his drunken and loutish behavior, the actor appeared CONTRITE but it was clear that he was sorry only for having been caught.

157. Problem

(PROB-luhm), noun

A question proposed for consideration or solution; a perplexing or difficult matter.

NOUNS

conundrum (kuh-NUN-drum). A riddle or puzzle.
"I don't understand anything," Stan said, in the months following graduation.
"Now that I'm out on my own, my whole life is one big CONUNDRUM."

dilemma (dih-LEM-uh). An argument necessitating a choice between equally unfavorable or disagreeable alternatives.
"Our DILEMMA is that we hate change and love it at the same time; what we really want is for things to remain the same but get better."—Sydney Harris, American journalist

exigency (EKS-ih-jen-see). A condition of some urgency requiring an immediate effort to alleviate or solve it.
"We should never despair, our Situation before has been unpromising and has changed for the better, so I trust, it will again. If new difficulties arise, we must only put forth New Exertions and proportion our Efforts to the EXIGENCY of the times."—George Washington

imbroglio (im-BRO-lee-oh). Colloquially referred to as a "sticky situation" —a predicament that is difficult to get out of.
Our inability to decide which New Year's Eve party to attend created an IMBROGLIO that disrupted our social calendar for months.

parameter (pah-RAM-ih-terr). A factor or variable that must be taken into account when solving a problem or understanding a situation.
The weight of Paul's grand piano is a PARAMETER that must be considered when building the mansion's new music room and ballroom.

predicament (prih-DIK-ih-muhnt). A condition or situation that is dangerous, unpleasant, or embarrassing; quandary.
Having moved in with Max, Alice now faced the PREDICAMENT of wanting to be alone.

quagmire (KWAG-myr). A thorny problem for which there is no ready solution; a messy situation from which there is no expeditious means of escape.
After years of fighting during which no visible progress occurred, the media and many vocal opponents started to refer to the Afghan War as a QUAGMIRE.

ANTONYMS

exposition (ek-spuh-ZISH-uhn). A setting forth of facts; detailed explanation.
"People who lean on logic and philosophy and rational EXPOSITION end by starving the best part of the mind."—William Butler Yeats, Irish dramatist and poet

resolution (rez-uh-LOO-shun). A solving, as of a puzzle; answering, as of a question; solution.
"Through the centuries, men of law have been persistently concerned with the RESOLUTION of disputes in ways that enable society to achieve its goals with a minimum of force and maximum of reason."—Archibald Cox, American lawyer

158. Punishment

(PUHN-ish-muhnt), noun

The act or fact of punishing; a penalty imposed on an offender for a wrongdoing.

ADJECTIVES

baculine (BAK-yuh-lin). Concerning a rod or stick, or with punishment administered with a rod.
It wasn't that long ago when BACULINE discipline was common in American schoolrooms.

NOUNS

ferule (FARE-uhl). A stick used to punish children; punishment.
Spare the FERULE and spoil the child.

reparations (reh-par-AYE-shuns). Payments made by nations defeated in war to the victors, who impose these payments to recover some of the costs of battle.
After World War I, REPARATIONS of 132 billion gold marks were imposed on Germany by the French.

forfeiture (FOR-fih-cher). A forfeiting; payment of a penalty or fine.
The vandal's FORFEITURE was thirty days of public service and six months probation.

mortification (mor-tuh-fi-KAY-shun). The practice of penitential discipline by controlling physical desires and passions.
In modern times, the practice of MORTIFICATION has either decreased or manifests itself differently from bygone days.

penance (PEN-uhns). A punishment undertaken or imposed as repentance for a sin or wrongdoing.
As PENANCE, Matt chose to give up chocolate ice cream.

retribution (ret-ruh-BYOO-shun). Punishment (as from God) for past wrongdoing.
Some saw the Mafia don's debilitating illness as a form of divine retribution for a life of crime.

sanction (SANGK-shun). A penalty as discipline or punishment.
The United Nations imposes SANCTIONS on countries that violate international rules or regulations.

VERBS

amerce (uh-MERSS). To punish, especially to punish with a monetary amount set by a court.
Barbara always watches her speed since she was AMERCED to the tune of a week's pay.

ANTONYMS

dispensation (dis-puhn-SAY-shun). A release from obligation; special exemption or remission; the suspension of a statute for extenuating circumstances.
Fortunately for him, William received a DISPENSATION and he was able to complete the building although it violated use restrictions of the town.

impunity (im-PYOO-nih-tee). Freedom from punishment or penalty.
We cannot let such an act of naked aggression stand with IMPUNITY.

159. Quash

(KWAHSH), verb

To repress or subdue completely.

ADJECTIVES

defunct (dih-FUNKT). An institution, object, etc., that has ceased to exist.
"Practical men, who believe themselves to be quite exempt from any intellectual influence, are usually the slaves of some DEFUNCT economist."
—John Maynard Keynes, British economist

hapless (HAP-liss). Unlucky and unfortunate.
"Exile is the noble and dignified term, while a refugee is more HAPLESS."
—Mary McCarthy, American author

pejorative (pih-JOR-uh-tiv). Insulting; meant as a put-down or to belittle the other person.
"Wordsmith" is a corporate term used to denote someone who is a good writer, but professional writers see it as PEJORATIVE.

vapid (VAH-pid). Dull; void of intellectual curiosity or intelligence; lacking spirit and enthusiasm; dull, routine, unchallenging.
What irked him most about his sister-in-law was her VAPID stares in response to simple questions, conversation, and jokes.

NOUNS

bête noire (bett-NWAR). A thing for which one has an intense dislike or great fear; a dreaded enemy or foe.
Sunlight was Dracula's greatest BÊTE NOIRE.

ordinance (OR-dih-nance). A specific law or regulation.
The lavish tree house Roger built for his kids was in clear violation of at least half a dozen local ORDINANCES.

VERBS

impugn (ihm-PYOON). To attack as false or wrong.
"I do not IMPUGN the motives of any one opposed to me. It is no pleasure to me to triumph over any one."—Abraham Lincoln

proscribe (pro-SKRYB). To forbid or prohibit; frequently confused with the word "prescribe."
State law PROSCRIBES the keeping of wild animals as house pets.

quell (KWELL). To suppress or extinguish; or, to quiet one's own or another's anxieties.
"O the orator's joys! / To inflate the chest, to roll the thunder of the voice out from the ribs and throat, / To make the people rage, weep, hate, desire, with yourself, / To lead America—to QUELL America with a great tongue."
—Walt Whitman, American poet and humanist

raze (RAYZ). To tear down or demolish.
We had to RAZE our Cape Cod home and rebuild it entirely, due to some structural damage to the home caused by high winds.

ANTONYMS

approbation (ap-ruh-BAY-shun). Official approval or commendation.
"In a virtuous and free state, no rewards can be so pleasing to sensible minds, as those which include the APPROBATION of our fellow citizens. My great pain is, lest my poor endeavours should fall short of the kind expectations of my country."—Thomas Jefferson

inurement (in-UR-ment). Acceptance without resistance or fighting back of punishment, poor treatment, or unpleasant circumstances or conditions.
Perhaps others might respond to this treatment with INUREMENT, Eloise hissed, but I will buy my diamonds at another boutique from this point forward.

malleable (MAL-yah-bull). Easily molded into different shapes; easily influenced to change one's opinion or actions.
"I did not know that mankind was suffering for want of gold. I have seen a little of it. I know that it is very MALLEABLE, but not so MALLEABLE as wit."
—Henry David Thoreau, American author and transcendentalist

160. Quotidian

(kwo-TID-ee-an), adjective

Familiar; commonplace; nothing out of the ordinary.

ADJECTIVES

colloquial (kah-LOW-kwee-ul). Informal, conversational, everyday language.
"COLLOQUIAL poetry is to the real art as the barber's wax dummy is to sculpture."—Ezra Pound, American expatriate poet

orthodox (OR-thuh-docks). Mainstream; conventional; adhering to the strictest interpretation of a law or religion.
ORTHODOX medicine has long ignored the obvious effect diet and nutrition have on health and illness.

pro forma (pro-FOR-muh). Standard; following a commonly accepted format or process.
"Don't worry about reading the fine print," the manager told the young singer as he shoved the contract in front of him and put a pen in his hand. "It's just PRO FORMA."

trumpery (TRUM-puh-ree). Something without value; a trifle.
The TRUMPERY that the Smythingtons collect and call "art" is, clearly, distasteful dreck.

utilitarian (you-till-ih-TAYR-ee-an). Showing preference for things and ideas that are practical and utterly pragmatic while eschewing the fanciful and useless.
Paul's UTILITARIAN mindset makes him an ideal trader on Wall Street.

NOUNS

ennui (on-WEE). Apathy and lack of energy caused by boredom and disinterest.
"And he spoke of ENNUI, of jaded appetites, of nights and days aboard a moonstone vessel as large as a city."—Harlan Ellison, American author

homeostasis (ho-me-oh-STAY-sis). A dynamic system in which balance between input and output has been achieved, so no net changes take place.
When HOMEOSTATIS is achieved in a sealed biosphere, the animals and plants can live without outside air, food, or water.

ANTONYMS

arcane (ar-KAYN). Strange and mysterious; understood by only a few.
Bill's ARCANE knowledge of all Lexus models and their accessories is just a waste of gray matter.

clandestine (klan-DES-tin). Pertaining to activities that are secret, covert, and perhaps not fully authorized or sanctioned.
"CLANDESTINE steps upon imagined stairs / Climb through the night, because his cuckoos call."—Wallace Stevens, American poet

maverick (MAH-ver-ik). An unorthodox or unconventional person who does what it takes to get things done.
"The rugged individualist is too often mistaken for the misfit, the MAVERICK, the spoilsport, the sore thumb."—Lewis H. Lapham, former editor of Harper's Magazine

ruritanian (roor-ih-TAYNE-ee-in). Anything related to a romantic adventure or its environment.
The two lovers found Barbados to be a RURITANIAN paradise.

161. Rash

(RASH), adjective

Acting too hastily without deliberation or caution; reckless.

ADJECTIVES

brash (brash). Impudent; hasty; acting impetuously and quickly.
The action you have taken is BRASH; you will regret your recklessness.

foolhardy (FOOL-har-dee). Rash; hasty; unthinking.
Mack's FOOLHARDLY decision to leave his job and visit Trinidad and Tobago for two years was apparently the result of a chance encounter with a palm reader he met in a Greyhound station in West Covina, California.

improvident (ihm-PRAHV-ih-dent). Not planning for the future; acting without thinking.
It was cute when he was younger, but now Mike's IMPROVIDENT behavior just makes him look like a total loser.

impulsive (im-PUHL-siv). Inclined to act without conscious thought.
Teenagers tend to be IMPULSIVE, but most learn from their actions and grow up to be rational adults.

quixotic (kwik-SOT-ik). Impractical; foolishly impulsive; rash; unpredictable in the manner of Cervantes's character Don Quixote.
We all loved Arthur dearly, but could not support his continual QUIXOTIC quests to save the environment.

reckless (REK-less). Disregarding consequences.
Jane's approach to affairs of the heart was RECKLESS and she invariably paid a terrible price.

NOUNS

temerity (tuh-MAIR-uh-tee). Rashness; recklessness.
You have the TEMERITY to ask for a raise after showing up late forty percent of the time over the last three months?

ANTONYMS

discreet (dih-SKREET). Careful about what one says or does; prudent.
"We are DISCREET sheep; we wait to see how the drove is going, and then go with the drove."—Mark Twain, American humorist and writer

judicious (joo-DISH-uhs). Having or applying sound judgment; wise and careful.
"Originality is nothing but JUDICIOUS imitation. The most original writers borrowed from one another."—Voltaire, French philosopher and writer

162. Raze

(RAYZ), verb

To tear down or demolish.

ADJECTIVES

asunder (ah-SUN-derr). Split into parts; separated, as a former union.
His marriage torn ASUNDER, Mike decided to quit his job, move to Tangiers, and become a year-round beach bum.

deleterious (dell-ih-TEER-ee-us). Harmful; damaging.
Smoking has been proven to have a DELETERIOUS effect on one's health.

defunct (dih-FUNKT). An institution, object, etc., that has ceased to exist.
"Practical men, who believe themselves to be quite exempt from any intellectual influence, are usually the slaves of some DEFUNCT economist."
—John Maynard Keynes, British economist

NOUNS

cannonade (kan-uh-NAYD). A continuous, relentless bombardment or effort.
A CANNONADE of questioning greeted Eva's statement that she was quitting the club's tennis team.

maelstrom (MAYL-struhm). A situation marked by violence, turbulence, and uncertainty.
Many families who lost their fortunes during the MAELSTROM of the 1929 stock market crash are still trying to regain their social status today.

tabula rasa (TAB-yuh-luh RAH-suh). A clean slate; lacking preconceived notions, prejudices, beliefs, and attitudes; receptive to instruction and information.
"Classic writer's fear of the blank page: call it TABULA-RASA-phobia."
—John Jerome, American nonfiction writer

VERBS

decimate (DESS-ih-mayt). To reduce something greatly, to the point of wiping it out.
"Every doctor will allow a colleague to DECIMATE a whole countryside sooner than violate the bond of professional etiquette by giving him away."
—George Bernard Shaw, Irish playwright

efface (ih-FAYSS). To erase, obliterate, make inconspicuous.
"It is also true that one can write nothing readable unless one constantly struggles to EFFACE one's own personality. Good prose is like a windowpane."
—George Orwell, British author

expunge (eks-PUNJ). To rid oneself of an annoyance; to cast out; to get rid of; to forcibly eject.
"There is no man, however wise, who has not at some period of his youth said things, or lived in a way the consciousness of which is so unpleasant to him in later life that he would gladly, if he could, EXPUNGE it from his memory."
—Marcel Proust, French novelist, essayist, and critic

quash (KWAHSH). To repress or subdue completely.
She quickly QUASHED the rebellion of the other members of the PTO by reminding them of the superiority of her social contacts.

quell (KWELL). To suppress or extinguish; or, to quiet one's own or another's anxieties.
"O the orator's joys! / To inflate the chest, to roll the thunder of the voice out from the ribs and throat, / To make the people rage, weep, hate, desire, with yourself, / To lead America—to QUELL America with a great tongue."
—Walt Whitman, American poet and humanist

ANTONYMS

ameliorate (uh-MEEL-yuh-rayt). To correct a deficiency or defect; to make right a wrong; to take actions that make up, at least in part, for negative actions or failure to take action previously.
After you insulted her mother, I don't think even the most expensive piece of jewelry will be enough to AMELIORATE your relationship with Marcia.

bulwark (bull-WARK). A defensive, protective barrier, wall, or force.
"Since he aims at great souls, he cannot miss. But if someone should slander me in this way, no one would believe him. For envy goes against the powerful. Yet slight men, apart from the great, are but a weak BULWARK."
—Sophocles, Greek tragedian

immutable (im-MYOO-tuh-bull). Unchanging; not able to be changed.
"I don't know what IMMUTABLE differences exist between men and women apart from differences in their genitals."—Naomi Weisstein, American feminist

163. Real

(REEL), adjective

Existing or happening in fact; actual; true; authentic; genuine.

ADJECTIVES

bona fide (BO-nah-fyed). Legitimate, the real thing, the genuine article.
He may not come across as particularly intelligent, but Brian's Phi Beta Kappa key is, in fact, BONA FIDE.

corporeal (kor-PORE-ee-ul). Tangible; having material existence.
The estate sold the late author's CORPOREAL assets, but it retained the copyright of all his intellectual properties, both published and unpublished.

de facto (dih-FAK-toe). Existing in fact, but without official title.
Although we eschew titles, Sasha clearly is the DE FACTO head of our arts-patronage club.

equable (ECK-wuh-bull). Unvarying, steady, and free from extremes.
"He spake of love, such love as spirits feel / In worlds whose course is EQUABLE and pure."—William Wordsworth, British Romantic poet

palpable (PAL-pah-bull). Capable of being touched, felt, or handled; tangible.
When Alistair did not give Lorissa the luxury watch she was expecting for her birthday, the silence was PALPABLE.

veritable (VER-ih-tah-bull). Genuine; perfect as a specimen or example.
"For me, the child is a VERITABLE image of becoming, of possibility, poised to reach towards what is not yet, towards a growing that cannot be predetermined or prescribed."—Maxine Greene, American philosopher and educator

viable (VY-uh-bull). Capable of occurring or working; practicable; real; capable of living.
Mike argued quite persuasively that the only VIABLE solution to the company's financial dilemma was for it to go public and raise money by selling stock.

VERBS

corroborate (kuh-ROB-uh-rayt). To make more certain; to confirm.
The witness was able to CORROBORATE the defendant's testimony.

substantiate (sub-STAN-shee-ayt). To give substance or true existence to: to show to be real or true by giving evidence; prove; confirm.
Jack tried for years to SUBSTANTIATE his rightful claim to ownership of the property.

vet (VET). To appraise or evaluate for authenticity.
The campaign manager thoroughly VETTED the short list of vice presidential candidates.

ANTONYMS

conjectural (kuhn-JEK-chur-uhl). Of the nature of guesswork; involving inference and theories.

"The present policy path makes current promises, at least in real terms, highly CONJECTURAL."—Alan Greenspan, former chairman of the Federal Reserve

incorporeal (in-core-PORE-ee-al). Lacking form.

The moanings and low rumblings in the old house suggested INCORPOREAL visitors to Kate.

164. Reduce

(ri-DOOS), verb

To lessen in any way, such as size, amount, number etc.

ADJECTIVES

curtate (KUR-tayt). Reduced; shortened; abbreviated.

The committee could not get a good idea of the building plans from the CUR-TATE descriptions at the luncheon.

NOUNS

diminution (dim-ih-NOO-shen). Reduction or decrease due to outside influence.

The stock fell in value by 75 percent in just over three hours; few issues can fully recover from such DIMINUTION.

VERBS

abate (uh-BAIT). To reduce or eliminate a tax, claim, fine, etc.; to diminish, subside.

John sold his car in February and, when he received a bill for the year's excise tax, asked the town to ABATE the amount.

curtail (ker-TALE). To abridge or truncate; to lessen, usually by taking or cutting away from.
His new office's 8:00 A.M. meetings meant Dwight would have to CURTAIL his late-night television watching.

decimate (DESS-ih-mayt). To reduce something greatly, to the point of wiping it out.
"Every doctor will allow a colleague to DECIMATE a whole countryside sooner than violate the bond of professional etiquette by giving him away."
—George Bernard Shaw, Irish playwright

dilute (die-LOOT). To make something, such as a mixture, thinner or weaker by adding additional objects, ingredients, compounds, etc. to it; to reduce force, strength, or effectiveness of.
Frederica never DILUTES her words. She'll tell you exactly how she feels.

extenuate (ik-STEN-yoo-ayt). To reduce in seriousness, external aspect, or extent; to make a fault or error less grave.
The case was dismissed because circumstances EXTENUATED his negligence.

ANTONYMS

accretion (uh-KREE-shun). Growth in size, especially by addition or accumulation.
"The most successful men in the end are those whose success is the result of steady ACCRETION."—Alexander Graham Bell, Scottish-American inventor

aggrandizement (uh-GRAN-diz-muhnt). An increase in power, position, riches, etc.; widening in scope or intensity.
Margaret had a well-developed skill for self-AGGRANDIZEMENT.
See also: Change, Harm

165. Refulgent

(rih-FULL-jent), adjective

Radiant, gleaming; shining brightly.

ADJECTIVES

effulgent (ih-FULL-jent). Shining brightly; glowing; radiant.
The lightning storm made the evening sky positively EFFULGENT.

luciferous (loo-SIH-fuh-ruhs). Providing insight or enlightenment; illuminating.
Blake did not find the Ivy League LUCIFEROUS, so he decided to devote his life to world travel instead.

nitid (NIHT-id). Bright and lustrous.
Brock and Jenny flew through NITID moonbeams in Brock's new Gulfstream GIV personal jet.

resplendent (reh-SPLEN-dent). Garbed or decorated in lush fabrics and rich, vibrant colors.
The bride was RESPLENDENT in a beaded silk gown.

NOUNS

élan, (a-LON). Enthusiasm, energy, flair, zest.
Bryanna reacted with ÉLAN when she was tapped to be part of a feature for Elite Travel Magazine.

exemplar (ig-ZEM-plar). A role model, a shining example of a desired state, status, or behavior.
"The system—the American one, at least—is a vast and noble experiment. It has been polestar and EXAMPLAR for other nations."—Phyllis McGinley, American poet

felicity (fih-LISS-ih-tee). A state of blissful happiness.
"Never lose sight of the fact that all human FELICITY lies in man's imagination, and that he cannot think to attain it unless he heeds all his caprices."
—Marquis de Sade, French aristocrat and revolutionary

VERBS

zonk (ZAWNK). To stun or stupefy.
We were positively ZONKED by Marie's choice of couture for the very important Sanderson gala.

ANTONYMS

austere (aw-STEER). Stern; grim and lacking humor or warmth; clean and unornamented; severe or strict in manner.
In the movie Dead Poets Society, *Robin Williams clashes with an AUSTERE headmaster at a private boys' school.*

innocuous (ih-NAHK-yew-us). Not harmful or offensive; innocent, incidental, and hardly noticeable.
"I know those little phrases that seem so INNOCUOUS and, once you let them in, pollute the whole of speech."—Samuel Beckett, Irish writer, dramatist, and poet

166. Regret

(ree-GRET), verb, noun

To feel sorrow over; mourn for; to feel remorse for.

ADJECTIVES

penitent (PEN-ih-tent). Feeling sorry and regretful that you have done something wrong.
According to Ambrose Bierce's jaded view, the PENITENT are typically those undergoing or awaiting punishment.

rueful (ROO-full). Regretful; pitiable.
In the terminal, Jean gave a RUEFUL sigh as she stared at the plane that was to carry her away from San Francisco forever.

NOUNS

compunction (kum-PUNK-shun). Unrest or uneasiness arising out of a feeling of guilt; a sensation of remorse or uncertainty about a decision or course of action.
I will sign her dismissal notice myself without COMPUNCTION; she is easily the most incompetent salesperson I have ever worked with.

contrition (kuhn-TRISH-uhn). A feeling of remorse for sins or guilt.
"I shall never send for a priest or recite an Act of CONTRITION in my last moments. I do not mind if I lose my soul for all eternity."—Mary McCarthy, American author

qualm (KWAHM). A sudden feeling of uneasiness, often linked to a pang in one's conscience.
Of course we feel no QUALMS about wanting the finest things in life; that is the legacy our forefathers bequeathed to us.

repentance (rih-PEN-tense). A feeling of sorrow for a wrongdoing.
"Prostitutes have very improperly been styled women of pleasure; they are women of pain, or sorrow, of grief, of bitter and continual REPENTANCE, without a hope of obtaining a pardon."—Anonymous

VERBS

bemoan (bih-MOWN). To regret passionately or to complain about an ill turn of events.
Joel could not stop BEMOANING the fact that he was only three numbers off of the Powerball jackpot.

ANTONYMS

appeased (uh-PEEZED). Placated; soothed or satisfied.
Sally was easily APPEASED, rarely feeling negative emotions or behaving in a way that would cause regret.

complacent (kum-PLAY-suhnt). Satisfied with oneself; smug; content.
Brian was so COMPLACENT during the practice scrimmages before the big game that his coach considered benching him and playing the backup quarterback instead.
See also: Sad

167. Relationship

(ri-LAY-shun-ship), noun

A state of being related; a connection or association.

ADJECTIVES

collegial (kuh-LEE-juhl). Of a working relationship among colleagues characterized by collective responsibility and minimal supervision.
The COLLEGIAL structure of the organization is one reason there's very little turnover there.

consanguineous (con-san-GWIN-ee-us). Related by blood; of common lineage.
The two brothers learned of their CONSANGUINEOUS relationship after a series of blood tests.

filial (FILL-ee-ull). That which is due from or befitting a son or daughter; pertaining to a son or daughter.
Mother considered it my FILIAL responsibility to take over the family business when I graduated, but I wanted to pursue a career of my own.

platonic (pluh-TAWN-ik). Free of sexual or romantic relations; also refers to the ideal form of something.
Emily knew that her relationship with Paul had to remain PLATONIC if they were going to continue working together.

symbiotic (sim-bee-OTT-ik). Characteristic of an intimate or mutually advantageous relationship, especially (in biology) one between dissimilar organisms.
In ocean life you often see SYMBIOTIC relationships between large and small fish, in which the smaller feed off of organisms existing on the larger, thereby keeping the larger fish clean and healthy.

NOUNS

dalliance (DAL-ee-ehnss). A brief, casual flirtation with or interest in someone or something; the act of tarrying rather than proceeding swiftly and deliberately.
Her DALLIANCE with the pool boy made her husband angry and jealous.

détente (day-TAWNT). From the French, meaning "to slacken," a loosening of strained relations.
After Graham and Heather stopped yelling at and started listening to each other, the DÉTENTE between them began.

liaison (lee-A-zawn). An adulterous relationship; or, a kind of illicit sexual relationship.
LIAISONS are much more common within our group than are stable marriages.

lineage (LIN-ee-ij). Ancestry; family tree.
We still consider Rachel nouveau riche because her family can only trace its American LINEAGE to the mid-eighteenth century.

nepotism (NEP-uh-tiz-um). The practice of favoring relatives.
The company practiced shameless NEPOTISM, regularly passing up qualified applicants and hiring the underqualified sons, daughters, and cousins of board members.

rapport (rah-PORE). A trusting and harmonious relationship.
Although the Wilsons found their neighbors odd at first, the four soon developed a strong RAPPORT.

rapprochement (rah-prosh-MOHN). Re-establishment of friendly relations between nations following a period of hostility.
Lydia spoke at length about how RAPPROCHEMENT between the United States and some former Soviet nations has been a real boon to her family's prestige and wealth.

schism (SKIZ-um). A division; a break or rupture of relations, especially one due to ideological or political differences.
The SCHISM in the party over the issue of slavery reflected a division in the country itself.

scion (SY-uhn). A descendant or heir.
"SCION of chiefs and monarchs, where art thou? / Fond hope of many nations, art thou dead?"—Lord Byron, British Romantic poet

sociometry (so-see-OM-uh-tree). The determination of preference among members of distinct social groups.
What we found is that the brand's success or failure in a given area was due not mainly to income level, but to SOCIOMETRY.

VERBS

correlate (KORE-uh-layt). To relate logically or systematically; to link.
I believe I can demonstrate convincingly that the increased cancer rate in the town can be directly CORRELATED to the dumping practices of your firm over the past twenty years.

ANTONYMS

estrange (ih-STRAYNJ). To alienate or remove from a position or relationship.
Michelle's refusal to give up her self-destructive habits ESTRANGED her brother.

misanthrope (MISS-en-throwp). A person of antisocial nature who dislikes other people and thinks poorly of them until they give him reason not to.
Harold has become a veritable MISANTHROPE since Anabelle refused to go on any more dates with him.

168. Relieve

(rhi-LEEV), verb

To ease, lighten, reduce, or free from pain, anxiety, etc.

NOUNS

anodyne (an-uh-DYNE). Anything that relieves or lessens pain; something that soothes.
"Novels so often provide an ANODYNE and not an antidote, glide one into torpid slumbers instead of rousing one with a burning brand."—Virginia Woolf, British novelist

unguent (UNG-gwent). A locally applied ointment or salve.
In treating poison ivy, calamine lotion or some similar UNGUENT is usually recommended.

VERBS

alleviate (uh-LEEV-ee-ayt). To make more bearable; to relieve.
The only thing that will ALLEVIATE the fatigue I'm feeling right now is a good night's sleep.

assuage (uh-SWAYJ). To ease; to make less severe; to mitigate.
Gary tried to ASSUAGE his grief at the loss of his lover by taking a long trip to Europe.

palliate (PAL-ee-ayt). To treat a patient so that his symptoms abate even though he still has the disease.
We introduced Amanda to Roberto, in attempt to PALLIATE the broken heart that Amanda suffered over her breakup with one of the scions of the Chesterfield family.

salve (SAVV). To soothe as with salve (medicinal ointment).
Luckily for Jim, roses would usually SALVE his wife's distress whenever he forgot their anniversary.

temper (TEM-per). To moderate or mitigate; soften.
After the accident, Paul found that the monetary settlement was able to TEMPER his discomfort to a great extent.

ANTONYMS

aggravate (AG-ruh-vayt). To make worse or more severe; to intensify.
"Truth is neither alive nor dead; it just AGGRAVATES itself all the time."
—Mark Twain, American humorist and writer

foment (foe-MEHNT). To rouse or incite.
Many social advocates have been considered as rebellious and often are arrested for attempting to FOMENT trouble.

169. Repeat

(ree-PEET), verb

To say, utter, do, or make again; to reproduce.

ADJECTIVES

recursive (ree-KURSS-iv). Pertaining to a process in which each step makes use of the results of the earlier steps.
The study of mathematics is a RECURSIVE learning experience.

NOUNS

iteration (it-uh-RAY-shun). The process of performing a series of instructions or steps repeatedly; also refers to one repetition of those repeated steps.
"Thou hast damnable ITERATION, and art indeed able to corrupt a saint."
—William Shakespeare

tautology (taw-TALL-uh-jee). A needless repetition of an idea or statement; redundancy.
After his wealthy father's death, Gerald consistently referred to his mother with the TAUTOLOGY, "widow woman."

VERBS

echo (EK-oh). To resound with an echo; reverberate; to repeat another's words or ideas.
"Kind words are short and easy to speak, but their ECHOES are truly endless."—Mother Teresa

perpetuate (purr-PETCH-oo-ayt). To make everlasting; to prolong memory or use (of a thing).
The rumor that I am resigning has been PERPETUATED by a number of sources, all completely unreliable.

recapitulate (ree-kuh-PITCH-uh-layt). To repeat something, but in a more concise form.
"To RECAPITULATE: always be on time for my class," the professor told his freshman class on the first day of the semester.

replicate (REP-li-kayt). To duplicate, repeat, or reproduce, particularly for experimental purposes.
John had successfully developed a cure for the common cold, but could not REPLICATE the process.

ANTONYMS

conclusive (kuhn-KLOO-sive). Able to settle a question; definitive; final.
Mary was tired of continually arguing with her parents about responsibility and felt that getting a full-time job would be a CONCLUSIVE demonstration.

unambivalent (un-am-BIV-uh-luhnt). Not ambivalent; definite; certain.
The score at the end of the game gave UNAMBIVALENT testimony of our team's superiority.

170. Replace

(ri-PLAYSS), verb

To place again; put back in the previous position; to provide a substitute or equivalent for.

ADJECTIVES

supposititious (sup-poz-ih-TISH-uhs). Spuriously substituted or pretended; fraudulent; not genuine.
The cook prepared the dessert according to a SUPPOSITITIOUS list of ingredients.

tantamount (TAN-tuh-mownt). Equivalent in value or effect.
Eleanor considered our snub of her TANTAMOUNT to betrayal, and, in truth, she was correct.

ADVERBS

vicariously (vye-KAIR-ee-uss-lee). Through another, as enjoying imagined feelings and experiences by observing or hearing about another person's life and adventures.
Married for over twenty-five years, Roger often told his single friends that he lived VICARIOUSLY through them.

NOUNS

quid pro quo (KWID-pro-kwo). A fair exchange of assets or services; a favor given in return for something of equal value.
In a QUID PRO QUO, Stephen helped Alex with his math homework, while Alex did Stephen's chores.

prosthesis (pross-THEE-sis). An artificially constructed member meant to replace a damaged or missing part of the human body.
Several months after the accident, Greg was fitted for a PROSTHESIS for his lower left leg that would allow him to walk again.

subrogation (sub-roe-GAY-shun). The substitution of one person for another with respect to a lawful claim or right.
The SUBROGATION clause in the lease says that if the landlord cannot collect rent from the tenant, she has the right to collect from the co-signer of the leasing agreement.

VERBS

supersede (su-per-SEED). When one thing takes the place of another or renders the former obsolete.
"The classical laws [of physics] were SUPERSEDED by quantum laws."
—Stephen Hawking, British theoretical physicist

supplant (suh-PLANT). To take the place of.
"If we would SUPPLANT the opinions and policy of our fathers in any case, we should do so upon evidence so conclusive, and arguments so clear, that even their great authority fairly considered and weighted, cannot stand."
—Abraham Lincoln

ANTONYMS

abiding (uh-BYD-ing). Continuing without change; enduring.
"Only on paper has humanity yet achieved glory, beauty, truth, knowledge, virtue, and ABIDING love."—George Bernard Shaw, Irish playwright

perdure (per-DYOOR). To continue or last permanently; endure.
Kevin knew that his life would change and friends would come and go, but his relationship with Jane would PERDURE.

171. Reputation

(rep-yuh-TAY-shun), noun

The estimation in which a person is commonly held, whether favorable or not; character in the view of others; repute; fame.

NOUNS

calumny (KAL-um-nee). The act of libel or slander; besmirching of a person's reputation by spreading false statements and rumors.
"To persevere in one's duty and be silent is the best answer to CALUMNY."
—George Washington, American president

innuendo (in-yu-ENN-doe). A subtle intimation; an indirect insinuation.
Through hints and INNUENDO her opponent managed to plant seeds of doubt about Governor Williams's past.

libel (LIE-bull). A written, printed, or pictorial statement or assertion that is unjustly negative, defaming, or hurtful to one's character and reputation.
Several celebrities have sued the supermarket tabloid for LIBEL, but the parade of lurid and preposterous headlines has continued unabated.

VERBS

exonerate (ig-ZON-uh-rayt). To clear or free from blame or guilt; to restore (one's reputation).
After the charges were thrown out and Brian was completely EXONERATED, he was free to continue his work in the securities industry.

insinuate (in-SIN-yu-ayt). To hint at darkly; to suggest (typically, with negative connotations).
I hope you don't mean to INSINUATE that my husband is seeing another woman.

slander (SLAN-dur). To make an untrue and malicious statement intended to damage the reputation of another.
If you continue to SLANDER my father, Mr. Caen, you will be hearing from my attorney.

ANTONYMS

notoriety (no-tuh-RY-ih-tee). The state of being widely and unfavorably known.
"It takes very little fire to make a great deal of smoke nowadays, and NOTORIETY is not real glory."—Lousia May Alcott, American author

unsavory (un-SAYV-err-ee). Distasteful; unpleasant; disreputable; of dubious reputation.
"Our future is inextricably linked to what happens in Washington, D.C., and we know that is a very UNSAVORY reality."—Don Libey, direct marketing advisor

172. Responsibility

(ri-spon-suh-BIL-uh-tee), noun

The condition or state of being responsible; obligation; duty.

ADJECTIVES

onerous (OH-nerr-us). Difficult; imposing heavy responsibility.
Caring for his son's large aquarium quickly went from an interesting hobby to an ONEROUS burden.

NOUNS

onus (OH-nuss). Obligation, responsibility, duty, or burden.
The ONUS for choosing the color scheme for our new lacrosse uniforms fell ultimately to Tabitha, who had previously chosen the design for our polo uniforms.

VERBS

ascribe (uh-SKRYB). To attribute or assign causal responsibility to a person or thing.
This work has been ASCRIBED to Rousseau, but his authorship now seems uncertain.

ANTONYMS

abdicate (AB-dih-kayt). To formally give up a position or responsibility; to step down from a high government office or other powerful position.
The King, as we all know, ABDICATED rather than give up the woman he loved.

dereliction (dair-uh-LIK-shun). Willful neglect; shirking of responsibility; the knowing failure to perform one's duty.
The sergeant's inaction that night led to troubling accusations of DERELICTION of duty.

exculpate (EK-skull-payt). To remove responsibility or guilt from.
The fact that I was convicted is immaterial; I have been fully EXCULPATED.

fickle (FIK-uhl). Changeable or unstable in interest or affection; capricious.
"O, swear not by the moon, the FICKLE moon, the inconstant moon, that monthly changes in her circle orb, Lest that thy love prove likewise variable."
—William Shakespeare, English dramatist

remiss (rih-miss). Negligent or careless.
Jon was REMISS in his relationships, never thanking anyone for the kindnesses he received.

sociopath (SO-see-uh-path). A person who, because of mental illness, lacks restraint or moral responsibility toward fellow members of society.
Although motion pictures and popular fiction have shown an unending fascination with serial killers, the fact is that such SOCIOPATHS are quite rare.

173. Revenge

(rih-VENJ), verb

To inflict punishment, damage, or injury in return for an insult, injury, etc.

ADJECTIVES

vindictive (vin-DIK-tiv). Mean-spirited; eager for revenge.
When angered, Lynn can be quite VINDICTIVE; those who work with her know that the most painless course is to stay on her good side.

NOUNS

nemesis (NEM-ih-sis). An act or agent of retribution; an opponent motivated by revenge.
Things looked bleak: Harold's nemesis, Mike, was in charge of all hiring decisions.

reprisal (rih-PRYZ-uhl). An instance or the act of retaliation.
Peter was confident that he was correct, but was just as sure he faced a REPRISAL for speaking up during the meeting.

retribution (ret-ruh-BYOO-shun). Deserved punishment for evil done.
Some saw the Mafia don's debilitating illness as a form of divine RETRIBUTION for a life of crime.

vendetta (ven-DETT-uh). A bitter feud or grudge, especially one involving vengeance for a wrongdoing.
Mark's arguments against my proposed project had less to do with its merits than with the VENDETTA he has waged against me since I was hired for the job he wanted.

VERBS

reciprocate (rih-SIP-ruh-kayt). To give or act in turn following the lead of another; to reply in kind.
We cannot ignore an act of aggression; if we are attacked, then we must RECIPROCATE.

requite (rih-KWYT). To return; to retaliate for an actual or assumed wrong.
"Certain sets of human beings are very apt to maintain that other sets should give up their lives to them and their service, and then they REQUITE them by praise"—Charlotte Brönte, British novelist

ANTONYMS

condone (kuhn-DOHN). To forgive, pardon, or overlook something.
*"One who CONDONES evil is just as guilty as the one who perpetrates it."
—Martin Luther King, Jr., American minister and civil-rights leader*

vindicate (VIN-dih-kayt). To clear from criticism, censure, suspicion, etc.; to justify or defend.
"Have patience awhile; slanders are not long-lived. Truth is the child of time; ere long she shall appear to VINDICATE thee."—Immanuel Kant, German philosopher

174. Reverence

(REV-er-uhns), noun

A feeling of deep respect, awe, and love; veneration.

NOUNS

deification (DEE-if-ih-kay-shin). The process of making someone or something into—and worshipping them as—a god.
"Poetry is the DEIFICATION of reality."—Edith Sitwell, British poet

fetish (FETT-ish). Any object, idea, leader, etc. inspiring unquestioned awe and reverence.
"It sickens me," Nora said, "how so many colleges have made a FETISH of high grades on standardized tests."

VERBS

exalt (ig-ZAWLT). To raise in honor, character, quality; to praise.
"Civilization degrades the many to EXALT the few." Amos Bronson Alcott, American reformer and philosopher

extol (ik-STOHL). To praise highly; laud.
When talking about his new girlfriend, Larry would EXTOL her virtues in reverential terms.

hallow (HAL-low). To establish as holy; to sanctify.
"But, in a larger sense, we can not dedicate, we can not consecrate, we can not HALLOW this ground."—Abraham Lincoln, Gettysburg Address

lionize (LIE-uh-nize). To praise excessively; to idolize.
For years young baseball fans LIONIZED Babe Ruth, whose many indiscretions were usually overlooked by the press.

venerate (VEN-uh-rayt). To regard or treat with reverence.
"The way the United States VENERATES celebrities can be quite annoying," Sylvia said.

ANTONYMS

desecrate (DESS-ih-krayt). To abuse the sacred character of a thing; to treat disrespectfully or irreverently.
Such profane language from our organization's current leader serves only to DESECRATE the memory of the founder.

impiety (im-PY-ih-tee). Lack of reverence for sacred things; disrespect for persons or things to which one should be devoted.
"To be in anger is IMPIETY; But who is man that is not angry?" William Shakespeare, English dramatist

175. Ridicule

(RID-ih-kyool), verb

To make fun of; to make the object of contempt; mock.

NOUNS

contumely (kon-TYOO-muh-lee). A rude display in speech or deed; contemptuous behavior; humiliating derision.
No matter how long he had held the grudge against Aaron, his CONTUMELY at the wedding was uncalled for.

VERBS

caricature (KAR-ih-kuh-chur). To exaggerate the peculiarities or defects of someone or something for purposes of ridicule.
Zealots of all stripes tend to CARICATURE those they despise in order to make them seem less powerful and frightening.

decry (dih-CRY). To condemn, ridicule, or denounce as harmful.
It is unconscionable to DECRY due process just because the system is sometimes abused.

deride (dih-RYD). To ridicule with cruelty; to laugh at and make fun of.
His classmates DERIDED Joe for wearing argyle socks to the prom.

lampoon (lam-POON). To mock or satirize.
Many felt that Trina was cruel to LAMPOON Jessica's performance, including her nervous tic.

pillory (PILL-uh-ree). To subject someone to merciless public ridicule or abuse.
I sipped my morning coffee as the respective parties' pundits PILLORIED each other.

scoff (SKAWF). To show mocking contempt; scorn.
"You may SCOFF all you want," Dave told the crowd as he climbed into the basket of the hot air balloon "but you'll see who gets to the wedding first."

ANTONYMS

applaud (uh-PLAWD). To express approval; acclaim; give praise.
"It often happens that those who in their lives were APPLAUDED and admired, are laid at last in the ground without the common honor of a stone."
—Samuel Johnson, English poet and critic

esteem (ih-STEEM). To value highly; have great respect and regard for; prize.
"The harder the conflict, the more glorious the triumph. What we obtain too cheap, we ESTEEM too lightly, it is dearness only that gives everything its value."—Thomas Paine, English-American writer and political pamphleteer

176. Sad

(SAD), adjective

Having or expressing sorrow, grief, or low spirits; melancholy; mournful.

ADJECTIVES

disconsolate (dis-KON-suh-lut). Beyond consolation; unable to be comforted; deep in grief or sorrow.
Jamie was DISCONSOLATE after missing what should have been the game-winning field goal.

doleful (DOLE-full). Causing or expressing grief or affliction.
I decided to rescue Rex from the animal shelter because I was entranced by his DOLEFUL expression.

lachrymose (LAK-rih-mose). Inclined to cry easily.
She was so LACHRYMOSE, she cried at commercials for long-distance phone companies.

morose (muh-ROHSS). Gloomy and ill-humored.
Now that his parents have taken away his private plane, Anthony has become positively MOROSE.

plangent (PLAN-jent). Having an expressive and particularly plaintive quality.
The PLANGENT locomotive whistle made Henry drop a tear in his beer.

sepulchral (suh-PUHL-kruhl). Suggesting a tomb; funereal or dismal.
The SEPULCHRAL tones of the organ emphasized the solemnity of the service.

woeful (WOH-full). Filled with sorrow or woe; in a sorry state.
When the home team lost the game in the final seconds, the WOEFUL crowd gasped, then went silent.

NOUNS

pathos (PAY-thoss). A quality arousing or evoking pity or sorrow or eliciting tender sympathy from an observer.
Chaplin's development of PATHOS as a component of film comedy was one of his most significant achievements.

tribulation (trib-yuh-LAY-shun). Great misery or distress, as from oppression.
"Rivers of wings surround us and vast TRIBULATION."—John Ashbery, American poet and critic

weltschmerz (VELT-shmertz). A lingering sorrow that some believe is a given in life.
When we snubbed Margaret for buying so many fashion knockoffs, her WELTSCHMERZ lasted until we forgave her.

VERBS

bewail (bih-WAYL). To express deep sorrow or regret over something, usually by weeping.
After his marriage ended, Chuck spent months BEWAILING his fate.

commiserate (kuh-MIZ-uh-rayt). To share in another's sorrow or disappointment.
Jane and Anita COMMISERATED with Frank over the failure of the business.

ANTONYMS

ebullient (eh-BULL-yuhnt). Feeling joy and positive emotions at an extreme level; the state of being wildly enthusiastic about something.
Lorne was EBULLIENT when he found that his mother had given the college enough money to overturn his rejection.

jubilant (JOO-buh-luhnt). Joyful and triumphant; elated.
After a hard-fought game, the winners were JUBILANT.
See also: Regret

177. Sapient

(SAY-pee-ent), adjective

Wise.

ADJECTIVES

erudite (AIR-yu-dyte). Sophisticated; well educated; deeply learned; knowledgeable; scholarly.
Beneath his ERUDITE image, Dr. John Brinkley was a money-grubbing con man.

omniscient (ahm-NIH-shent). All-knowing.
"The god of love, if omnipotent and OMNISCIENT, must be the god of cancer and epilepsy as well."—George Bernard Shaw, Irish playwright

venerable (VEN-err-uh-bull). Respected and revered, sometimes because of achievement, intelligence, or character, but just as often as a result of being around a long time.
"Is the babe young? When I behold it, it seems more VENERABLE than the oldest man."—Henry David Thoreau, American author and transcendentalist

NOUNS

hypothesis (hy-POTH-uh-sis). A principle derived from limited evidence, seen as sensible based on an analysis of available data, but not proven to the point where it is an accepted theory, rule, or law.
"In order to shake a HYPOTHESIS, it is sometimes not necessary to do anything more than push it as far as it will go."—Denis Diderot, French philosopher

literati (elit-uh-RAH-tee). The segment of society comprised of learned or literary men and women.
We attract the LITERATI because of our constantly carefree and exciting exploits.

sagacity (suh-GASS-ih-tee). Wisdom; soundness of judgment.
"Our minds are endowed by nature with such activity and SAGACITY that the soul is believed to be produced from heaven."—Quintilian, Roman rhetorician

VERBS

adjudicate (uh-JOO-dih-kayt). To preside over or listen to opposing arguments and help two parties settle their difference and come to an agreement.
As my daughters pummeled each other while screaming at top volume I tried desperately to ADJUDICATE their quarrel.

educe (ee-DYOOCE). To come to a conclusion or solve a problem through reasoning based on thoughtful consideration of the facts.
After Roger's family purchased a Mercedes C class, rather than its usual Mercedes E class, we EDUCED the Wallertons were enduring financial difficulties.

ANTONYMS

fatuous (FATCH-oo-us). Trivial, silly, absurd, unimportant, pointless.
"I'm sick of pretending that some FATUOUS male's self-important pronouncements are the objects of my undivided attention."—Germaine Greer, Australian writer and scholar

jejune (jih-JOON). Thoughts and actions that are not well thought out or fully formed; a poor performance or inferior work.
Samantha snidely informed Blake that her JEJUNE entertaining efforts might someday grow to maturity.

non compos mentis (non KAHM-puhs MEN-tiss). Crazy; insane; not in one's right mind.
When Bryce suggested he was considering the ministry, rather than joining the family bond business, we were certain he was NON COMPOS MENTIS.

tyro (TIE-roh). A beginner or novice.
Though a TYRO, Madeline quickly mastered cross-country skiing during her jaunt to Switzerland.

178. Science

(SY-ehnss), noun

A body of knowledge concerned with establishing facts, principles, and methods through experimentation and study.

NOUNS

biogenesis (by-oh-JEN-ih-siss). The process of life arising from other living things.
BIOGENESIS involves an unending regenerative cycle of life and death.

entomology (en-tuh-MOL-uh-jee). The study of insects.
Judy's little boy so loved to collect bugs from the garden that we wondered if he might grow up to study ENTOMOLOGY.

eustasy (YEW-stah-see). A change in sea level caused by melting of ice, movement of ocean floors, or major deposits of sediment.
Global warming is already triggering EUSTASY by melting the polar ice caps.

kinesiology (kih-nee-see-OL-uh-jee). The science of muscles and their function, physical movement, and muscular development.
As a body builder, he studied both nutrition and KINESIOLOGY.

morphology (moe-FALL-uh-jee). The study of something's form or structure.
We spent a surprisingly interesting few minutes discussing the MORPHOLOGY of the duck-billed platypus.

nanosecond (NAN-oh-sek-uhnd). A time period equal to one-billionth of a second.
Certain processes can now be measured in NANOSECONDS.

ornithology (or-nih-THOLL-uh-jee). The study of birds.
Her lifelong love of birds led Stella to seek a degree in ORNITHOLOGY.

taxonomy (tak-SON-uh-mee). The science of formal classification and naming.
The newly discovered insect was dubbed "Lilliput" by the researchers, although its formal name was a question of TAXONOMY that no one felt hurried to resolve.

xenogamy (zih-NAHG-uh-me). Cross-pollination among plant species.
The secret of our award-winning formal gardens is the careful use of XENOGAMY.

ANTONYMS

sorcery (SOR-suh-ree). The use of supernatural powers and evil spirits; witchcraft.
"The teaching of the church, theoretically astute, is a lie in practice and a compound of vulgar superstitions and SORCERY."—Leo Tolstoy, Russian novelist, philosopher

wizardry (WIZ-er-dree). The art of a wizard; magic; sorcery.
Brian was an accomplished politician; his diplomatic and rhetorical skills approached WIZARDRY.

179. Secret

(SEE-krit), adjective, noun

To keep from public knowledge; something not revealed.

ADJECTIVES

clandestine (klan-DES-tin). Pertaining to activities that are secret, covert, and perhaps not fully authorized or sanctioned.
"CLANDESTINE steps upon imagined stairs / Climb through the night, because his cuckoos call."—Wallace Stevens, American poet

cryptic (KRIP-tik). Having a hidden or ambiguous meaning; mysterious, secret.
In an effort to make their messages interesting, advertisers have made them more CRYPTIC so that, at times, it's unclear what is being advertised or why.

incognito (in-cog-NEE-toe). Hidden or unknown; with an intentional change in appearance to make one's real identity unknown.
The novelist wore sunglasses in hopes of remaining INCOGNITO at restaurants, but he was still pestered by autograph hounds.

surreptitious (suh-rep-TISH-us). Done in secret.
With little more than SURREPTITIOUS glances, Alison was able to entice Quentin to her side at the spring gala.

NOUNS

cache (KASH). Something hidden or stored.
Everyone was jealous when they learned of Moira's CACHE of acceptances to the finest schools.

machination (mak-uh-NAY-shun). A conniving plot; a crafty scheme meant to achieve an illicit end.
Carrie was familiar with Desmond's MACHINATIONS when it came to winning raises.

VERBS

encipher (en-SY-fur). To scramble or convert data into a secret code, prior to transmission, thereby making it impossible for unauthorized users to understand or decipher.
Mathematicians were employed by the Army to crack ENCIPHERED messages during the war.

ANTONYMS

candid (KAN-did). Honest; outspoken.
"Blame where you must, be CANDID where you can, and be each critic the good-natured man."—Robert Burns, Scottish poet

overt (oh-VURT). Open, public, and observable.
The enemy's OVERT acts demonstrated a bravado indicating their complete confidence in success.

180. Sensuous

(SEN-shoo-us), adjective

Affecting, appealing to, or perceived by the senses; enjoying the pleasures of the senses.

ADJECTIVES

epicurean (ep-ih-kyoo-REE-uhn). Fond of luxury and indulgence in sensual pleasures.
Peter was fond of EPICUREAN delights of all kinds, but could only afford the most basic.

hedonistic (heed-in-IS-tik). Characteristic of a belief that pleasure or happiness is the chief goal in life.
We were all amazed that our small-town friend could grow up and adopt such a HEDONISTIC lifestyle.

luxurious (lug-ZHOOR-ee-us). Characterized by luxury; loving luxury or pleasure.
"The sixties were an oyster decade: slippery, LUXURIOUS, and reportedly aphrodisiac they slipped down the historical throat without touching the sides."
—Julian Barnes, British critic and author

sybaritic (sih-bar-IT-ik). Relating to self-indulgent sensuous luxury and pleasure.
Selena rubbed the suntan lotion over her tanned middle slowly, and the whole thing had an erotic, SYBARITIC quality that made the men's eyes pop out of their heads.

toothsome (TOOTH-suhm). Voluptuous and sexually alluring.
Dorienne is TOOTHSOME thanks mainly to her plastic surgeon and her family's fortune.

voluptuous (vuh-LUP-chew-us). Anything arising from or giving extreme sensory or sensual pleasure.
A VOLUPTUOUS banquet was the highlight of the Masterlys' Thanksgiving gala.

ANTONYMS

astringent (uh-STRIN-jent). Severe; harsh; austere.
Her ASTRINGENT style was a perfect complement to the cold, chaste main character.

austere (aw-STEER). Severe in appearance or nature; self-disciplined or strict to a high degree.
George chose an AUSTERE lifestyle because he believed it was more wholesome and healthy.
See also: Sex

181. Sex

(SEKS), noun

The division by gender; the manifestation of the physical and emotional attraction between individuals.

ADJECTIVES

Dionysian (die-uh-NIH-she-un). Frenzied; uninhibited; hedonistic; orgiastic; unrestrained.
The fraternity's DIONYSIAN exploits were fun for a while, but when they resulted in his failing two classes, Emmett decided to go back to the quiet life.

lascivious (luh-SIV-ee-us). Interested in and eager to engage in sexual activity; sexual in nature.
"An impersonal and scientific knowledge of the structure of our bodies is the surest safeguard against prurient curiosity and LASCIVIOUS gloating."
—Marie Carmichael Stopes, British scientist and birth-control pioneer

lubricious (loo-BRISH-us). Arousing or suggestive of sexual desire; lustful.
All corporations require employees to attend a workshop on harassment in order to curb latent LUBRICIOUS instincts.

nubile (NOO-bile). Sexually mature and/or prepared for marriage; sexually attractive.
Art looked at his "baby" daughter Marie and realized that she had somehow become a NUBILE young woman of eighteen.

phallic (FAL-ik). Of or pertaining to the phallus, or penis; reminiscent of a penis; reminiscent of the life-giving force of nature, as in ancient Dionysian festivals that made the phallus a central element.
According to Freud, PHALLIC symbols (such as the sword of Unferth used by Beowulf) abound in both ancient and modern literature.

prurient (PROOR-ee-ent). An excessive focus on sex.
"The idea," Judge Cotlin wrote, "that Joyce's Ulysses is designed mainly to excite the reader's PRURIENT interest is absurd."

salacious (suh-LAY-shuss). Having an unhealthy, obsessive, or addictive interest in sex.
For weeks, the society pages were rife with SALACIOUS gossip, which turned out to originate from Mallory, who had lost her beau to Jeannette.

scabrous (SKAB-russ). Indelicate; risqué; salacious.
Joe believed that SCABROUS jokes were the most humorous.

sultry (SUL-tree). Suggestive of passion or smoldering sexuality.
Marjorie did nothing to accentuate her figure or appearance, but she still incurred the wrath of many women in the office who considered her to be naturally SULTRY.

tantric (TAN-trik). Related to views of sex as a sacred and deeply spiritual act.
"Both religions [Hinduism and Buddhism] were patronized by the same kings, ministers, and merchants, many of whom indulged in the same TANTRIC hetero-doxies."—William Dalrymple, Scottish historian and author

wanton (WAHN-tuhn). Loose, lascivious, and lewd.
Robert is so WANTON that women stay away from him in spite of his family's connections.

NOUNS

androgynous (an-DRAWJ-eh-nus). Something or someone who is of indeterminate sex; or hermaphrodite (having characteristics of both a male and a female).
The models at fashion week were so ANDROGYNOUS that Katherine couldn't tell if the clothes were designed for men or women.

coitus (KO-uh-tus). Sexual intercourse.
Professor Wells sternly informed me that he would prefer that I use the term "COITUS" in describing the activities of the test couples, rather than the less formal "making whoopee."

concupiscence (kon-KYOO-pih-suhns). Unbridled lust in the extreme; horniness.
"You're talking to a young vampire, a fountain of CONCUPISCENCE."
—Mario Acevedo, American fantasy author

debauchery (de-BAW-chuh-ree). Frequent indulgence in sensual pleasures.
"The geniuses, the mad dreamers, those who speak of DEBAUCHERY in the spirit, they are the condemned of our times."—Harlan Ellison, American author

demimonde (DEMM-ee-mond). Women who are considered to have loose morals due to their indiscreet or promiscuous behavior.
Unless you're trying to get yourself labeled a DEMIMONDE, Sylvia, you need to stop hanging out with guys like Roger.

flagrante delicto (fluh-GRAN-tee di-LIK-toh). In the act of committing an offense; most widely used today to describe a couple caught in the act of sexual intercourse.
"No cheating spouse, no teen with a wrecked family car, no mayor of Washington, D.C., videotaped in FLAGRANTE DELICTO has ever come up with anything as farfetched as U.S. farm policy."—P.J. O'Rourke, American satirist

hermaphrodite (hur-MAFF-ruh-dite). One who possesses both male and female reproductive organs.
Sheldon brought back miniature statues of the island's mythic hero, a HERMAPHRODITE warrior.

lothario (lo-THAR-ee-oh). A man who seduces women.
Ryan is friendly, I'll admit, but he is certainly no LOTHARIO.

necrophilia (nek-ruh-FILL-ee-uh). An erotic attraction to corpses.
For the lover concerned about rejection, NECROPHILIA may be the answer.

panderer (PAN-dur-ur). A person who obtains prostitutes for clients or supplies clients to prostitutes; a pimp.
Ralph was so inept at meeting women that he seriously considered getting advice from a PANDERER.

roué (roo-A). A licentious man; a libertine or lecher.
Although Ernest's dalliances might have been understandable when he was a young man, they were more difficult for his family to forgive in his later years, when he came to resemble nothing so much as a tired and lonely old ROUÉ.

sapphism (SAFF-iz-im). Lesbianism.
After several failed relationships with men, Martha was ready to try SAPPHISM.

saturnalia (sat-uhr-NAY-lee-uh). Unrestrained, licentious merrymaking.
Anyone looking at the party's aftermath the next day would have thought it was a SATURNALIA, not a fairly quiet reunion of five old friends.

satyr (SAY-ter). A lascivious, lecherous man.
Harold's graceful manners disappear once he has had a few glasses of champagne, and he becomes a veritable SATYR.

VERBS

eroticize (ih-ROT-uh-syz). To take something "tame" and sexualize it.
There's no need to EROTICIZE Shakespeare because his works are already filled with bawdy—sometimes downright filthy—puns.

philander (fih-LAN-der). To engage in amorous flirtations or exploits with someone whom one cannot or does not intend to marry.
These accusations of PHILANDERING, whether based in fact or not, have little to do with the question of whether the candidate will serve our state well in the United States Senate.

ANTONYMS

celibacy (SELL-ih-buh-see). The quality of being chaste; the state of abstaining from sexual activity.
Although he took Holy Orders, David eventually found that he could not live a life of CELIBACY and left the priesthood.

chaste (CHAYST). Not indulging in sexual activity; virginal; celibate.
"Too CHASTE a youth leads to a dissolute old age."—Andre Gide, French writer
See also: Love

182. Shape

(SHAYP), noun

The quality of a thing that defines its external surface and physical form; something seen in outline; contour.

ADJECTIVES

conoidal (kuh-NOYD-uhl). Shaped like, or nearly like, a cone.
My son's paintings of CONOIDAL objects are all the rage in his preschool.

infundibular (in-fuhn-DIB-yoo-lar). Having the shape of a funnel.
From years of erosion by rapidly moving water, the valley has acquired an INFUNDIBULAR appearance.

lunate (LOO-nayt). Crescent-shaped.
Looking like a partially eaten cookie, the LUNATE moon rose over the lake.

ovoid (OH-void). Having the shape of an egg.
The OVOID droppings were left by an unidentified but fastidious animal.

pyriform (PIR-uh-form). Having a pear shape.
With their PYRIFORM outline, the apples looked like pears from a distance.

serriform (SAIR-uh-form). Shaped like a saw-edge; having ridges reminiscent of saw-teeth.
The two SERRIFORM pieces fit together perfectly, making a solid joint.

sigmoid (SIG-moid). Having a double curve like the letter "S."
The rather large serpent was resting in the classic SIGMOID position.

sinuous (SIN-yoo-uhs). Bending in and out; having many curves; wavy.
Flowing slowly across the plain, the great river followed a SINUOUS path to the ocean.

spheroidal (sfi-ROID-uhl). In the shape of a sphere.
Seemingly without effort, the toddlers were able to transform the SPHEROIDAL ball into one that was distinctly ovoid.

symmetrical (sih-MET-rih-kul). Characterized by a regularity of features and form; well-proportioned; agreeably arranged.
The tree was so perfectly SYMMETRICAL that we wondered if it was real.

tauriform (TAWR-uh-form). Having the shape of a bull or the head or horns of a bull.
Arthur was temporarily stumped when asked to draw an object with a TAURIFORM shape.

xiphoid (ZIE-foid). Shaped like a sword.
We can always spot Carlson's private plane because it is covered with the same XIPHOID shapes that adorn his family's crest.

ANTONYMS

amorphous (ah-MORE-fis). Without definite shape, substance, or form; lacking definition and boundaries.
"Of course the illusion of art is to make one believe that great literature is very close to life, but exactly the opposite is true. Life is AMORPHOUS, literature is formal."—Françoise Sagan, French novelist and playwright

incoherent (in-koh-HEER-uhnt). Not logically connected; disjointed; rambling.
"Dreams are nothing but INCOHERENT ideas, occasioned by partial or imperfect sleep."—Benjamin Rush, American physician and political leader

183. Short-lived

(SHORT-LYVD), adjective

Living only a short time.

ADJECTIVES

caducous (kuh-DOO-kuss). Transitory; short-lived; perishable.
"Some thing, which I fancied was a part of me, falls off from me and leaves no scar. It was CADUCOUS."—Ralph Waldo Emerson, American poet, essayist, and transcendentalist

deciduous (dih-SIJ-oo-uhs). Not permanent.
After meeting Martha, Arnold was content to give up all of his DECIDUOUS pleasures.

ephemeral (eh-FEM-er-uhl). Describes a short-lived condition, temporary event, or fleeting moment.
"There remain some truths too EPHEMERAL to be captured in the cold pages of a court transcript."—Irving Kaufman, Chief Judge, United States Court of Appeals

evanescent (ev-eh-NESS-ent). Having the qualities of a mist or vapor, capable of vanishing seemingly into thin air.
"Nobody thinks it's silly to invest two hours' work in two minutes' enjoyment; but if cooking is EVANESCENT, well, so is the ballet."—Julia Child, American cook, author, and television personality

fugacious (fyoo-GAY-shuss). Fleeting, transitory, short-lived.
The FUGACIOUS mid-summer cold snap was a welcome relief from the heat.

transitory (TRAN-si-tor-ee). Lasting only a short time; not permanent.
"All forms of beauty, like all possible phenomena, contain an element of the eternal and an element of the TRANSITORY—of the absolute and of the particular."—Charles Baudelaire, French poet

ANTONYMS

incessant (in-SES-uhnt). Not stopping; never ceasing; continuing without end.
"The longest absence is less perilous to love than the terrible trials of INCESSANT proximity."—Edna St. Vincent Millay, American poet and dramatist

perdurable (per-DURE-uh-bull). Extremely durable or lasting; permanent; imperishable.
Oscar's aphorisms always expressed a PERDURABLE truth.

perennial (puh-REN-ee-uhl). Lasting for a long time; enduring.
"Folly is PERENNIAL and yet the human race has survived."—Bertrand Russell, English logician and philosopher

184. Similar

(SIM-uh-ler), adjective

Having a general resemblance or likeness; nearly but not exactly the same.

ADJECTIVES

akin (uh-KIN). Showing a similar feature or quality; comparable or related in some important way.
I feel that Harry's repeated falsification of his records is much more than a breach of policy: it is AKIN to outright perjury.

alliterative (uh-LIT-er-uh-tive). Using the repetition of initial consonant sounds in language.
"Peter Piper picked a peck of pickled peppers" is an ALLITERATIVE tongue-twister.

analogous (an-AL-uh-gus). Similar or comparable in some respects.
Nikki tried to argue that attending public school in Manhattan was ANALOGOUS to attending the prestigious boarding school in the country, but her argument was weak and her grandmother wasn't buying it.

derivative (deh-RIV-uh-tiv). Copied or adapted from others.
"Only at his maximum does an individual surpass all his DERIVATIVE elements, and become purely himself."—D.H. Lawrence, British author

isomorphic (aye-seh-MAWR-fik). Having a similar form, shape, or structure.
Jerry enjoyed traveling before all cities seemed to become endless mazes of ISOMORPHIC structures.

NOUNS

metaphor (MET-uh-for). A sentence or phrase in which a word ordinarily associated with one thing is applied to something else, to indicate that in some way they are similar.
"If we are a METAPHOR of the universe, the human couple is the metaphor par excellence, the point of intersection of all forces and the seed of all forms."
—Octavio Paz Lozano, Mexican writer, poet, and diplomat

parity (PAIR-ih-tee). The condition of everyone being more or less equal.
The firemen received a raise to help them achieve pay PARITY with the sanitation workers and police department.

propinquity (pro-PING-kwi-tee). Nearness in time or place; an affinity of nature.
As more and more of the small ranches in his neighborhood were knocked down and replaced by mansion-like dwellings, Ralph felt wealthy by virtue of PROPINQUITY.

similitude (sih-MIL-ih-tood). Likeness or similarity.
Bea and Rosa have a SIMILITUDE of habits when it comes to cooking.

simulacrum (sim-yuh-LAY-krum). A minor, unreal, or eerie similarity.
The boy possessed only the barest SIMULACRUM of the classic DeBerris brow, but something told me his claim to be a descendant was valid.

ANTONYMS

heterogeneity (het-uh-roh-juh-NEE-ih-tee). Characterized by dissimilarity; disparateness.
HETEROGENEITY is found throughout the animal and plant world with each individual virtually unique.

imparity (im-PAIR-ih-tee). Inequality or disparity.
Joyce was continually amazed by the IMPARITY of her children.

185. Skilled

(SKILD), adjective

Having a particular ability from training or experience.

ADJECTIVES

adroit (uh-DROYT). Skilled or clever in a particular pursuit.
"It's kind of sad," Betty said to Barbara, "that Will thinks his being ADROIT as an opera singer will impress women."

consummate (KON-suh-mitt). Complete or perfect; showing supreme skill.
"[John F. Kennedy is] a new star with a tremendous national appeal, the skill of a CONSUMMATE showman."—Russell Baker, American author

efficacious (eff-ih-KAY-shuss). Capable of having a desired effect.
"Example is always more EFFICACIOUS than precept."—Samuel Johnson, British moralist and poet

habile (HAB-ill). Skillful and able; handy.
Our HABILE gardener has helped render our topiary into the shapes of dollar and pound signs.

NOUNS

demiurge (DEM-ee-urj). A powerful creative force or a creative personality.
After trying a few different professions, Jackson realized that his ability with artifice, combined with his family connections, would make him a DEMIURGE of the marketing world.

journeyman (JUR-nee-man). A person who, although not a top master of his profession, has become extremely competent, through long years of practice, at a particular craft or skill.
"So this is happiness, / that JOURNEYMAN."—Anne Sexton, American poet and author

virtuoso (vir-choo-OWE-so). A supremely skilled artist.
Geena is a piano VIRTUOSO who has won dozens of competitions.

ANTONYMS

inept (in-EPT). Without judgment, discretion, aptitude, or skill.
Williams, an INEPT craftsman, soon found that his goods would never fetch top dollar.

jejune (jih-JOON). Not well thought out or fully formed; poor in performance.
Samantha snidely informed Blake that her JEJUNE entertaining efforts might someday grow to maturity.

186. Sleepy

(SLEE-pee), adjective

Inclined to sleep; characterized by an absence of activity; drowsy; idle.

ADJECTIVES

hypnopompic (hip-nuh-PAHM-pik). Having to do with the semiconscious state that precedes wakefulness.
With all of her partying at exclusive clubs, Madison spends most of her life in a HYPNOPOMPIC state.

lassitude (LASS-ih-tood). Having little energy or motivation; weariness.
"We know what boredom is: it is a dull / Impatience or a fierce velleity, / A champing wish, stalled by our LASSITUDE, / To make or do."—Richard Wilbur, American poet

lethargic (luh-THAR-jik). Drowsy and sluggish; lacking vigor.
"Great talents, by the rust of long disuse, / Grow LETHARGIC and shrink from what they were."—Ovid, Roman poet

logy (LOW-gee). Characterized by lethargy and sluggishness.
"To be scared is such a release from all the LOGY weight of procrastination, of dallying and pokiness! You burn into work. It is as though gravity were removed and you walked lightly to the moon like an angel."—Brenda Ueland, American author

oscitant (OSS-ih-tuhnt). Drowsy, inattentive; dull.
Before 10:00 A.M., any lecture hall on any campus will be filled with OSCITANT students.

recumbent (rih-KUM-bent). Inactive, idle; lying down.
During our Italian cruise, we spent most of our time RECUMBENT on the bow of the yacht, soaking up the sun's rays.

somniferous (som-NIFF-er-us). Inducing sleep.
The professor's SOMNIFEROUS voice caused many students to fall asleep during her lectures.

somnolent (SOM-nuh-lunt). Tired, sleepy.
Having worked all night on the paper, Gaylord dragged himself into the lecture hall and spent the hour casting a well-meaning but SOMNOLENT gaze in the direction of his professor.

soporific (sop-uh-RIFF-ik). Boring, tedious, or exhausting such that it brings on sleep.
If Cassandra weren't such an important social contact, her SOPORIFIC speech would surely cause us to avoid her.

NOUNS

inertia (in-UR-shuh). Sluggishness; the quality of being inert.
It is not a lack of opportunity that has hampered you, Jackson, but simple INERTIA.

narcoma (nar-KO-muh). A hazy state between sleep and wakefulness reminiscent of or signaling use of narcotics.
Because she had worked in a city emergency room for four years, Ellen knew that the boy had slipped into NARCOMA.

opiate (OPE-ee-ut). An addictive narcotic, especially one with numbing or sleep-inducing qualities; anything that causes dullness or inaction.
Whenever Roger was agitated by overwork, he would relax with classical music and allow its calming effect to act like an OPIATE on his mind.

torpor (TORE-pur). Temporary loss of the power of motion or sensation; dormant; apathy; indifference.
"A multitude of causes unknown to former times are now acting with a combined force to blunt the discriminating powers of the mind, and unfitting it for all voluntary exertion to reduce it to a state of almost savage TORPOR."
—William Wordsworth, British Romantic poet

ANTONYMS

animated (AN-uh-mate-id). Vigorous; lively.
Their discussion was ANIMATED by the assurance that each was correct and the others were fools.

astir (uh-STUR). In motion; in excited activity.
My uncle's energy was such that he was constantly ASTIR; he even talked in his sleep.

187. Small

(SMAWL), adjective

Little; of less than the usual quantity, size, amount, value, importance, etc.

ADJECTIVES

diminutive (dih-MIN-yuh-tiv). Small in stature.
Marcia's forceful personality overcomes her DIMINUTIVE stature.

exiguous (ex-IG-yu-uss). Meager; small; scanty.
Dinner turned out to be an EXIGUOUS offering of two thin slices of chicken, three green beans, and a potato—albeit quite artistically arranged.

infinitesimal (in-fin-uh-TESS-ih-mull). So small that it can't accurately be measured.
Which color lipstick to wear tonight is an INFINITESIMAL, not a major, issue, so let's get going already!

Lilliputian (lil-uh-PEW-shen). Small in stature; tiny in comparison to one's peers.
Jules Verne's LILLIPUTIAN appearance made people treat him like a child.

minuscule (MIN-uss-kyool). Extremely small.
Sometimes, trying to decipher the MINUSCULE names, numbers, and signs on a map only makes me feel more lost.

nominal (NOM-ih-nuhl). Relatively minor in importance; insignificant as an amount or volume of something.
For a NOMINAL fee, the store delivers your new wide-screen TV to your home and sets it up for you.

trifling (TRY-fling). Insignificant; unimportant; trivial.
The fact is, you are unlikely to be called in for an audit over such a TRIFLING amount of money.

NOUNS

globule (GLOB-yewl). A small globe or ball.
"In yourself is the law of all nature, and you know not yet how a GLOBULE of sap ascends."—Ralph Waldo Emerson, American poet, essayist, and transcendentalist

iota (eye-OH-tuh). A minute quantity; an extremely small amount.
The fact that the prisoner's reprieve omits his middle initial doesn't matter one IOTA, Warden Holloway.

microcosm (my-kruh-KAHZ-uhm). A representation of something on a very small scale.
"Each particle is a MICROCOSM, and faithfully renders the likeness of the world."—Ralph Waldo Emerson, American poet, essayist, and transcendentalist

minutiae (mih-NOO-she-ee). Small, trifling matters that one encounters on an average day.
The MINUTIAE of golf, tennis, and spa treatments at the club can become utterly tiresome.

modicum (MAWD-ih-kuhm). A modest amount; a small quantity.
"To be human is to have one's little MODICUM of romance secreted away in one's composition."—Mark Twain

paucity (PAW-si-tee). A lack of something, a small supply or limited selection.
"It is very strange, and very melancholy, that the PAUCITY of human pleasures should persuade us ever to call hunting one of them."—Samuel Johnson, British moralist and poet

pittance (PIT-unce). A very small amount.
My allowance in those days, of course, was a PITTANCE compared to my brother's.

scintilla (sin-TILL-uh). A spark; a tiny trace amount.
"The air twittered with bright SCINTILLAS of fading light."—Harlan Ellison, American author

smattering (SMAT-er-ing). A little bit; a small amount of something.
Dean picked up a SMATTERING of Italian during his visit to Venice.

tincture (TINK-chur). A trace amount or slight tinge.
The tragic opera was leavened with a TINCTURE of comic relief.

VERBS

dwindle (DWIN-dul). To become smaller; to shrink or waste away; to decrease.
I had planned to run away forever, but my supply of cookies and pennies DWINDLED, forcing me to return home by nightfall.

truncate (TRUN-kayt). To shorten by cutting (a segment).
The director left the long passage about the "willow that grows aslant the brook" intact, but decided to TRUNCATE an earlier scene that had something to do with Hecuba.

ANTONYMS

ponderous (PON-der-us). Massive; heavy.
"Ever since I was a boy, I regarded opera as a PONDEROUS anachronism, almost the equivalent of smoking."—Frank Lloyd Wright, American architect

prodigious (proh-DIJ-is). Extraordinary in size, extent, amount, degree, bulk, etc.; enormous; monstrous.
Clark's PRODIGIOUS collection of old movie posters led many of his friends to ask whether he had once owned a theatre.

188. Sojourn

(SO-jern), noun

A temporary visit or stay.

ADJECTIVES

bucolic (byoo-KALL-ik). A peaceful, serene, rural object, place, or environment.
We bought a weekend place in a BUCOLIC little village in the country.

desultory (DES-ul-tor-ee). Acting without plan or purpose; activity that seems random or haphazard.
"Find time still to be learning somewhat good, and give up being DESULTORY."—Marcus Aurelius, Roman Emperor

halcyon (HAL-see-un). Calm, peaceful, carefree, prosperous.
"It was the most HALCYON summer I ever spent."—Rick Bass, American author and environmental activist

NOUNS

convalescence (con-vah-LESS-ense). The time spent recovering from an illness and getting back to full health, often while being taken care of by others.
"CONVALESCENCE is the part that makes the illness worthwhile."
—George Bernard Shaw, Irish playwright

dalliance (DAL-ee-anss). A brief, casual flirtation with or interest in someone or something; the act of tarrying rather than proceeding swiftly and deliberately.
Her DALLIANCE with the pool boy made her husband angry and jealous.

dilettante (DILL-ih-tont). A person who studies a subject in a casual fashion, learning the topic for the fun of it rather than to apply it to solve real problems.
Joseph Priestly could be considered a DILETTANTE, and yet his work led to the discovery of oxygen.

hedonism (HEE-duh-niz-im). The nonstop pursuit of personal pleasure as one's primary goal.
"[Bad] taste supervenes upon good taste as a daring and witty HEDONISM. It makes the man of good taste cheerful, where before he ran the risk of being chronically frustrated."—Susan Sontag, American literary theorist, philosopher, and political activist

hiatus (hi-A-tuss). An interruption or break in time or continuity.
Lorelei's coming-out party was a welcome HIATUS in our otherwise uneventful social calendar.

wanderlust (WAWN-der-lust). A strong and innate desire to travel far from home.
*"In our WANDERLUST, we are lovers looking for consummation."
—Anatole Broyard, literary critic for the* New York Times

VERBS

disport (dih-SPORT). To amuse oneself.
Felicia loved to DISPORT with the proprietors of her favorite boutiques by arguing over price.

meander (me-AN-duhr). To wander aimlessly.
We fired that particular servant because he MEANDERED far too slowly from task to task.

ANTONYMS

edacious (ih-DAY-shuss). Greedy, eager, and consumed with consumption.
It's not fair to label Rosella EDACIOUS because she only wants the same luxury items the rest of us desire.

histrionics (hiss-tree-AWN-iks). Over-the-top, unnecessarily dramatic behavior.
"Enough with the HISTRIONICS!" his mother scolded, immediately shutting off the flow of tears and silencing his bawling.

189. Solution

(suh-LOO-shun), noun

The method or act of solving a problem; explanation; clarification; answer.

NOUNS

catholicon (kuh-THOL-ih-kuhn). A universal remedy; panacea.
Money is often considered a CATHOLICON for many of the world's ills.

elixir (e-LIX-ur). A solution meant to be used for medicinal purposes; in medieval times, a supposedly curative drink made from mixing alcohol and drugs in water.
Dr. Callahan's ELIXIR of Life, a patent medicine popular in Kansas in the late 1880s, may have owed part of its popularity to the coca leaves used in its preparation.

panacea (pan-uh-SEE-uh). A universal solution for all problems, diseases, or woes.
Parents today see buying their kids everything they want as a PANACEA for misery, boredom, and unhappiness.

VERBS

elucidate (ee-LOO-sih-dayt). To lecture, explain, or pontificate about a subject in great detail so as to make it exceedingly clear.
"It [was] the mission of the twentieth century to ELUCIDATE the irrational."
—Maurice Merleau-Ponty, French philosopher

ratiocinate (rash-ee-OSS-inn-ayt). To work toward the solution of a problem through logical thinking and reason.
Since the dawn of humanity, our best minds have failed to RATIOCINATE a method of proving God's existence.

ANTONYMS

impasse (IM-pass). A situation that seems to offer no solution or escape; a point of stalemate. Literally, a dead-end street or passage.
Tom realized that his relationship with Betty had come to an IMPASSE; divorce was now on her mind, and he knew it.

nostrum (NAH-strum). An untested and questionable remedy made of secret ingredients; an ineffective solution.
"America's present need is not NOSTRUMS but normalcy."—Warren G. Harding

190. Sound

(SOWND), noun

That which can be heard; the sensation produced when the organs of hearing are stimulated by vibrations transmitted through the air or another medium; noise.

ADJECTIVES

euphonious (yu-FONE-ee-uss). Pleasing to the ear.
The low, EUPHONIOUS thrumming of the crickets outside my window those summer nights always put me to sleep quickly.

guttural (GUTT-er-ul). Harsh or raspy; reminiscent of deep sounds produced in the throat.
The dog let out a low, GUTTURAL growl that was likely to give pause to whoever was standing on the other side of the door.

plangent (PLAN-jent). Resounding loudly and, typically, sorrowfully.
The locomotive whistle is considered by many to be a PLANGENT sound.

polyphonic (poll-ee-FAHN-ik). Having many different sounds.
"The guitar is a small orchestra. It is POLYPHONIC. Every string is a different color, a different voice."—Andres Segovia, Spanish classical guitarist

sonorous (SAWN-er-uss). A deep, rich, resonant sound.
The B-flat bass saxophone is the most SONOROUS member of the saxophone family, with the baritone saxophone coming in a close second.

stentorian (sten-TOR-ee-un). A sound characterized as loud and powerful.
The announcer's STENTORIAN voice could be heard even after a storm knocked out the power to his microphone.

strident (STRY-duhnt). Harsh; obtrusively grating.
Dennis's appeals for money became more common—and more STRIDENT—as the year wore on.

NOUNS

cacophony (kuh-KOFF-uh-nee). Harsh, unpleasant sounds that can create a disturbing feeling.
The CACOPHONY of the nearby construction site made it almost impossible for me to get any work done.

crescendo (kruh-SHEN-doe). A gradual increase in volume or intensity (used especially in relation to musical works).
As the orchestra reached a thundering CRESCENDO, my six-year-old son continued to sleep peacefully by my side.

knell (NELL). The sound of a bell, especially when rung solemnly at a funeral.
"They are of sick and diseased imaginations who would toll the world's KNELL so soon."—Henry David Thoreau, American author and transcendentalist

sibilance (SIB-uh-lence). A hissing sound.
Electronic engineers try mightily to eliminate any SIBILANCE introduced by sound-reproduction equipment.

spirant (SPY-ruhnt). A sound produced by the passage of breath through the partially closed oral cavity; fricative.
The "sh" and "v" sounds are both SPIRANTS.

susurration (suss-uh-RAY-shun). A soft, whispering sound.
I sat there on the porch of my parents' farmhouse, listening to the SUSURRATION of wind-driven stalks of wheat.

timbre (TAM-bur). A quality of sound, usually musical, determined by its overtones; a distinctive quality or tone.
I feel that the haunting TIMBRE of the oboe, when played by a master, is more moving than that of any other musical instrument.

tintinnabulation (tin-ti-nab-yuh-LAY-shun). The sound of ringing bells.
In my old neighborhood, we were always woken on Sunday mornings by the TINTINNABULATION of the local churches.

tremolo (TREMM-uh-lo). A quality of musical sound marked by rapid repetition of one or two notes.
The pianist played extravagantly, adding embellishments and trills of TREMOLO far too often for my taste.

VERBS

crepitate (KREP-uh-tayt). To crack, crinkle, or pop.
Joe jumped up and sat down several times, as if to prove that his chair—and not he—was CREPITATING.

ANTONYMS

aphonic (a-FON-ik). Not sounded; having aphonia, loss of voice.
In certain English words, the initial "k" is APHONIC.

inaudible (in-AW-duh-bull). unable to be heard.
The storm passed far to the south; we could see the lightning flashes but the thunder was INAUDIBLE.

191. Speech

(SPEECH), noun

The act of speaking; communicating or expressing thoughts and ideas by spoken words, sounds, and gestures.

ADJECTIVES

bombastic (bom-BAS-tik). Characterized by haughty, overblown, or pompous talk or writing.
We expected a compelling argument from our attorney, but he came to court offering little more than a BOMBASTIC harangue.

discursive (dis-KER-siv). A manner or style of lecturing in which the speaker rambles between many topics.
Paul's DISCURSIVE lectures on American history jumped from century to century, yet it all came together in an understandable and fresh fashion.

extemporaneous (eks-tem-puh-RAYN-ee-us). Off the cuff; done without preparation.
His EXTEMPORANEOUS delivery made everyone in the public speaking class wonder why he had enrolled.

grandiloquent (grand-IL-oh-kwent). Having a pompous, overly inflated, hyperbolic, or pretentious way of presenting oneself in speech and mannerism.
The architect waxed GRANDILOQUENT about the visionary design of his new skyscraper.

laconic (luh-KAWN-ik). Of few words; expressing oneself with an economy of words.
Harold may be LACONIC, but when he does speak, he is worth listening to.

prolix (pro-LIKS). Tediously wordy; long and verbose.
The report was so PROLIX, I gave up trying to finish reading it.

reticent (REH-tih-sent). Reluctance to openly express one's thoughts, feelings, and personal business to other people; uncommunicative; behaving like an introvert in social situations.
"The shorter poems tend to be RETICENT, psychologically acute love poems about the shifting inequalities of love."—Edward Mendelson, Professor of English and Comparative Literature at Columbia University

sententious (sen-TEN-shuss). Tending to use many clichés or maxims in order to enlighten others.
Polonius's SENTENTIOUS manner of speaking clearly irritates Hamlet in this scene.

NOUNS

elocution (el-oh-KEW-shun). The ability to deliver a public speech in a clear and persuasive manner.
He's a brilliant man, but he needs to work on his ELOCUTION.

euphony (YU-fun-ee). The arrangement or emphasis of words or phrases so they are pleasing to the ear and roll off the tongue with greater ease.
In finishing school, Alsace learned the art of EUPHONY, and she has parlayed that into a hobby of earning roles in television commercials.

filibuster (FILL-ih-bus-ter). A prolonged speech used to delay legislative actions or other important decisions.
The room breathed a collective sigh when the senator finally ended his eight-hour FILIBUSTER.

locution (low-KEW-shin). A person's manner and style of speaking.
Neil prides himself on his precise LOCUTION, but some of the guys think he sounds rather prissy.

malapropism (MAL-uh-prop-ism). Misuse of a word or mangling of the English language, often done for comic effect.
Since Emily refused to take elocution lessons like the rest of us, her speech is constantly marred by ridiculous MALAPROPISMS.

metaphor (MET-uh-for). A sentence or phrase in which a word ordinarily associated with one thing is applied to something else to indicate that in some way they are similar.
"If we are a METAPHOR of the universe, the human couple is the metaphor par excellence, the point of intersection of all forces and the seed of all forms."
—Octavio Paz Lozano, Mexican writer, poet, and diplomat

mot juste (MOE-zshoost). The perfect word or phrase to communicate pre-cisely what you mean to say.
Years of elocution lessons have left Paulina capable of leavening every occasion with a suitable MOT JUSTE.

orator (OR-ah-ter). A skilled and persuasive public speaker.
Tom overestimated his abilities as an ORATOR and, consequently, stayed at the podium far longer than the audience wanted him to.

palaver (pa-LAH-ver). A rambling, meandering monologue spoken to prove or make a point.
Don't ask Eileen about collecting art. The result will be twenty minutes of mind-numbing PALAVER.

parlance (PAR-lunss). Vernacular or jargon used by a particular industry, profession, or group.
By using the terms "discourse," "pedagogy," and "literary criticism," the professors spoke in the PARLANCE of academia.

patois (PAT-wah). Rural speech or jargon; any language that deviates from standard usage.
"I've given up trying to follow the PATOIS of teenagers," the teacher complained.

periphrasis (puh-RIF-ruh-sis). The use of many words where one or a few would suffice.
The lecture always ran late due to the professor's habit of PERIPHRASIS.

raconteur (RAK-on-tur). Someone who enjoys telling stories, does so frequently, and is good at it.
"O'Hara writes as a poetic one-man band, shifting rapidly among his roles as RACONTEUR, sexual adventurer, European traveler . . ."—Edward Mendelson, Professor of English and Comparative Literature at Columbia University

soliloquy (suh-LIL-ih-kwee). A dramatic or literary monologue in which a character reveals his innermost thoughts.
The most famous SOLILOQUY in all of literature is the "To be or not to be" speech in Hamlet.

VERBS

pontificate (pon-TIF-ih-kayt). To speak in a dogmatic or pompous manner.
Can I assume the Senator now intends to PONTIFICATE on the many virtues of our current trade policy?

ANTONYMS

censor (SEN-ser). To examine, review, and change or delete a word or passage from a written work based on moral or political grounds.
"If in other lands the press and books and literature of all kinds are censored, we must redouble our efforts here to keep them free."—Franklin D. Roosevelt, American president

inarticulate (in-ar-TIK-yuh-lit). The inability to express oneself; lacking clear and expressive speech.
"The INARTICULATE speak longest."—Japanese proverb
See also: Language, Talk

192. Stupid

(STOO-pid), adjective

Lacking normal intelligence, understanding, or keenness of mind; slow-witted; dull; foolish.

ADJECTIVES

asinine (ASS-ih-nine). Showing a very noticeable lack of intelligence and/or good sense.
I left halfway through the latest thriller because I could feel its ASININE plot depleting my brain cells.

benighted (bih-NY-tid). To be lost, ignorant, or unenlightened.
The medieval period was a BENIGHTED era of superstition.

besotted (bih-SOT-ed). Made foolish, stupid, or dull due to infatuation.
Aline thinks Jake is BESOTTED with her, but he's really BESOTTED with her father's stock portfolio.

inane (in-ANE). Pointless or lacking in substance; empty; vacuous.
Among other INANE suggestions, Jeff proposed painting the lunchroom in a polka-dot pattern.

obtuse (ob-TOOCE). Lacking understanding, intelligence, and perception; unable to comprehend; having a dense mind.
Thomas was so OBTUSE, he didn't realize his inappropriate behavior was making his friends uncomfortable.

vacuous (VAK-yoo-uss). Characterized by emptiness; devoid of emotion or intelligence; stupid; moronic.
The VACUOUS stare from her two eyes, looking like raisins pushed into a lump of dough, made him shiver with loathing and contempt.

NOUNS

duffer (DUFF-uhr). An incompetent or ineffectual person.
Maxwell can't help being a DUFFER. After all, his family has only been wealthy for two generations.

lummox (LUM-ux). A dim-witted or clumsy person; an oaf.
Sherman had a heart of gold, but when it came to social etiquette, he was something of a LUMMOX.

nescience (NESH-uhns). Lack of knowledge; ignorance.
Sociologists were sent to the region to determine if the inhabitants' poverty resulted in their NESCIENCE or vice versa.

yokel (YOH-kuhl). A gullible inhabitant of a rural area; bumpkin.
"[A human being] is the YOKEL par excellence, the booby unmatchable, the king dupe of the cosmos."—H.L. Mencken, American magazine editor, essayist, and critic

ANTONYMS

acuity (uh-CUE-ih-tee). Keenness of perception; the ability to make quick, accurate decisions and evaluations.
Jane's mental ACUITY enabled her to think and respond quickly in a crisis.

ingenious (in-JEEN-yuhs). Having great mental ability; clever; resourceful; inventive.
"It will be found, in fact, that the INGENIOUS are always fanciful, and the truly imaginative never otherwise than analytic."—Edgar Allan Poe, American writer and critic

193. Style

(STYL), noun

A manner of expression or custom of behaving; manner of conduct.

ADJECTIVES

fin de siècle (fan-deh-see-ECK-luh). Related to the fashions, art, ideas, etc. associated with the end of the nineteenth century.
Martin is an aficionado of FIN DE SIÈCLE European art.

sartorial (sar-TOR-ee-al). Related to clothing, especially tailored clothing.
Jonathan's personal tailor always makes sure that Jonathan radiates SARTORIAL splendor.

soigné (swahn-YEY). Well taken care of, well-groomed, well-dressed.
Arthur enjoyed interacting with the staff at the best hotels, even the SOIGNÉ parking attendants.

tawdry (TAW-dree). Gaudy, showy, and cheap, as clothes; or, base and mean, as motives.
"Far from being the basis of the good society, the family, with its narrow privacy and TAWDRY secrets, is the source of all our discontents."—Sir Edmund Leach, British author

urbane (ur-BAYN). Suave, sophisticated, refined, cosmopolitan, and well versed in the ways of high society.
Even in his knock-around tennis whites, Brett always manages to appear URBANE.

NOUNS

couture (ko-TOOR). Clothing in the latest and most popular styles created by in-vogue fashion designers.
If Alyssia does not have the latest COUTURE prior to its debut on Paris runways, she will not deign to consider wearing it.

dishabille (dis-uh-BEEL). Casual dress, or a casual manner.
Jensen is such a stickler for proper attire that he feels he is in a state of DISHABILLE if he leaves the house without an ascot.

haute couture (OAT-ko-TOOR). Highly fashionable clothing on the cutting edge of the latest design fads and trends.
"HAUTE COUTURE should be fun, foolish, and almost unwearable."
—Christian Lacroix, French fashion designer

haut monde (oh-MOND). High society.
"The literary wiseacres prognosticate in many languages, as they have throughout so many centuries, setting the stage for new HAUT MONDE in letters and making up the public's mind."—Fannie Hurst, American novelist

panache (puh-NASH). A distinctive flair or style; a flamboyant manner.
Rosamund was swept away by the charming stranger's PANACHE—he seemed so dashing and romantic.

savoir faire (SAV-whar FAIR). Tact or social skill.
I'm afraid Helen just doesn't have the SAVOIR FAIRE necessary to build coalitions in such a fractious organization.

ANTONYMS

dowdy (DOW-dee). Lacking stylishness or smartness; old-fashioned.
After my grandmother retired, she dropped her DOWDY pantsuits and began to wear skirts and shoulder-exposing blouses.

passé (pah-SAY). No longer fashionable or current.
Marge's insistence that platform shoes were PASSÉ led me to believe that she hadn't been keeping up with fashion trends.
See also: Tasteful

194. Subservient

(sub-SUR-vee-ehnt), adjective

Acting or serving in a subordinate capacity; subordinate.

ADJECTIVES

ancillary (AN-sih-lair-ree). Secondary or subordinate; serving an auxiliary or supportive function.
He took a great deal of pride in his work, even though the pay was poor and most of his duties were ANCILLARY to those of the regional director.

obsequious (uhb-SEE-kwee-us). Subservient; eager to listen to and please others to an excessive degree; behaving in the manner of a servant or slave.
"[The political mind] is a strange mixture of vanity and timidity, of an OBSEQUIOUS attitude at one time and a delusion of grandeur at another time.—Calvin Coolidge, American president

sequacious (si-KWAY-shuss). Given to following another person, especially without reason.
The king drew much of his strength from the SEQUACIOUS peasants.

servile (SUR-vil). Overly eager to serve; slavish.
Marion's uncharacteristically SERVILE demeanor can only mean one thing: He wants a raise.

subaltern (sub-AWL-turn). Lower in position or rank; secondary in importance.
Stop giving me all these SUBALTERN reasons for your behavior and tell me what your true motivation is!

tractable (TRACK-tuh-bull). Easygoing; compliant; easily managed.
The occasional kind comment seems rather enough to keep our servants TRACTABLE.

NOUNS

minion (MIN-yuhn). A follower of someone in an important position.
The boss's MINIONS were all yes-men, blindly faithful and protective of their position in the company hierarchy.

underling (UHN-der-ling). A person with little authority or rank in comparison to the person he serves; subordinate.
The police knew that the crime families were fighting because of all the UNDERLINGS who disappeared.

VERBS

genuflect (JEN-yu-flect). To bend one knee to the floor; to act in a servile or overly reverential way toward someone else.
"The way Harold GENUFLECTS to Mr. Thomas at staff meetings just makes me want to barf," Alice said.

prostrate (PROSS-trayt). To lie face down on the ground due to being weary, overthrown, or helpless, or as an act of humility.
We were all embarrassed when Milt almost PROSTRATED himself in front of the boss.

subjugate (SUB-juh-gayt). To cause to become subservient; to bring under complete control.
The dictator's attempts to SUBJUGATE his country's smaller neighbors will end in failure; mark my words.

truckle (TRUK-uhl). To submit obsequiously to a command.
We have trained our servants to TRUCKLE to our every whim.

ANTONYMS

eminent (EM-ih-nent). Prominent or noted; of high esteem; outstanding and distinguished.
I found the prospect of studying physics under an EMINENT professor like Dr. Maxwell, who had just won a Nobel Prize, daunting to say the least.

supercilious (su-per-SILL-ee-us). Feeling superior to others; haughtily disdainful or contemptuous.
Linda grew up surrounded by wealth and privilege and consequently adopted a SUPERCILIOUS attitude with everyone she met.

195. Support

(suh-PORT), verb

To give comfort, courage, faith to; to approve; maintain; help; strengthen.

NOUNS

adherent (ad-HEER-unt). Someone who adheres to an opinion; one who is devoted to or strongly associated with a cause or opinion.
The measure's ADHERENTS were outspent by its opponents.

benediction (ben-ih-DIK-shun). A formal blessing, an expression of good wishes.
As the priest pronounced the BENEDICTION, Julia thought about how it would help her face the arduous day ahead.

succor (SUCK-ur). Aid or assistance; relief.
Although she did not participate in the crime, Mrs. Helm was sentenced to five years in prison for giving SUCCOR to men she knew to be kidnappers.

VERBS

abet (uh-BET). To encourage or assist a plan or activity; to entice or help, usually in a misdeed.
Though Michael did not participate in the actual kidnapping, he ABETTED the perpetrators by hiding them from the police.

advocate (AD-voe-kayt). To plead in favor of another; recommend publicly.
If you need a recommendation, I'd be happy to ADVOCATE for you.

buttress (BUT-riss). To support; to strengthen by adding supportive features.
The spokesman was prepared to BUTTRESS the president's argument for shutting down the branch office with a list of statistics.

espouse (ih-SPOWZ). To advocate as though one's own.
Do you have any idea how complicated it would be to implement the plans you are ESPOUSING?

underwrite (UN-dur-ryt). To support as by subsidy; to support in full as though undertaking (a risk or venture) oneself.
A group of philanthropists UNDERWRITES our drama department's annual playwriting competition.

ANTONYMS

discommode (dis-kuh-MOHD). To inconvenience; trouble; disturb.
Elizabeth turned over all the forms and paperwork for her business to her lawyer so it would not DISCOMMODE her any further.

interdict (in-ter-DIKT). To prohibit; forbid the use of something.
The border patrol attempts to INTERDICT the flow of illegal or banned substances.
See also: Approval, Help

196. Sweet

(SWEET), adjective

Having the flavor or taste characteristic of sugar or honey; not sour, bitter, or salty.

ADJECTIVES

cloying (KLOY-ing). Sickeningly sweet, sappy, or sentimental.
"Minerva save us from the CLOYING syrup of coercive compassion!"
—Camille Paglia, American author, feminist, and social critic

mellifluous (muh-LIF-loo-us). Flowing sweetly and smoothly.
Jane's MELLIFLUOUS cello playing was the envy of the other musicians.

saccharine (SAK-er-in). Very sweet to the taste; sickeningly sweet.
There is a lucrative market for SACCHARINE books and television programs.

NOUNS

confection (kuhn-FEK-shun). A sweet food of no nutritional value; a frivolous or amusing artistic work.
She knew the play was merely a CONFECTION for the masses, but Beatrice enjoyed the music and acting immensely.

VERBS

dulcify (DULL-suh-fy). To sweeten; to make more agreeable.
Adding enough sugar will DULCIFY almost anything.

edulcorate (ih-DUHL-kuh-rayt). To make pleasant; to free from harshness; to free from impurities by washing.
The ambassador hoped to EDULCORATE the relationship with his intransigent hosts.

mull (MUHL). To heat, sweeten, and flavor with spices.
Betsy loved to MULL cider; it filled her house with a wonderful aroma.

ANTONYMS

acerbic (uh-SUR-bik). Sour in taste; severe or harsh.
Many people, oblivious to his quiet attention, were crushed completely by Dan's ACERBIC wit.

piquant (PEE-kuhnt). Biting or tart; pungent; stimulating.
Mary loved the PIQUANT flavor of salsa and used it on almost everything.

T

197. Take

(TAYK), verb

To get possession of by skill or force; seize; capture.

ADJECTIVES

rapacious (ruh-PAY-shuss). Given to plunder or the forcible overpowering of another.
The foe we face is a RAPACIOUS one who thinks nothing of overrunning the weak if it suits his purposes.

NOUNS

brigand (BRIG-und). One who lives as a bandit, plundering riches.
The BRIGANDS held up the stagecoach and terrified the passengers.

usurper (yu-SIR-per). A person who seizes a position of power through illegal means, force, or deception.
"A USURPER in the guise of a benefactor is the enemy that we are now to encounter and overcome."—William Leggett, American poet and fiction writer

VERBS

arrogate (AIR-uh-gayt). To demand something for oneself or to take control without authority.
The way Nelson ARROGATES office meetings drives his coworkers crazy!

despoil (dih-SPOIL). To deprive of possessions, things of value, etc. by force; rob; plunder.
The unarmed citizens could only watch as the soldiers DESPOILED their town.

expropriate (eks-PRO-pree-ayt). To seize property or wealth from its owner for the public's use or benefit, as when the state takes someone's home under eminent domain to build a road through it.
The Bradfords are still reeling from the fact that the state EXPROPRIATED a portion of their gardens for a new highway.

garnish (GAR-nihsh). To legally take a portion of a person's wages, property, and assets to pay his debts.
If you do not pay your taxes within thirty days, the county reserves the right to GARNISH a portion of your wages until the back taxes are paid in full.

maraud (muh-ROD). To loot or invade for treasure.
The ship was waylaid by pirates MARAUDING on the fourteenth of May.

procure (pro-KYOOR). To seek and eventually gain ownership of something.
My book dealer recently PROCURED, at considerable expense, a first edition of Great Expectations *for our library.*

usurp (yoo-SURP). To assume forcibly and/or without right; to take over.
The authority of Congress was indeed USURPED by Lincoln during the war, but legislators briskly reasserted themselves once the crisis was past.

wrest (REST). To pull away; to take something by force or threat.
"WREST once the law to your authority: / To do a great right, do a little wrong."
—William Shakespeare

ANTONYMS

inalienable (in-AY-lee-un-a-bull). Incapable of being taken away.
Although I have always believed freedom of speech to be the INALIENABLE right of every American, I must admit that the diatribes of those who preach hate and violence against members of my race are awfully tough to stomach.

proffer (PROF-er). To place (something) before someone; to offer.
John self-consciously PROFFERED his homework to the teacher as if it were a valuable gift.

198. Talk

(TAWK), verb

To put thoughts into and communicate by spoken words; speak; converse.

ADJECTIVES

loquacious (loh-KWAY-shuss). Verbose; chatty; the habit of talking nonstop.
Amy and Donna are each so LOQUACIOUS, their average phone call lasts ninety minutes.

orotund (OR-uh-tund). Distinguished by strength, fullness, and clearness, as a voice.
In a beguilingly OROTUND voice, the conductor offered a synopsis of the evening's opera.

voluble (VOL-yuh-bull). Characterized by a ready flow of words; talkative; glib.
We chose a VOLUBLE candidate for the important public relations position.

NOUNS

garrulity (gah-ROO-lih-tee). The habit of talking way too much.
"The interview is an intimate conversation between journalist and politician wherein the journalist seeks to take advantage of the GARRULITY of the politician and the politician of the credulity of the journalist"—Emory Klein, American journalist

phraseology (fray-zee-AH-lo-jee). The way phrases and words are employed.
With her excellent diction, articulation, and PHRASEOLOGY, Holly had a gift for public speaking and debate.

somniloquence (som-NIL-oh-kwence). The act of talking in one's sleep.
Jean's SOMNILOQUENCE was responsible for revealing much more of her past than she had intended.

VERBS

aver (uh-VER). To assert the truthfulness of a statement.
"'Has she no faults, then (Envy says), sir?'/ Yes, she has one, I must AVER: / When all the world conspires to praise her, / The woman's deaf, and does not hear."—Alexander Pope, British poet

blather (BLATHE-r). To gabble or talk ridiculously; to talk nonsense or discuss meaningless issues for extended periods.
We tried to leave the party, but Mark insisted on BLATHERING endlessly to the hostess about his new car.

bloviate (BLOH-vee-ate). To speak pompously and at length.
Maxwell BLOVIATES about his "excellent" golf game, but everyone knows he cheats outrageously.

confabulate (kuhn-FAB-yuh-layt). To chat or converse informally.
Jarod proceeded to CONFABULATE about the wines most recently added to the family cellar.

descant (des-KANT). To talk freely and without inhibition.
Eloise is always more than willing to DESCANT concerning her past liaisons.

elide (ee-LYD). To leave out a sound or syllable when speaking; to eliminate the distinctive barrier separating levels.
When Catherine ELIDES the "g" at the end of certain words, she betrays her Southern origins.

elucidate (ee-LOO-sih-dayt). To lecture, explain, or pontificate about a subject in great detail so as to make it exceeding clear.
"It [was] the mission of the twentieth century to ELUCIDATE the irrational."
—Maurice Merleau-Ponty, French philosopher

enunciate (ee-NUN-see-ayt). To pronounce words carefully and clearly; to speak in a manner that makes you easily understood.
No one will listen to him until he stops mumbling and learns to ENUNCIATE.

expatiate (ik-SPAY-she-ayt). To speak or write in detail or at length.
I just tuned out Tyrone as he began to EXPATIATE again on his troubled relationship with Mavis.

gesticulate (jes-TIH-cue-layt). To use gestures when talking, especially when eager or excited to get ideas across.
"Okay, the man in the yellow shirt," the seminar leader said, pointing to an audience member who was GESTICULATING wildly.

natter (NATT-er). To talk ceaselessly; babble.
The way Emily NATTERS endlessly about her family's new yacht is revolting to those of us who have owned several yachts over the years.

perorate (PER-uh-rayt). To speak at length; to conclude a speech.
While Lincoln could be concise, Edward Everett was known for his ability to PERORATE.

prattle (PRAT-l). To babble; to talk nonstop without regard as to whether what you are saying makes sense or is of any interest to the listener.
"Infancy conforms to nobody: all conform to it, so that one babe commonly makes four or five out of the adults who PRATTLE and play to it."—Ralph Waldo Emerson, American poet, essayist, and transcendentalist

reiterate (re-IT-uh-rayt). To restate or say again; to repeat.
Let me REITERATE: There will be no exception to the official policy on removing unauthorized recordings from the studio.

ANTONYMS

mute (MYOOT). Unable or unwilling to speak; silent.
Throughout the long and contentious trial, the defendant remained impassive and MUTE.

tacit (TAS-it). Making no sound; silent; saying nothing.
Seeking every advantage, Carolyn offered a TACIT prayer before her physics exam.
See also: Language, Speech

199. Tasteful

(TAYST-fuhl), adjective

Having or showing a good sense of aesthetic discernment, judgment, or appreciation.

ADJECTIVES

decorous (DEK-er-us). Behaving in a manner acceptable to polite society; having good taste and good manners.
*"Another week with these DECOROUS drones and I'll jump out the window,"
the young girl complained to her mother of her fellow debutantes.*

discriminative (dih-SKRIM-uh-nay-tiv). Discriminating; discerning; making distinctions.
We appreciated Alan's DISCRIMINATIVE sensibilities and looked to him for guidance before any gastronomic outing.

genteel (jen-TEEL). Well-bred and possessing a refined temperament.
"[I am] a journalist in the field of etiquette. I try to find out what the most GENTEEL people regularly do, what traditions they have discarded, what compromises they have made."—Amy Vanderbilt, American etiquette expert

NOUNS

epicure (EP-ih-kyoor). One who cultivates refined tastes, especially in reference to food and drink; connoisseur.
Matt, who never seemed at all interested in gourmet dining, has suddenly become something of an EPICURE.

punctilio (pungk-TIL-ee-o). A fine point of etiquette.
"Don't use dessert forks during the main course, please," my grandmother intoned, refering to one of her favorite PUNCTILIOS.

ANTONYMS

brassy (BRASS-ee). Brazen; cheap or showy.
The promotional campaign struck a BRASSY, daring tone that instantly won consumer attention.

crass (KRASS). Coarse and crude in actions, manner, and language.
Will you please remember that you're over fifty and stop being so CRASS?

ribald (RIB-uld). Lewd; off-color, as humor.
"It is . . . useful to distinguish between the pornographic, condemned in every society, and the bawdy, the RIBALD, the shared vulgarities and jokes, which are the safety valves of most social systems."—Margaret Mead, American cultural anthropologist

uncouth (un-KOOTH). Crude, without manners, unrefined.
Carl had an unfortunate way of belching loudly in public places, guessing (accurately and loudly) whether or not someone he just met had undergone plastic surgery, and otherwise acting in an UNCOUTH manner in front of strangers.

unsavory (un-SAYV-err-ee). Distasteful; unpleasant; disreputable; of dubious reputation.
"Our future is inextricably linked to what happens in Washington, D.C., and we know that is a very UNSAVORY reality."—Don Libey, direct marketing advisor
See also: Style

200. Teem

(TEEM), verb

To abound or swarm.

ADJECTIVES

rife (RYF). Prevalent, abundant, abounding.
The hotel was RIFE with tourists, so we quickly went upstairs to the penthouse.

NOUNS

brouhaha (BROO-ha-ha). A confusing, exciting, and turmoil-rife event.
Madeline caused a BROUHAHA when she told her parents she was eschewing Harvard for a state school in order to be closer to her boyfriend.

melee (MAY-lay). A confused struggle involving many people.
"The man who is in the MELEE knows what blows are being struck and what blood is being drawn."—Woodrow Wilson

VERBS

disseminate (diss-SEM-in-ayt). To distribute something so as to make it available to a large population or area.
The Internet is rapidly replacing newspapers as the primary medium for the DISSEMINATION of news.

harry (HAIR-ee). To torment with constant attacks.
"At middle night great cats with silver claws, / Bodies of shadow and blind eyes like pearls, / Came up out of the hole, and red-eared hounds / With long white bodies came out of the air / Suddenly, and ran at them and HARRIED them."
—William Butler Yeats, Irish poet and dramatist

ANTONYMS

insular (IN-suh-ler). Self-contained and therefore isolated from the world and unaffected by outside influences, usually to one's detriment.
The Pricewaters moved from the family's tradition enclave to a more INSULAR compound further up the coast.

isolationism (eye-so-LAY-shin-iz-um). A foreign policy in which a country deliberately keeps its relationships and interactions with other nations to a bare minimum, effectively isolating itself from world affairs.
In the early twentieth century, American ISOLATIONISM stopped the U.S. from joining the League of Nations.

sequester (see-KWESS-ter). To remove and isolate a portion from a larger whole.
"A great deal of genetic engineering must be done before we have carbon-eaters SEQUESTERING carbon in sufficient quantity to counteract the burning of fossil fuels."—Freeman Dyson, English-born American physicist and mathematician

201. Tenacious

(tuh-NAY-shuss), adjective

Persistent, stubborn, obstinate.

ADJECTIVES

dauntless (DAWNT-liss). Fearless, intrepid, and bold.
"For Thought has a pair of DAUNTLESS wings."—Robert Frost, American poet

indefatigable (in-deh-FAT-uh-guh-bull). Capable of continuing along one's current course of action without wavering, tiring, or faltering.
"We are truly INDEFATIGABLE in providing for the needs of the body, but we starve the soul."—Ellen Wood, British playwright

intractable (in-TRAK-tuh-bull). Difficult to control or manage.
"It is precisely here, where the writer fights with the raw, the INTRACTABLE, that poetry is born."—Doris Lessing, British author

NOUNS

avarice (AV-uh-riss). The insatiable desire to have a lot of money, greed.
"What you call AVARICE," Mary said, "I just call getting my share."

leverage (LEV-er-ij). Possessing an advantage or extra degree of influence in a given situation.
With his family's connections, Eldridge required no LEVERAGE to obtain a sinecure in the financial industry.

VERBS

beleaguer (beh-LEE-gir). To persistently surround, harass, or pester until you get what you want.
To the embarrassment of her friends, Kristen BELEAGUERED the sommelier until he brought her a satisfactory Bordeaux.

wrest (REST). To pull away; to take something by force or threat.
"WREST once the law to your authority: / To do a great right, do a little wrong."
—William Shakespeare

ANTONYMS

abjure (ab-JOOR). To renounce or turn your back on a belief or position you once held near and dear.
Once Jodi tasted my mouth-watering, medium-rare filet mignon, she ABJURED the vegetarian lifestyle forever.

perfunctory (per-FUNK-ter-ee). Implemented or executed quickly, without much care or thought put into it.
"The tale is so contrived and PERFUNCTORY that many readers will be tempted to skip to the real story in the second half of the book."—Tim Parks, British novelist

temporize (TEM-puh-ryz). To gain time by being evasive or indecisive.
When an officious socialite tries to get too close to us, we do not feel the need to TEMPORIZE with our response; we simply remind her of her place.

202. Think

(THINK), verb

To exercise rational judgment; to produce ideas, decisions, memories, etc.; to reflect upon.

NOUNS

metaphysics (met-uh-FIZ-iks). The study of abstract ideas and principles that cannot be demonstrated through physical evidence.
"During my METAPHYSICS final, I cheated by looking into the soul of the person sitting next to me."—Woody Allen, American film director, writer, and comedian

VERBS

cogitate (KOJ-ih-tayt). To think about or ponder seriously.
The president, never one to be pressured into a decision, closed the discussion by saying he needed another week to COGITATE on the matter.

educe (ee-DYOOCE). To come to a conclusion or solve a problem through reasoning based on thoughtful consideration of the facts.
When we noticed that their house appeared to be abandoned, we EDUCED that the Wallertons were enduring financial difficulties.

excogitate (ex-KAWJ-ih-tayt). To think something through carefully; to devise.
Dad spent so much time EXCOGITATING a route to the airport that we missed our flight.

muse (MYOOZ). To meditate on; to consider closely.
Phyllis MUSED over the advertising campaign for some days before finally approving it.

ruminate (ROO-muh-nayt). To ponder or review; to go over in the mind repeatedly.
Elaine was still RUMINATING over whether or not to attend college in the fall.

speculate (SPEK-yoo-layt). To consider possible future events; to conjecture. To invest money in a stock market or business venture.
"There are two times in a man's life when he should not SPECULATE: when he can't afford it, and when he can."—Mark Twain, American humorist and author

surmise (sur-MYZ). To guess; to come to a conclusion (often without strong evidence).
We SURMISED that Leanna had declined the invitation to Arthur's birthday party simply because she didn't want to buy him a gift.

ANTONYMS

disregard (dis-rhi-GARD). To pay little or no attention to; neglect.
"Painting is a faith, and it imposes the duty to DISREGARD public opinion."
—Vincent van Gogh, Dutch painter

inconscient (in-KON-shuhnt). Mindless; unconscious.
Alan acted with INCONSCIENT abandon at school and was consequently expelled.
See also: Learn, Understanding

203. Time

(TYM), noun

The period between two events during which something happens, exists, or acts; duration considered as that in which events occur and succeed each other; a system to measure the relation between the occurrence of events.

ADJECTIVES

biennial (by-EN-ee-hl). Happening every second year.
Ms. Webster argues that the summer Olympics, which now occurs every four years, should become a BIENNIAL event.

coeval (koh-EE-vuhl). Of the same period, having the same duration, or being of the same age.
It's interesting to think that the squeaky clean Cleavers of Leave It to Beaver *and the society-shunning members of the Beat Generation were COEVAL.*

diurnal (dy-UR-nuhl). Taking place or being active during daylight hours.
The house staff knows not even to approach Nora's bedroom door before twilight because she totally rejects a DIURNAL lifestyle.

ephemeral (ih-FEM-uh-ruhl). Lasting only a short while.
Our school's joy at winning the state basketball championship turned out to be EPHEMERAL, as the title was suspended when officials learned of the presence of an ineligible player on the team's roster.

mensal (MEN-suhl). Monthly.
The board established MENSAL meetings.

prevenient (pruh-VEEN-yuhnt). Coming before; preceding.
It was necessary to hold a PREVENIENT meeting to prepare for the primary meeting.

quondam (KWAHN-dumm). Former; at-one-time.
You should not hire the Wilkersons' QUONDAM servant because she has been known to break many objets d'art.

quotidian (kwo-TID-ee-uhn). Familiar; commonplace; occurring every day.
Despite closets full of the latest Parisian couture, Alison's QUOTIDIAN complaint is that she has "nothing to wear."

neolithic (nee-oh-LITH-ik). Of or pertaining to the latter part of the Stone Age, when ground stone weapons and tools first came into use; unsophisticated; outdated; passé.
In these days of computers and word processors, many consider the old-fashioned manual typewriter positively NEOLITHIC.

retrograde (RET-ruh-grayd). Reverting to an earlier state, condition, or style; harkening to an earlier time and place.
William was unable to recognize his family or remember any events of his past due to a case of RETROGRADE amnesia.

senescent (si-NESS-uhnt). Growing old; aging; characteristic of old age.
His SENESCENT viewpoint put him at a disadvantage when competing with younger candidates.

sesquicentennial (ses-kwuh-sen-TEN-ee-uhl). Pertaining to a period of 150 years.
A committee was formed to plan Civil War SESQUICENTENNIAL events for the town.

synchronous (SING-kruh-nus). Taking place at the same time.
The Smythingtons and the Lyttons caused quite a stir among their social contacts after they scheduled SYNCHRONOUS galas.

temporal (TEM-por-uhl). Relating to time.
"Science is the language of the TEMPORAL world; love is that of the spiritual world."—Honoré de Balzac, French novelist and playwright

topical (TOP-ih-kuhl). Having to do with issues of current or local interest.
Glenda is always reading magazines so she can keep up with TOPICAL issues and have something to say when encountering new clients.

transient (TRAN-zee-unt). Temporary; lacking permanence.
*"To the artist is sometimes granted a sudden, TRANSIENT insight which serves in this matter for experience. A flash, and where previously the brain held a dead fact, the soul grasps a living truth! At moments we are all artists."
—Arnold Bennett, English novelist*

ultimo (UL-tih-mo). Of or in the calendar month preceding the current one.
On the 23rd ULTIMO, I was informed by counsel that an indictment would be forthcoming.

vernal (VER-nul). Related to spring.
"One impulse from a VERNAL wood / May teach you more of man, / Of moral evil and of good, / Than all the sages can."—William Wordsworth, British Romantic poet

NOUNS

equinox (EK-wih-nox). The point in a year when the sun crosses the equator, causing night and day to be of roughly equal length everywhere on Earth.
The vernal (or spring) EQUINOX generally occurs around March 21; the autumnal equinox, around September 22.

hiatus (hi-A-tuss). An interruption or break in time or continuity.
Lorelei's coming-out party was a welcome HIATUS in our otherwise uneventful social calendar.

moratorium (mor-uh-TOR-ee-um). An authorized period of delay.
The city council voted to place a six-month MORATORIUM on new commercial development.

nanosecond (NAN-o-sek-und). One billionth of a second; an extremely short period of time.
It seemed the phone was on the hook for only a NANOSECOND before it rang again.

respite (RESS-pit). A reprieve; a temporary delay; an instance of temporary relief.
The accused was granted a RESPITE before serving his sentence.

solstice (SOUL-stiss). A day of the year during which the sun is at its highest or lowest point in the sky, causing the shortest day of the year on December 21 (winter solstice) and the longest day of the year on June 21 (summer solstice).
We open our lake house for the summer season every year at the SOLSTICE.

VERBS

temporize (TEM-puh-ryz). To gain time by being evasive or indecisive; to suit one's actions to the time or occasion; to agree or comply temporarily.
I unleashed a longwinded backstory in an effort to TEMPORIZE while I came up with a logical explanation for my behavior.

ANTONYMS

amaranthine (am-uh-RAN-thin). Unfading; undying; deathless; everlasting.
Sally vowed her AMARANTHINE love to Brian.

infinite (IN-fuh-nit). Lacking limits or bounds; of an unmeasurable duration.
The recital lasted just forty-five minutes, but for Joyce, listening to the screeching violins and discordant tones, it seemed INFINITE.

204. Travel

(TRAV-uhl), verb

To go from one place to another; take a trip; journey.

ADJECTIVES

errant (AIR-unt). Given to travel; wandering about aimlessly.
The buzzing of ERRANT flies practically wrecked the contentment I had been feeling while sitting on the dock.

itinerant (eye-TIN-er-unt). Traveling from place to place with a purpose.
While I was between jobs, I worked as an ITINERANT farmer.

peripatetic (per-ih-pa-TET-ik). Wandering without a clear goal or definiteness of purpose.
While waiting to receive his trust fund at age thirty, Giles lived a PERIPATETIC lifestyle.

wayfaring (WAY-fair-ing). Traveling on foot.
We spent many WAYFARING weekends during our month-long jaunt in France last year.

NOUNS

conveyance (kuhn-VAY-unts). A device that serves to transport something or someone.
Our visit to the "wild west" site was greatly enhanced by a ride on an authentic CONVEYANCE: a Conestoga wagon.

jaunt (JAWNT). A short journey taken for pleasure.
Nicole plans to take a JAUNT across the southern tip of Africa next year.

sojourn (SO-jern). A temporary visit or stay.
The Israelites' SOJOURN in the desert lasted for forty long years.

wanderlust (WAWN-der-lust). A strong and innate desire to travel far from home.
"In our WANDERLUST, we are lovers looking for consummation."—Anatole Broyard, literary critic for the New York Times

VERBS

amble (AM-bul). To walk in an easy or leisurely manner; to saunter or stroll.
The day's last customer AMBLED from one end of the shop to the other; no amount of staring from the clerk, it seemed, could make him come to the register.

gallivant (GAL-uh-vant). To wander about seeking amusement or pleasure; to go about indiscreetly with members of the opposite sex.
Because he required little sleep, Mark could GALLIVANT almost continuously.

gambol (GAM-bull). To run, skip, or jump about in a playful or joyous fashion.
"We all have these places where shy humiliations GAMBOL on sunny afternoons."—W. H. Auden, Anglo-American poet

maraud (muh-ROD). To wander in search of booty; to loot or invade for treasure.
The ship was waylaid by pirates MARAUDING on the fourteenth of May.

meander (me-AN-duhr). To wander aimlessly.
We fired that particular servant because he MEANDERED far too slowly from task to task.

perambulate (puh-RAM-byuh-layt). To walk around; to stroll or saunter.
The elderly couple PERAMBULATED the city streets every night after dinner.

peregrinate (PER-ih-gruh-nayt). To travel about on foot.
The ascetics preferred to PEREGRINATE, eschewing all motorized travel.

saunter (SON-tur). To walk leisurely or for pleasure.
On Sunday afternoons, Mr. Weeks would SAUNTER through Central Park gathering material for his short stories.

skulk (skulk). To move about furtively or quietly.
After she lost her job, Lea SKULKED around the town at odd hours, hoping to avoid her former colleagues.

wend (WEND). To go; to proceed.
"As they WEND away / A voice is heard singing / Of Kitty, or Katy, / As if the name meant once / All love, all beauty."—Philip Larkin, British poet, novelist, and jazz critic

ANTONYMS

bide (BYD). To abide; dwell; wait; remain.
Martin did not like to travel but would BIDE at home without the least curiosity about other places.

tarry (TAR-ee). To delay; linger; loiter; be tardy.
"The life of man is a long march through the night, surrounded by invisible foes, tortured by weariness and pain, towards a goal that few can hope to reach, and where none may TARRY long."—Bertrand Russell, English logician and philosopher

205. True

(TROO), adjective

In accordance with fact; agreeing with reality; not false; loyal; faithful.

ADJECTIVES

incontrovertible (in-kahn-trah-VER-tih-bull). Beyond question or dispute.
"Some minds are as little logical or argumentative as nature; they can offer no reason or "guess," but they exhibit the solemn and INCONTROVERTIBLE fact."—Henry David Thoreau, American author and transcendentalist

veritable (VER-ih-tuh-bull). Authentic; true; undeniably legitimate or actual.
The cardboard boxes contained a VERITABLE treasure trove of Civil War artifacts, probably worth tens of thousands of dollars.

NOUNS

paradox (PAIR-uh-doks). A seemingly absurd and self-contradicting situation that seems impossible but may in fact be true.
The article profiled a man who was a real PARADOX; he was grossly overweight, yet had tremendous athletic stamina.

veracity (ver-ASS-ih-tea). The characteristic or habit of being truthful and conforming to accepted standards of behavior.
"The world is upheld by the VERACITY of good men: they make the earth whole-some."—Ralph Waldo Emerson, American poet, essayist, and transcendentalist

verisimilitude (ver-uh-si-MIL-ih-tood). Having the appearance of truth; probability.
The speech, while obviously heartfelt, unfortunately lacked VERISIMILITUDE.

ANTONYMS

aspersion (uh-SPUR-zhun). False accusation; slander.
I will not allow you to cast these ASPERSIONS on a man whose career has been so distinguished.

fabulist (FAB-yuh-list). A liar; someone who tells outrageously untrue stories.
Sir Gerald, a notorious FABULIST, was not consulted for an authoritative account of the crime.

mendacity (Men-DA-sit-tee). A tendency toward or habit of being dishonest.
"The human condition is composed of unequal parts of courage, friendship, ethics, self-sacrifice, brutality, degeneracy, and MENDACITY."—Harlan Ellison, American author

206. Umbrage

(UM-brij), noun

To take exception to and be offended by a comment or action seen as a slight or insult.

ADJECTIVES

acrimonious (ak-rih-MOAN-ee-us). Angry; bitter; disputed.
"There is something about the literary life that repels me, all this desperate building of castles on cobwebs, the long-drawn ACRIMONIOUS struggle to make something important which we all know will be gone forever in a few years . . ."—Raymond Chandler, American author

bellicose (BELL-ih-kohss). Belligerent, surly, ready to argue or fight at the slightest provocation.
Doug is so touchy about his new Jaguar that he'll instantly grow BELLICOSE if you so much as brush against it.

importunate (ihm-PORE-chuh-nitt). Urgent and persistent in solicitation, to the point of annoyance.
"Sisters are always drying their hair. / Locked into rooms, alone, / They pose at the mirror, shoulders bare, / Trying this way and that their hair, / Or fly IMPORTUNATE down the stair / To answer the telephone."—Phyllis McGinley, American poet

NOUNS

contretemps (KON-treh-tahn). An inopportune occurrence with embarrassing results.
"Pan had been amongst them . . . the little god Pan, who presides over social CONTRETEMPS and unsuccessful picnics."—E.M. Forster, English novelist

imprecation (IM-pre-kay-shun). A curse spoken aloud.
Thomas muttered IMPRECATIONS as he circled the airfield, waiting for clearance to land his Airbus 380.

VERBS

deprecate (DEPP-rih-kayt). To express severe disapproval of another's actions.
"Those who profess to favor freedom and yet DEPRECATE agitation, are men who want crops without plowing up the ground."—Frederick Douglass, American abolitionist and orator

execrate (EK-sih-krayt). To loathe; to subject to scorn and derision.
We EXECRATED William for weeks due to his casual rejection of an invitation to join Yale's Skull and Bones.

impugn (ihm-PYOON). To attack as false or wrong.
"I do not IMPUGN the motives of any one opposed to me. It is no pleasure to me to triumph over any one."—Abraham Lincoln

ANTONYMS

badinage (bah-dih-NAHZH). Light, good-natured, even playful banter.
"If you don't care for me, you can move out now. I'm frankly not up to BADINAGE."—Harlan Ellison, American author

conciliatory (kon-SILL-ee-ah-tore-ee). Actions or words meant to settle a dispute or resolve a conflict in a manner that leaves no hard feelings on either side.
"If you are not very clever, you should be CONCILIATORY."—Benjamin Disraeli, British statesmen and literary figure

innocuous (ih-NAHK-yew-us). Not harmful or offensive; innocent, incidental, and hardly noticeable.
"I know those little phrases that seem so INNOCUOUS and, once you let them in, pollute the whole of speech."—Samuel Beckett, Irish writer, dramatist, and poet

207. Uncaring

(uhn-KAR-ing), noun

The state of unconcern; lack of worry; inattentiveness; thoughtlessness; apathy.

ADJECTIVES

cavalier (kav-uh-LEER). Unconcerned with what is considered important; nonchalantly unengaged, especially with regard to serious matters.
His CAVALIER attitude toward financial management may be his company's undoing.

cursory (KUR-suh-ree). Performed with haste and without care.
Mrs. Wallace avoided giving tests on the Friday before a vacation, as she knew her students' efforts would be CURSORY at best.

desultory (DEH-sul-tor-ee). Lacking guidance or progressing randomly; aimless; fitful.
Unable to believe it was his last day on the job, Bill's DESULTORY thoughts wandered through his mind.

feckless (FEK-less). Ineffective; careless; lacking definitiveness of purpose.
Some accuse us of being FECKLESS, but they have no idea how difficult it is to live a wealth-infused lifestyle.

incogitant (in-KOJ-uh-tuhnt). Thoughtless, inconsiderate.
Bill never became accustomed to Ann's continual INCOGITANT acts.

indolent (IN-duh-lnt). Lazy, as a way of life; inactive and unlikely to exert oneself.
Peter, an INDOLENT young man, spent his young days gazing out the window daydreaming.

insensate (in-SENS-ayt). Without human feeling, or lacking judgment and good sense.
Owen's INSENSATE behavior the morning after their tryst made Amy realize she'd made a mistake in asking him to stay the night.

insouciant (in-SOO-see-unt). Acting as if one has not a care in the world; free of worry and angst.
We are never INSOUCIANT about our wealth because we must work at all times to ensure its protection.

intemperate (in-TEM-prit). Refers to a person who indulges his own whims and fancies without regard to other people's feelings or inconvenience.
"Certainly it was ordained as a scourge upon the pride of human wisdom, that the wisest of us all, should thus outwit ourselves, and eternally forego our purposes in the INTEMPERATE act of pursuing them."—Laurence Sterne, Irish-born English novelist and Anglican clergyman

lackadaisical (lack-uh-DAY-zih-kuhl). Lazy and indolent; lacking determination.
No matter how many times a week her father allows her to go on a spending spree, Millicent is never LACKADAISACAL about her trips to Cartier.

laggard (LAG-uhrd). Moving sluggishly and reacting slowly.
"Reviewers . . . must normally function as huff-and-puff artists blowing LAGGARD theatergoers stageward."—Walter Kerr, American theater critic

perfunctory (per-FUNK-ter-ee). Implemented or executed quickly, without much care or thought put into it.
"The tale is so contrived and PERFUNCTORY that many readers will be tempted to skip to the real story in the second half of the book."—Tim Parks, British novelist

remiss (rih-miss). Negligent or careless.
Our servants know that if they ever are REMISS in their duties, we will quickly fire them.

supine (SOO-pine). Apathetic; indolent; passive.
Damon found the marketing department SUPINE when it came to implementing ideas.

NOUNS

ennui (on-WEE). Apathy and lack of energy caused by boredom and disinterest.
"And he spoke of ENNUI, of jaded appetites, of nights and days aboard a moonstone vessel as large as a city."—Harlan Ellison, American author

fainéant (fay-nay-AHNT). Someone who is lazy and idle.
I spent my vacation as a FAINÉANT, so I found it hard to focus on work once I returned to my "real life."

improvidence (im-PRAH-vih-dense). A rash action performed without careful consideration or deliberation.
"This made him think of all the nights . . . spending his youth with the casual IMPROVIDENCE of a millionaire."—Richard Matheson, American science fiction writer

lotus-eater (LOH-tus-ee-ter). A person who leads a life of indolence and ease, unaware of reality and duty.
Raymond considered adopting the lifestyle of a LOTUS-EATER, but could not reconcile his income to the task.

torpor (TORE-purr). Temporary loss of the power of motion or sensation; dormancy; apathy; indifference.
*"A multitude of causes unknown to former times are now acting with a combined force to blunt the discriminating powers of the mind, and unfitting it for all voluntary exertion to reduce it to a state of almost savage TORPOR."
—William Wordsworth, British Romantic poet*

ANTONYMS

discernment (dih-SURN-muhnt). The power of discerning; keen perception or judgment; insight.
*"The supreme end of education is expert DISCERNMENT of all things."
—Samuel Johnson, English poet and critic*

solicitude (suh-LIS-ih-tood). The state of being concerned and anxious.
Amy's SOLICITUDE for John's welfare while he was overseas demonstrated a newfound concern for him as a friend.

208. Understanding

(uhn-der-STAN-ding), noun

The mental state and process of a person who understands; comprehension; discernment.

ADJECTIVES

cognizant (KOG-nih-sint). Aware of the realities of a situation.
Amanda is always COGNIZANT of her acquaintances' pedigrees.

implicit (im-PLIH-set). understood but not stated directly.
"The vanity of men, a constant insult to women, is also the ground for the IMPLICIT feminine claim of superior sensitivity and morality."—Patricia Meyer Spacks, American literary critic

lucid (LOO-sid). Intelligible; clear to the understanding.
The documentary gave a lucid account of the underlying causes of the events.

luciferous (loo-SI-fuh-ruhs). Providing insight or enlightenment; illuminating.
Blake did not find his college courses LUCIFEROUS, so he decided to devote his life to world travel instead.

recondite (REHK-un-dite). Beyond typical knowledge and understanding.
For most people, opera, polo, and fine wine remain RECONDITE subjects.

tacit (TASS-it). Implied; understood without being openly explained or expressed.
The men took their sergeant's harsh language toward Ned as TACIT approval of their own abusive behavior toward him.

NOUNS

perspicacity (per-spih-KASS-ih-tee). Insightfuness; keen understanding.
The problem was a complex one that required the analysis of someone with great PERSPICACITY.

profundity (pruh-FUN-dih-tee). Depth of reasoning or insight; great under-standing and intellectual incisiveness.
A paper's length is no indication of its PROFUNDITY.

savoir faire (SAV-wahr-FAIR). An evident sense of confidence, optimism, and proficiency in the task at hand.
Eileen hosted a charity luncheon for forty people with her usual SAVOIR FAIRE.

VERBS

peruse (puh-ROOZ). To read through with attention; to examine with an eye to detail.
The witness PERUSED the document for some time, then declared that it was not the one he had signed.

ANTONYMS

transcendent (tran-SEN-dent). Beyond the realm of normal experience or understanding; transcending customary bounds of perception.
While the astronauts reacted in different ways to the TRANSCENDENT experience of space travel, all were profoundly affected by the experience.
See also: Judgment, Learn, Think

209. Unreal

(uhn-REE-uhl), adjective

Not real or actual; imaginary; fantastic; illusory; false; artificial.

ADJECTIVES

incorporeal (in-core-PORE-ee-al). Lacking form.
The moanings and low rumblings in the old house suggested INCORPOREAL visitors to Kate.

ineffable (in-EF-uh-bull). So fantastic, incredible, or difficult to grasp it cannot be described in words.
Poet Ezra Pound wrote of "the infinite and INEFFABLE quality of the British empire."

intangible (in-TAN-juh-bul). Incapable of being touched, felt, or calculated.
Friends berated me for breaking up with Matthew, but there was something INTANGIBLE missing from the relationship, something I couldn't do without.

spectral (SPEK-trul). Reminiscent of ghosts or spirits; gruesome and otherworldly.
Scrooge's SPECTRAL visitors take different forms, but each is interested in the same thing: the redemption of the old man's heart.

surreal (suh-REEL). Possessing a quality that makes something seem unreal; strange; bizarre; almost other-worldly.
"He seemed to toss them all into the mixed salads of his poetry with the same indifference to form and logic, the same domesticated SURREALISM, that characterized much of the American avant-garde of the period."—Frank O'Hara, American poet

NOUNS

chimera (kih-MEER-uh). An illusion or fabrication; an imaginary monster.
"What a CHIMERA then is humankind. What a novelty! What a monster, what a chaos!"—Blaise Pascal, French philosopher

dystopia (diss-TOPE-ee-uh). An imaginary society characterized by human misery, squalor, fear, oppression, and hunger.
A popular genre of motion pictures features the postapocalyptic DYSTOPIA.

eidolon (eye-DOH-luhn). A phantom or apparition; or, the image of an ideal
"By a route obscure and lonely, / Haunted by ill angels only, / Where an EIDOLON, named Night, / On a black throne reigns upright."—Edgar Allan Poe, American author and poet

nonentity (non-EN-tih-tee). A person or thing considered completely unimportant or that exists only in the imagination.
You may safely regard this clause of the contract as a NONENTITY; it is obsolete and completely unenforceable.

phantasmagoria (fan-taz-muh-GORE-ee-uh). A dreamlike, constantly changing series of visions.
The avant-garde film had no dialogue or plot in the traditional sense; it was essentially a PHANTASMAGORIA set to music.

philter (FIL-tur). A magical love potion.
Thinking the glass contained Evian water, Veronica drained the PHILTER to its dregs; her eyes met those of the startled butler, and she melted with tenderness.

phoenix (FEE-niks). A mythical bird about the size of an eagle, but with brilliantly colored plumage, that dies by fire and then is reborn from the ashes.
One day the PHOENIX appeared in the forests of France, and legend has it that all the other birds become instantly jealous.

thaumaturge (THAW-mah-turj). A person who works miracles.
If you were ever to see Hannah early in the morning, just after she has awoken, then you would know her personal make-up artist is the epitome of a THAUMATURGE.

Triton (TRY-ton). A mythical creature, similar to a mermaid, with a human torso and arms, gills under the ears, and a tail like a dolphin.
TRITONS served Neptune as his attendants.

utopia (you-TOE-pee-uh). A perfect or ideal society.
Many of us who are accustomed to wealth have learned to accept that we must make our own UTOPIAS, rather than to rely on the actions of outside forces or agencies.

Xanadu (ZAN-uh-dyoo). A place of perfect, idyllic beauty.
"In XANADU did Kubla Khan / A stately pleasure-dome decree: / Where Alph, the sacred river, ran / Through caverns measureless to man / Down to a sunless sea"—Samuel Taylor Coleridge, English poet

yeti (YEH-tee). The (legendary) Abominable Snowman.
Carl claims to have photographic evidence of the Loch Ness Monster, several UFOs, and a large gray YETI, but I have yet to see any of it.

ANTONYMS

de facto (dee-FAK-toe). Existing in fact but not officially.
Although we eschew titles, Sasha clearly is the DE FACTO head of our arts-patronage club.

substantive (SUHB-stuhn-tiv). Existing independently; having a real existence; actual.
After the election, the local blogs were full of criticism written by people who did not vote and had no SUBSTANTIVE complaints.

210. Utopia

(you-TOE-pee-uh), noun

A perfect or ideal society.

ADJECTIVES

halcyon (HAL-see-un). Calm, peaceful, carefree, prosperous.
"It was the most HALCYON summer I ever spent."—Rick Bass, American author and environmental activist

luciferous (loo-SI-fuh-ruhs). Providing insight or enlightenment; illuminating.
Blake did not find the Ivy League LUCIFEROUS, so he decided to devote his life to world travel instead.

salutary (SAL-you-tore-ee). To have a soothing or healing effect; helping recover or benefit from a situation.
Tuberculosis patients were often sent to the mountains, where the fresh air was thought to have a SALUTARY effect on their condition.

sybaritic (sih-bar-IT-ik). Relating to self-indulgent sensuous luxury and pleasure.
Selena rubbed the suntan lotion over her tanned middle slowly, and the whole thing had an erotic, SYBARITIC quality that made the men's eyes pop out of their heads.

NOUNS

eidolon (eye-DOH-luhn). A phantom or apparition; or, the image of an ideal.
"By a route obscure and lonely, / Haunted by ill angels only, / Where an EIDOLON, named Night, / On a black throne reigns upright."—Edgar Allan Poe, American author and poet

panacea (pan-uh-SEE-uh). A universal solution for all problems, diseases, or woes.
Parents today see buying their kids everything they want as a PANACEA for misery, boredom, and unhappiness.

VERBS

consecrate (KON-seh-KRAYT). To declare something sacred, true, sacrosanct, or involuble.
"It is regarded as normal to CONSECRATE virginity in general and to lust for its destruction in particular."—Karl Kraus, Austrian writer

ANTONYMS

Draconian (drah-KONE-ee-an). Strict; mean-spirited; excessively harsh; cruel; punishment or restriction meant to cause misery to those receiving it.
Ophelia was distraught over the DRACONIAN way that her father forced her to stay with her chaperone throughout their vacation on the Greek Isles.

211. Verdant

(VUR-dant), adjective

Lush with trees, bushes, ferns, and other green foliage.

ADJECTIVES

bucolic (byoo-KALL-ik). A peaceful, serene, rural object, place, or environment.
We bought a weekend place in a BUCOLIC little village in the country.

effusive (eh-FEW-siv). Profuse and overflowing, without reservation.
In an effort to butter up the senator, the lobbyist was transparently EFFUSIVE in his praise of the new bill.

florid (FLOOR-id). Excessively ornate and showy, as prose.
"All men are really most attracted by the beauty of plain speech, and they even write in a FLORID style in imitation of this."—Henry David Thoreau, American author and transcendentalist

jocund (JOE-kund). Having a lust for life; possessing a positive attitude and desire to enjoy life to the fullest.
Ron's JOCUND façade shattered when he found himself the victim of identity theft.

NOUNS

fecundity (Fe-KUN-di-tee). A person, organization, resource, or activity that is exceptionally productive, creative, fertile, or fruitful.
"Blistering heat suddenly took the place of Carboniferous moisture and FECUNDITY."—Simon Winchester, British author and journalist

fruition (froo-ISH-un). The completion of a task; the achievement of a goal as the result of significant and persistent effort.
John Nash, a mathematician whose life was featured in A Beautiful Mind, *received the Nobel Prize for the FRUITION of his work in game theory decades after he completed it.*

renaissance (REN-ah-sonce). A period of great learning, thinking, and creativity—in art, literature, science, economics, and philosophy.
We were so pleased by the RENAISSANCE of wealth acquisition that arose during the closing years of the twentieth century.

ANTONYMS

defoliate (dee-FOH-lee-ayt). To strip bare of leaves.
During the Vietnam War, the U.S. military DEFOLIATED large parts of the country.

hoary (HOAR-ee). Impressively old; ancient.
"Feminism has tried to dismiss the femme fatale as a misogynist libel, a HOARY cliché. But the femme fatale expresses women's ancient and eternal control of the sexual realm."—Camille Paglia, American author, feminist, and social critic

stagnation (stag-NAY-shin). The condition of being inactive or the slowing of forward progress or lessening of activity.
"Economists' statistical techniques are not refined enough to analyze unambiguously the causes of this long-term STAGNATION."—Jeff Madrick, director of policy research at the Schwartz Center for Economic Policy Analysis, The New School.

212. Virtuous

(VUR-choo-us), adjective

Having or characterized by righteousness or moral virtue.

ADJECTIVES

exemplary (ig-ZEM-pluh-ree). Serving as an example or model; worth imitating by others.
William's EXEMPLARY behavior was repeated so frequently and embellished so enthusiastically, that the rest of us eventually turned to a life of crime.

inculpable (in-KUHL-puh-bull). Blameless; guiltless.
Because John wasn't at the drinking party, he was deemed INCULPABLE.

seraphic (si-RAF-ik). Characteristic of a seraph; angelic.
Underneath her SERAPHIC appearance, Marjorie actually had a heart of gold.

NOUNS

probity (proh-bi-tee). Integrity; uprightness in one's dealings with others; complete honesty.
The new parents were convinced that by setting a good example, their child would grow up to embrace the virtues of cleanliness and PROBITY.

rectitude (REHK-ti-tood). Conduct according to moral principles; moral virtue; strict honesty; rightness.
"The mind that's conscious of its RECTITUDE, / Laughs at the lies of rumor."
—Ovid, Roman poet

veracious (vuh-RAY-shuss). Honest; truthful.
Your Honor, I ask that the defense's assertion that none of the prosecution's witnesses are VERACIOUS be stricken from the record.

ANTONYMS

nefarious (nih-FAIR-ee-us). Inherently evil, malicious, and unjust.
"Only a government that is rich and safe can afford to be a democracy, for democracy is the most expensive and NEFARIOUS kind of government ever heard
of on earth."—Mark Twain, American humorist and writer

peccadillo (pek-uh-DIL-oh). A slight offense; trifling fault, indiscretion.
Bob knew that shoplifting the package of gum was just a PECCADILLO, but his secret tormented him for his entire adult life.

213. Visage

(VIZ-aj), noun

Face or overall appearance.

NOUNS

countenance (KOWN-teh-nanss). Appearance, particularly the expression on one's face.
Cervantes's Don Quixote is sometimes referred to as the Knight of the Doleful COUNTENANCE.

face (FAYSS). The front part of the head, including the forehead, eyes, nose, cheeks, mouth, and chin. One's facial expression.
Your FACE reminds me of the expressions on classical statues from ancient Greece. Your expression is timeless.

mien (MEEN). A person's look or manner.
Dan's country-bumpkin MIEN effectively hides his shrewd business tactics.

physiognomy (fizz-ee-AH-no-mee). One's face as an expression of one's character. The features of your face that show what kind of a person you are.
"You're either sexy or you're not. I'm very self-conscious about my PHYSIOGNOMY."—Bobby Darin, American singer

tête-à-tête (TET-ah-tet). A face-to-face meeting.
Some of us had begun to believe that our servants were pilfering from us, so we sat down with the allegedly guilty parties and had a TÊTE-À-TÊTE.

VERBS

envisage (en-VIZ-ij). To envision, imagine, or create a mental picture.
"I don't ENVISAGE collectivism. There is no such animal, it is always individualism."—Gertrude Stein, American author

overlook (OH-ver-LUK). Don't notice, either unintentionally or, more often, intentionally.
Robert was so devoted to his two-year-old son that he tended to OVERLOOK the boy's exhibitions of spoiled brattiness.

ANTONYMS

androgynous (Ann-DRAH-gen-us). Something or someone who is sexless; of indeterminate sex; or hermaphrodite (having characteristics of both a male and a female).
The models at fashion week were so ANDROGYNOUS that Katherine couldn't tell if the clothes were designed for men or women.

efface (ih-FAYSS). To erase, obliterate, make inconspicuous.
"It is also true that one can write nothing readable unless one constantly struggles to EFFACE one's own personality. Good prose is like a windowpane."
—George Orwell, British author

W

214. Waif

(WAFE), noun

A stray person or animal.

ADJECTIVES

bereft (beh-REFT). Lacking a certain characteristic, possession, or trait; isolated and lonely.
"A woman moved is like a fountain troubled. / Muddy, ill-seeming, thick, BEREFT of beauty, / And while it is so, none so dry or thirsty / Will deign to sip or touch one drop of it."—William Shakespeare

impecunious (im-puh-KYOON-ee-us). To be poor or broke; to have little or no money.
Alex has been raving about his IMPECUNIOUS state ever since his trust fund was cut from $25,000 to $20,000 per month.

Lilliputian (lil-ee-PEW-shun). Small in stature; tiny in comparison to one's peers.
Jules Vern's LILLIPUTIAN appearance made people treat him like a child.

pusillanimous (pyoo-suh-LAN-ih-muss). Being mild or timid by nature; a shrinking violet; a person who seeks to avoid conflict, challenge, and danger.
Frank L. Baum's most PUSILLANIMOUS fictional creation is the Cowardly Lion of Oz.

wan (WAHN). Showing or suggesting ill health or unhappiness.
"So shaken as we are, so WAN with care, / Find we a time for frighted peace to pant."—William Shakespeare

NOUNS

gamine (gah-MEEN). A girl with a boyish demeanor and mischievous nature who is somehow still appealing.
Her GAMINE behavior and looks only made her that much more attractive to teenage boys her age.

paucity (PAW-city). A lack of something, a small supply or limited selection.
"It is very strange, and very melancholy, that the PAUCITY of human pleasures should persuade us ever to call hunting one of them."—Samuel Johnson, British moralist and poet

VERBS

debilitate (dih-BILL-uh-tayt). To make weak or feeble.
Several hours on the polo fields are enough to DEBILITATE even the most robust player.

ostracize (OS-truh-size). To exclude from society, friendship, community, etc.
Once we learned that Sasha had been planting stories about us in the society pages, we, of course, had to OSTRACIZE her permanently from our group.

scarify (SKAIR-ih-fy). To wound with harsh criticism.
We deemed it necessary to SCARIFY Eileen for having the nerve to criticize our fashion sense.

ANTONYMS

hermetic (her-MET-ik). Isolated, or unaffected by outside influences.
"Reality, whether approached imaginatively or empirically, remains a surface, HERMETIC."—Samuel Beckett, Irish writer, dramatist, and poet

insouciant (in-SOO-see-unt). Acting as if one has not a care in the world; free of worry and angst.
We are never INSOUCIANT about our wealth because we must work at all times to ensure its protection.

vivacious (vy-VAY-shuss). Joyful; happy, spirited; possession a positive attitude about and enthusiasm for life; a person who lives life to the fullest.
Even after her family maintained some steep revenue losses, Sandra retained her VIVACIOUS character.

215. Warn

(WAWRN), verb

To caution others about a danger, impending evil, misfortune, etc.; to urge or advise to exercise care; caution.

ADJECTIVES

premonitory (preh-MAHN-ih-tor-ee). Strongly indicative of or intuiting that something is going to happen.
The Harrisons sold their stock in that company because they had a PREMONITORY vision that the company would soon go bankrupt.

NOUNS

caveat (KAV-ee-ott). A precaution or warning.
Before Arthur applied to college, his sister offered him a CAVEAT: "Many of us do not consider Columbia to be a true Ivy League school."

harbinger (HAR-bin-jer). A forerunner or warning sign of a future event or trend.
The asteroid's shadow blotted out the sun as it speeded on a collision course with Earth, a HARBINGER of impending doom.

portent (POR-tent). A warning sign that something bad is going to happen.
In Ray Bradbury's novel Something Wicked This Way Comes, *the carnival coming to town is a PORTENT of evil things to come.*

VERBS

admonish (ad-MON-ish). To warn; caution against specific faults; to advise; exhort.
On our first day, the counselor ADMONISHED all campers to avoid the poison ivy, the deep end of the lake, and the scrambled eggs.

betoken (bee-TOE-ken). To serve as a warning.
For Mary and Paul, the breakdown of their new car while they were still two hours away from their summer home BETOKENED a disastrous vacation.

presage (press-ij). To foretell or indicate.
Such provocation may PRESAGE armed conflict in the region.

ANTONYMS

dissemble (diss-SEM-bul). To act with an insincere or disguised motive.
Although many on the committee were convinced that the undersecretary was DISSEMBLING about how much he knew of rebel activities, there was no hard proof to support this view.

obscure (uhb-SKYOOR). To make unclear or conceal by confusing.
The official explanation OBSCURED the fact that a number of people had been hurt by using the product in the way it was intended.

216. Wayfaring

(WAY-fair-ing), adjective

Traveling on foot.

ADJECTIVES

circuitous (sir-CUE-uh-tuss). Extremely twisty and winding; indirect.
Blanche called it a shortcut, but her CIRCUITOUS directions caused us to arrive very late at the debutante ball.

peripatetic (per-ih-pa-TET-ik). Wandering from career to career, job to job, company to company, or place to place, seemingly without a clear goal or definiteness of purpose.
While waiting to receive his trust fund at age thirty, Giles lived a PERIPATETIC lifestyle.

serpentine (SUR-pen-teen). Snake like in shape or movement.
"For it is not possible to join SERPENTINE wisdom with columbine innocency, except men know exactly all the conditions of the serpent."—Francis Bacon, English philosopher, author, and statesman

NOUNS

wanderlust (WON-dehr-lust). A strong and innate desire to travel far from home.
"In our WANDERLUST, we are lovers looking for consummation."—Anatole Broyard, literary critic for the New York Times

VERBS

meander (me-AN-duhr). To wander aimlessly.
We fired that particular servant because he MEANDERED far too slowly from task to task.

ANTONYMS

geostationary (JEE-oh-STAY-shin-air-ee). Pertaining to a satellite in orbit 22,300 miles above the Earth's surface so that the satellite is always directly over the same spot of ground.
Arthur C. Clark was the first to propose that three GEOSTATIONARY satellites orbiting Earth could provide a global communications network effectively covering every location on the planet.

immutable (im-MYOO-tuh-bull). Unable, or unwilling, to change.
"I don't know what IMMUTABLE differences exist between men and women apart from differences in their genitals."—Naomi Weisstein, American feminist

insular (IN-suh-ler). Self-contained and therefore isolated from the world and unaffected by outside influences, usually to one's detriment.
The Pricewaters moved from the family's tradition enclave to a more INSULAR compound further up the coast.

sedentary (SED-n-tair-ee). Resting a great deal and taking little exercise.
All we have to do is hire a personal trainer if our SEDENTARY habits begin to have negative effects on our well-being.

217. Weak

(WEEK), adjective

Not strong; having no strength, stamina, vigor, power, etc.

ADJECTIVES

anemic (uh-NEE-mik). Of or pertaining to a medical condition in which one's blood is deficient in red corpuscles; extraordinarily weak.
I made a few ANEMIC efforts to get some work done last night, but I couldn't really focus on the job at hand.

decrepit (di-KREP-it). Enfeebled or weakened by old age; worn out; infirm.
The car's DECREPIT appearance was deceiving; Colin found it capable of 75 mph on the highway, and it got very good mileage.

flaccid (FLASS-id). Lacking firmness, stiffness, vigor, or force.
The candidate's FLACCID speech left the listeners unimpressed.

languid (LANG-gwid). Characterized by weakness and fatigue; or, lacking spirit and animation.
"In doing good, we are generally cold, and LANGUID, and sluggish; and of all things afraid of being too much in the right."—Edmund Burke, Anglo-Irish statesman, orator, and author

pallid (PAL-id). A wan, sickly, washed-out appearance indicating illness or weakness, or lack of energy, strength, and vitality.
Many of us maintain a PALLID pallor because we want to make it clear that we do not need to go outdoors unless we so choose.

NOUNS

infirmity (in-FUR-mih-tee). A physical weakness or ailment; mental or moral weakness.
Randall, get over yourself. An ingrown toenail is annoying. It's not an INFIRMITY. You cannot park in the handicapped spot!

lassitude (LASS-ih-tood). A lack of energy or motivation; weariness.
"We know what boredom is: it is a dull / Impatience or a fierce velleity, / A champing wish, stalled by our LASSITUDE, / To make or do."—Richard Wilbur, *American poet*

VERBS

attenuate (a-TEN-you-ayt). To weaken or reduce; spread thin; to cause a decrease in amount, value, power, or severity.
Jim's strategy was to ATTENUATE the impact of Joan's accusations of harassment by suggesting that she had somehow invited his overtures.

debilitate (dih-BIIL-ih-tayt). To enfeeble or weaken; to devitalize or deplete strength.
Fran's DEBILITATING illness slowly sapped her will to live.

dilute (die-LOOT). To thin or weaken by adding additional ingredients; to reduce the force, strength, or effectiveness of.
Frederica never DILUTES her words. She'll tell you exactly how she feels.

enervate (EN-ur-vayt). To weaken; to deprive of vitality, strength, or endurance.
The vacation's whirlwind pace actually served to ENERVATE Madge.

ANTONYMS

omnipotent (ahm-NIP-uh-tuhnt). All powerful.
"An OMNIPOTENT God is the only being with no reason to lie."
—Mason Cooley, *American author*

puissant (PYOO-uh-suhnt). Powerful; mighty.
"Methinks I see in my mind a noble and PUISSANT nation rousing herself like a strong man after sleep, and shaking her invincible locks."—John Milton, *English poet and historian*

218. Work

(WURK), noun

Physical or mental effort exerted to do or make something; labor; toil; employment.

ADJECTIVES

laborious (luh-BORE-ee-us). Requiring a great deal of hard work and perseverance.
Even though the years in school were LABORIOUS, they were worth the effort when I earned my PhD.

operose (OP-uh-roass). Laborious; tedious; industrious.
What's the point of taking on OPEROSE work when our social connections help us to achieve success with little effort?

sedulous (SEJ-yuh-luss). Done or crafted with perseverance, diligence, and care.
The teen's SEDULOUS labors at the desert site were rewarded by the discovery of triceratops bones in the third week of the dig.

yeoman (YOH-muhn). Pertaining to or one who performs arduous tasks in a loyal and workmanlike manner.
We promoted Helga to upstairs maid because of her YEOMAN work ethic.

NOUNS

métier (MAY-tee-yay). One's occupation, profession, field of work, etc.
Since her family started one of Wall Street's most profitable houses, it's only natural that Ellen's MÉTIER would be finance.

moil (MOYL). Hard, grinding work.
The MOIL of paperwork made Sheila long for early retirement.

sinecure (SIN-eh-KYOOR). A job or office without regular duties but with regular pay; a position requiring minimal labor but conveying prestige or status to one who holds it.
Being elected as the new president of his trade association bestowed on Bill a much-needed SINECURE.

travail (truh-VALE). Hard work, especially work causing physical pain; the labor of childbirth.
It is not surprising that, given the TRAVAILS of the long journey westward, some settlers opted to return East rather than try to make a life on the frontier.

VERBS

lucubrate (LOO-kyoo-breyt). To work, study, or write laboriously, particularly at night.
A night owl, Phyllis always LUCUBRATED into the wee hours.

ANTONYMS

disport (dih-SPORT). To amuse oneself.
Felicia loved to DISPORT with the proprietors of her favorite boutiques by arguing over price.

diversion (dih-VUR-zhuhn). A pastime; amusement.
"Politics is the DIVERSION of trivial men who, when they succeed at it, become important in the eyes of more trivial men."—George Jean Nathan, American journalist and critic

219. Worthless

(WURTH-lis), adjective

Without value or worth; of no use or importance.

ADJECTIVES

brummagem (BRUHM-uh-juhm). Describes something that looks great but performs poorly.
"Our press is certainly bankrupt in . . . reverence for nickel plate and BRUMMAGEM."—Mark Twain

nugatory (NOO-guh-tore-ee). Trifling, worthless, and ineffective.
We spend our time with the NUGATORY pastimes of polo, tennis on grass courts, and weekends in Europe.

paltry (PAHL-tree). Trivial; insignificant; worthless.
The PALTRY sum found in the cash register made us regret having picked this store for our first robbery.

picayune (pik-ee-YOON). Petty; trifling or unimportant.
Mr. Franks apparently couldn't be bothered with such PICAYUNE concerns as what color shirt to wear.

NOUNS

chaff (chaff). Worthless stuff; material to be cast away.
I usually write for an hour straight in my journal, knowing full well that much of what comes out will be drivel, and allowing myself to go back later and separate the wheat from the CHAFF.

cipher (SIE-fur). A person or thing without meaning or value; a mystery; literally, the mathematical symbol for zero.
Despite the best efforts of the intelligence community to gather evidence against him, Doctor Lysenko remained a CIPHER.

dregs (DREGS). The leftover, least appealing or valuable part.
Though many in her town looked on ex-convicts as the DREGS of society, it was Debbie's job as a social worker to try to rehabilitate everyone who came through her door, regardless of past history.

gimcrack (JIHM-krack). A showy object of little or no value.
"Haul them off! Hide them! / The heart winces / For junk and GIMCRACK, / for jerrybuilt things."—Richard Wilbur, American poet

inutility (in-yoo-TIL-ih-tee). Something that's useless.
The puddle of oil beneath the car confirmed that it had become a very expensive INUTILITY.

kitsch (KIHCH). Art, artifacts, or other objects of a cheap or junky nature produced by the popular culture.
His room was filled with KITSCH: lava lamps, Farrah Fawcett and Cheryl Tiegs posters, and plastic models of Frankenstein and Dracula.

obsolescence (ob-suh-LESS-uhnts). The state of being no longer current or useful.
Roderick found, to his dismay, that some of the new Maserati models had lapsed into OBSOLESCENCE almost as soon as they hit the showroom floor.

trumpery (TRUHM-puh-ree). Something without value; a trifle.
The TRUMPERY that the Smythingtons collect and call "art" is, clearly, distasteful dreck.

VERBS

marginalize (MAR-jin-ul-eyes). To dismiss something as less important than it actually is.
Francine has too many connections for us to snub her completely, but we have done our best to MARGINALIZE her influence.

nullify (NUHL-uh-fy). To make something valueless or ineffective.
We keep our collections under lock and key because, sometimes, merely breathing on them NULLIFIES their value.

ANTONYMS

heirloom (AIR-loom). A possession of commercial or sentimental value handed down from generation to generation.
As the oldest child, I was given the most precious family HEIRLOOM, our old grandfather clock, when my mother passed away.

valuation (val-you-AYE-shun). The calculated worth or value of an asset, based on a rigorous appraisal.
One of the accounting firm's services is business VALUATION, which provides an accurate appraisal of what your business would sell for if acquired.

220. Writing

(RY-ting), noun

The act of a person who writes; something written, such as a book, letter, document, inscription, etc.

ADJECTIVES

verbose (ver-BOHS). Describes a person or composition using more words than are needed to get the point across.
Long-winded and VERBOSE, Mitch made his team members groan whenever he stood up to speak at a charity event.

NOUNS

elegy (EL-eh-gee). A poem of lament and praise for the dead.
"Modern ELEGIES tend to be unconvincing because the poet so clearly believes in the immortality that an ELEGY traditionally claims for its subject."—Edward Mendelson, Professor of English and Comparative Literature at Columbia University

kenning (KEN-ing). A metaphorical compound word or phrase, used often in epic poetry.
Cliff's letter to Natasha included such KENNINGS as "pearl-eyed dove" and "crinkly gowned angel." It's no wonder she broke up with him soon after.

missive (MISS-iv). An official or formal letter.
He sent out a MISSIVE informing all employees that, henceforth, there would be no smoking in their quarters—but he forgot to remove the ashtrays.

passim (PASS-im). A word used to indicate that a given source or element is used frequently throughout a written work.
References to a fictitious writer named Kilgore Trout appear PASSIM in a number of Kurt Vonnegut's novels.

verbiage (VER-bee-ij). Words; in particular, prose written to fill space and impress others rather than communicate ideas and information.
"There's some white space on the back page of the sales brochure," the marketing manager told his ad agency, "so let's fill it with some VERBIAGE about service and quality."

vers libre (VERSS-LEE-breh). Free verse, a style of poetry requiring no rhyme or meter.
H.L. Mencken observed that VERS LIBRE is "a device for making poetry easier to write and harder to read."

VERBS

elucubrate (ih-LOO-kyoo-brait). To produce a written work through lengthy, intensive effort.
Thanks to a few hundred bucks passed along to a classmate, Miles did not have to ELUCUBRATE a term paper and could, instead, attend parties with us.

euphuism (YOU-few-iz-im). Ornate, flowery, overly elaborate language, often making the exact meaning difficult to discern.
Felicia's words are full of EUPHUISM, particularly when describing the architecture of her family's various houses.

indite (in-DITE). To write or compose a literary work.
"But if, both for your love and skill, your name / You seek to nurse at fullest breasts of Fame, / Stella behold, and then begin to INDITE."—Sir Philip Sidney, English courtier, soldier, and poet

limn (LIM). To outline in detail, portray in words.
With all of the expressive terms he could muster, the theologian proceeded to LIMN an exposition of the pious life.

paraphrase (PAIR-uh-frayz). A restatement of a text or passage with a new meaning or as a clarification.
To call this work a new translation of the original Greek texts is an overstatement; it is a capable, but by no means groundbreaking, effort to PARAPHRASE existing English editions.

ANTONYMS

legible (LEJ-uh-bull). Capable of being read.
John's handwriting was LEGIBLE but his prose was incomprehensible.

peruse (puh-ROOZ). To read through with attention; to examine with an eye to detail.
The witness PERUSED the document for some time, then declared that it was not the one he had signed.
See also: Language

221. Xenophile

(ZEN-uh-file), noun

Someone who is attracted to foreign styles, customs, manners, etc.

ADJECTIVES

geopolitical (gee-oh-poh-LIH-tih-kull). Anything having to do with the politics affecting the relationships of two or more countries, especially when influenced by geographical factors.
GEOPOLITICAL instability in the Middle East is fueling rising crude oil prices.

geostationary (GEE-oh-STAY-shin-air-ee). An object orbiting a larger body that synchronizes its movement with that of the body so it always remains in the same position relative to it.
Arthur C. Clarke was the first to propose that three GEOSTATIONARY satellites orbiting Earth could provide a global communications network effectively covering every location on the planet.

NOUNS

acculturation (ah-kul-chuh-RAY-shin). The process of adapting to a different culture.
Just because sushi makes me queasy doesn't mean I'm opposed to ACCULTURATION.

gazetteer (gaz-ih-TEERr). A geographical index or dictionary of places organized by name.
The Rothschilds prefer their pilot simply head for the sun, rather than consult a GAZETTEER prior to short flights.

globalization (glow-bull-ih-ZAY-shin). The movement toward a true world economy with open and free trading across national borders.
"Proponents of GLOBALIZATION insist that, as trade and investment move across borders, economic efficiencies raise the standards of living on both sides of the exchange."—Arthur Goldwag, American author

humanism (HEW-man-iz-um). The philosophy or belief that the highest ideals of human existence can be fulfilled without regard to religion or supernatural intervention.
"The four characteristics of HUMANISM are curiosity, a free mind, belief in good taste, and belief in the human race."—E.M. Forster, English novelist

jaunt (JAWNT). A short journey taken for pleasure.
Nicole plans to take a JAUNT across the southern tip of Africa next year.

VERBS

gallivant (GAL-ih-vant). To wander widely; to constantly travel to many different places, without an itinerary or plan; to freely go wherever and whenever the mood strikes you, and doing so frequently.
Some accuse us of GALLIVANTING around the world, but cultural knowledge is de rigueur for cocktail conversation.

ANTONYMS

apartheid (uh-PART-hyt). South Africa's former government-sanctioned policy of segregation and racial discrimination.
Since APARTHEID ended in 1994, South Africa has elected three native African presidents.

insular (IN-suh-ler). Self-contained and therefore isolated from the world and unaffected by outside influences, usually to one's detriment.
The Pricewaters moved from the family's tradition enclave to a more INSULAR compound further up the coast.

jingoism (JIN-go-iz-um). Extreme nationalism, backed up by the explicit or implied threat of military force; more broadly, extreme enthusiasm and support for an idea or position without being open to contrary arguments or notions.
We cannot countenance JINGOISM, especially since it has such a negative impact on overseas markets.

xenophobic (zee-nuh-FOE-bik). Having an irrational fear of foreigners and immigrants.
We are not XENOPHOBIC; we dislike all strangers, regardless of their backgrounds, unless they are brought to us by other social contacts.

yokel (YOH-kuhl). A gullible inhabitant of a rural area.
"[A human being] is the YOKEL par excellence, the booby unmatchable, the king dupe of the cosmos."—H.L. Mencken, American magazine editor, essayist, and critic

Y

222. Yare

(YAIR), adjective

Quick and agile; lively.

ADJECTIVES

adroit (uh-DROYT). Skilled or clever in a particular pursuit.
"It's kind of sad," Betty said to Barbara, "that Will thinks his ADROIT opera-singing abilities will impress women."

ebullient (eh-BULL-yuhnt). Feeling joy and positive emotions at an extreme level; the state of being wildly enthusiastic about something.
Lorne was EBULLIENT when he found that his mother had given the college enough money to overturn his rejection.

effervescent (ef-ur-VESS-ent). Bubbly; upbeat; cheerful; possessing a positive attitude and joyful personality.
After getting the acceptance letter from Cornell, Sabrina was EFFERVESCENT and celebrated with a trip to Neiman Marcus.

effusive (eh-FEW-siv). Profuse and overflowing, without reservation.
In an effort to butter up the senator, the lobbyist was transparently EFFUSIVE in his praise of the new bill.

jocund (JOE-kund). Having a lust for life; possessing a positive attitude and desire to enjoy life to the fullest.
Ron's JOCUND façade shattered when he found himself the victim of identity theft.

NOUNS

élan, (a-LON). Enthusiasm, energy, flair, zest.
Bryanna reacted with ÉLAN when she was tapped to be part of a feature for Elite Travel Magazine.

fillip (FILL-uhp). Something that revives or arouses excitement.
"Faithful horoscope-watching, practiced daily, provides just the sort of small, but warm and infinitely reassuring FILLIP that gets matters off to a spirited start."—Shana Alexander, American author

VERBS

gambol (GAM-bull). To run, skip, or jump about in a playful or joyous fashion.
"We all have these places where shy humiliations GAMBOL on sunny afternoons."—W.H. Auden, Anglo-American poet

ANTONYMS

bovine (BO-vyn). Anything related to or reminiscent of cows or other dull, docile, slow-moving, grazing mammals.
"The cow is of the BOVINE ilk; One end is moo, the other, milk."—Ogden Nash, American poet

enervate (EN-er-vayt). To rob a person, organization, place, or thing of its energy, strength, and vitality.
Greenhouse gases ENERVATE the protective ozone layer surrounding the Earth.

etiolate (EE-tee-uh-layt). To cause to become weak and appear sickly.
Over time, Brad's excesses—and his refusal to see a plastic surgeon— increasingly ETIOLATED his once-handsome appearance.

lugubrious (loo-GOO-bree-us). Pessimistic, emotionally downtrodden, spiritually low, sad, or depressed.
Prozac failed to ameliorate the patient's LUGUBRIOUS outlook on life.

morose (muh-ROHSS). Gloomy and ill-humored.
Now that his parents have taken away his private plane, Anthony has become positively MOROSE.

223. Zephyr

(ZEFF-uhr), noun

A gentle breeze.

ADJECTIVES

bucolic (byoo-KALL-ik). A peaceful, serene, rural object, place, or environment.
We bought a weekend place in a BUCOLIC little village in the country.

caducous (kuh-DOO-kuss). Transitory; short-lived; perishable.
"Some thing, which I fancied was a part of me, falls off from me and leaves no scar. It was CADACOUS."—Ralph Waldo Emerson, American poet, essayist, and transcendentalist

gossamer (GOSS-uh-muhr). Something delicate, light, and flimsy that will flutter in the slightest breeze.
Fairies flitted among the flowers on GOSSAMER wings.

VERBS

burgeon (BURR-jin). To sprout, to grow; to blossom and flourish.
Natalia does her part for the BURGEONING "green" movement by having her gardener turn manure from her stables into fertilizer.

ANTONYMS

miasma (my-AZ-mah). An unhealthy atmosphere or environment; an unpleasant feeling pervading the air.

"These appearances, which bewilder you, are merely electrical phenomena not uncommon—or it may be there they have their ghastly origin in the rank MIASMA of the tarn."—Edgar Allan Poe, American author and poet

odoriferous (oh-duh-RIFF-er-us). Bad-smelling; foul.

Eleanor believed she would enjoy her weekend trek through the South American rainforest, but she found the animals too noisy, the constant rain unpleasant, and the forest's ODORIFEROUS vegetation distasteful.

Index

Note: Page numbers in **bold** indicate main entries.